CRIMINAL EVIDENCE

GLENCOE CRIMINAL JUSTICE SERIES

Allen/Simonsen: **Corrections in America: An Introduction (Second Edition)**

Bloomquist: **Marijuana: The Second Trip**

Brandstatter/Hyman: **Fundamentals of Law Enforcement**

Coffey/Eldefonso: **Process and Impact of Justice**

Eldefonso: **Issues in Corrections**

Eldefonso: **Readings in Criminal Justice**

Eldefonso/Coffey: **Process and Impact of the Juvenile Justice System**

Eldefonso/Hartinger: **Control, Treatment, and Rehabilitation of Juvenile Offenders**

Engel/DeGreen/Rebo: **The Justice Game: A Simulation**

Gourley: **Effective Municipal Police Organization**

LeGrande: **The Basic Processes of Criminal Justice**

Lentini: **Vice and Narcotics Control**

Kamon/Hunt/Fleming: **Juvenile Law and Procedures in California (Revised Edition)**

Melnicoe/Mennig: **Elements of Police Supervision (Second Edition)**

Nelson: **Preliminary Investigation and Police Reporting: A Complete Guide to Police Written Communication**

Pursley: **Introduction to Criminal Justice**

Radelet: **The Police and the Community (Second Edition)**

Radelet/Reed: **The Police and the Community: Studies**

Roberts/Bristow: **An Introduction to Modern Police Firearms**

Simonsen/Gordon: **Juvenile Justice in America**

Waddington: **Arrest, Search, and Seizure**

Waddington: **Criminal Evidence**

Wicks/Platt: **Drug Abuse: A Criminal Justice Primer**

General Editor:

G. DOUGLAS GOURLEY

Professor and Chairman
Department of Criminal Justice
California State University at Los Angeles
Los Angeles, California

CRIMINAL EVIDENCE

LAWRENCE C. WADDINGTON
Judge of the Municipal Court
Los Angeles, California

GLENCOE PUBLISHING CO., INC.
Encino, California

Collier Macmillan Publishers
London

Printed in the United States of America

Chapter 2, "Detention and Arrest"; Chapter 3, "Arrest"; Chapter 4, "Search"; Chapter 6, "Search Incident to Arrest"; Chapter 7, "Consent Searches"; and Chapter 8, "Searches without Warrants" are reprinted from ARREST, SEARCH, AND SEIZURE by Lawrence C. Waddington.

Glencoe Publishing Co., Inc.
17337 Ventura Boulevard
Encino, California 91316
Collier Macmillan Canada, Ltd.

Library of Congress Catalog Card Number: 76-4062

First printing 1978

ISBN 0-02-479510-0

CONTENTS

Preface

The needs of a police officer to understand the law of evidence do not always coincide with those of a lawyer. In this volume, the materials have been selected with the needs of the police officer in mind. First, the volume contains basic principles of evidence which every officer must know. Second, it includes principles which may be applied to every criminal investigation, not only to assure that evidence will be admissible in court, but also to increase the weight, or importance, of the evidence. Third, this book stresses the need for obtaining evidence in a way that is consistent with the requirements of the Fourth, Fifth, and Sixth Amendments to the United States Constitution. And fourth, it contains special sections on the laws of evidence affecting specific types of investigation—driving under the influence of alcohol and homicide. Throughout the volume, principles of evidence are clearly illustrated by means of hypothetical examples and actual court cases.

The most dramatic evidence in a criminal case is generally the physical evidence seized by the officers. The guns, the knives, the stolen property, or the narcotics which are offered in evidence at trial vividly portray what words cannot. But officers must obtain this evidence lawfully. If the arrest of a suspect or the search and seizure of evidence is not lawful, the evidence obtained as a result will be excluded in a court of law, and the loss of such evidence severely damages the prosecution's case. For this reason, several chapters on this subject are included to enable the officer to understand the basic principles of arrest, search, and seizure.

In some crimes, witnesses are the only link in connecting the defendant to the crime. An interview with a witness to obtain a physical description of the suspect is critical, and a careless report of the interview can severely damage any subsequent prosecution. An understanding of the rules of evidence affecting witnesses improves an officer's ability to strengthen the prosecution's case. The competency of witnesses, the potential for contradicting their testimony, the need to corroborate their testimony, the possibility that their testimony will be privileged against disclosure, and their character are all important considerations which should be weighed and dealt with well in advance of trial.

In other crimes, no eyewitnesses may be available, and only a thorough investigation can connect the defendant to the crime. The officer must know the kind of evidence, usually circumstantial, that can be admitted in court. Such evidence may include hearsay, expert testimony, or documentary and physical evidence.

This volume attempts to combine those rules of evidence which an officer must know with the practicalities of everyday law enforcement. The real world of experience teaches that a weak pre-trial preparation can severely damage any subsequent prosecution. A few years of experience in trial courts will educate officers to the types of weaknesses in a case that defense attorneys will attempt to exploit. Hopefully this volume will provide much of that experience for the officer beforehand.

A Guide to Case Citations

All court cases are referred to by full citation to enable the reader to locate materials from several sources. Readers desiring to read a case in full will need access to a law library. Citations to state court cases start with the state citation followed by reference to the West Report system. For example: 71 C. 2d 602, 76 Cal. R. 636, 452 P. 2d 924 indicates that the case cited may be found in the official California Reports (Volume 71, Second series, page 602) or in the California Reporter series (Volume 76 of California Reports, page 636), or in the West Reporter system in Volume 452 of the Pacific Second series, page 924. The West Reporter system collects cases decided by state courts in various regions of the United States.

A sample United States Supreme Court case is cited as follows: 101 U.S. 63, 19 L. Ed. 2d 804, 45 S. Ct. 63. This citation refers to a case which can be found in Volume 101 of the United States Reports on page 63. The same case is also found in Volume 19, Second Edition of the Lawyers Edition of United States Supreme Court Reports on page 804. The Lawyers Edition also contains notes collecting other cases similar to the one decided. The case may also be found in the Supreme Court series, Volume 45, page 63. Any law librarian can assist the reader in locating a particular book cited.

The law of evidence varies from state to state, and not all courts and legislatures agree on the same rules or on the interpretation of those rules. Court cases in this volume have been selected with as broad a consensus as possible, but naturally the courts from larger states render more decisions. In those cases interpreting rules of evidence which are constitutionally based rather than statutorily based, United States Supreme Court decisions have been cited.

1 Detention and Arrest

Chapter Objectives

After reading this chapter, you will be able to:

1. Explain the role of the Fourth Amendment as applied to the detention of a suspect without arrest.

2. Describe the evidence necessary to establish a lawful detention.

3. Discuss the rules governing the limited search of a suspect for weapons and the secondary search to remove weapons.

The Fourth Amendment to the U.S. Constitution provides: "The right of the people to be secure in their persons, houses, papers, and effects, against unreasonable searches and seizures, shall not be violated, and no warrants shall issue, but upon probable cause, supported by oath or affirmation, and particularly describing the place to be searched, and the persons or things to be seized."

The Fourth Amendment is the source of all the rules that govern the arrest, search, and seizure of persons and/or property. Despite state and federal statutes that define arrest and search authority, the Fourth Amendment is the ultimate yardstick. Because the issue of arrest and search emerges almost exclusively in criminal trials, or in proceedings of an essentially criminal nature, judges must determine whether governmental agents obtained evidence in violation of the provisions of the Fourth Amendment. Without any statute to refer to, judges must resort to previous decisions of state and federal courts that interpret the constitutional language. These cases, which are reported and published, articulate the rules of arrest, search, and seizure.

Detention—the Stop

Confrontations between citizens and peace officers are manifold in variety and purpose. The spectrum fluctuates from the casual friendly conversation between beat officer and shopkeeper to the violence incident to the arrest of an armed-robbery suspect. In some cases the initial meeting may begin routinely enough, but may erupt quickly into violence. To the officer who reads about or is aware of public hostility to law enforcement, every confrontation contains the seeds of violence. The routine inquiry addressed to a pedestrian on the street, the familiar traffic stop, the service of a traffic warrant—any of these daily minor acts may suddenly become hazardous. Law enforcement's concern for personal welfare is a relevant factor and an important consideration in measuring the reasonableness of the steps officers take under these circumstances. On the other hand, to assume that every citizen is potentially hostile is unreasonable.

What have the courts to do with police-citizen confrontations? Although various state and federal statutes authorize civil suits for money damages against peace officers for alleged violations of civil rights, in an ensuing criminal trial the courts will rule on the admissibility of any evidence seized as a consequence of the confrontation. If the confrontation violates a person's Fourth Amendment right to personal security, the court will exclude evidence seized as a consequence of the violation. Accordingly, it becomes extremely important to focus on the initial contact between citizen and police officer. If that contact is incompatible with Fourth Amendment requirements, any subsequent arrest or search may be tainted and important evidence excluded. For example, a search otherwise valid under the Fourth Amendment may become unlawful if the seized evidence was a product of an earlier unlawful detention.

Right to Detain—Forcible Detention

Police attention is drawn to a person for any number of reasons, some quite evident and others dependent on intuition. Whatever factors alert the officer's suspicion, the issue is whether the officer has any right to stop and possibly question the person. The officer may not have seen sufficient evidence to justify an arrest for a specific crime, but he or she may have seen enough to suggest the possibility of a recently committed crime or the preparation of a crime. How does the Fourth Amendment come into play in such instances?

In 1968, the U.S. Supreme Court decided *Terry* v. *Ohio*. In *Terry*, a veteran police officer testified that he had been assigned to patrol a location in downtown Cleveland. He observed standing on the corner of an intersection two men whom he had never seen before. He saw one of the men leave the other and walk past some stores. "The man paused for a moment and looked into a store window, then walked a short distance, turned around and walked back toward the corner, pausing once again to look into the same store window. He rejoined his companion at the corner, and the two conferred briefly. Then the second man went through the same series of motions, strolling down the same street, looking in the same window, walking on a short distance, turning back, peering in the store window again, and returning to confer with the first man at the corner. The two men repeated this ritual alternately between five and six times apiece—in all roughly a dozen trips. At one point while the two were standing together on the corner, a third man approached them and engaged them briefly in conversation. This man then left the two others and walked away. The first two men resumed their measured pacing, peering, and conferring. After this had gone on for several minutes, the two men walked off together following the path taken earlier by the third man.'' Believing the two men to be ''casing'' the store, the officer approached the three men, identified himself, grabbed Terry, spun him around, and commenced a cursory search of his clothing. His search yielded a concealed weapon, whereupon the officer arrested Terry. Subsequently, Terry was convicted of carrying a concealed weapon.

After his conviction, Terry appealed. He contended that his detention was a ''seizure'' of the person in the sense of the Fourth Amendment and therefore had to be based on a quality of evidence that would constitute probable cause to arrest. Further, he contended that in the absence of evidence justifying an arrest, no invasion of personal security could be judicially approved.

The State of Ohio responded that the thrust of the Fourth Amendment is ''reasonableness'' and that, even if a detention is a ''seizure'' in the constitutional sense, the act should be measured in terms of balancing the personal security of the citizen against the need to investigate possible criminal activities.

Support of the latter rule prevailed. The Supreme Court held that indeed the forcible detention of a citizen by an officer constituted an invasion of personal security and was therefore a ''seizure'' within the meaning of the Fourth Amendment. Consequently, any such intrusion must be compatible with the Fourth Amendment command that people are to be free from unreasonable searches and seizures. Using the balancing test of reasonableness, the Court held that the detection of crime and its prevention were obvious governmental interests. And if the facts, objectively viewed, revealed that the detention was reasonably related to achieving that objective, the invasion would be constitutionally sanctioned. The Court in *Terry* ruled that ''a police officer may in appropriate circumstances and in an appropriate manner approach a person for the purpose of investigating possible criminal behavior even though there is no probable cause to make an arrest.''

In a later case decided in 1972 (*Adams* v. *Williams*), the Court stated that the Fourth Amendment does not require a policeman to shrug his shoulders and allow a crime to occur or a criminal to escape simply because he lacks the precise level of information necessary to establish probable cause to arrest. On the contrary, continued the Court, ''it may be the essence of good police work to adopt an intermediate response. A brief stop of a suspicious individual in order to determine his identity, or to maintain the status quo momentarily while obtaining more information, may be most reasonable in light of the facts known to the officer at the time.''

Terry and *Adams* thus confirm the right of police to stop—that is, ''seize'' citizens short of actually effecting an arrest. The right to ''stop'' was approved; the ''frisk,'' which the Court held was a ''search,'' was also approved—under proper circumstances (see section entitled Limited Search—the Frisk).

Most states authorize arrests by statute, but, until *Terry,* few jurisdictions statutorily authorized officers to forcibly detain citizens. The practice of detention, short of sufficient evidence to justify arrest, was widespread throughout the United States, however. *Terry* held that these confrontations were subject to the Fourth Amendment guarantee of personal security and that any evidence seized as a consequence of the detention must be measured against that standard. The court approved the detention of citizens based on a quality of evidence less than the ''probable cause'' required for arrest. (See chapter 2, Arrest.) As a shorthand phrase, the Court approved a doctrine of ''probable cause to detain.''

Many police contacts with citizens have nothing to do with suspected criminal activity. Neighborhood noise, domestic quarrels, lost children—all occupy a substantial portion of police time. Just as frequently, officers routinely stop motorists for moving traffic violations or defective vehicular equipment. If officers encounter possible criminal activity in either of these contexts of apparently noncriminal activity, they may escalate their response from investigation to forcible detention. And further investigation may lead to arrest. Because police contact with citizens is so diverse, the Supreme Court in *Terry* constitutionally approved a range of flexible police responses reasonably related to the incident at hand. When an arrest ensues as the result of the contact, the court will scrutinize the officer's entire conduct to determine if his or her acts were reasonably related to the perceived objective. If a person was detained on evidence insufficient to establish that the person's conduct merited investigation for criminal activity, the detention will be held constitutionally unlawful and any evidence seized as a consequence thereof will be excluded.

Right to Detain—Investigative Detention

In *Terry,* the Supreme Court reviewed facts that reflected an officer's forcible detention of a suspect without prior questioning. The officer had seen enough to justify a reasonable suspicion that an armed robbery was about to take place. Suppose an officer observes suspicious activity that appropriately merits investigation but only wants to ask the person questions. *Terry* apparently confirms the right of officers to detain for questioning—often called an investigative seizure, although the Court did not specifically discuss this issue since the case involved forcible detention based on facts that clearly evidenced possible criminal activity. Where observed conduct is equivocal and not so clearly criminal, officers may merely want to question without necessarily physically detaining the person and subjecting him or her to a search.

The *Terry* rule, however, suggests that officers do possess the right to detain a person involuntarily and to subject the person to questioning, even if probable cause to arrest for a specific crime is lacking. For example, both California and New York grant officers the right constitutionally to detain a suspect for questioning if the circumstances would indicate to a reasonable person in a like position that the detention is necessary to the proper discharge of the officers' duties. Of course this right to detain is measured against an objective standard and must be based on articulated facts and circumstances—not on a hunch. The California rule appears in *People* v. *Mickelson:* ''In this state, however, we have consistently held that circumstances short of probable cause to make an arrest may still justify an officer's stopping pedestrians or motorists on the streets for questioning. If the circumstances warrant it, he may in self-protection request a suspect to alight from an automobile or to submit to a superficial search for concealed weapons. Should the investigation then reveal probable cause to make an arrest, the officer may arrest the suspect and conduct a reasonable incidental search.''

Standard of Detention

The right to detain without necessarily arresting has a salutary effect: it wards off pressure on officers to make an arrest when only an investigation is required. Through such an investigation, officers may dispel or corroborate their suspicions without haste. Detention permits them reasonable investigation commensurate with the circumstances that confront them and allows them legal flexibility to dispose of a bewildering variety of street encounters. At the same time, officers are required to articulate facts that distinguish the innocent citizen from the possibly guilty one, thereby insuring all citizens that the judiciary will scrutinize the detention and demand that it pass constitutional muster before any evidence seized is permitted in court. Court decisions sanctioning or disapproving a particular detention frequently present a kaleidoscopic pattern. Although this fact is disconcerting, the average observer of court opinions understands that any attempt to write an undeviating rule of ''stop and frisk'' is inherently inconsistent. First, the English language is not equal to the task for writer or reader; second, the very flexibility that the rule is designed to accommodate necessarily precludes any other result. What the courts seek from officers is a clear articulation of their observation and knowledge sufficient to validate their judgment objectively.

In *Terry* the Court stated that the test for a lawful detention was: ''Would the facts available to the officer at the moment of seizure . . . warrant a man of reasonable caution in the belief that the action taken was appropriate?'' Although this standard is not altogether free from vagueness, it requires a threefold test:

1. a rational suspicion by a peace officer that some activity out of the ordinary is or has been taking place;
2. some evidence to connect the person under suspicion with the unusual activity;
3. some suggestion that the activity is related to crime.

It is the last requirement that probably is most crucial and on which a peace officer must focus attention.

In attempting to meet the requirement that the observed activity is related to crime, officers can use evidence obtained by any of their senses, evidence obtained from other sources, relevant surrounding circumstances known to them, as well as their expertise and experience. All these factors, which, incidentally, are identical with those that justify an arrest, may be relied on to establish a reasonable basis for detention—that is, probable cause to detain. Since probable cause to detain rests on the same kind of factors that provide probable cause to arrest, but to a lesser degree, these factors will be considered in the section on Probable Cause to Arrest. (See chapter 2, Arrest.)

Although each case must ultimately depend on the specific facts involved, common sense dictates that some consideration be allotted to the gravity of the crime under investigation. Balancing the interest of personal security against the social need for protecting or detecting crime is more than an academic exercise. Approaching an armed robber differs substantially from arresting the possessor of marijuana cigarettes. Courts have said as much, and a general judicial consensus recognizes the need for instant and flexible police response to danger.

Most cases involving the detention of a person for suspected criminal activity arise from personal observation by the officer. In *Terry,* for example, the defendant was observed by the officer while he walked along a public sidewalk in front of a commercial store. His conduct was ambiguous at best, but clearly suspicious. Contrast Terry's action with that of the defendants in the following cases:

Police officers were sent to the airport to investigate a telephoned report from an airline that an employee had discovered what appeared to be marijuana in a passenger's baggage. When the passenger (Cauwels) came to the storage room to claim his package, he was arrested. One of the officers observed the number on the baggage tag attached to the arrestee's package. After the arrest, the officer left the storage room in the baggage area to see whether the arrestee was accompanied by anyone else. He observed the defendant (Irwin) "just standing" in the lobby about fifteen feet outside a glass door separating the baggage area from the lobby, which led to the sidewalk. "The defendant was standing next to three pieces of baggage, consisting of two pieces of luggage and a paper bag. Attached to one piece of luggage was a baggage tag bearing the next sequential number to the tag of the arrestee's cardboard box.

"[The officer] asked the defendant to accompany him to the storage room in the baggage claim area. In response to the officer's question, the defendant said he had no baggage. After leaving the defendant where his partner could 'keep an eye on him,' the officer went back to the lobby 'to examine the baggage.' He picked up the paper bag and detected an odor similar to the odor which came from the arrestee's baggage. He then took the bag and the two pieces of luggage back to the storage room, where he examined the bag, and found clothing, an envelope with defendant's name, and 'six paper-wrapped packages . . . each containing a green, plant material.' " The officer then arrested the defendant.

The Court said: "Although the discovery that the arrestee (Cauwels) had shipped a box of marijuana showed criminal activity, there was nothing *unusual in the activity* of the defendant who was standing close to baggage near the baggage area in the airport. The basis of [the officer's] initial decision to see if the arrestee was accompanied by anyone else did not appear in the record; the court had to assume that the officer had a "hunch" that marijuana shippers might be traveling in pairs. Certainly there was nothing in the defendant's activity to distinguish him from any other embarking or debarking passenger at the airport.

"Nor does the circumstance that one of the pieces of luggage near where [the defendant] was standing contained the next-numbered tag to the arrestee's baggage tag rationally suggest criminal activity by [the defendant], or provide a *rational connection to* [the arrestee's] *criminal activity*. The most that can be said of this circumstance, in isolation, is that the defendant was the next passenger in line at the baggage check-in counter.

"Even assuming that it could be inferred that [the defendant] stood behind [the arrestee] in line and further inferred that [the defendant] knew [the arrestee], the next inference that [the defendant] was *involved in* [the arrestee's] *criminal activity* is based on nothing more substantial than inarticulate hunches. There is no evidence that the officer had any additional information about [the arrestee] or [the defendant], or had any tip that persons traveling in pairs were shipping marijuana." (*Irwin* v. *Superior Court.*)

Compare this example: "An experienced narcotic officer responded to the call of a private citizen who had discovered a kit containing apparatus used in administering narcotics. The kit was found in a flower planter box adjacent to the sidewalk in front of his place of business, and had not been there 24 hours prior to the report. The officer . . . proceeded to examine the premises, and while at the back thereof [the defendant] Reulman was observed driving a Cadillac through the alleyway at the rear of the building.

The officer 'felt' that [the defendant] was out of place in the Cadillac and the alleyway and for that reason gave particular attention to his movements. He noticed [the defendant] was nervous and that he watched the officers in the rear view mirror as the car passed beyond. [The defendant] drove to the end of the alleyway, turned right to the street on which the building fronted, turned right again to the front of the building and parked immediately across the sidewalk from the point where the kit had been discovered. From that time on he was under constant surveillance by the officers. He left his automobile and walked along the sidewalk in the direction from which the car had approached. He peered into a window of a barbershop and then returned in the direction of his automobile. At this point the officers detained him and requested his identification.'' Was the detention lawful?

''The officers observed only that [the defendant] was nervous, appeared to be wary of them, and that he parked his car adjacent to the point where the kit was found and thereafter took a rather aimless walk in the near vicinity. Further observations by the arresting officer to the effect the defendant looked like an untruthful person and as though he did not belong in the Cadillac are not impressive and appear to add little to create any real suspicion, even considering that the officer was an experienced narcotics investigator familiar with the conduct of suspects in like circumstances. There is little, if anything, to distinguish the defendant from any other harried citizen who may have innocently parked his automobile in the same spot as did Reulman.''

Suppose we change the facts: At 10 A.M., ''an officer observed [the defendant] Moore in a telephone booth [near a refreshment stand at the corner of an intersection]. The officer had made several narcotic arrests in the area and testified that addicts go to this location to make purchases from street peddlers. As the police car drove into an adjacent parking lot, [the defendant] appeared to be talking on the telephone, seemed to observe the police car, moved from a comfortable position in the telephone booth, and turned his back on the police car. [The defendant] appeared nervous. The officer thought that [the defendant] 'was trying to avoid' him and due 'to the area and the surrounding circumstances . . .' thought it was suspicious.

''The officer left his car, went to the telephone booth, and asked [the defendant] his name and several questions. He asked [the defendant] if he had ever used narcotics in the past. The defendant said he had but not since he left jail. The officer then asked defendant if he might inspect the latter's arms.'' Was the detention for questioning lawful?

''The only suspicious circumstances relied upon by the officer were that the area was one where narcotic transactions had taken place in the past, and, that [the defendant], upon seeing the officers' car, turned his back on them, moved from a comfortable position, and appeared nervous. [The defendant] was talking on a telephone in a booth at ten in the morning, and, again, there seems little to distinguish him from any other citizen who may have been making a telephone call at that time and place. To hold that police officers should, in the proper discharge of their duties, detain and question all persons in that location, or all those who act nervous at the approach of officers, would, for practical purposes involve an abrogation of the rule requiring substantial circumstances to justify the detention and questioning of persons on the street.'' (*People* v. *Moore*.)

Whether or not a reasonable basis exists to detain someone for investigation of criminal activity depends largely on the context of the time, place, and circumstances of the detention. ''Probable cause to detain'' is shaped largely by the context in which it emerges. Thus, in the first example, the defendant Irwin was detained in a public airport frequented by thousands of people. He stood in the passenger area and did nothing to distinguish himself from other passengers. Although a crime had been reported, another person had already been arrested, and no evidence connected Irwin with that crime. In the second example, a crime had also been reported as having occurred on a public street, but no one had been arrested for its commission. Yet aside from his proximity to the location of the crime, the defendant was walking on a public street like anyone else. The officer could only describe a general nervousness—clearly not enough to meet a standard of detention which requires some observed activity out of the ordinary and related to crime. ''Nervousness'' is not sufficiently incriminating to justify a detention.

It should be noted that a frequent justification for detention is the officer's testimony that he or she observed evasive gestures or movements. ''Furtive conduct'' can be an additional factor that justifies detention, or possibly arrest, since an inference can be drawn that the person detained is attempting to conceal or dispose of seizable evidence. This topic is relevant here, but is discussed in chapter 2, Arrest.

In the last of the preceding case examples, the officers added a significant factor to ''mere presence'': a high incidence of narcotic sales in the area. But that fact alone was not sufficient to warrant the detention of someone who happened to be in the area. Yet this case does mark the transition between unlawful and lawful detention. By adding other circumstances, or other factors, officers approach the required standard of detention: unusual activity relating to crime.

Suppose these facts occur: At 4:30 P.M., three officers were cruising in an unmarked police car near a public park, an area of known narcotics activity. The officers were in plain clothes. One officer testified that he first observed the defendant walking away from the area of a rest room. He noticed that the defendant held a wadded object that protruded about an inch from his clenched fist. (The officer had admittedly a purely speculative idea that the object might be a narcotics kit.) The car in which the three officers were riding drove past the defendant and ahead of him. It appeared that the defendant was going to cross the street had he continued on his course. However, the defendant looked in the direction of the police car and abruptly changed his direction by traveling away from the car and thus away from the street which he would have crossed had he continued in his prior course. The car containing the officers passed the defendant. At this point, the defendant changed the object from one hand to another. At all times the defendant kept looking at the car containing the police officers. The car passed the defendant again, at which point the officer put the car in reverse, and the defendant walked away from the police car, reversing his direction from westbound to eastbound. The officer put the car in forward gear, pulled alongside the defendant, and stopped. He then called to the defendant, "Come here." When he opened the car door, the defendant started running. The officer testified that he did not identify himself as a peace officer or state his purpose of wanting to talk to the defendant because he did not have a chance to do so. The officer then chased the defendant, who ran out of the park and into the backyard of a nearby house. On the way the defendant bumped into a hedge. He was finally stopped. The officers went back to the hedge (the other officer having seen the defendant throw an object at the time he hit the hedge), and found a wadded piece of magazine paper that contained two rubber balloons and six paper bindles of heroin, plus three five-dollar bills. The officer testified that the packaging of narcotics as described was the way narcotics were normally packed for sale.

In such a case, the court will bear in mind the officer's specialized knowledge and will consider the specific and articulable facts available to them, together with reasonable inferences to be drawn from those facts, to ascertain whether or not the action of the officer in saying "Come here" was such an intrusion into the life of the defendant as to be constitutionally impermissible. If the officer had the right to say to the defendant, "Come here," then the defendant's actions in running away would be an additional circumstance that would obviously allow the subsequent detention and arrest. (While it might be argued with considerable merit that the mere speaking to an individual by a police officer, as was done in this case, is not a sufficient intrusion into that individual's life to put into effect the rules of detention, assume that the words used in this case were a sufficient show of authority to apply the rules.)

Consider these factors: First, the area—an area known to the officers to be one of considerable narcotics activity. For the trained officer, the sight of someone passing a transparent bag containing a leafy substance to another and receiving money in exchange is evaluated together with the environment in which the transaction takes place. Seeing that transaction take place in an area of known narcotics activity is a suspicious circumstance. Seeing the same transaction take place on the floor of a Chicago Grain Exchange would probably (and hopefully) be meaningless.

Second, the appearance of the officers. When evaluating the conduct of the officers, the court will keep in mind the concurrent conduct of the defendant and the officers' awareness of that conduct. Those involved in the narcotics trade are a skittish group—literally hunted animals to whom everyone is an enemy until proven to the contrary. Thus, the average law-abiding citizen seeing three grown men sitting in a slow-moving car at 4:30 in the afternoon would probably give them no more than a passing glance. But to the person involved in the narcotics traffic, three men in plain clothes, riding in an unmarked car, cruising at a slow speed in an area of high narcotic activity are about as inconspicuous as three bull elephants in a backyard swimming pool. Any normal person in the narcotics subculture would assume them to be "narcs."

With these first two factors in mind, pass to the third factor—the activity of the defendant in this case. There were others in the park whom the officers studiously avoided. It was the activity of the defendant that brought him to their attention. On seeing the officers' car, the defendant did not give it the passing glance of the upright, law-abiding citizen. His eyes were glued on that car. To him, it represented danger until proven otherwise. When it appeared that the car was going to intercept him if he continued on his path, he changed his course of travel and walked away. When the car again neared him, he again altered his course and proceeded in a different direction. At the same time he was making these changes in his course of travel and watching the police car closely, he changed an object in his hand (which the officer without any articulable reason thought was a narcotics kit) to another hand. By this time there was obviously no question in the defendant's mind as to who the three gentlemen in the car were. When the officer shouted, "Come here," it was, to him, a show of authority. Just as obviously, the defendant knew that they were police officers, as reflected by his subsequent and almost instantaneous behavior. This detention is lawful.

Observations alone will often suggest that a person is engaged in some kind of unusual activity. But relating that unusual activity to crime may require that the observation be supplemented by other evidence. For example: "About 2:30 P.M., two police officers, [using binoculars], saw the defendants, whom they did not know, seated on the grass in a public park. They appeared to be dividing objects which shone in the sunlight. One officer who observed the defendants testified they appeared to be counting coins and passing them back and forth. He could not actually see coins, but when one of the defendants got up, the officer saw him put what appeared to be a roll of coins in his pocket. The defendants then walked to a parked car and drove off, driving in a normal fashion and observing the traffic laws. The police officers followed in a patrol car, then drove alongside the defendants, identified themselves, and ordered the defendants to stop their vehicle. At that time, [one of the occupants] leaned forward and appeared to put something under the front seat and the car continued about three hundred feet before stopping." (*People* v. *Henze*.)

This case is close, but if the officers could have testified to additional facts, the case for a lawful detention would have been strengthened. If this incident had taken place during the hours of darkness, its timing alone might have provided a sufficient extra factor to justify temporary detention for investigation. The law in many instances draws a sharp distinction between the controls that may be exercised by peace officers during the nighttime and those to which they are limited during daylight hours. Most of the cases upholding temporary detention for investigation and questioning have arisen out of incidents that occurred at night.

Yet nighttime activity is not essential to the validity of temporary detention. Other factors may provide a sufficient basis for temporary detention:

"Had the officers had a report of a current burglary, that factor might have furnished sufficient added suspicion to justify detention. But here the officers had no knowledge of any burglary, either at the time of their original observations or at the time of the detention.

"Had the park where the police observed the defendants been known as a place where crimes, such as the sale of narcotics, had frequently and currently taken place, this might have provided sufficient justification for the detention.

"Had the police received information that criminal activity was scheduled to take place in the park of a type consistent with what the suspects were seen doing, this might have justified the detention.

"Had these officers known of a rash of recent petty burglaries in the neighborhood, this, too, might have provided the necessary additive to justify temporary detention.

"Had the officers known that one of the defendants had previously been convicted of burglary, this might have provided sufficient reason for the detention.

"Had the defendants been observed driving their car in an erratic or suspicious fashion, this might have provided sufficient justification for stopping them.

"Had the defendants been sitting in a parked car at an unusual time and place, this might have justified their detention.

"Had the defendants given the officers cause to believe that they were violating the motor vehicle laws, this, too, would have justified their detention for investigation."

Almost every case of detention occurs on public streets and is based on conduct observed by the officer. But suppose that the officer is told by someone else that criminal activity is taking place. Must the officer corroborate this statement by personal observation in order to detain a person, or may the officer act on the informant's statement alone?

For example: "An officer, driving alone early in the morning on patrol duty in a high-crime area, was approached by a person known to him and informed that an individual seated in a nearby vehicle was carrying narcotics and had a gun at his waist.

"After calling for assistance on his car radio, the officer approached the vehicle to investigate the informant's report. He tapped on the car window and asked the occupant, one Williams, to open the door. When the occupant rolled down the window instead, the officer reached into the car and removed a fully loaded revolver from his waistband. The gun had not been visible to the officer from outside the car, but it was in precisely the place indicated by the informant. The occupant was then arrested by the officer for unlawful possession of the pistol. A search incident to that arrest was conducted after other officers arrived."

In *Adams* v. *Williams,* the U.S. Supreme Court held that the officer acted justifiably in responding to his informant's tip. "The informant was known to him personally and had provided him with information in the past. This is a stronger case than in the case of an anonymous telephone tip. The informant here came forward personally to give information that was immediately verifiable at the scene. Thus, while the informant's unverified tip may have been insufficient for an arrest or search, the information carried enough reliability to justify the officer's forcible stop.

"[In reaching its conclusion], the Court rejected the defendant's argument that reasonable cause for a stop and frisk can only be based on the officer's personal observation, rather than on information supplied by another person. Informants' tips, like all other clues and evidence coming to a policeman on the scene, may vary greatly in their value on reliability. One simple rule will not cover every situation. Some tips, completely lacking in reliability, would either warrant no police response or require further investigation before a forcible stop of a suspect would be authorized. But in some situations—for example, when the victim of a street crime seeks immediate police aid and gives the description of his assailant, or when a credible informant warns of a specific impending crime—the police may respond appropriately."

Officers, therefore, can use personal observation, information obtained from others, and inferences drawn from the time and place of the confrontation to approach and detain a person for investigation of criminal activity. But whether the official purpose of the involuntary detention is to question or to forcibly detain, the reasons for the detention must be articulated.

Extent of Detention

Just as the original circumstances must justify an intrusion of personal security, there must be factors to justify the extent or duration of that intrusion. Generally speaking, the scope of police investigation during a forcible or involuntary detention must be reasonably related to the circumstances that justified the initial stop. Whether stopped for a traffic citation or detained as a pedestrian, a citizen cannot be detained an unreasonable length of time for "further investigation" unless other factors justify investigation of a different crime.

For example, two officers were patrolling at about 7:30 A.M. "They saw a person standing alone next to a road sign. His only observable possession, a green back pack, strapped closed, was 'leaned up against a road sign' and he was 'eighteen inches to two feet away.'

"It is a local police practice to talk to hitchhikers who appear to be under age, ask them for identification, and advise them of the dangers of hitchhiking. [The officers] believed that the defendant 'looked to be a juvenile' and they alighted from their patrol car and approached him. One of the officers asked for identification, and the defendant produced it. His identification established that he was over 18 years of age.

"At this juncture defendant was asked if he had 'any weapons—knives or guns or explosives.' He replied that he had 'three knives.' He was requested to produce them, and he withdrew one pocket knife from his coat pocket and another from his pants pocket. After the officers examined the two knives, they were returned to him. They inquired about the third knife, and the defendant stated that it was in the pack. [One of the officers] asked if he could see it. Defendant answered 'yes and walked over and started opening his pack:

"Without looking into the pack, [the officer] reached into the small pocket on the underside of the flap and brought out a book and a road map. On reaching into the pocket a second time, he withdrew a 'roach clip.' [The officer] thought he detected a brown residue on the teeth of the clip. The officer then turned his attention to the main part of the pack and pulled out a pair of bluejeans. In the back pocket of the jeans he found a 'Corina Mini' cigar box. He indicated that he was not looking for the third knife in that small box, but he did open it and discovered its contents to be two cigars and nineteen hand-rolled cigarettes. Suspecting that the cigarettes contained marijuana, the officers [placed the defendant under arrest]. . . .

"[One officer] testified that throughout the period of street detention the defendant appeared somewhat nervous and uneasy, but not more so than 50 percent of other persons stopped and questioned by the officers. The defendant did not make any furtive motions while under observation and did not appear to be under the influence of drugs or alcohol. Until the officers discovered the 'roach clip,' they perceived nothing that caused them to believe the pack contained contraband. [The officer] further stated that he was not apprehensive of being attacked by the defendant during the period of time he was in contact with him. . . .

"No hard and fast rule can be formulated for determining the reasonableness of the period of time elapsing during a detention. The dynamics of the detention-for-questioning situation may justify further investigation, search, or arrest. The significance of the events, discoveries, and perceptions that follow an officer's first sighting of a candidate for detention will vary from case to case. Nevertheless, in determining the reasonableness of further detention, favorable answers, observations, or perceptions must be regarded by the detaining officer as suspicion-allaying, rather than suspicion-heightening." (*Pendergraft* v. *Superior Court.*)

In this case, the defendant established he was over eighteen years of age, thus dispelling the officer's suspicion about his age. No other evidence suggests any reason for the officer to continue his detention other than curiosity.

In this chapter, detention has been isolated from all other factors that present themselves when an officer confronts a citizen. And the term has been used to describe detention for investigation of criminal activities. Often, however, the officer's initial contact with the person may arise in a noncriminal context—that is, when the officer is responding to a request for medical assistance or merely stopping a motorist for a minor traffic violation. The brief period incidental to noncriminal investigation may reveal additional factors that reflect criminal activity. Under these circumstances, the officer may escalate his or her response from "mere contact" to detention. Although in a fast-moving situation the distinction may blur between mere contact, detention for investigation of criminal activity, traffic infraction, misdemeanor, or felony, all the factors will be sorted out later in the courtroom.

Limited Search—the Frisk

It has become routine to discuss the topic of detention as "stop and frisk." The possible misinterpretation implicit in this joinder of words is that if the "stop" is lawful, a "frisk" is automatically legitimated. The U.S. Supreme Court has clearly held that a stop does not necessarily authorize a frisk. A stop is a *seizure* within the meaning of the Fourth Amendment, and a frisk is a *search* within the meaning of the Fourth Amendment. Each must be based on constitutionally adequate grounds and each must be separately evaluated. Analytically, the frisk should be discussed as a search, albeit a limited search (see chapter 3, Search). For reasons of convenience of discussion, however, and because the two acts have become so closely related, it will be discussed here.

Again the leading case is *Terry* v. *Ohio*. In *Terry* the officer forcibly detained the defendant based upon facts which, objectively viewed, indicated that Terry was about to enter a store and rob it. Simultaneous with the detention, the officer ran his hands over the outer clothing of Terry to determine whether weapons were on his person. The Court had to decide whether such conduct constituted a search within the meaning of the Fourth Amendment. The Court observed that this frisk, which followed the act of forcible detention, was a separate act invading personal security and that it had to be considered apart from the detention. The Court agreed that running the hands over the outer clothing was not a search in the full sense of the word. But such conduct was nevertheless an invasion of personal security that had to be balanced against the governmental interest of preventing crime. Reviewing the history of violence of American criminals, the justices agreed that police protection against guns and knives was an overwhelming social concern. Because detention in itself may elicit an emotional response, the Court ruled that street confrontations must be conducted in an atmosphere conducive to the officer's safety: "We cannot blind ourselves to the need for law enforcement officers to protect themselves and other prospective victims of violence in situations where they may lack probable cause for arrest. When in situations where they may lack probable cause for arrest. When an officer is justified in believing that the individual whose suspicious behavior he is investigating at close range is armed and presently dangerous to the officer or to others, it would appear to be clearly unreasonable to deny the officer the power to take necessary measures to determine whether the person is in fact carrying a weapon and to neutralize the threat of physical harm."

The Court reasoned, however, that even a limited search of the outer clothing for weapons constitutes "a severe, though brief, intrusion upon cherished personal security, and it must surely be an annoying, frightening, and perhaps humiliating experience." The Court authorized "a narrowly drawn authority to permit a reasonable search for weapons for the protection of the police officer, where he has reason to believe that he is dealing with an armed and dangerous individual, regardless of whether he has probable cause to arrest the individual for a crime. The officer need not be absolutely certain that the individual is armed; the issue is whether a reasonably prudent man in the circumstances would be warranted in the belief that his safety or that of others was in danger. . . ."

The Court said, too, that due weight should be given, not to inchoate and unparticularized suspicions or hunches, but to the specific reasonable inferences which the officer is entitled to draw from the facts in the light of personal experience. The Court also warned that the search must be "confined in scope to an intrusion reasonably designed to discover guns, knives, clubs, or other hidden instruments potentially usable in the assault of the police officer."

To disable a person from potential violence is entirely reasonable, and the initiating Court has approved a narrowly drawn constitutional authority for police to conduct a limited search for weapons—only if there is a reasonable basis for assuming that the person stopped is armed and dangerous. Of course the believing officer need not be positive, but he or she must be able to articulate the basis for this belief.

If officers confront someone whom they reasonably believe to be armed and dangerous, they may undertake precautionary steps to determine the validity of the suspicion. Normally this includes a brief patting down of the outer clothing, or in some cases perhaps a cursory search into a nearby area accessible to the individual detained, for example, a limited search of the car. If the pat-down reveals to the sense of touch the possibility of a dangerous weapon inside the clothing, a further intrusion into the pockets or clothing is authorized for the purpose of neutralizing the danger. The *Terry* case, and subsequent state court cases, indicate that the first intrusion on the suspect's outer clothing does not automatically authorize a second intrusion inside the clothing unless the first search reasonably reveals the basis for a more intensive quest. The act of reaching inside the pockets or clothing of a person is a separate search in the constitutional sense and must be founded on constitutionally adequate ground. If the pat-down reveals the possibility of a concealed weapon, this factor is constitutionally adequate to authorize a further limited search and removal of the weapon. The discovery of the invisible object may dispel the officer's concern for personal safety—in which case a more intensive search is unnecessary. Or, if the object removed is a weapon, grounds for arrest may emerge. Generally speaking, the scope and intensity of the frisk must be reasonably related to the need to remove a source of danger to the officer. Beyond that, no further invasion of personal security is permissible.

Would the officer be justified in frisking under the following circumstances? An officer testified that while he was patrolling his beat in uniform, he observed the defendant "continually from the hours of 4:00 P.M. to 12:00, midnight . . . in the vicinity of a major intersection. [He stated that] during this period of time he saw the defendant in conversation with six or eight persons whom the officer knew from past experience to be narcotics addicts. The officer testified that he did not overhear any of these conversations, and that he did not see anything pass between the defendant and any of the others. Late in the evening the defendant entered a restaurant. The officer saw the defendant speak with three more known addicts inside the restaurant. Once again, nothing was overheard and nothing was seen to pass between the defendant and the addicts. The defendant sat down and ordered pie and coffee, and, as he was eating, the officer approached him and told him to come outside. Once outside, the officer said, 'You know what I am after.' According to the officer the defendant 'mumbled something and reached into his pocket.' Simultaneously, the officer thrust his hand into the same pocket, discovering several glassine envelopes, which, it turned out, contained heroin."

In this case the officer's observations of unusual activity relating to crime were marginal at best. But assuming they were adequate to detain the defendant, the nature and scope of the officer's search were so clearly unrelated to the detention as to render the heroin inadmissible. "The search for weapons approved in *Terry* consisted solely of a limited patting of the outer clothing of the suspect for concealed objects which might be used as instruments of assault. Only when he discovered such objects did the officer in *Terry* place his hands in the pockets of the men he searched. In this case, with no attempt at an initial limited exploration for arms, the officer thrust his hand into the defendant's pocket and took from him envelopes of heroin. His testimony shows that he was looking for narcotics, and he found them. The search was not reasonably limited in scope to the accomplishment of the only goal which might conceivably have justified its inception—the protection of the officer by disarming a potentially dangerous man.'' (*Sibron* v. *New York.*)

Suppose the case for detention is stronger: Two veteran narcotic officers, working in plain clothes, assumed a vantage point near a refreshment stand in an area of high narcotic activity. ''One of the officers, who was seated facing the street, observed the defendant and a companion walking towards him. His suspicion aroused by 'the manner in which they were walking up the sidewalk and talking to each other and looking around. . . . looking back and to the side as to see if anyone was watching,' one officer told his partner to 'keep an eye' on the suspects as they passed the hot dog stand and proceeded toward a nearby park—the direction in which his partner was facing. 'Having some experience in this type of thing concerning the area,' both officers agreed that by looking around, the suspects were 'acting in a suspicious manner . . . being apprehensive about someone observing them.' The officer observed the defendant and his companion, apparently engaged in conversation, walk 40 to 50 feet east of the refreshment stand and stop.

''Although his view was somewhat obscured by the park chain-link fence, the officer saw the suspects continue to look around; noticed that the defendant laughed and that the companion leaned against a parked car; observed each of the suspects reach into his pants pocket. The companion appeared to extract an object—although the officer could not actually see an object—while the defendant extracted what appeared to be money. The two placed their hands together in an apparent exchange. Having then observed the suspects for a total of three to four minutes, the officer told his partner, 'Okay, the deal has gone down.'

''The officers left the refreshment stand and approached the suspects, who were walking toward them. The officers identified themselves and asked 'Were you two dealing?' After receiving a negative reply they ordered the suspects to return to the site of the suspected transaction 'to determine whether or not a narcotic transaction had been made.' One officer reached into the defendant's pocket, pulled it up, observed balloons subsequently determined to contain heroin, shoved the balloons back into petitioner's pocket, and handcuffed him.'' (*Cunha* v. *Superior Court.*)

Assuming that the officers' observations were insufficient to justify an arrest for sale or narcotics, the facts were sufficient to warrant detention. Absent probable cause to *arrest* (which would allow an unlimited incidental search of the person), officers can only conduct a limited search for weapons. The purpose of the frisk incidental to a detention is the removal of weapons, not the seizure of evidence. And the frisk is only authorized if there is a reasonable basis to believe the suspect is armed and dangerous. No evidence of the officers' belief that defendants were armed and dangerous appears from their testimony. The pat search, therefore, was unwarranted by the circumstances and evidence seized from their person was excluded.

Because observation of conduct possibly reflecting sale or possession of narcotics may not be significantly different from innocent conduct, officers must use particular care in distinguishing criminal activity from innocent activity. But detention for suspected criminal activity, even in narcotic cases, will not justify a frisk without evidence that the officer believes the defendant to be armed and dangerous. Because narcotics are so easily disposed of or concealed, the officer's task in detaining and simultaneously preventing the loss of possible evidence is difficult.

Assume now that the detention of a suspect is reasonable and that the officer reasonably believes the suspect to be armed and dangerous. The officer is authorized to make a cursory search of the exterior of the suspect's clothing. If the cursory search reveals a lump in the shirt pocket, may the officer remove the object?

In balancing the safety of police officers against the Fourth Amendment's proscription of unreasonable intrusions, *Terry* and *Sibron* concluded that in searching a legally detained individual reasonably suspected of being armed, a police officer must be limited to "a careful exploration of the outer surfaces of [the] person's clothing" until and unless he or she discovers specific and articulable facts reasonably supporting the suspicion. Only then may an officer exceed the scope of a pat-down and reach into the suspect's clothing for the limited purpose of recovering the object thought to be a weapon.

"Feeling a soft object in a suspect's pocket during a pat-down, absent unusual circumstances, does not warrant an officer's intrusion into a suspect's pocket to retrieve the object. A pat-down must 'be confined in scope to an intrusion reasonably designed to discover guns, knives, clubs, or other hidden instruments for the assault of the police officer.' The obvious purpose of holding that officers cannot go beyond exploration of the surfaces of a suspect's clothing without being 'able to point to specific and articulable facts which, taken together with rational inferences from those facts, reasonably warrant that [additional] intrusion' is to ensure that the scope of such a search cannot be exceeded at the mere discretion of an officer, but only upon discovery of tactile evidence particularly tending to corroborate suspicion that the suspect is armed. To permit officers to exceed the scope of a speculation that the object might be a razor blade concealed in a handkerchief, a 'sap,' or any other atypical weapon would be to hold that possession of any object, including a wallet, invites a full search of an individual's person. Such a holding would render meaningless *Terry's* requirement that pat-downs be limited in scope absent articulable grounds for an additional intrusion.

"Accordingly, an officer who exceeds a pat-down without first discovering an object which feels reasonably like a knife, gun, or club must be able to point to specific and articulable facts which reasonably support a suspicion that the particular suspect is armed with an atypical weapon which would feel like the object felt during the pat-down. Only then can judges satisfy the Fourth Amendment's requirement of a neutral evaluation of the reasonableness of a particular search by comparing the facts with the officer's view of those facts. Thus, for example, an officer who believes a soft object is a 'sap' in the form of a small bag of sand must be able to point to its weight and consistency to justify an intrusion into the suspect's pocket.'' (*People* v. *Collins*.)

One of the most difficult legal problems for police and the courts is the skyrocketing use of contraband narcotics, drugs, and marijuana. The distinctive packaging of heroin in tinfoil or condoms is common to police experience. Officers quickly learn to detect the telltale feel of tinfoil or tightly packed contraceptives containing heroin. If an officer carefully manipulates the outer clothing of someone whom he or she has detained and detects the presence of these distinctive containers inside the clothing or in pockets, the officer is instantly alerted to the possible presence of contraband. Can these concealed materials be seized as evidence?

The answer is not easy. On the one hand, an officer is entitled to remove concealed objects from inside the clothing if acting on a belief that the object is a potential lethal weapon. Tinfoil and condoms are not in that category. On the other hand, if the officer's sense of touch reveals the presence of contraband, an arrest should ensue for possession of an illegal substance. A crime is being committed in the officer's presence. If the Constitution does indeed authorize a set of flexible police responses to varying situations, then the officer may escalate the searching authority according to the circumstances. Thus, if an officer initially entertains a reasonable basis for believing a suspect is armed and dangerous, a pat search for weapons is authorized—but not a search for contraband. If the frisk reveals facts that lead the officer to conclude the suspect is carrying contraband instead, the officer must articulate the reasons for this belief. This basis probably could not be supported by the sense of touch alone since the officer cannot verify the belief until he or she observes the concealed item. For this reason, many courts are reluctant to approve a search inside a suspect's clothing based on the officer's opinion that sense of touch revealed the presence of contraband on the suspect's person. Some judicial reticence to accept such testimony stems from an unwillingness to allow the right to pat-search for weapons to be expanded too broadly. The courts will often demand corroborating facts. Aside from the officer's experience in the detection of narcotics—which is relevant if the officer observes a person's dilated eyes, needle marks on the arm, slurred speech, or other indicia of heroin or narcotic use—these factors are important in corroborating the sense of touch. As these corroborating factors increase, the likelihood of judicial approval of a search for contraband inside the clothing is increased; as these corroborating factors decrease, the opposite result is likely. An officer who can catalog the factors corroborating sense of touch and articulate them at trial is most likely to convince the court that the search inside the clothing or of the pockets was reasonably based.

CASES AND MATERIALS

Tiffany, McIntyre and Ratenburg, *Detection of Crimes,* Little, Brown & Co., Boston (1967).

Wayne R. LaFave, "Street Encounters and the Constitution," 67 *Michigan Law Review* 40 (1968).

Detention

Adams v. *Williams,* 407 U.S. 143, 32 L. Ed. 2d 612, 92 S. Ct. 1921.

Commonwealth v. *Berrios,* 437 Pa. 338, 263 A. 2d 342.

Commonwealth v. *Meadows,* 293 A. 2d 365 (Pennsylvania).

Cunha v. *Superior Court,* 2 C. 3d 352, 466 P. 2d 704.

Ingram v. *State,* 264 So. 2d 109 (Florida).

Irwin v. *Superior Court,* 1 C. 3d 423, 462 P. 2d 12.

Pendergraft v. *Superior Court,* 15 Cal. App. 3d 237, 93 Cal. R. 155.

People v. *Collins,* 1 C. 3d 658, 463 P. 2d 403.

People v. *Henze,* 253 Cal. App. 2d 986, 61 Cal. R. 545.

People v. *La Grange,* 40 Mich. App. 342, 198 N.W. 2d 736.

People v. *Mack,* 26 N. Y. 2d 311, 258 N.E. 2d 703.

People v. *Manis,* 268 Cal. App. 2d 653, 74 Cal. R. 423.

People v. *Mickelson,* 59 C. 2d 448, 380 P. 2d 658.

People v. *Moore,* 69 C. 2d 674, 446 P. 2d 800.

People v. *One 1960 Cadillac Coupe,* 62 C. 2d 92, 396 P. 2d 706.

People v. *Rivera,* 14 N. Y. 2d 441, 201 N.E. 2d 32.

People v. *Taggart,* 20 N. Y. 2d 335, 229 N.E. 2d 581.

Sibron v. *New York,* 392 U.S. 40, 80 S. Ct. 1889, 20 L. Ed. 2d 917.

State v. *Onishi,* 499 P. 2d 657 (Hawaii).

Terry v. *Ohio,* 392 U.S. 1, 88 S. Ct. 1868, 20 L. Ed. 2d 889.

1. Officers properly stop a vehicle for a minor traffic violation, but observe no conduct by the motorist indicating that he poses any threat to the officers. The officer asks the motorist to alight from the vehicle and enter the patrol car. When the motorist enters the car, the officer notices him drop a bundle of heroin. Would the seizure of the evidence be reasonable? What authority does the officer have to request that the motorist leave his vehicle under these circumstances? If no such authority exists, the motorist has been unlawfully seized and the subsequent observations may be unreasonable. (*People* v. *Robles,* 28 Cal. App. 3d 739, 104 Cal. R. 907.)

2. Defendant, holding an airplane ticket for a domestic flight, passes through a magnetometer prior to entering the airplane. The magnetometer, a device which reflects the presence of metal on the person, reacts positively. The defendant is prevented from boarding the plane and frisked. No weapons are found. His luggage is then opened and officers observe contraband narcotics. May a seizure follow even if no weapons were found?

Suppose a prospective passenger fits the "highjacker profile." May he be stopped and frisked, without more evidence, prior to boarding an airplane? What about a search of his luggage?

("Airport Searches and the Fourth Amendment," 71 *Columbia Law Review* 1039.)

3. "While his car was stopped at a traffic light at 1:45 A.M., a police officer observed the front seat passenger of a following vehicle pick up what appeared to be a beer can, drink from it, and then put the can out of view. A few moments later the police car's red light was activated, causing the other automobile to stop. The purpose was to see if there was an open container, or drinking, of an alcoholic beverage in violation of the Vehicle Code. The driver of each vehicle left his car. Asked by the police officer what his passenger was drinking the driver said that it was an 'orange drink.' The officer testified, 'He said that he would like to show me.' He walked back to the vehicle, opened the left front door and said, 'Officer, come here, look for yourself.' At that point I did approach the left front door that was open. I looked inside and observed the person in the right front seat, which was Padgett, holding a Fanta brand name orange can in his left hand; and also on the seat next to his left leg was what appeared to be a six-inch .38 revolver.

"Obviously considering the probability that the gun was loaded the officer 'backed up, and pulled [his] service revolver [and] advised [his] partner that there was a gun in the car. [They] ordered the occupants to get out.' "

Was the original detention lawful?

(*People* v. *Superior Court* [Acosta], 20 Cal. App. 3d 1085, 98 Cal. R. 161.)

4. At approximately 10:45 A.M., an officer and his partner, wearing sport clothes and driving in an unmarked vehicle, were on patrol duty. When they were approximately thirty to forty yards away, they observed a parked vehicle adjacent to the roadway and saw three males (one of whom was defendant) standing near the rear of the parked car. As the officer approached the vehicle, the young men started to leave. The officer stopped the police vehicle; he and his partner alighted and announced that they were police officers. With guns in hand they walked up to the three persons, directed them to turn toward the parked car, and made a cursory search of their persons for weapons.

The officer testified that in the pat-down he did not feel any weapons. He testified that, as to one of these three (not the defendant), he could "observe . . . numerous half dollars, the silver variety, which aren't in circulation any more." He said he also could see "an extremely large amount of currency in his left front pants pocket which bulged considerably being folded once."

Was this a reasonable detention? Why would the officers approach with drawn guns under these circumstances? Did they fail to articulate their reasons adequately?

5. Two officers were proceeding southbound on a boulevard at approximately 12:30 A.M. in an unmarked police car when they observed a vehicle parked on a street near the northwest corner of an intersection.

"As they approached the vehicle, the officers noticed that it was occupied by three men who were looking across the street in the direction of a motel. One officer testified that as they passed the vehicle, the occupants 'looked at us and their heads seemed to follow us as our vehicle passed theirs, and after we had passed them, the headlights went on; we then pulled in to the curb across the other side of the street.'

"The officers continued to observe the car and saw the headlights 'go out again'; the three occupants again appeared to direct their attention towards the area of the motel. After approximately five minutes, defendant's vehicle left the scene and made a right turn. The officers turned their car around and saw defendant turn left into another street. The officers turned on their red light and defendant stopped his car. There is no indication that defendant's car had been driven otherwise than in a legal manner during this period.

"As the officer approached the car on foot, defendant got out of the car, but the other occupants remained seated therein. All three were asked to identify themselves. They showed various papers and stated that they had just been driving around for about an hour. Defendant, who had been driving the car, admitted ownership.

"The officers proceeded to search the car, and in addition to two open beer bottles found lying on the floor behind the front seat, they discovered five shotgun shells in the glove compartment and a sawed-off shotgun hidden in the ventilator shaft under the dashboard. This gun was not visible from outside the car, nor from the vantage point of a person seated in a normal fashion on the front seat."

Were the officers' actions reasonable?

(*People* v. *Cowman,* 223 Cal. App. 2d 109, 35 Cal. R. 528.)

2 Arrest

Chapter Objectives

After reading this chapter, you will be able to:

1. Explain the Fourth Amendment's requirement that all arrests must be supported by probable cause.

2. Define probable cause and its components: observation, information, circumstantial evidence, and opinions.

3. Describe the rules governing the use of statements by informants.

4. Explain the special requirements covering delayed arrests and arrests with warrants.

Statutory Requirements

Early English common law authorized certain designated persons to arrest subjects for the purpose of securing their presence at trial for an alleged criminal offense. But the English and colonial tradition of maximum freedom from governmental interference reflects concern over the potential abuse of such awesome power. Because of this concern, English and American legal history records a continuing attempt to strike a balance between the need to preserve individual freedom and the need to allow the state to prevent injury to the person and property of its citizenry. It has not always been easy to achieve this balance, yet perhaps the tension between freedom and authority helps maintain it.

No one can forget the legacy of oppression facilitated by indiscriminate arrest power. The extensive statutory definitions of arrest power—that is, requirements of notice of the reason for arrest, immediate delivery of the arrestee to the magistrate, provisions for bail, the right to be present with counsel at trial, the right to testify and present evidence, and the right to confront accusers—all flow directly from the initial arrest. Legislatures have attempted not only to define carefully the arrest itself, but also to assure that any subsequent conviction be obtained in open court before an impartial tribunal. ''Fair trial'' is only the final stage that originated with the arrest.

Of course, countless arrests never result in any subsequent trial, but the forcible jailing of anybody nevertheless triggers a series of judicial responses. Incarceration of a person is subject to judicial review by writ of habeas corpus, in which law enforcement agencies must justify custody of the arrestee to the court. Or a magistrate will review the circumstances of the custody, even if no crime is charged as yet, to determine whether bail is authorized. And, in some cases, the arrest may be the subject of a federal suit alleging violation of civil rights. Lastly, the arrest record impairs the academic and employment application of an arrestee so that he or she may seek to expunge the record by judicial relief.

The power of a peace officer, or in some cases of a private person, to arrest and thereby involuntarily deprive a citizen of liberty is universally defined by statute. Generally speaking, peace officers are authorized to arrest for the commission of at least two classes of crimes: misdemeanors and felonies. The states differ widely as to the kinds of crimes that constitute misdemeanor or felony, but the former includes minor offenses subject to fine, or brief imprisonment, or both; the latter involves more serious offenses, often warranting imprisonment for longer periods of time.

The power to arrest for either class of offense is related to the nature of the offense. Officers may arrest for misdemeanors only when these misdemeanors are committed in their presence. The usual misdemeanor offense is not a sufficiently grave risk to person or property to justify an arrest based on statements by another person, or even if the officer personally believes the offense was committed at an earlier time. Under such circumstances, when a misdemeanor offense is not committed in the officer's presence, the remedy is to obtain a warrant from the court authorizing the arrest.

Incidentally, with the extensive growth of vehicular traffic, a new classification of crimes has emerged: the infraction. Because most traffic violations are classified as misdemeanors, that is, crimes, the entire array of procedural and substantive criminal law is invoked. Yet most traffic violations are negligent acts, not intentional violations of the law, and motorists are dismayed to be enmeshed in a procedure that was never designed to apply to them. The increasing use of traffic citations, easy bail forfeiture, and a traffic court is a response to the absurd ritual of criminal trials for traffic offenders. The use of the term *infraction* has evolved to avoid burdening the courts with vehicular trivia.

Whatever the merits of the new classification of infraction, the term only becomes important here in the context of search and seizure. As discussed earlier in chapter 1, Detention and Arrest, the officer's initial contact with the citizen often is the result of a traffic violation. If the traffic violation is a misdemeanor, the offense is committed in the officer's presence, therefore authorizing the arrest. Many state statutes, however, specifically describe the procedure to be followed when an officer detains for the purpose of issuing a citation. Normally the motorist must be released on a promise to appear unless the statute authorizes arrest on some other ground, such as the motorist's demand to be taken before a magistrate immediately or an inability to provide satisfactory evidence of a driver's license, vehicle registration, or identification.

Many courts have been reluctant to classify this brief detention as an arrest, although functionally speaking the motorist has been involuntarily deprived of personal liberty. Yet the routine traffic offense has created a significant legal issue that highlights the distinction between *statutorily* authorized arrest and *constitutionally* authorized arrest, or seizure. The right to search incidental to detention for a traffic violation flows from constitutional origin, that is, the Fourth Amendment, and not from statutory authority (see chapter 3, Search). For our purposes, it should be noted that an arrest for a traffic violation authorized by statute must still be examined constitutionally to determine whether the detention was a seizure within the meaning of the Fourth Amendment.

Felonies constitute the other major category of crimes. Arrests may be effected even if these more serious crimes are not committed in the officer's presence. If the officer has probable cause to believe that a felony has been committed, he or she may arrest. In this instance, the officer relies not solely on personal observation of the crime, but on information provided by others, or on a strong suspicion that a felony has been committed. Or, in many cases, the officer acts on a combination of these factors. Because the Fourth Amendment also requires that arrests, or seizures, must be based on reasonable cause, the following section of this chapter is especially relevant.

Constitutional Requirements

The lawfulness of an arrest does not depend merely on compliance with a statute defining or authorizing an arrest. It is the court's responsibility to determine whether the arrest was lawful constitutionally, not statutorily. Just as a detention is a seizure within the meaning of the Fourth Amendment, so also an arrest is a seizure in the constitutional sense.[1] An arrest, which is an act invading a citizen's personal security, may be effected only in conformity with the constitutional command that citizens are to be secure against unreasonable searches and seizures.

In order for an arrest to be reasonable within the meaning of the Fourth Amendment, the seizure must be based on *probable cause*. In the absence of sufficient evidence of probable cause, the arrest will be held unlawful, and any evidence seized as a consequence thereof will be excluded. Requiring all arrests to be founded on probable cause prevents officers from using the arrest as a pretext to conduct a search. The court must implement the constitutional requirement of probable cause by reviewing any invasion of personal security that resulted in the seizure of evidence subsequently offered at trial.

Probable Cause Defined

We have noted that peace officers are usually authorized by statute to arrest misdemeanants only if the offense is committed in the officer's presence. Because misdemeanors normally involve no injury or damage to person or property, officers must either see the offense committed or obtain a warrant. For more serious crimes, officers are usually statutorily authorized to arrest based on probable cause to believe that a crime has been committed. The Fourth Amendment also requires that all arrests be based on probable cause, however, and therefore a state statute cannot authorize an arrest on a standard less strict than that required by the Constitution. The standard of probable cause must be consistent with the Fourth Amendment as interpreted by the courts and particularly by the U.S. Supreme Court.

Probable cause has been defined as follows: facts and circumstances within the knowledge of the officer, and of which he or she had reasonably trustworthy information, which were sufficient to warrant a prudent person in believing that an offense had been committed or was being committed.

Another court has said: "There is no exact formula for the determination of reasonableness. Each case must be decided on its own facts and circumstances and on the total atmosphere of the case. Reasonable cause has been generally defined to be such a state of facts as would lead a man of ordinary care and prudence to believe and conscientiously entertain an honest and strong suspicion that the person is guilty of a crime. Probable cause has also been defined as having more evidence for than against; supported by evidence which inclines the mind to believe, but leaves some room for doubt." (*People* v. *Ingle*).

It is important to note that the standards for evidence that proves the guilt of an arrestee differ from those for evidence that establishes probable cause to arrest. Guilt must be proved beyond a reasonable doubt under established rules of evidence. The law of evidence—which is defined either by statute or by cases decided by courts of each state—has developed through attempts to filter the truth by excluding certain kinds of evidence that could prejudice or mislead the jury. On the other hand, probable cause deals with probabilities, that is, factual and practical considerations of everyday life on which reasonable and prudent people act. Probable cause is a practical, nontechnical conception that affords a compromise between the citizen's privacy and the officer's execution of the law.

Probable or reasonable cause is a legal test measuring the quality of evidence. When the issue is presented to the judge, he or she must determine whether there are sufficient facts and circumstances that would warrant a reasonable person in believing that an offense has been committed. The court bears the responsibility for determining whether the officer has testified to facts sufficient to support a finding of probable cause. In the majority of cases, the validity of the arrest is critical at trial when the prosecution offers evidence seized by the officers at the time of arrest. If the court finds that the arrest was not supported by probable cause, the search incidental to arrest will not be reasonable within the meaning of the Fourth Amendment, and the seized evidence will be excluded.

As in detention for investigation of criminal activity, probable cause is shaped by the context in which it emerges. Yet some patterns can be outlined. But first, let us consider some examples which illustrate the doctrine of probable cause itself:

An officer testified that he was at home in his apartment at about 1 P.M. "He had just finished taking a shower when he heard a noise at his door. He looked through the peephole into the hall, and saw 'two men tiptoeing out of the alcove toward the stairway.' He immediately called the police, put on some civilian clothes and armed himself with his service revolver. Returning to the peephole, he saw 'a tall man tiptoeing away from the alcove and followed by this shorter man, toward the stairway.' The officer testified that he had lived in the 120-unit building for 12 years and that he did not recognize either of the men as tenants. Believing that he had happened upon the two men in the course of an attempted burglary, the officer opened his door, entered the hallway and slammed the door loudly behind him. This precipitated a flight down the stairs on the part of the two men, and the officer gave chase. His apartment was located on the sixth floor, and he apprehended the defendant between the fourth and fifth floors. The defendant explained his presence in the building to the officer by saying that he was visiting a girl friend. However, he declined to reveal the girl friend's name, on the ground that she was a married woman. The officer patted the defendant down for weapons, and discovered a screwdriver in his pocket.

"By the time the officer caught up with the defendant on the stairway between the fourth and fifth floors of the apartment building, he had probable cause to arrest him for attempted burglary. The officer heard strange noises at his door which apparently led him to believe that someone sought to force entry. When he investigated these noises he saw two men, whom he had never seen before in his 12 years in the building, tiptoeing furtively about the hallway. They were still engaged in these maneuvers after he had called the police and dressed hurriedly. And when the officer entered the hallway, the men fled down the stairs. It is difficult to conceive of stronger grounds for an arrest, short of actual eyewitness observation of criminal activity." (*Peters* v. *New York*).

In this example the officer's observation of unusual conduct led to a strong suspicion that a burglary was being attempted in his presence. But in other cases, probable cause must necessarily rest on inferrence and deduction from known facts. Consider the following example.

"On three prior occasions, purchases of marijuana cigarettes had been made by an undercover agent from one Garcia. On the night of the arrest, the agent again purchased marijuana cigarettes from Garcia. On each of these occasions the same general plan of operation was followed. The agent would obtain money with which to make the purchases, he would then drive to Garcia's house, Garcia would come to his car, the latter would give Garcia this money for the purpose of purchasing marijuana, Garcia would take the money and leave, returning in 15 or 20 minutes. On his return he would hand marijuana cigarettes to the agent. Garcia's car was a 1948 maroon-colored Chevrolet. The automobile in which the defendant was seated at the time of arrest was that used by Garcia in these transactions. On each occasion another officer, while keeping the defendant under observation, saw Garcia's car pull into the driveway in front of his house, observed someone leave the house and approach the car on the driver's side, and observed that shortly thereafter the car would leave. On one occasion there were two separate trips made by Garcia to purchase cigarettes for the agent, and Garcia's Chevrolet was twice observed in the defendant's driveway at those approximate times. The time during which the agent waited for Garcia to return coincided with the time required for him to make the trip to the defendant's house and return. The cigarettes contained marijuana.

"On the night of the arrest the agent again met Garcia at the latter's premises and stated he wanted to buy marijuana, giving him an envelope containing $20 in currency. This money, consisting of two $5.00 and ten $1.00 bills, had been placed in the agent's envelope after the serial numbers thereon had been listed. At approximately 7 P.M. Garcia received this envelope and departed. He returned about 8:10 P.M. About 7:15 Garcia's car was seen pulling in the defendant's driveway, someone approached the car and after a short delay the car left. When Garcia returned to the agent's car, he handed him 36 marijuana cigarettes. At that moment the agent signaled waiting police officers that the marijuana had been delivered. Garcia was immediately arrested. He had returned on foot, his car was not in the driveway, and the officers set out at once to look for it. A few minutes later they found it half a block away occupied by the defendant and a known addict whom they immediately arrested.

"At that moment the officers knew that the defendant was a peddler and user of marijuana. He was definitely implicated in the purchases, and the presence of himself and a companion in the car at that particular time and place, under all of these circumstances, motivated the officers in making the arrest and search of both men, although they had no previous knowledge as to the defendant.

"Was the sole ground for the defendant's arrest the fact that he was sitting in an automobile with a known dope user and peddler? No. Officers arrested the defendant not merely because he was sitting in an automobile at night with a known addict, or because the automobile was parked in a neighborhood where the narcotics trade was known to flourish. These arresting officers had just participated in the arrest of Garcia. They knew that a narcotics transaction had just taken place in which Garcia, Garcia's car and the defendant's house were directly implicated. They knew that contraband had just been transported in that car. They knew that the defendant's companion was not only a peddler but a user. They had reasonable grounds for inferring that the narcotics sold to the agent had been purchased from the defendant or from someone with whom he was then working.'' (*People* v. *Ingle*.)

Probable cause must be based on facts that directly, or circumstantially, lead to a strong suspicion that a crime has been committed. Suppose officers attempt to combine observation and inference, as in the following case:

An officer testified that ''he observed one Edwards step out of an automobile containing two women and some small children and hold a conversation in the street with one Gould, whom the officer knew to be a burglar. He afterwards examined police records and ascertained that Edwards also had a burglary record. By tracing the license number of the car, the officer obtained the address of defendant's home. Later that day officers commenced a surveillance of defendant's home and saw Edwards and some small children entering and leaving the house at various times over a period of three days. Three days later, about 9 P.M., the officer with six or seven other officers gathered in the street opposite defendant's home. None of the officers was in uniform and they were all dressed in 'rough clothing.' They saw Edwards and the defendant at the window of a front bedroom looking in their direction. The officers proceeded across the lawn, knocked on the front door, and 'almost instantly . . . the lights went out.' They called out that they were police officers and receiving no response, they kicked in the front door. The officers arrested Edwards. . . . At the time of Edwards' arrest, none of the officers knew of any specific burglary or had reason to believe that Edwards had committed a burglary or any other felony.

''The question of probable cause to justify the arrest of Edwards and the search of the premises incident thereto must be tested upon the facts which the record shows were known to the officers at the time the arrest was made. Those facts were: 1. Some days before the arrest Edwards was seen talking to a known burglar; 2. police records showed that Edwards had a previous record for burglary; 3. Edwards, the defendant and their children over a period of three days were seen in and about defendant's home; 4. when seven or eight men wearing rough clothing walked across the lawn, after seeing Edwards and defendant looking out of a bedroom window, and knocked at the door the lights went out, and when they identified themselves as police officers there was no immediate response. Taken separately or all together, these facts could not constitute reasonable cause to believe that Edwards had committed a felony so as to justify his arrest without a warrant. The facts that Edwards had a burglary record and was seen talking to a known burglar, while relevant, are not sufficient to constitute reasonable cause to believe that Edwards had committed a burglary or any other felony. The conduct of Edwards in entering and leaving the defendant's home is not shown to have been accompanied by any suspicious conduct of any sort. There is nothing to support a reasonable belief that any man, no matter how bad his past record, has committed a felony simply because he is seen going in and out of a private home in a normal manner. This leaves only the turning out of lights and the failure briefly to respond to the call of 'police officers' after seven or eight roughly dressed men crossed the lawn in a body and knocked at the door in the darkness of night. While evasive conduct upon the approach of police officers may under proper circumstances justify an arrest and search, the observed approach to a private home in the nighttime of a party of seven or eight roughly dressed men and their knocking on the door might reasonably lead the most innocent of persons to extinguish the lights hoping that they would depart. And their subsequent announcement that they were police officers might reasonably arouse a degree of skepticism that would lead the occupants to make no immediate response or indeed any response at all, except possibly to telephone for the aid of those whom they knew with certainty to be police.

"Whether or not Edwards and Gould are characterized as 'professional burglars' because they both had a past burglary record, whether or not their street conversation is characterized as 'making a meet' (thus by a semantic slant putting an aura of criminality about what so far as the police officers knew was an entirely innocent conversation), and whether or not the additional fact is that a large number of burglaries were committed in the area, the evidence is insufficient to connect either of them or the defendant with the commission of any one or more burglaries." (*People* v. *Privett.*)

In this case, the inferences drawn from what the officers observed and what they knew did not constitute a strong suspicion that a felony had been committed. And if they had found incriminating evidence inside the house, such evidence could not have been used to support probable cause. Probable cause must be based on facts known to the officers *prior* to an arrest. Facts that are discovered subsequent to the arrest are not admissible.

For example: An officer testified that he had received information that a "shooting gallery" (the smoking of marijuana) was to take place at a particular address. Two officers drove to the address and parked nearby at about 1:20 A.M. The building appeared to consist of an upper and lower flat. No lights shone in it. Four men entered the building. The officers called for two more policemen, and the four officers approached the steps leading to the building entrance. Two of the men who had recently entered came through the front door. An officer called to them, identifying himself as a policeman. One of the men called out "cops." Both reentered and slammed the door against the police, who promptly broke it in, pursued the two men upstairs, and arrested all four men in the apartment.

In this case, even assuming there was some basis for detention, no evidence of probable cause to arrest existed prior to the officers' observation of the men (the information, as discussed later in this chapter, was wholly inadequate to justify arrest). The furtive conduct of the suspects, therefore, cannot be substituted for the lack of probable cause. The conduct was in response to an unlawful display of authority and is inadmissible on the issue of probable cause.

Similarly, if officers went to an apartment, lacking probable cause, they could not demand to be admitted. If the occupants opened the door and then learned the identity of the officers, their response of slamming the door cannot be construed as anything more than an indirect demand for a search warrant. The act, although uncivil, was in response to an unlawful show of authority.

Probable cause is composed of bits and pieces of evidence, the sum total of which yields a strong suspicion that a crime is being or has been committed. Probable cause cannot be based on a hunch or intuition; rather, the officer must articulate those facts and circumstances, known prior to the arrest, which equaled a "strong suspicion." These facts and circumstances can arise from several sources and may be classified as *factors of probable cause*.

Observational Probable Cause

This category includes all kinds of evidence that are presented directly to the officer's senses: what the officer sees, hears, smells, or touches. In the case of such evidence, the officer is a witness to the events and can testify to facts directly perceived. Most often the officer will testify to what he or she saw. These observations will be measured at trial against the standard of probable cause to determine whether the officer saw enough to warrant a strong suspicion that a crime was being committed.

The same facts that justify an arrest may also reliably justify a detention. Since the standard for the quality of evidence necessary to detain is less strict than that for probable cause to arrest, officers can often detain a person and utilize the detention to establish additional evidence to arrest. Or officers can use the detention to dispel their original suspicions and effect a release of the suspect immediately instead of making an arrest. If the circumstances allow, a detention should always precede an arrest so that officers can develop additional evidence during this investigative stage without risking a premature arrest.

Furtive Movements Perhaps the most frequent observation used to establish probable cause is the officer's testimony that he or she observed an arrestee's "furtive movements." This phrase is verbal shorthand to describe the conduct of an arrestee when confronted by an officer. If the arrestee attempts to dispose of, conceal, or destroy evidence when confronted by the officer, the prosecutor can logically argue that such conduct was sufficiently incriminating to warrant the officer's "strong suspicion" that a crime had been committed. Attempting to prevent the officer's discovery of contraband or other seizable evidence certainly suggests guilty knowledge that qualifies as probable cause, even if the officer could not point to the specific crime involved. And the courts have tended to agree that furtive gestures do imply guilt at least sufficient to justify arrest, although not necessarily sufficient to convict.

Difficulty arises in determining what constitutes "furtive conduct." At the outset, the courts have said that the officer cannot intentionally induce such conduct in another. For example, if an officer confronts someone on the street for no reason and threatens to search this person, any furtive conduct by the person in response is unlawfully induced. Any evidence seized as a consequence would be inadmissible as a product of an unlawful arrest.

In the vast majority of cases, the officer testifies that he or she observed a motorist or passenger make a furtive movement when the officer signaled the vehicle to stop. Note at this point the legal analysis: The officer observes a traffic violation—usually a misdemeanor—committed in his or her presence. The statute authorizes an arrest, or at least the temporary immobilization of the vehicle for the purpose of issuing a citation. In the constitutional sense, this detention constitutes at least as much a seizure as the temporary detention of a pedestrian in *Terry*. (See chapter 1, Detention and Arrest.) If the momentary detention reveals additional evidence of possible criminal activity, a different misdemeanor offense or a felony may emerge. The significance of a furtive gesture during or after the traffic stop escalates a traffic offense into a possible felony, that is, possession of contraband. The distinction between arrest authority and search authority, to be considered in more detail later, is clear in this example: The misdemeanor was committed in the officer's presence and justified an arrest on that basis. The felony—possession of contraband—is implied from the conduct of the occupant of the vehicle even if the officer did not see the object of suspicion. The "furtive conduct" establishes the strong suspicion necessary to prove probable cause to arrest for a felony.

"The difficulty is that from the viewpoint of the *observer*, an innocent gesture can often be mistaken for a guilty movement. He must not only perceive the gesture accurately, he must also interpret it in accordance with the actor's true intent. But if words are not infrequently ambiguous, gestures are even more so. Many are wholly nonspecific, and can be assigned a meaning only in their context. Yet the observer may view that context quite otherwise from the actor: not only is his vantage point different, he may even have approached the scene with a preconceived notion—consciously or subconsciously—of what gestures he expected to see and what he expected them to mean. The potential for misunderstanding in such a situation is obvious.

"It is because of this danger that the law requires more than a mere 'furtive gesture' to constitute probable cause to search or to arrest. The United States Supreme Court recently reaffirmed this rule in the case of

Sibron v. *New York:* 'deliberately furtive actions and flight at the approach of strangers or law officers are strong indicia of guilt, and when coupled with specific knowledge on the part of the officer relating the suspect to the evidence of crime, they are proper factors to be considered in the decision to make an arrest.' That knowledge, of course, may be derived from the usual twin sources of information and observation; it is the information known to the police officers or the suspicious circumstances which turn an ordinary gesture into a furtive one, but in the absence of information or other suspicious circumstances, a furtive gesture alone is not sufficient.

"A few distinguishable examples will serve to set the scene. A furtive gesture coupled with prior reliable information may constitute probable cause, i.e., the downward motion of a juvenile sitting with others in a car parked in an area where officers had been told to expect a gang fight. Detention, or possibly arrest, may also be predicated on a furtive gesture coupled with an actual observation of contraband in the portion of the vehicle to which the gesture was directed, i.e., the downward motion of an occupant of a parked car, followed by the officer's observation of a marijuana cigarette under the seat. And the officer need not even see recognizable contraband so long as he observed the suspect in the act of deliberately hiding a package or box which, in the circumstances, it is reasonable to believe contains contraband, i.e., a motorist and his companions refused to leave a service station at 3 A.M.; when officers arrived and asked for identification, he was seen to take a small white package from his pocket and drop it into the open motor of a parked car.

"In each of the foregoing cases the gesture of the suspect could reasonably be given a guilty connotation from prior reliable information, or from the officer's personal observation of contraband, or a deliberate act of concealment under otherwise suspicious circumstances. It is true that to reach a conclusion of probable cause in each instance the officer was required to draw certain inferences from the known facts; but the inferences were eminently reasonable, and the chain of his deductions was correspondingly strong and compelling.

"In the typical case, an officer on patrol observes a motorist commit a routine traffic violation, and turns on his siren or red light to stop the violator's car and issue a citation; upon giving such a signal, the officer sees the driver or other occupant of the car suddenly 'lean forward' or 'bend down' or otherwise reach toward the dashboard or floor. Assuming these are the only 'facts known to the officer' at that moment, do they give him probable cause to believe that the person he observed moving in the car is in possession of contraband? Careful analysis reveals there are too many weak links in the officer's chain of deductions to support that conclusion. The flaws may be conveniently grouped around two assumptions.

"First, the argument assumes that the movements in question were purposeful responses to the officer's appearance on the scene. But the person observed might not in fact have seen the police car, in which event any movements he made would be irrelevant. If he did see a vehicle following, he might not have recognized it to be a police car; many of the 'furtive gesture' cases have arisen in the dark of night, with the officer's car some distance behind. If he recognized it as such, he might not have understood that the police were attempting to bring his own car to a halt. If he correctly inferred the intent of the police, his movements might not have been made in *response* to that awareness; they might simply have been movements he was on the point of making in any event. And if his movements were responsive to the situation, they still might not have been *purposeful:* i.e., when suddenly facing an imminent confrontation with the police for some unknown misdeed, many citizens with nothing to hide will nevertheless manifest an understandable nervousness by means of random, undirected gestures or movements.

"Secondly, the argument assumes that only the guilty will react in the described manner to a policeman's signal to stop their car. To begin with, every motorist knows that the approaching police officer will in all likelihood ask to see his driver's license, and probably also the registration card of the car. The observed movement, therefore, might well be nothing more than the driver's act of reaching for his wallet so as to have his license ready for inspection, or reaching for the steering post or glove compartment to obtain the registration card. And as many women drivers keep their handbag—containing their license and other identification—next to them on the floor or between the seats, a reaching motion in that direction would be no less natural for them.

"Furthermore, every motorist knows that the officer will wish to speak with him, however briefly; simple preparations for that conversation are therefore to be expected. It may be necessary, for example, for the driver to roll down his window. If the radio is playing at the time, the driver or a passenger might lean forward to reduce the volume or turn off the set. If the driver was smoking, he might well reach down to extinguish or store his cigarette in the car's ashtray. And if an occupant of the vehicle was consuming food or beverages, similar movements would probably follow.

"Additionally, many motorists expect to alight from their car, whether voluntarily or upon request, when they are stopped by the police. Again, certain preparations are usually in order: seat belts may have to be unbuckled; passengers may have to remove road maps, packages, folded coats, or infants from their laps; and clothing may have to be adjusted, shoes or hats put on, belts tightened, and outer garments buttoned.

"Finally, when a driver stops his car in a situation in which he knows he may alight from the vehicle, it is both customary and prudent for him to apply his parking brake. Yet in many automobiles the parking brake handle or lever is on or below the dashboard, and the driver is therefore compelled to lean forward or downward in order to apply it.

"Each of the foregoing gestures in some degree resembles—and could reasonably be mistaken for—the movements of a person engaged in secreting contraband inside a car. Yet each is wholly innocent, and has been made at one time or another by virtually every driver or passenger on the roads today.

"Of the various circumstances, perhaps the most persuasive is a driver's failure to stop his car promptly when a police officer signals him to do so. Even this fact, however, is subject to interpretation. Little difficulty is experienced when the motorist in this situation continues to drive for a substantial distance and makes sharp turns or other unusual maneuvers; such conduct can fairly be deemed evasive action, implying consciousness of guilt. Yet in other instances a delay in stopping may well be reasonable. It is a motorist's duty to use due care at all times, and when requested to pull over by a police officer he should do so at the first *safe* opportunity. But road conditions, speed, or other traffic may sometimes compel him to proceed a short way before bringing his car to a halt. The line may be a fine one in certain cases, but it must be drawn realistically and in light of all the facts.

"A second circumstance is that the confrontation took place in the nighttime. Here, however, the possibility of mistake is greater. As distinguished from a deliberate delay in stopping his car, the fact that it is night when the police appear is not 'conduct' of the motorist 'in response to' the officer's signal. The significance of this fact should therefore be appraised with caution; it does not, without more, transform an innocent gesture into a culpable one furnishing probable cause to search." (*People* v. *Supreme Court* [Keifer].)

Other circumstances bearing on the question of whether the furtive gesture has a criminal connotation include the remoteness of the area where the confrontation takes place; a report of a recent crime of violence in the neighborhood, with a description of the suspect; the damaged condition of a car giving ground for belief that it might be stolen; the motorist's lack of a driver's license and other identification; erratic or dangerous driving by the operator of the suspected car; and "nervousness" of the motorist while under police investigation.

By requiring a more patient investigation subsequent to an observed furtive movement, the courts prevent an arrest predicated on a tenuous interpretation of criminal misconduct. Normally the traffic stop allows the officer sufficient time to develop additional facts to corroborate or dispel his or her original impression. Undeniably an experienced officer can intuitively detect the presence of contraband or suspect the recent commission of a crime. But these suspicions must be rational, and they must be articulated. Otherwise the constitutional requirement of probable cause would evaporate under subjective evaluation. What is necessary is the officer's verbalization of the arrestee's criminally significant conduct. That testimony need not be confined only to the conduct observed; the officer may combine other factors of probable cause to corroborate suspicions. Thus, the suspect's overheard statement, observed the conduct and behavior, the smelled odor of contraband, the officer's experience in detecting narcotic violations—all such factors of probable cause may be invoked.

Arrest for Grand Theft Auto Closely related to the arrest of motorists in the context of furtive movements, although not necessarily so, are arrests for grand theft auto. Often these arrests begin also with the temporary detention of the motorist to issue a citation. If the license plate of the vehicle is not listed on a "hot sheet," the officer must determine whether the vehicle has been stolen based on a record check or on his or her own field investigation. Given the widespread use of computers to determine vehicle theft, most officers resort to these resources instantly. Absent any affirmative information, the officer must proceed solely upon the field investigation.

Officers tend to conclude that the inability of a motorist to produce a driver's license or satisfactory evidence of vehicle registration indicates theft. Obviously both these factors suggest that judgment. Yet officers often fail to take any additional steps to fortify their conclusions. The danger exists that a court may conclude that absence of a license or registration is easily explained by many innocent drivers. In fact, failure to produce a valid driver's license or registration certificate is an extremely trivial offense, and often the motorist can avoid a penalty merely by presenting the correct papers later in court. At most, a small fine is levied. Aside from turning up the revoked or canceled license, however, little significance is attached to these offenses. Thus, officers who rely solely on these two factors may find courts disapproving arrests and subsequent searches based on such a slim thread. To prevent such a result, officers can often use their detention time to develop additional evidence that will substantiate evidence of theft. Usually the driver's conflicting statements, demonstrable falsehoods, or inability to identify the owner of the car, coupled with an attempt by the officer to verify lawful possession of the vehicle, will be sufficient corroborating evidence of grand theft.

Street Sales of Narcotics The following case closely parallels a situation described in chapter 1 on Detention. Compare this apparent narcotic transaction to that on pages 17–18.

During the daytime, a police sergeant was parked in an unmarked police vehicle at a street intersection adjacent to a high school and near a location designated by the school as a smoking spot for students. "The defendant, age 20, was leaning against a chain-link fence about 40 feet from the police officer's vehicle. A young man wearing a red and white shirt and carrying a notebook folder walked up to the defendant, and the two appeared to converse. The defendant then handed Red and White Shirt 'some type of paper currency . . . green in color.' Red and White Shirt reached into his notebook folder and pulled out a package 'five inches long, about an inch and a half to two inches wide. It appeared to be flat and wrapped in wax paper.' He gave it to the defendant who put it in his right rear pocket. After further brief conversation, Red and White Shirt entered the school campus. . . .

"The sergeant, commander of the vice and narcotic bureau, had participated in approximately 500 narcotic arrests. In his experience, marijuana is normally packaged in waxed paper bags when sold to young people in $5 and $10 quantities. The sergeant waited a few minutes for the arrival of an assistant and then arrested the defendant for possession of marijuana. In the latter's right rear pocket he found a folded waxed paper bag containing marijuana.

"In this case, an experienced police officer saw the defendant and another engage in conversation and then saw the defendant hand the other person paper currency and receive back a flat waxed paper package of the size and appearance used for the sale of marijuana in small quantities. The sergeant's observations differed in degree of specificity from those, for example, where a suspicious package is observed, but neither money nor merchandise is seen to change hands. In contrast, the sergeant observed all the elements of a completed sale—preliminary negotiation, a delivery of paper currency, and a reciprocal delivery of a suspicious package, specifically, a waxed paper package of a type known by him to be commonly used for marijuana sales.

"It is difficult to imagine what further visual evidence of a street sale of narcotics could be required to establish reasonable cause for an arrest, for here the officer observed each element in the sale carried out before his eyes. Of course, it is possible that on close examination the subject matter of the sale might turn out to be something other than contraband—as for example alfalfa grass, catnip, pipe tobacco, balsam needles, or aromatic herbs. But reasonable cause for arrest requires probabilities only, not certainties, and the circumstances make it highly unlikely that the waxed paper package contained anything other than contraband, for noncontraband items in waxed paper bags are not normally exchanged for paper currency on street corners." (*People* v. *Garrett*.)

Use of Other Senses A more difficult problem occurs when the officer relies on the sense of smell to justify an arrest. For example: Officers lawfully entered a temporarily unoccupied house and observed a closed bag lying on the table. The strong odor of marijuana alerted the officers to the presence of contraband inside the bag although they could not verify their belief until they opened the bag. One court has said that officers cannot rely solely on their sense of smell to *search*. Since no one was present in the house, there was no arrest. Consequently, the court held that the sense of smell was not sufficient by itself to justify a warrantless search.

Had an occupant been present, however, the significant odor emanating from the bag might well have been probable cause to arrest.

This doctrine, therefore, would not apply to an arrest of the occupants of a car. If after lawfully stopping a motor vehicle, officers detect the odor of marijuana emerging from inside the car, the sense of smell would constitute a strong suspicion that the occupants were committing, or had committed, a crime, thereby establishing probable cause for their arrest and an incidental search for the contraband.

The odor of marijuana can also be detected from outside an apartment or dwelling place when officers approach the door. May entry and arrest follow? If there is a reasonable basis for believing that the dwelling place is occupied, the odor of marijuana constitutes probable cause to arrest the occupants. If the dwelling place is unoccupied, the odor is only evidence that contraband is present, but no occupant is subject to arrest. The odor may provide probable cause to search—in which case a search warrant will be necessary—but it does not authorize entry in the absence of someone to arrest.

Most courts are reluctant to approve arrests based on probable cause supported by the use of the sense of smell. Their reluctance is partly attributable to a concern that such testimony is not susceptible to effective cross-examination and is thus open to abuse. This same judicial reluctance to allow an arrest appears when probable cause is supported by evidence of the officer's sense of touch. An officer cannot verify completely what he or she smells or touches until it is seen. As noted earlier (see Limited Search—the Frisk in chapter 1), the sense of touch is often unreliable without some corroboration. Therefore, in developing probable cause to arrest from the sense of touch or smell, officers should proceed cautiously. They are well advised to employ temporary detention, rather than arrest, to obtain corroboration of the sense of smell or touch, even if they are positive in their own minds. Officers must remember that their opinions alone are not sufficient; they must convince the court of the validity of their strong suspicions. This responsibility can be best accomplished by presenting as many corroborating factors of probable cause as possible.

Informational Probable Cause Although most arrests are based on conduct personally observed by officers, other kinds of evidence are also admissible to establish probable cause. Information received from other officers, victims, witnesses, and informants is relevant and admissible to establish the strong suspicion necessary for probable cause.

Information received from others, however, is a classic example of hearsay, and several judicial rules have been created to require at least a minimum reliability for this kind of evidence. Statements made by others to peace officers would not normally be admitted in evidence at trial on the issue of guilt. Such statements are hearsay and would not be admitted because hearsay rules generally require the witness to testify to what he or she saw, did, or heard. By requiring witnesses or victims to testify to events they observed, or to statements they heard, the court is able to observe their demeanor and assess their credibility in person. Defense attorneys can cross-examine witnesses in an attempt to contradict or modify their statements. If statements from absent witnesses or informants are to be admitted at all, the courts must maintain some control so that the fact-finding process is not subverted.

Hearsay, that is, statements by parties who are not witnesses at trial, may be received and are admissible to establish probable cause to arrest. But such statements are inadmissible to establish guilt of the charge. Largely for this reason, the court determines the lawfulness of an arrest in the absence of the jury. The task of separating statements into admissible and inadmissible forms is probably too difficult a one to demand of a lay jury. In addition, probable cause is a question of law for the court, not an issue for the jury. Thus, hearsay statements can be offered in evidence to establish the lawfulness of the arrest without seriously impairing the defendant's right to a fair trial on the issue of guilt.

Officers receive information from a variety of sources. For purposes of analysis, it is useful to classify informants according to the source. Informants may be categorized as criminal informants and citizen informants.

Criminal Informants Although the characterization of someone as a criminal informant is not entirely accurate, the term generally connotes a person who supplies information to law enforcement agencies in exchange for pay, immunity from arrest, or a promise of lenient treatment. Because this kind of informant is often heavily involved in illicit activities, his or her information must be subjected to careful scrutiny. History testifies to careless or sinister use of informants, and courts will not allow reports from such sources to be received without some verification. And that verification cannot be supported by a subsequent arrest and search that confirms the informant's statement. Probable cause must be established prior to an arrest—not after.

Most courts admit hearsay statements related to an officer by an informant if there is a reasonable basis for relying on the informant's credibility. In other words, an arrest may be based on such information if the informant is "reliable." The reliability of an informant is usually established by the officer's previous experience with this person. If an informant has reported criminal activities that have proved accurate on prior occasions, it is reasonable to rely on a present statement of criminal activity. The accuracy of the previous information can be established by testimony from the officer that a specific number of arrests and/or convictions were obtained based on the informant's statement. It is not critical that criminal *convictions* result from the informant's reports, but that arrests and subsequent trials were held based on the informant's reports. The quantity of arrests or trials that resulted from the informant's information is not decisive; the decisive factor is the quality of this person's evidence. That quality can be improved by supplementing the informant's statements with the officer's own investigation, observation, experience, and other information.

If an officer testifies to facts that lead the judge to conclude there is a reasonable basis for the informant's reliability, the first step in establishing probable cause to arrest is completed. The courts require, however, that the reliable informant must not be repeating hearsay from others. The informant must speak from personal knowledge of the events that are related to the officer. When the officer-witness testifies in court that an informant reported certain incriminating facts about the defendant, the court must determine whether the informant *personally* saw or heard the facts. Moreover, the facts that the informant relates to the officer cannot simply be innocent or meaningless facts, such as a description of the car, or of the suspect, or of the suspect's companions. The informant must inform the officer about personal knowledge of incriminating facts, that is, those facts that strongly indicate the commission of a criminal act.

The second category of criminal informant may be characterized as the untested informant. Probable cause to arrest cannot be supported by information from an anonymous or untested informant unless the information is corroborated. The corroboration required here is not that which is often required to corroborate an accomplice's testimony at trial. The rule of corroboration of an untested informant requires officers to validate and confirm information furnished by a source whose reliability is unknown or untested.

Corroboration can be obtained from a variety of sources: information from other untested informants; observation of the defendant; prior record of the defendant; information from other officers who have known the defendant; information from official records. Again the decisive factor is not so much the quantity of information as its quality. An unverified tip is not equivalent to a strong suspicion that a crime has been committed. The "strong suspicion" must emerge from several factors, none of which may be significant in itself, but which in conjunction with each other indicate probable cause. Corroborating an untested informant gives that person a status equivalent to that of a reliable informant—and then an arrest may be made.

For example: "An officer received information from two untested informants that one 'Al' was selling narcotics, 'mainly dangerous drugs.' The informants gave the officer Al's physical description, indicated that he drove a dark blue Mustang convertible, and gave the address of the apartment where he allegedly carried on his unlawful activity. The officer and his partner went to the address given by the informants and observed on the mailbox for apartment 207 the names 'Sutherland' and 'A. Fein.' A blue Mustang convertible was parked in the carport to the rear of the apartment.

"The officer went to the door of apartment 207, knocked and a female voice from inside asked 'Who's there?' The officer stated, 'Police officers. Narcotics Investigation.' The reply from the same female voice was 'Just a minute.' The officer then heard noises from within the apartment which sounded like people moving about and running, together with a noise described as 'like a plastic type vial landing or falling to a hard floor surface.' After a lapse of about 30 seconds, the door was opened about 1½ feet by a codefendant. When the officer asked if 'Al' was there, she opened the door completely, stepped backwards and said, 'Yes, he's the one on the couch.' The officer observed defendant seated on the couch in the apartment, stepped in the apartment about three feet and stated that he, the officer, had a complaint concerning the use and selling of narcotics at the location. The officer could observe lying on an end table what appeared to him to be two burnt marijuana seeds. The officer retrieved these two seeds from the end table, placed them in an envelope and then in his pocket. Thereupon, he arrested defendant. A search revealed contraband.

"If the officers had reasonable cause to arrest defendant, the search would have been justified as incident to a lawful arrest. Although the information which the officers received from their untested informants justified further investigation, that information standing alone was not sufficient to constitute reasonable cause for an arrest or search. Information given by an untested informant may be sufficient if corroborated in essential respects by other facts, sources or circumstances. It could be argued that the informants' reliability was corroborated by the fact that certain information furnished by them proved to be correct, such as defendant's first name, his presence at the apartment, and the presence of the blue Mustang. However, in order for corroboration to be adequate, it must pertain to defendant's alleged *criminal* activity; accuracy of information regarding the suspect in general is insufficient.

"Even if there are two informers, the statements of one do not necessarily corroborate the statements of the other. The quantification of the information does not necessarily improve its quality; the information does not rise above its doubtful source because there is more of it. Although there may be circumstances where corroborative information from separate, unrelated sources will thereby establish its credibility, nevertheless in the instant case there is no showing of what information each informer furnished the officers, or whether the information was furnished independently by each informer. Accordingly, there is no basis for holding that their statements were truly corroborative.

"Cases have held that suspicious conduct observed by officers may furnish the necessary corroboration for an untested informer. Without attempting to set forth a rule of general application, the sounds heard here by the arresting officer do not sufficiently corroborate the informers' statements that defendant was selling narcotics. The apartment door was opened shortly after the officers announced their presence, no plastic vial was discovered by them, and the sounds described by the officer were wholly consistent with innocent activity.

"Does the officer's observation of what he thought were two burnt marijuana seeds sufficiently corroborate the information furnished by the informants and afford reasonable cause for defendant's arrest? It is apparent that evidence of prior marijuana *use* is not strongly corroborative of information regarding alleged *sales* of narcotics, 'mainly dangerous drugs.' Secondly, it seems clear that the mere presence of two burnt marijuana seeds would not give rise to a reasonable inference or strong suspicion that the occupants of the apartment in which the seeds were found were presently guilty of a crime. Evidence of useless traces or residue of narcotic substances do not constitute sufficient evidence to sustain a conviction for possession of narcotics. Although the presence of two burnt marijuana seeds might reasonably suggest that defendant or another occupant of the apartment formerly possessed and used marijuana, that inference would not justify their arrest for present use, possession or sale.

"Apart from searches of automobiles, and other movable property, it is the general rule that probable cause to believe that a search will reveal contraband does *not* justify a warrantless search. Therefore, even if the presence of two burnt marijuana seeds could, under the circumstances in the instant case, have supported an inference that a search would uncover larger, usable quantities of drugs, that inference should have been drawn by a neutral and detached magistrate and not solely by the officer. However strongly convinced officers may be that a search will reveal contraband, their belief does not justify a search without a warrant.

"It follows that ordinarily an arrest may not be based solely upon suspicion that a subsequent search will reveal contraband. It is settled that an arrest may not be used as a pretext to search for evidence, and that an arrest cannot be justified by the fruits of a subsequent search." (*People* v. *Fein.*)

With regard to the requirement that an informant speak from personal knowledge, the officer-witness faces a dilemma. The officer often desires to conceal the identity of the informant from the defendant because disclosure would end the informant's usefulness or possibly subject this person to retaliation from the defendant or others. By careful cross-examination, the defendant can readily determine the time, place, and persons present when the informant obtained personal knowledge of the crime. By a process of elimination, the defendant may be able to ascertain indirectly the informant's identity. This dilemma is unavoidable in many cases, but the officer must be aware of the possibility of indirect disclosure and tailor the investigation accordingly. The more knowledge the officer can acquire independently of the informant, the stronger the case and the less the officer will need to rely on the informant.

The U.S. Supreme Court has indicated that an informant need not be disclosed on the issue of probable cause. But many courts have held that disclosure will be required if the informant is a material witness on the issue of guilt. In most cases the informant's information will be admissible on both issues. Because the informant must have personal knowledge of incriminating facts, this person becomes, in effect, a witness to the crime. The defendant can easily argue that due process requires disclosure of material witnesses on the issue of guilt. Thus, even though disclosure could be withheld on the issue of probable cause, concealing the informant's identity on the issue of guilt may not be possible. In California, a statute authorizes the judge to hold a special hearing on the issue of disclosure in the absence of the defendant and his or her counsel. After hearing prosecution evidence, including the possibility of naming the informant, the court may deny disclosure to the defendant and order the transcript of the hearing sealed. The sealed transcript may be opened only by a reviewing court.

Just as the officer must inform the magistrate about the source of information that amounted to probable cause to *arrest,* he or she must supply similar information in the affidavit for a warrant to *search*. Whatever object the officer intends to seize under the authority of a warrant, he or she must inform the magistrate about the source of information. If the source of information for the warrant is an informant, the officer must also recite sufficient evidence of the informant's reliability and personal knowledge of the facts related.

If this information does not inevitably tend to disclose the identity of an informant whom the officer wishes to conceal, the defendant can still attempt to challenge the factual accuracy of the affidavit. Some state courts allow the defendant to offer evidence of the officer's misunderstanding of the facts related by the informant, or even evidence that the informant's statements are false. This type of inquiry further removes the cloak of secrecy from the informant. And even disclosure of the informant's identity does not improve the defendant's legal position. The informant's identity, without the ability to locate this person, is an empty gesture. What the defendant will demand is the production of the informant in court as a potential witness. In reality, the defendant realizes that a demand for disclosure and production forces the prosecuting attorney into a dilemma. If the prosecutor refuses to disclose the name of an informant who is a material witness, the defendant is denied the right to due process, and the officer's statement or testimony of probable cause will be stricken. If the officer does disclose, at the very least the informant's further usefulness disappears.

One state has held that if the officer uses an informant as an active agent, arrangements must be maintained that will enable officials to locate the informant and subject this person to the process of the court if he or she is a material witness. Failure to do so deprives the defendant of due process of law because testimony cannot be obtained from a material witness.

Whether a court will order disclosure, and perhaps production, of informants depends on judicial policy more than state legislatures. The "fair trial" concept reposes considerable discretion in the courts to determine these issues. The competing choices are difficult: crimes often can be investigated and solved only by drawing on those people who know the most about their perpetration. The average citizen is ignorant about crime and criminal offenders. The person possessed of such knowledge is frequently closely associated with crime. The credibility of such a witness, however, is often weak. In order to solve crimes, particularly so-called "victimless" crimes, informants are indispensable. But once disclosed, their utility—and perhaps their lives—are gone.

Ultimately the judiciary must decide the issue of disclosure and production of informants. Statutes are too rigid, and only in a discretionary setting can the issue be resolved. The closed hearing at which the judge hears evidence only from the prosecutor is an attempt to allow judicial discretion. Inevitably the case will arise where the defendant must be allowed to cross-examine on the issue of disclosure just as he or she would on the issues of probable cause or guilt. Perhaps on balance the closed hearing offers the best compromises. Much confidence is thereby reposed in judicial discretion, but who else is suited for impartial judgment?

There are those who claim that the use of informants to enforce victimless crimes further compromises the police and the courts; that such crimes are not violent and pose no threat to person or property; that disproportionate police resources—and use of informants—could be redirected. Whether society is prepared to adopt such a policy is immaterial here except insofar as a reduction in the quantity of informants is concerned. Yet the criminal law will continue to require the use of informants for crimes of violence and for those victimless crimes that clearly cannot be approved as a way of life.

Citizen Informants The courts have recognized a distinction between those who regularly supply information to the authorities and others who provide information openly and without expectation of any reward or immunity. The latter informant has been characterized as a "citizen informant." Most often a citizen informant is a victim or witness of a crime involving injury to person or damage to property. This person's report, often easily verifiable from the circumstances, may properly constitute the sole source of probable cause to arrest. Because a citizen informant's statement can be easily corroborated, and because such a report is openly submitted, the courts have approved arrests solely upon this source of information. A single citizen informant can provide sufficient evidence of probable cause as long as he or she has personal knowledge of the facts related. All the officer needs to establish is the informant's status as a "citizen."

In most cases the status of an informant is obvious from the circumstances. The injured liquor store operator who shouts for help after a robbery is a clear example of a citizen informant. But, on occasion, a citizen informant may provide information about clandestine crimes not involving violence or damage. The prevalence of marijuana, drugs, and narcotics is such that few people are unaware of this illicit traffic. But familiarity with indicia of drug use is not automatically converted to expertise. Officers need to exercise caution when receiving reports from citizen informants about narcotic use. Careful questioning is essential in order to evaluate the informant's ability to identify contraband. Often a supplemental investigation will be necessary to corroborate the informant's report. This is probably routine police practice in any event, but the courts will scrutinize the informant's report in order to determine whether the source is an informed citizen or merely an uncorroborated, untested informant.

Official Channels An arrest, or detention, is not always made on the officer's personal knowledge or on what an informant told the officer. Modern law enforcement requires radio communication, in which the authority to arrest is directed from a central transmitting facility. Or, in some cases, one officer delegates arrest authority to another. In either case, the arresting officer cannot testify to any facts that qualify as probable cause. To allow arrests without the original information would open the door to abuse. Consequently, the courts hold that although an arrest is lawful even if the arresting officer personally lacks probable cause, the defendant may demand to cross-examine whoever possessed the probable cause initially. The source may be a victim, a witness, an informant, or another peace officer. Consider the following.

"At 8 o'clock in the morning an officer, while sitting in his radio car, saw two men, the defendant and another person, standing and talking with one another in the alley bordering a service station. The two men walked over to the service station attendant, then walked away from the attendant in opposite directions from each other. The officer approached the attendant and asked him if he knew the two men and what they were doing there. The attendant replied that he did not know them, and 'I was just going to call the station because they had been hanging around acting suspicious.' This colloquy constitutes the entire conversation between the officer and the attendant. The attendant did not testify at the trial. Another employee of the service station arrived on the scene in time to see the defendant and his companion parting from each other and walking away from the station. The officer called out to the defendant asking him to come back because he wanted to talk to him. Defendant kept on walking. This officer radioed another officer who was driving a different patrol car, and told him "to stop a male Negro that was walking northbound in the alley, that he was a suspicious person." The officer drove his radio car down the alley to stop the defendant. The officer patted the defendant down for weapons and felt what appeared to be a pistol inside his waistband on the right side.

"The direction by one officer to another to pick up the defendant was not, standing alone, justification for the detention. An order by one officer to another insulates the complying officer from assuming personal responsibility for the acts done in obedience to the order, but the order did not itself supply legal cause for the detention any more than the fact of detention supplies its own cause. If the first officer had adequate cause to detain the defendant, he could properly delegate the detention to the other officer, but if he did not have cause to detain the defendant, he could not create such cause simply by relaying an order to a fellow officer.'' (*People* v. *Hunt.*)

Circumstantial Factors Whether relying on informants or on personal observation, officers should attempt to detail specific circumstances that are significant to them, even if not to the average person. Officers can testify to experience, training, or education that enabled them to attribute criminal significance to otherwise seemingly innocent conduct. Their expertise can be valuable in giving meaning and direction to facts observed and heard.

In addition, the officers can articulate other factors—circumstantial factors—that again may not be significant in themselves, but together form an incriminating pattern. In some cases, the combination of otherwise unrelated factors may be significant. Thus, some of the following circumstances should be considered as possible factors: location, time of day, number of people, previous knowledge of the suspect, knowledge of the suspect's associates, knowledge of the area, conduct at the time of observation (sometimes called ''furtive conduct.'' Certain gestures or movements of a suspect may be significant, particularly in narcotic arrests. As we have noted earlier, however, the officer cannot induce the furtive conduct by threatening actions and then rely on the suspect's response). In summary, the officer must paint the picture of probable cause with as many factors as possible and should not overlook neutral circumstances that may be significant.

Examine the facts in the following case in which the officers combine their observation, information, and other factors known to them in an attempt to develop probable cause to arrest.

At night, two undercover officers were standing in front of a restaurant on a main city street. ''One officer observed defendant standing outside talking with a 'hippie-type' male; she looked around 'over either shoulder,' removed a tinfoil package from her purse, and then 'nodded in a motion that they both go inside.' The officers could not tell what was inside the tinfoil package. Both officers followed the couple inside. The officers approached the defendant who was standing next to a table and said, 'Why don't we go outside and have a talk.' At about the same time, his partner reached into the defendant's purse and removed the package from it.

''The other officer had not seen the defendant holding the tinfoil package outside. As they approached the defendant he noticed a tinfoil package in her purse; he could see only the large tinfoil wrapping, and not the individually wrapped packets contained inside the larger wrapping. He reached into her purse and removed the tinfoil package. The package contained Seconal tablets individually wrapped in tinfoil. . . .

''One officer further testified that he had been working with a special platoon in the department for about two months prior to and including the date of the arrest, and that he had made 'numerous arrests' for narcotic violations during that period. He also testified that he had been informed by other officers that defendant was selling dangerous drugs, but that he did not know of any officers who ever purchased narcotics from defendant and that he did not know whether the basis of this information was an informer or some officer who observed defendant make a sale; he did not see a 'rap sheet' or any other official department records that dealt with defendant. The officer described the area of arrest as having 'a reputation with the Police Department as being an area where there is a great deal of drug traffic. . . .' Finally, he testified that in his experience dangerous drugs were packaged either in plastic baggies or in tinfoil.

"The first officer testified that a few weeks prior to the arrest he had briefly discussed with the other officer a previous arrest of defendant for assault and possession of dangerous drugs, and that the officer—who 'handled' the previous case—had indicated that defendant was not actually involved in the assault but that large quantities of pills were found in the apartment where the assault occurred and in defendant's possession. The officer testified that he had seen the 'rap sheet' which reflected the above arrest, and that he recalled no other arrests of defendant; however, he had made no attempt to determine whether the above charges against defendant had been dropped, and, in fact, at the time of the hearing was unaware that the charges against the defendant had been dismissed at [an earlier hearing]. . . ." Finally, the officer testified that his experience was that Seconal tablets are usually packaged in tinfoil.

"The evidence indicated that there was only one prior arrest of defendant; that there was no evidence offered at the earlier hearing as to any drugs found in the apartment where the defendant was arrested, other than those found in another person's pockets; that the charges against defendant were dismissed at the earlier hearing; and that the dismissal was prior to defendant's arrest in the instant case. In addition, the prosecutor conceded that during the prior arrest no dangerous drugs were found on the person of the defendant.

"In the abstract, no implication of guilt can be drawn from the fact that a suspect indicates an apparent concern with privacy by looking around to see whether anyone is observing him, and that a showing that an area is known to be the site of frequent narcotics traffic cannot convert into sufficient cause to arrest circumstances that are as consistent with innocence as with criminality, although specialized knowledge may render suspicious what would appear innocent to a layman, the test remains whether the circumstances would warrant a man of reasonable caution—who possessed such knowledge—in the belief that the action taken was appropriate.

"The act of showing a tinfoil package to a companion is even less suspicious than that of engaging in a sidewalk sale. Neither officer was able to see the contents of the package or any impressions on the tinfoil wrapping, and both admitted that for all he knew at the time he approached defendant, the tinfoil package could have contained cookies. Defendant exhibited little concern with her surroundings; and her apparent concern was consistent with innocent activity—such as keeping an eye out for acquaintances.

"The fact that the area is known to be the site of frequent narcotics traffic cannot convert circumstances as innocent as those involved in this case—an individual being generally concerned with her surroundings while displaying a tinfoil package to a companion—into sufficient cause to arrest."

What about the special knowledge and experience of the arresting officers that dangerous drugs are often packaged in tinfoil? "Even if dangerous drugs are often packaged in tinfoil, so many other legitimate items—such as foods or tobacco—are packaged in tinfoil that a tinfoil package is not a suspicious circumstance, and a man of reasonable caution who possesses the knowledge that dangerous drugs are often packaged in tinfoil would not be justified in assuming, upon seeing a tinfoil package, that it is likely to contain drugs.

"It is thus clear that in itself a tinfoil package is so commonly used for legitimate purposes that it is not a suspicious circumstance. And the officers heard nothing of the conversation between defendant and [her] companion, and the record evidences nothing which would distinguish a layman's estimate of the suspiciousness of defendant's behavior from the officers' estimate. . . .

"[As to the defendant's criminal record:] It is well settled that while it may be perfectly reasonable for officers in the field to make arrests on the basis of information furnished to them by other officers, when it comes to justifying the total police activity in a court, the People must prove that the source of the information is something other than the imagination of an officer who does not become a witness. To hold otherwise would permit the manufacture of reasonable grounds for arrest within a police department by one officer transmitting information purportedly known by him to another officer who did not know such information, without establishing under oath how the information had in fact been obtained by the former officer. If this were so, every utterance of a police officer would instantly and automatically acquire the dignity of official information; 'reasonable cause' or 'reasonable grounds,' . . . could be conveniently fashioned out of a two-step communication; and all Fourth Amendment safeguards would dissolve as a consequence.

"In sum, when an officer furnishes to another officer information which leads to an arrest, the People must show the basis for the former officer's information. More specifically in relation to the instant case, when an officer furnishes to another officer information as to alleged prior criminal activity of an individual relied upon for an arrest relating to subsequent activities of that individual, then the People must show the basis for the former officer's information. The absence of such a requirement would allow a police officer to manufacture reasonable grounds to arrest while circumventing the necessity of pointing to 'specific and articulable facts' justifying his suspicions.

"The officer had known nothing about defendant's 'criminal record'—i.e., her arrest for assault and possession of dangerous drugs, the charges having been dismissed for lack of evidence. He testified that he had known nothing of defendant's prior activities other than what other officers had told him—that defendant sold dangerous drugs. He did not see a 'rap sheet' or any other department records that dealt with defendant, nor did he know of any officers who had ever purchased drugs from defendant. Indeed, he did not know whether the basis of the information given him was an informer or some officer who observed defendant make a sale. The prosecution did not produce any of the officers who allegedly had informed the officer about defendant's narcotics sales.

"In such a situation, the officer's testimony as to his knowledge of defendant's activities cannot be utilized as an ingredient in the probable cause equation. To do so would permit the manufacture of a known criminal background—in this case, sales of dangerous drugs by defendant—within a police department by one officer transmitting information to another officer without establishing the basis for his information.

"One officer testified that he had been informed by his partner that during the prior arrest large quantities of pills (dangerous drugs) had been found in the apartment where defendant had been arrested and in defendant's possession. This testimony can be given no weight, since it was conceded by the prosecutor at the hearing that no dangerous drugs had been found on defendant and that no evidence had been produced at the ensuing preliminary hearing as to any drugs found in the apartment, other than those found in another person's pockets.

"The officer also testified that he had seen the 'rap sheet' reflecting defendant's prior arrest, but that he had made no attempt to determine whether the charges against defendant had been dropped and did not even know at the time of the hearing that the charges against defendant had been dismissed.

"A prior related *conviction,* when known by the arresting officers, has at best only a slight tendency to establish a present violation of the law; obviously, a prior related *arrest* where there is no conviction must have even less than a 'slight tendency' to establish a present violation of the law. Where, as in this case, the charges upon which the prior arrest had been based were dismissed, not because of any legal technicality unrelated to the merits of the charges against defendant, but because the charges had been held to be unfounded—because, in other words, defendant had been found innocent of the charges—the officer's knowledge of that arrest should be given no weight. As defendant states, to allow an arresting officer's knowledge of a suspect's prior arrest to convert into probable cause circumstances that otherwise would not constitute probable cause when the prior charges were dismissed because of insufficient evidence is to hold that persons arrested on unfounded charges would thereafter become second-class citizens, with lesser rights than other citizens." (*Remers* v. *Superior Court.*)

This case illustrates that a combination of observation, information, and other factors will not always justify an arrest unless care is taken to develop all the facts in the officer's possession that add up to a strong suspicion that a felony has been committed. Sometimes, of course, the evidence is simply insufficient—as in the case just reviewed.

Delay in Arrest

Not all arrests are made immediately after the crime has been committed—even if committed in the officer's presence. Serious problems of fairness arise.

For example: " 'Charles H.' was hired by a local police department to work as an undercover agent in a narcotic 'buy' program. [In June] he went to defendant's apartment to attempt to purchase marijuana. Later that evening, H. purchased a quantity of marijuana from defendant. No arrest was made at the time but this sale was the basis for a complaint which was subsequently issued for the arrest of the defendant.

"The complaint against defendant was filed in mid-November of the same year and defendant was arrested shortly thereafter. Another officer testified at the preliminary hearing that defendant was not arrested sooner because H. was working on a number of other cases as an undercover agent, and the police department did not want H.'s identity disclosed until they were ready to make all the arrests connected with the 'buy' program."

The preliminary hearing was held in December. The defendant moved to dismiss on the ground that there was an unreasonable delay between the time of the alleged offense and the time of arrest.

"In cases involving narcotic 'buy' programs, there is no hard and fast rule establishing how much of a delay in defendant's arrest constitutes a denial of due process to him. Each case must be resolved by balancing public interest and the rights of the defendant. The necessity of using undercover agents to detect violations of the narcotic laws is obvious. It is within the realm of common knowledge and common sense that uniformed or otherwise known policemen are unable to penetrate the *sub rosa* world of the narcotics peddler. Extensive, time-consuming investigations by undercover operatives, who daily risk their lives, are required to get to the retail and wholesale sources of illicit narcotics. It is equally obvious that the effectiveness of such an agent does not survive the time it becomes known that he is a policeman. The public thus has a substantial interest in keeping the officer's identity secret for a reasonable period of time while he continues his investigations. This public interest is a legitimate reason for delaying the arrest of an individual wrongdoer. The courts have recognized this fact, and the cases are legion which have upheld the use of narcotic 'buy' programs as acceptable police practice.

"This does not mean, however, that the public interest must always prevail. The accused has substantial rights which must be protected, and the delay between the alleged offense and the time of arrest must not result in a deprivation of due process. Delaying the arrest of the accused may hinder his ability to recall or reconstruct his whereabouts at the time the alleged offense occurred. The accused has no way of knowing, to say nothing of proving, where he was at the time and on the day the policeman says his diary shows he made a sale of narcotics to the policeman. An additional problem resulting from such delays is misidentification, where an undercover officer saw the accused only occasionally and then for brief periods of time. There is no doubt that under certain circumstances the delay in filing the accusation makes it difficult or impossible for an accused to adequately prepare his defense.

"But the fact that the question in this type of case must be resolved by balancing interests does not mean that there are no guidelines for a court to follow. An accused must show two things to establish 'unfairness' resulting from claimed delay in his arrest: that there was no legitimate reason for the delay, and that he was prejudiced by the delay." (*People* v. *Wright.*)

Arrest with Warrant

An arrest warrant is a process, issued in the name of a legal authority and directed to a law enforcement officer, commanding this person to take the named individual into custody. In most jurisdictions the procedure for an application to obtain a warrant, the form of the warrant, and the service of the warrant are set forth by statute. Yet the Fourth Amendment, which states that "no warrant shall issue but upon probable cause, supported by oath or affirmation, and particularly describing the . . . person . . . to be seized," supersedes any statute. An arrest is a seizure within the meaning of the Fourth Amendment, and any arrest pursuant to an arrest warrant must be effected pursuant to the constitutional provision.

Until recently, most state as well as federal courts routinely issued arrest warrants without seriously considering the necessity of establishing probable cause to support the warrant. But, in 1957, in *Giordenello* v. *United States,* the U.S. Supreme Court examined a federal warrant that had been issued ordering the defendant's arrest for possession of contraband. The warrant provided as follows: "The undersigned complainant being duly sworn states: that on or about January 26, 1956, at Houston, Texas in the Southern

District of Texas, Veto Giordenello did receive, conceal, etc., narcotic drugs, to-wit: heroin with knowledge of unlawful importation; in violation of Section 174, Title 21, United States Code.''

The officer executed the warrant and, incidental to the defendant's arrest, seized contraband on his person.

Federal Rules of Criminal Procedure provide that an arrest warrant may be issued only upon a written and sworn complaint (1) setting forth ''the essential facts constituting the offense charged,'' and (2) showing ''that there is probable cause to believe that [such] an offense has been committed and that the defendant has committed it. . . .'' In *Giordenello,* the Court said the provisions of ''these Rules must be read in light of the constitutional requirements they implement. The language of the Fourth Amendment, that '. . . no Warrants shall issue, but upon probable cause, supported by Oath or affirmation, and particularly describing . . . the persons or things to be seized,' applies to arrest as well as search warrants. The protection afforded by these Rules, when viewed against their constitutional background, is that the inferences from the facts which lead to the complaint '. . . be drawn by a neutral and detached magistrate instead of being judged by the officer engaged in the often competitive enterprise of ferreting out crime.' The purpose of the complaint is to enable the appropriate magistrate, here a Commissioner, to determine whether the 'probable cause' required to support a warrant exists. The Commissioner must judge for himself the persuasiveness of the facts relied on by a complaining officer to show probable cause. He should not accept without question the complainant's mere conclusion that the person whose arrest is sought has committed a crime.

''When the complaint in this case is judged with these considerations in mind, it is clear that it does not provide any basis for the Commissioner's determination that probable cause existed. The complaint contains no affirmative allegation that the affiant spoke with personal knowledge of the matters contained therein; it does not indicate any sources for the complainant's belief; and it does not set forth any other sufficient basis upon which a finding of probable cause could be made. These deficiencies could not be cured by the Commissioner's reliance upon a presumption that the complaint was made on the personal knowledge of the complaining officer. This is illustrated by the facts of this case, for the agent's testimony later showed that he had no personal knowledge of the matters on which his charge was based. In these circumstances, the Commissioner could not be expected to assess independently the probability that the defendant committed the crime charged. If the complaint in this case were upheld, the substantive requirements would be completely read out of the rules, and the complaint would be of only formal significance entitled to perfunctory approval by the Commissioner. This would not comport with the protective purposes which a complaint is designed to achieve.''

In *Giordenello,* the U.S. Supreme Court interpreted the Federal Rules of Criminal Procedure and, arguably, were not applying Fourth Amendment standards. If such were the case, the decision would only apply to federal arrests and not to arrests by state officers. But the issue was apparently resolved a short time later when the Court summarily disposed of a similar question involving an arrest warrant under a state statute. In any event, the clearly safer practice is to issue a warrant of arrest in harmony with the requirements of the Fourth Amendment. How can this be done?

In California, the magistrate issues arrest warrants only if accompanied by a "constitutionally adequate" complaint or declaration. The declaration must recite sufficient facts to enable the magistrate to determine the existence of probable cause. Establishing probable cause to support an arrest warrant parallels establishing probable cause necessary to arrest. Or, more specifically, probable cause to support an arrest warrant must be shown just as probable cause to issue a search warrant must be presented. A mere recital of a violation of a statute in the language of the statute is insufficient.

If an arrest is made pursuant to a constitutionally defective complaint, any evidence seized incidental to the arrest will be excluded. Yet the prosecution can still validate the arrest on alternative grounds, because the legality of an arrest cannot depend exclusively on the validity of the warrant since an arrest without a warrant may stand if based on probable cause. In *Giordenello* v. *United States,* the government had argued to the Supreme Court that "the arrest was justified *apart* from the warrant." The Court held that in the event of a new trial the government could seek to justify the defendant's arrest without relying on the warrant. In other words, if the prosecution can establish probable cause to arrest without a warrant, the invalid warrant will not void a lawful search incident to the arrest.

A search undertaken pursuant to an invalid search warrant, which could otherwise be upheld as incident to an arrest based on probable cause, presents an analogous problem. In *Marron* v. *United States,* police officers conducted a search of the defendant's business premises pursuant to a *valid* search warrant but seized items which were not specified by the warrant. After stating that: "The requirements that warrants shall particularly describe the things to be seized makes general searches under them impossible and prevents the seizure of one thing under a warrant describing another," the Supreme Court held the seizure valid on the ground that the search by means of which the officers found the seized items was incident to the arrest of the defendant's agent, who was committing a crime on the premises in the presence of the officers.

Policy considerations for the rationale allowing the prosecution to validate an arrest independent of an invalid arrest warrant are: First: "Although certain nonwarrant arrests and searches are permissible, the policy of the law is to encourage officers to use search warrants. . . . Second: The rule which excludes evidence obtained by illegal searches was adopted [partially] for the purpose of eliminating the incentive for police officers to use illegal methods. That principle does not call for a rejection of the evidence. . . . Given a choice between a nonwarrant arrest and a search based upon a magistrate's warrant, officers will be impelled to forego the latter if a defect in the warrant procedure will invalidate an arrest and search which would have been legal without a warrant." (*People* v. *Chimel.*)

In addition to setting forth the probable cause that justifies the issuance of a warrant of arrest, the officers must provide a description of the arrestee. Officers do not always know the name, or even the alias, of the person suspected of committing the crime involved. "The weight of authority holds that to meet the constitutional requirements, a 'John Doe' warrant must describe the person to be seized with reasonable particularity. The warrant should contain sufficient information to permit his identification with reasonable certainty. This may be done by stating his occupation, his personal appearance, peculiarities, place of residence or other means of identification. Where a name that would reasonably identify the subject to be arrested cannot be provided, then some other means reasonable to the circumstances must be used to assist in the identification of the subject of the warrant. If a fictitious name is used the warrant should also contain sufficient descriptive material to indicate with reasonable particularity the identification of the person whose arrest is ordered." (*People* v. *Montoya.*)

CASES AND MATERIALS

Brinegar v. *United States,* 338 U.S. 160, 69 S. Ct. 1302, 93 L. Ed. 1879.

Carroll v. *United States,* 267 U.S. 132, 45 S. Ct. 280, L. Ed. 543.

Draper v. *United States,* 358 U.S. 307, 79 S. Ct. 329, 3 L. Ed. 2d 327.

Dyke v. *Taylor Implement Co.,* 391 U.S. 216, 88 S. Ct. 1472, 20 L. Ed. 2d 538.

Freeman v. *DMV,* 70 C. 2d 235, 449 P. 2d 195 ("presence").

Giordenello v. *United States,* 357 U.S. 480, 78 S. Ct. 1245, 2 L. Ed. 2d 1503.

Henry v. *United States,* 361 U.S. 98, 80 S. Ct. 168, 41 L. Ed. 2d 134.

Honore v. *Superior Court,* 70 C 2d 162, 449 P. 2d 169.

Marron v. *United States,* 275 U.S. 192, 48 S. Ct. 74, 72 L. Ed. 231.

McCray v. *Illinois,* 386 U.S. 300, 87 S. Ct. 1056, 18 L. Ed. 2d 62.

People v. *Chimel,* 68 C. 2d 436, 439 P. 2d 333.

People v. *Fein,* 4 C. 3d 747, 484 P. 2d 583.

People v. *Garrett,* 29 Cal. App. 3d 535, 104 Cal. R. 829.

People v. *Hunt,* 250 Cal. App. 2d 311, 58 Cal. R. 385.

People v. *Ingle,* 53 C. 2d 407, 348 P. 2d 577.

People v. *Miller,* 7 C. 3d 219, 496 P. 2d 1228.

People v. *Montoya,* 255 Cal. App. 2d 137, 63 Cal. R. 73.

People v. *Privett,* 52 C. 2d 330, 341 P. 2d 1.

People v. *Sesslin,* 68 C. 2d 418, 439 P. 2d 321.

People v. *Superior Court* (Keifer), 3 C. 3d 807, 478 P. 2d 449 (furtive conduct).

People v. *Superior Court* (Simon), 7 C. 3d 186, 496 P. 2d 1205 (car theft; traffic searches).

People v. *Wright,* 2 Cal. App. 3d 732, 82 Cal. R. 859.

Peters v. *New York,* 392 U.S. 40, 80 S. Ct. 1889, 20 L. Ed. 2d 917.

Remers v. *Superior Court,* 2 C. 3d 659, 470 P. 2d 11.

Rios v. *United States,* 364 U.S. 253, 80 S. Ct. 1431, 4 L. Ed. 2d 1688.

Roviaro v. *United States,* 353 U.S. 53, 77 S. Ct. 623, 1 L. Ed. 2d 639 (disclosure of informant).

United States v. *Santana,* 49 L. Ed. 2d 300.

Whitley v. *Warden,* 401 U.S. 560, 83 S. Ct. 407, 9 L. Ed. 2d 441.

Wong Sun v. *United States,* 371 U.S. 471, 83 S. Ct. 407, 9 L. Ed. 2d 441.

1. Officers arrest the defendant for vagrancy. At trial, officers testify that based upon the conduct they observed, no probable cause existed to arrest defendant for robbery. The court finds that the arrest for vagrancy was illegal but, despite the officers' opinion, probable cause did exist to arrest for robbery. How is probable cause measured? Must the officers *subjectively* believe the defendant is guilty of the crime they arrest this person for, or is probable cause measured by an objective evaluation of the facts? If an officer personally does not believe he or she has probable cause to arrest for a particular crime, why should the court validate an arrest that is objectively lawful?

2. While conducting an investigation of a burglary, officers remove unidentified palm prints from a windowsill. Several days later, a large number of juveniles are arrested, fingerprinted, and released. Subsequent investigation reveals that prints of one of the juveniles matches those found on the windowsill. The juvenile is rearrested. At trial he objects to the introduction of his fingerprints on the ground that they are the product of an unlawful search.

Are fingerprints, which are not physical evidence like personal property, subject to the exclusionary rule?

Does detention for the purpose of obtaining fingerprints require probable cause?

"Detention for fingerprinting may constitute a much less serious intrusion upon personal security than other types of police searches and detentions. Fingerprinting involves none of the probing into an individual's private life and thoughts that marks an interrogation or search. Nor can fingerprint detention be employed repeatedly to harass any individual, since the police need only one set of each person's prints. Furthermore, fingerprinting is an inherently more reliable and effective crime-solving tool than eyewitness identifications or confessions and is not subject to such abuses as the improper line-up and the 'third degree.' Finally, because there is no danger of destruction of fingerprints, the limited detention need not come unexpectedly or at an inconvenient time." Do you agree?

(See *Davis* v. *Mississippi,* 394 U.S. 721, 89 S. Ct. 1394, 22 L. Ed. 676.)

3. Officers receive information from a reliable informant that a specifically described individual will transport baggage containing marijuana on a particular flight. Later, officers observe a man resembling the description as he checks his baggage on the reported flight. When the luggage arrives in the baggage check room, the officer unleashes a dog specifically trained to detect marijuana. The dog instantly runs to the described luggage and barks furiously, scratching at the luggage. This reaction is in response to his training in the detection of marijuana. Is such evidence admissible on the issue of probable cause to search?

4. Four armed men robbed a residence. One of them was arrested. At the time of arrest, he was driving the defendant's car, and a search of the car produced property stolen in the robbery the day before. He admitted taking part in the robbery and implicated the defendant. He told the police that he was sharing an apartment with the defendant. He also stated that the guns used in the robbery and other stolen property were in the apartment.

One of the investigating officers then checked official records on the defendant, verifying his prior association with the arrestee, his age and physical description, his address, and the make of his car. The information the officer uncovered corresponded with the general descriptions by the robbery victims and the statements made by the arrestee.

Four officers went to the apartment, verified the address, and knocked. One of the officers testified: "The door was opened and a person who fit the description exactly of the defendant, as I had received it from both the cards and from the arrestee, answered the door. . . . We placed him under arrest for robbery."

After arresting the man who answered the door, they asked him whether he was the defendant and where the guns and stolen goods were. The arrestee replied that he was not the defendant, that his name was Miller, that it was the defendant's apartment, and that he was waiting for the defendant. The arrestee then produced identification indicating that he was in fact Miller, but the police were unimpressed, proceeded to search the apartment, and discovered incriminating evidence in plain sight.

Subsequent investigation confirmed that indeed the man was Miller and not the defendant.

The defendant was arrested later, and at his trial he contended the search of his apartment was unlawful since the mistaken arrest of Miller was not supported by probable cause to arrest Miller. Therefore, the defendant argued, the incidental search was unlawful. What should be the result?

5. Officers execute a federal arrest warrant and arrest the named arrestee after forcing entry into his apartment. While inside they observe contraband and seize it.

At his trial in the state court for possession of the contraband, the defendant attacks the validity of the federal warrant on which his arrest was originally authorized.

a) Can a state court declare a federal warrant invalid?

b) If so, does the unlawful warrant taint the entry and arrest?

c) Assuming the warrant is invalid, would the odor of burning marijuana smelled from outside the apartment by the officer make any difference? *People* v. *Rice,* 10 Cal. App. 3d 730, 89 Cal. R. 280.

6. A statute provides that anyone arrested pursuant to an arrest warrant must be arraigned in court within forty-eight hours after the arrest. The defendant is arrested on the authority of a warrant and sixty-two hours after his arrest tells officers that stolen property is in his house. He consents to their entry. He is then arraigned on the warrant. At trial, he objects to the introduction of évidence seized from his house on the ground that his statement was made after he should have been arraigned; if he had been arraigned within the forty-eight-hour period he would not have made such a statement. Or, in the alternative, the late arraignment was unduly coercive, contributed to an involuntary consent, and was not a free act of his will. What should be the result?

NOTES

1. On the constitutional significance of a traffic violation as an arrest, see chapter 1, Detention and Arrest.

3 Search

Chapter Objectives

After reading this chapter, you will be able to:

1. Give the definition of a search.
2. Describe the rules used to measure whether a search has been conducted.
3. Explain the role of privacy in evaluating the legality of a search.

The Fourth Amendment prohibits unreasonable searches. Before it can be determined whether an officer's action was unreasonable, the court must first ascertain whether or not there was a "search." A search, at least in the constitutional sense, is an act that a law enforcement officer undertakes with the intent to discover objects concealed from view.

The "Plain View" Doctrine

Because of this definition, the courts developed the "plain view" doctrine. Under this rule, an officer may seize any evidence that is open to view because the property is not concealed. Seizing property in plain view does not constitute a search, and it is therefore immaterial whether the officer's action was reasonable or unreasonable. Only if the officer's act disclosed items previously concealed, that is, if it were a search, would the issue of "reasonableness" arise.

The Right to View

Whether or not an object is open to view is not the only issue in determining whether a search was conducted. Officers must also have the right to be in a position to obtain the view. This rule requires the officer to justify the plain view of seizable evidence by establishing that he or she violated no other constitutionally protected rights of the suspect in obtaining this view. Thus, an officer could not forcibly enter a dwelling place on no basis whatsoever and then observe seizable evidence in plain view. Nor could the officer needlessly stop a motorist and obtain a view of the interior of the car to determine whether seizable evidence was in plain view. In other words, each investigative step prior to the officer's plain view will be scrutinized to determine whether the view was obtained in violation of any constitutional rights.

Overcoming the Trespass Objection

Often in narcotic investigations, officers will maintain close surveillance of premises in an attempt to observe conduct inside the house. Necessarily this involves entering the occupant's land, walking on the property, or perhaps standing on a porch step of the house in order to facilitate visual entry—as distinct from actual physical entry. Although some courts have said that the Fourth Amendment prohibits unreasonable searches—not trespasses—nevertheless a police officer's entry on private property without the consent of the owner is a factor in evaluating the officer's right to have a view. If the property is unfenced and no gate or other barrier prevents one from entering the property, the degree of trespass is significantly less than if the officer must open a locked gate or climb over a fence or shrubbery. Officers who intend to obtain visual entry to premises must overcome the trespass objection—preferably by establishing a reasonable basis for investigation that requires entry. That basis may rest on a neighbor's report, a report from a victim of or a witness to a crime, or a report from an informant. Establishing the basis for limited entry on the land reduces the trespass objection.

Assuming that the officers are reasonably on the land and thereby establish their right to be present, the usual technique is to peer into windows in an attempt to verify information or to obtain corroborating facts. The act of looking through a window and observing something in plain view would not constitute a search within the meaning of the definition. Nor would a view of the interior obtained by looking through an open door be a search. But officers cannot improve their view by removing any obstruction to their line of sight. To push aside a drape or to open a closed but unlocked screen door would be impermissible.

Nor can officers employ a ruse or trick to facilitate visual entry. Thus, if officers lacked probable cause to arrest prior to their visual or physical entry, any evidence they seized inside would be the product of a search because they obtained its disclosure by subterfuge. But there is nothing unlawful in tricking an occupant into opening the door if officers have previously developed probable cause to arrest. If probable cause to arrest exists, officers can forcibly enter in any event; subterfuge merely avoids the potential violence of a forcible entry.

The Right of Privacy

The courts, including the U.S. Supreme Court, have expressed some dissatisfaction with the classic definition of a search. Recent decisions hold that the "plain view" rule, and the rule that requires the officer to establish the "right to have the view," are not always a sufficient justification for visual searches conducted from the exterior of the house. The U.S. Supreme Court has held that the Fourth Amendment embodies a right of *privacy* that cannot be unreasonably invaded. In order to understand the relevance of this doctrine in the context of search, some background is necessary.

In *Hester* v. *United States,* the U.S. Supreme Court enunciated the "open fields" doctrine. In this case, officers had concealed themselves from fifty to one hundred yards from the house of Hester's father; they saw Hester leave the house and hand a bottle to one Henderson. When an alarm sounded, Hester and Henderson ran. Hester dropped a jug, which broke, and Henderson threw away the bottle. The officers retrieved the jug and bottle, as well as a broken jar that was thrown from the house, and recognized their contents as moonshine. The opinion states: "It is obvious that even if there had been a trespass, the [officers'] testimony was not obtained by an illegal search or seizure. The defendant's own acts, and those of his associates, disclosed the jug, the jar and the bottle—and there was no seizure in the sense of the law when the officers examined the contents of each after it had been abandoned. . . . The only shadow of a ground for bringing up the case is drawn from the hypothesis that the examination of the vessels took place upon Hester's father's land. As to that, it is enough to say that, apart from the justiciation, *the special protection accorded by the Fourth Amendment to the people in their 'persons, houses, papers, and effects,' is not extended to the open fields.*" (Italics added.)

Although many lower federal court decisions have applied the "open fields" doctrine of *Hester* v. *United States* in upholding the legality of a search or seizure, they contain conflicting statements as to whether the *ground* area of the curtilage,[1] or yard, is protected by the Fourth Amendment. Some, relying on *Hester,* have declared that the "grounds" or "enclosed or unenclosed . . . grounds or open fields around . . . houses are not included in the prohibition of the Fourth Amendment." Under the foregoing rule, it was held that the Fourth Amendment was not violated by the examination of a jug left on the ground under a car apparently parked by the porch of a shack belonging to one of the defendants or by the detection of an odor by the porch of the defendant's premises.

Several California decisions, in rejecting claims of unlawful searches and seizures, have stated that "the premises around a house" or "'enclosed or unenclosed grounds or open fields' around a house" are not protected by the Fourth Amendment. Other California cases have emphasized the degree of privacy the defendant enjoyed in the place in question.

In one case, an officer entered the side yard of a duplex through an open gate. A sidewalk went from the gate to a side porch that was unroofed; there were no bushes or hedges nearby. The officer stood on the first step of the side porch and looked through a window into the interior of the house where he observed certain matters. The court concluded that under the circumstances the officer's acts did not constitute an unconstitutional invasion of the defendant's privacy. The court said that looking through a window does not become an unreasonable search merely because a police officer may be on the defendant's premises when he or she makes the observation, and that the degree of privacy which defendant enjoyed in the place involved is an important factor in determining the reasonableness of the search.

The U.S. Supreme Court recognized in *Katz* v. *United States* that "the security of one's privacy against arbitrary intrusion by the police [is] at the core of the Fourth Amendment. The Fourth Amendment protects people, not places, and wherever an individual may harbor a reasonable 'expectation of privacy,' he or she is entitled to be free from unreasonable governmental intrusion . . ." In *Katz,* federal agents, by means of an electronic device, listened to and recorded the defendant's end of a conversation made from a public telephone booth, the door to which apparently had been closed by the defendant. The court held that "The Government's activities in electronically listening to and recording the petitioner's words violated the privacy upon which he justifiably relied while using the telephone booth and thus constituted a 'search and seizure' within the meaning of the Fourth Amendment," and that, in the absence of prior judicial authorization, the search and seizure were unreasonable. The Court also noted that, although it had occasionally described its conclusions in terms of "constitutionally protected area," it had "never suggested that this concept can serve as a talismanic solution to every Fourth Amendment problem."

Thus, the analysis of cases involving searches of open fields or grounds adjacent to a house no longer will be resolved on a trespass-plain-view theory. In answering the question: Did the officer have the right to have the view? the answer may well depend on whether there was a violation of the arrestee's reasonable expectation of privacy. The answer will vary, depending, in part, on whether there was a trespass. And, of course, the location of the officers when they observed either seizable evidence or unlawful conduct will be relevant, as well as the location of the observed evidence itself. Thus, although "trespass," "plain view," and "right to have the view" are no longer quick answers, they are still relevant in evaluating privacy.

For example: A police officer was contacted by a neighbor who lived next door to the defendants and who reported that about a week before he had seen on the defendants' back porch a large plastic bag containing described packages, one of which was torn and contained a dark green vegetable substance that appeared similar to alfalfa, but did not smell like alfalfa, and had a "small funny type seed." Officers walked down the railroad tracks behind the defendants' residence and entered into "the open back yard area" of that residence. There the officers observed three trash cans two or three feet from the back porch door. The officers did not have a search warrant. Inside one of the trash cans they found, among other things, a bag that contained marijuana.

Here the officers established a basis for being on the land because of the neighbor's report. They did not violate any rights of the defendant prior to observing the marijuana, and they committed only a minor trespass. They observed evidence in plain view. Despite this, the court said that the occupants reasonably expected privacy of the contents of their trash can. "The trash can was within a few feet of the back door of defendants' home and was an adjunct to the domestic economy. Placing the marijuana in the trash can, so situated and used, was not an abandonment unless as to persons authorized to remove the receptacle's contents, such as trashmen. So far as appears defendants alone resided at the house. In the light of the combined facts and circumstances it appears the defendants exhibited an expectation of privacy, and that expectation was reasonable under circumstances of the case. There are many reasons why residents would not want their castaway clothing, letters, medicine bottles or other telltale refuse and trash to be examined by neighbors or others, at least not until the trash had lost its identity and meaning by becoming part of a large conglomeration of trash elsewhere. Half-truths leading to rumor and gossip may readily flow from an attempt to read the contents of another's trash." (*People* v. *Edwards*.)

This case could have been decided differently if one assumes that no one reasonably expects privacy in their discarded papers. Yet in a different context, where there is no evidence that the property observed was abandoned, the right of privacy could not reasonably be expected. Consider the following example:

"Two police officers testified that they were on duty when they responded to a call to investigate a complaint by two youths, aged 17 and 18. The youths told them that they had met defendant and that he had invited them to his apartment. Accepting the invitation, the boys had accompanied defendant to his car, where they had seen a marijuana cigarette in a clip on the dashboard. At the apartment, defendant had offered them some marijuana. They became frightened and fled the apartment.

"The officers further testified that they returned to the apartment house around midnight with the two boys and two plainclothes officers. Upon arrival, the police officers and one of the boys went to the subterranean garage, where the boy pointed out defendant's automobile. Through the window of the locked car the police officers observed an object lying across the top of an open ashtray that appeared to be a partially smoked marijuana cigarette."

Apparently the apartment garage was a common area; the officers did not commit a trespass by entering it. Nor did the officers conduct an unreasonable search by looking in the window of the car. ''Defendant, on cross-examination of the apartment house manager elicted testimony that the garage 'was not a common area open to the public' but 'rather a private area not open to the public,' that '[i]n other words, the . . . garage . . . was not an enclosed piece of land that had been set aside for public or municipal use,' and that there were no spaces in the garage for parking by guests. The manager also testified that the garage was a 'common parking area for tenants of the apartment building.' One of the officers who entered the garage testified that there was no indication that the garage was a common area or public parking. His partner stated that the garage was big, that it would definitely hold 5 cars, but that he could not recall whether it would accommodate 105 cars.

''The garage, used in common by the tenants of the apartment building, is similar in nature to a common hallway of an apartment building. The officers apparently entered the garage without force. Defendant's car was parked in the garage and the marijuana was in plain sight on an open ashtray inside the car. Any expectation by the defendant of privacy as to objects in plain sight in the car would have been unreasonable, and no constitutionally protected right of privacy was violated when the officers looked through the window of the car.'' (*People* v. *Terry.*)

In this case, the entry into a common garage did not invade the defendant's right of privacy because he could not reasonably expect a significant degree of privacy in a facility shared in common with other tenants, most of whom he probably did not even know. Similarly, if visual entry of an apartment is made from a common hall or corridor, a defendant could not argue that he reasonably expected privacy unless special circumstances could be established.

Thus, the evolution of trespass, which is a law of real property, into ''privacy'' serves the Fourth Amendment better in assessing the officer's actions. What began as an ''open fields'' doctrine led to a doctrine that attempts to come to grips with visual entries of dwelling places. But the doctrine of privacy is not confined to dwelling places. For example, the leading case expanding the right of privacy emerged from electronic surveillance of the occupant of a telephone booth.

Although the most frequent application of the right of privacy results from entry and/or search of a dwelling place, the question also is important in clandestine observation of public rest rooms. It is generally conceded that when people leave their homes, they shed a substantial amount of privacy and must tolerate conduct from others that they would forbid in their own homes. Yet people do not surrender all of their right of privacy when they enter public property or places. Most courts that have considered the question have held that people retain a minimum amount of privacy when they enter public rest rooms and close the toilet door. Despite the well-known pattern of homosexuals in entering adjoining toilet stalls to engage in mutual masturbation, sodomy, and similar acts which violate penal laws, the courts have held that absent some basis to arrest the occupants prior to entering the toilet stalls, the act of spying and waiting to observe illegal conduct constitutes a "search" without probable cause in the constitutional sense and one that is consequently unreasonable. These rules necessarily reduce the use of spy holes, two-way mirrors, and similar police practices. Of course, if the conduct was open to the view of anyone inside the rest room, officers could arrest for a public offense committed in their presence. Because of these rulings, many public places have removed toilet stalls or restructured the premises to allow open surveillance. As a consequence, no one can enjoy privacy in the elimination of bodily waste. Curiously, this result occurred because the courts attempted to preserve privacy.

CASES AND MATERIALS

Bielicki v. *Superior Court,* 57 C. 2d 602, 371 P. 2d 388.

Britt v. *Superior Court,* 58 C. 2d 469, 374 P. 2d 817.

Coolidge v. *New Hampshire,* 403 U.S. 443, 91 S. Ct. 2022, 29 L. Ed. 2d 564.

Harris v. *United States,* 390 U.S. 234, 88 S. Ct. 992, 19 L. Ed. 2d 1067.

Hester v. *United States,* 265 U.S. 57, 44 S. Ct. 445, 68 L. Ed. 895.

Katz v. *United States,* 389 U.S. 347, 88 S. Ct. 507, 19 L. Ed. 2d 576.

McDowell v. *United States,* 383 F. 2d 599.

People v. *Edwards,* 71 C. 2d 1096, 458 P. 2d 713.

People v. *Sirhan,* 7 C. 3d 710, 102 Cal. R. 385.

People v. *Terry,* 70 C. 2d 410, 454 P. 2d 36.

1. Officers lawfully enter a home based on information that the defendant has just sold marijuana to an informant. Discovering no one inside, they observe a closed paper bag lying on the floor. This bag and its contents emit a strong odor of marijuana. On opening the bag, officers observe marijuana. Several hours later the defendant returns home and is arrested.

Was there a search?

2. Officers received untested information that the defendant possesses stolen property in his home. After securing approval of the adjoining landowner, they maintain a constant surveillance of the defendant's home from a vantage point in the second story of the neighbor's house. Unable to see clearly, they use binoculars to improve their view.

Is such conduct an unreasonable violation of the defendant's privacy? Suppose that the officers observe the defendant commit a homicide while they are seeking evidence of possession of stolen property? Would the legal analysis differ if they see only the stolen property?

3. "An officer testified that he received an anonymous telephone call. He was advised that a female Caucasian, about 20 years old with long blond hair, was engaged in prostitution at a specific apartment. Officers went to the above address to investigate the informer's tip. Upon arrival, the officers walked to the fourth floor of the building. No activity was observed in the hallway. A fire escape was located at the south end of the hallway next to defendant's apartment, and was attached to the outside of the building. To gain access to the fire escape it was necessary to pass through a doorway marked "Exit." Photographs of the fire escape, introduced into the record, indicated that the escape ladder could be reached by going directly through the exit door to the head of the descent ladder. The officer stepped out onto the fire escape and stepped to his left two or three feet, which placed him in front of a window of the apartment, through which he could observe the inside of that apartment. Looking through the window the officer observed defendant seated at a kitchen table. In front of her on the table was a clear plastic bag containing marijuana." While one officer was on the outside fire escape, the other officer went to the door of the apartment and knocked on the door. The door was opened, at which time the officer entered and placed the defendant under arrest for possession of marijuana. (*Cohen* v. *Superior Court,* 5 Cal. App. 3d 429, 85 Cal. R. 354.)

Was there a search?

4. An envelope was found by a police officer assigned to security at the rear of a certain residence to keep unauthorized persons away. The officer said that he made a "search" of the residence rear yard, at the back of which is a fence. Several boxes of trash were in the rear, and the officer stated that he found an envelope lying in a box of trash containing garbage and papers. The envelope was partly wadded up, lying in the trash. When subsequently asked by the prosecutor when he made the "search," he said that he had a paper cup and had walked over to drop it in the trash; it was at this time that he noticed the envelope. It had writing on it, and he picked it up out of curiosity, looked at it, and later delivered it to another officer.

Was this act an unreasonable invasion of privacy?

5. An officer received a call from the assistant superintendent of schools, who stated that he had reason to believe that there had been marijuana parties at a certain location. He and other officers went to the residence. One officer parked his car and walked along an alley behind the house. Music and voices were coming from inside, which indicated to him that a party was in progress. The officer walked around the side of the house through an orange grove to the front of the house where three windows opened in the dining room. He was aware that he and the other officers were on private property at the time.

"There were bushes along the house in front of the windows. The bushes were so close to the house that their branches touched the windows and house. To get a clear view through the windows, the officers stood between the bushes and the house.

Heavy drapes at the sides of the windows did not substantially obstruct the officer's view, and he could see what was going on inside through the thin curtains that covered the windows.

"[The officers] observed the activities in the dining room for about 15 minutes from this position. Two young women were seated at the dining room table and three or four men were standing towards the back of the room. . . . He observed two men smoking a cigarette in a manner that suggested it was a marijuana cigarette. The cigarette itself did not appear to be an ordinary cigarette. Finally, the officer recognized one of the men in the room as a person he had previously investigated in connection with a narcotics case. The officers then saw someone stagger, as though drunk, out the front door to a car. The officer left his position by the window and walked up to the front door." (*Mann* v. *Superior Court,* 3 C. 3d 1, 472 P. 2d 468.)

Will a search be lawful?

6. Early one morning police officers observed in a vacant lot a stripped, engineless Ford automobile that had not been there the day before. An immediate investigation disclosed that it had recently been stolen. The defendant, who was known to the officers, lived nearby, from which area the car could have "been pushed." He had, according to officers, "changed parts, put new car parts or newer car parts on old cars, old Fords."

Considering him a suspect, the officers went to his home. Alongside the house was a driveway about thirty feet in length, running from the sidewalk to the backyard. The officers walked up the driveway to the rear edge of the house, where, in the backyard, they saw bucket seats, an automobile transmission lying on the ground, and "a homemade wooden A-frame type of hoist with a chain hoist, and a Ford engine hanging from it." They also observed lying on the ground gas receipts and an automobile registration certificate on which could be seen the name of the owner. All of the things seen were in plain sight of the officers. There was no gate or fence between the sidewalk and the property seen in the backyard. From the sidewalk the subject property could not have been seen.

Was this a violation of the defendant's right of privacy in his backyard?

7. "A deputy sheriff, an experienced narcotics officer, was told by an informer of unknown reliability that defendant had marijuana in his house, was engaged in selling it, and was on parole for its possession. The informer also gave information concerning defendant's car. The next evening the same informer told the deputy that defendant was growing marijuana by a fig tree at the rear of his residence.

"After receiving this second report, he went to the defendant's address. The premises included a house that faced the street; a driveway that ran along the east of the house and terminated in a garage at the rear and east of the house; [the] defendant's residence which was attached to the rear of the garage; and a large 'fenced-in yard' to the west of defendant's residence. . . .

"The deputy, noticing that defendant's car was gone, believed he was away and went into the 'rear yard area' to investigate. There he saw a marijuana plant in a keg two or three feet from the base of a fig tree that was about 20 feet from defendant's door. The officer did not know if the tree was in the backyard of the owner (who presumably lived in the front house) or of defendant. It was necessary for the officer to be within almost a foot of the tree to distinguish the marijuana plant. According to the officer, the keg was 'partially covered by the leaves and the limbs of the fig tree.' When later asked if the 'marijuana plant was hidden under the fig tree,' the officer replied, 'I don't believe you could say exactly hidden, however, it was covered by foliage.' He did not have a search warrant."

The appropriate test is whether the person has exhibited a reasonable expectation of privacy, and, if so, whether that expectation has been violated by unreasonable governmental intrusion. "Measured by that test, the officer's discovery and seizure of the marijuana plants in the yard adjacent to defendant's residence did not violate the constitutional prohibitions against unreasonable searches and seizures. From the recited evidence it may be inferred that the marijuana plants were partially but not totally covered by foliage. It does not appear that the plants were covered by nontransparent material, and it may be inferred that at least part of the plants were in plain sight of anyone within a foot of the tree. Although they were in a rear yard that was fenced to an undisclosed extent, they were located a scant 20 feet from defendant's door to which presumably delivery men and others came, and the front house, as well as defendant's house, apparently had access to the yard. Under the circumstances it does not appear that defendant exhibited a subjective expectation of privacy as to the plants. Furthermore, any such expectation would have been unreasonable." (*People* v. *Bradley,* 1 C. 3d 80, 460 P. 2d 129.) Do you agree?

NOTES

1. It has been stated that "Whether the place searched is within the curtilage is to be determined from the facts, including its proximity or annexation to the dwelling, its inclusion within the general enclosure surrounding the dwelling, and its use and enjoyment as an adjunct to the domestic economy of the family. The word originally signified the land with the castles and outhouses, enclosed often with high stone walls, and where the old barons sometimes held their court in the open air. The presence of a fence or other boundary has been said to be an important, but not controlling, factor in determining the extent of the curtilage." (*McDowell* v. *United States.*)

4 Search Incident to Arrest

Chapter Objectives

After reading this chapter, you will be able to:

1. Define the right to search incidental to a lawful arrest.

2. Explain the three requirements for searches incidental to arrest: relatedness, contemporaneity, and limited scope.

3. Describe the rules governing the impound search of automobiles.

As a general rule, all searches must be conducted under the authority of a warrant unless there is some basis for a warrantless search. There are only a few recognized exceptions to the warrant requirement, but a warrantless search incidental to a lawful arrest is the most important. The courts have approved a search of an arrestee without a warrant because of demonstrated needs for such a rule. The rationale is that an officer can search an arrestee without a warrant to prevent escape, assault, or the destruction or concealment of evidence. Protection of the arresting officer and prevention of the loss of evidence are the twin underpinnings to a warrantless search of a person incidental to an arrest.

It should be noted that the full search of a person incident to arrest should be distinguished from a limited search of a person incident to detention (see Limited Search—the Frisk in chapter 1). The purpose of the frisk is to neutralize the possibility of an assault on the officer—not to discover otherwise seizable evidence. A detention is not an arrest, and consequently the warrantless frisk is limited to a weapons search only. If an arrest is made, a search for weapons as well as evidence related to the offense is justified, because if there is a strong suspicion that a person committed a crime (which is not the test for detention), it is reasonable to search the person, not only for weapons but for the proof of the crime itself. Whether the interference with a person's mobility constitutes a detention or an arrest will depend on what the officer said and did at the time. (See chapter 2, Arrest.)

Dispensing with the requirement of the warrant to search the person at the time of the arrest is entirely reasonable. The arrest itself deprives a person of freedom of movement in any event, and searching the person under such a circumstance involves no more serious invasion of privacy. Moreover, the justification for the warrantless search is based partly on the assumption that the arrestee will be booked in a jail facility where a full search is obviously necessary to prevent the introduction of weapons or contraband into jail. By searching in the field, the officer anticipates the booking search. But not all "arrests" in the field contemplate booking and custody. What difference does this factor make?

The First Requirement: Relatedness

Although the actual terminology differs, most jurisdictions do not consider the issuance of a traffic citation as an arrest in the traditional sense. Usually there is no search of the motorist; no custody is contemplated in the absence of injury to person or property; no booking is foreseen; and, most importantly, no evidence of the traffic offense will be yielded that would relate to the cited offense. Under these circumstances, the theoretical justification for a search incidental to an arrest disappears. Absent any concern about personal safety, the officer cannot accelerate a booking search that will not occur. Nor could the motorist conceal or dispose of any evidence related to the traffic offense, because there would be no incriminating evidence in any event. Thus, the first limitation on the right of the officer to search incidental to an arrest is that the search must be reasonably related to the arrest. In most cases, a search incidental to a traffic citation would be impermissible.

This principle applies only if there are no other circumstances involved in the issuance of the citation. If additional factors emerge, the officer may escalate the right to search provided that the search is reasonably related to the new circumstances. If there is some basis for believing that the motorist is armed and dangerous, a limited search of this person is authorized. If the investigation reveals the commission of a misdemeanor or a felony, further searching authority may be justified.

Consider other situations that may occur. Suppose that the officer arrests the driver for a traffic offense, and a statute authorizes custody rather than the mere issuance of a citation. Or, suppose that the officer determines that a traffic warrant is outstanding against the traffic violator. In either case, the officer intends to take the driver into custody. What is the officer's searching authority now? Keeping in mind that a search must be for evidence reasonably related to the arrest, custody alone would not alter the rule. No more evidence of the traffic offense would be admissible if the suspect were arrested than if this person were released. The only rationale for allowing a search of the traffic violator being taken into custody is the safety of the officer. Transporting anyone in a police car reasonably escalates the potential for resistance or violence, so that the officer can take some protective measures for personal welfare even if he or she does not entertain a reasonable basis for believing the arrestee is armed and dangerous. The circumstances demand the use of minimum security measures; at least a search for weapons would be reasonable although a thorough search might not. In this area, federal and state rules differ.

Can a thorough field search of the person be justified on the theory that the search is an anticipatory booking search? The answer will depend largely on the state's statute. Many states have initiated comprehensive legislation regulating the detention and arrest of traffic violators. If the statute requires the officer to deliver the arrestee to a magistrate, or to an officer authorized to admit the violator to bail, no real custody is contemplated. The violator is detained lawfully, but to be delivered to a magistrate—not to a jail cell. If the violator will not be jailed, he or she will not be "booked" and the booking search will not occur. Again, a field search cannot anticipate a booking search that will not occur.

This analysis assumes that only a traffic violation, or a warrant for a previous traffic violation, is involved. If investigation reveals a different offense, the searching authority may increase. Or if the circumstances of the violation involve alcohol, drugs, or injury to person or property by means of the automobile, the officer's searching authority of the person—and the vehicle—may be extended.

The rule that a search must be reasonably related to the arrest is exemplified in the arrest of a motorist for driving under the influence of alcohol. An arrest for this misdemeanor would authorize the search of the motorist's person for evidence related to the offense, that is, flasks or bottles of liquor. As will be seen later, a search of the vehicle itself would also be authorized in order to discover evidence of alcohol, or a search of the person and vehicle would also be authorized to discover any drugs that might have contributed to the motorist's erratic driving. Conversely, a search of a motorist's person, if the motorist were arrested for misdemeanor reckless driving, would not yield any evidence of reckless driving. Absent any custody as a consequence of the driving, no search of the person or vehicle for evidence of the offense would be fruitful.

In the case of felony arrests, generally an arrestee may be searched thoroughly for weapons and evidence regardless of the particular felony. This rule could be challenged if the specific felony was not committed by force or violence, and no evidence of the crime would conceivably be concealed on the person, for example, the theft of a valuable painting. But the vast majority of arrests for felonies automatically justify a search of the person for weapons and evidence. And in most cases, an arrest for a felony automatically authorizes jail custody, in which case a booking search would be perfectly proper.

The Second Requirement: Contemporaneity

The second limitation on the right to search incidental to arrest is that the search must be contemporaneous in time with the arrest and in the same place. This rule requires that an officer conduct a warrantless search at approximately the same time as the arrest and at substantially the same place. This rule harmonizes with the theory that a warrantless search of the person incidental to arrest is justified to prevent assault or destruction of evidence. Once these purposes have been achieved, the reason for the warrantless search elsewhere or at a later time disappears. Any further search would require a warrant. The rule of contemporaneity also exists to prevent using the arrest as a pretext to conduct an unlimited search. By circumscribing the time and place of the search, a general and unlimited search is prohibited.

If a person is arrested while walking on the street, the only principle that applies to a search of this person is the requirement that the search must be for evidence reasonably related to the arrest. Such a search is obviously at the same time and place. If a person is arrested in or near a vehicle, however, the issues become twofold: Is a search of the person justified? Is a search of the vehicle justified? The answer to the first question depends on whether the search is for evidence reasonably related to the arrest. The answer to the second question depends on this principle and also on the issue of contemporaneity. Specifically: Is a search of the vehicle, as an incident of the occupant's arrest, conducted at the same time and place?

If the only basis for the search of the vehicle is the arrest of the occupant, the court will assess the validity of the arrest first. If there is a basis for the arrest, the second question is whether the search of the vehicle—which we assume will be for evidence reasonably related to the arrest—is substantially contemporaneous with the arrest in time and in the same place. If the search of the vehicle is conducted on the street immediately after the defendant is placed in custody, the rule of contemporaneity is satisfied. More difficult cases arise when the defendant is separated from the vehicle and the car is searched at a later time and in a more convenient location—usually a police facility. Consider the following problems:

1. Officers observe the defendant drive up to his apartment, exit, and walk away from the car. As the defendant reaches the door to his apartment, officers lawfully arrest him. The officers return to the car and search it.

2. Officers observe the defendant driving her car on a public street and arrest her pursuant to a validly issued arrest warrant charging unlawful possession of narcotics. As they commence the search of the car, a large crowd forms and threatens injury to the officers. The officers tow the car away and search it shortly afterwards at the impound garage.

3. Officers arrest the driver of a car based on probable cause to believe that he had committed a felony. They observe two new television sets sitting on the back seat of the vehicle, each bearing the original price tag. Reluctant to remove the sets for fear of disturbing possible fingerprints, officers impound the car. Several days later police technicians enter, remove the sets, and examine them for fingerprints.

4. Officers arrest the defendant in Louisiana for a murder he allegedly committed in California. The murder was committed inside the car itself. Lacking jurisdiction to prosecute, the arresting officers transfer the vehicle to a freight car, seal it, and route the car to the demanding jurisdiction. On arrival, the vehicle is removed from the freight car and searched. Chemical analysis reveals incriminating evidence.

5. Officers, armed with a murder warrant, arrest the defendant. The arrest occurs when officers see him standing next to his car. Believing that there is incriminating evidence inside the car and that this evidence can be removed only by chemical analysis, officers seal the car and request an expert to subject the car to laboratory inspection. Several days later, chemists enter and remove incriminating evidence.

6. Officers attempt to arrest the defendant, whom they observe driving her car. The defendant abandons the car and flees. Being unable to apprehend the defendant, officers return to the car and search it, seizing incriminating evidence. Several days later the defendant is arrested.

The single thread that runs through these examples is the obvious reasonableness of the officers' conduct. None of the searches suggests an indifference to constitutional rights or an exercise of arbitrary police authority. In each case, the vehicle was searched after the occupant's personal liberty had been breached by arrest, and in all cases an immediate and thorough search at the time of arrest would have been justified. Yet the defendant has been separated from the car, and the search lacks contemporaneity.

Example 1: Although there is a tendency to apply the exclusionary rule mechanically, most courts have indicated that the Fourth Amendment is a rule of reasonableness. Despite the general rule that all searches must be contemporaneous in time and substantially identical in place (to avoid the possibility of an arrest justifying any kind of search), most courts have held that the rule of contemporaneity requires that the search be *substantially* contemporaneous in time and in the same place as the arrest. If the defendant is arrested near his car, a search of the car would be substantially contemporaneous. As long as there is some evidence that the defendant exercised control over the vehicle, an arrest of the defendant in the near vicinity of his car will justify an otherwise lawful search of the vehicle.

Example 2: Whether a search is contemporaneous with an arrest depends on the totality of circumstances. This rule lacks the precision of arithmetic, but it does provide the officer with an opportunity to develop those facts and circumstances that prevent or interfere with the usual requirement of an immediate search. Thus, an officer confronted by a threatening crowd need not press forward with a search while simultaneously pondering the prospect of assault. Under such circumstances, removing a car from the scene of arrest and subjecting it to search a short time later is quite reasonable. The officer had the right to search the car incidental to the arrest, but was foreclosed from executing the right to search by circumstances beyond the officer's control. By commencing the search at the location of arrest, discontinuing the search, and resuming the search as soon as possible thereafter, the officer established that the search was not delayed capriciously; rather, the search was commenced, discontinued briefly, and resumed shortly thereafter.

Example 3: Courts have encouraged law enforcement agencies to rely on scientific evidence as much as possible. This category of evidence is often most compelling and most reliable. But such evidence is also often difficult to obtain. When officers delay a search because they lack the skills or the facilities to conduct scientific tests, the court will frequently approve a delayed search of the vehicle. Thus, when officers observe new television sets with price tags affixed lying in the back seat of a car, the possibility of fingerprints on the sets is substantial. Although officers could remove the sets immediately in the street, such a course would not be reasonable. Aside from the inconvenience of transferring the sets from one vehicle to another, the potential loss of latent prints is increased. Courts would undoubtedly note that the officers did have the right to seize the sets at the moment of the arrest, but merely delayed executing that right until the circumstances allowed for removal at the laboratory.

Example 4: Similarly, if the defendant is arrested in a car that was an instrumentality of the crime of murder itself, officers could seize the car incidental to the arrest. Not only could the delayed examination of the car be justified under the previous theory, but also the entry by lab technicians can be considered constitutionally reasonable on the ground that the car was evidence of the crime itself and, like guns, contraband, or stolen property, could be seized as evidence. The entry of the car by lab personnel would not be a "search" at all because the car was evidence in police custody and could be subjected to examination just like any other piece of evidence. Such a theory is only sustainable if the vehicle is an instrumentality of the crime itself and not used as a mere carrier of seizable evidence.

Example 5: If officers desire to search a car incidental to an arrest, but desire to delay the search to facilitate laboratory examination, precautions should be taken to indicate the reasonableness of this conduct. Reports should clearly state the reasons why no immediate search was undertaken (for example, lack of skilled personnel and facilities); that, for these reasons, no entry of the vehicle was attempted; that the vehicle was sealed; that an entry was attempted as soon as possible by lab personnel (preferably in the presence of the arresting officer or the investigating officer).

Example 6: If officers establish probable cause to arrest for a felony, thereby simultaneously authorizing an incidental search of the arrestee, that right cannot be frustrated by an arrestee's escape. Even if the prospective arrestee's absence eliminates the theoretical need to search the car for weapons and destructible evidence, the car *could* have been searched if an arrest were affected. The suspect's flight cannot immunize the car from search. In many cases the defendant, when arrested, will contend that the officers also lacked the initial probable cause to arrest.

Alternative theories exist to validate a search of the car. There is a clear indication by the U.S. Supreme Court that if there is probable cause to search or seize the vehicle itself—regardless of probable cause to arrest the occupants—the car may be entered and searched without a warrant at a time and place remote from the arrest. This rule requires evidence of probable cause to believe that the car was used as an instrumentality of the crime or contained seizable evidence. This subject will be discussed separately (see Probable Cause to Search a Motor Vehicle in chapter 6, Searches without Warrants).

Impound Search

A frequent police practice is to inventory the contents of a vehicle after the driver has been arrested. Such an inventory is conducted at a police facility to allow a thorough search under reasonably safe conditions. If the inventory reveals the presence of seizable evidence, may the items be admitted in court?

Not all courts have agreed on the answer. One argument upholds the right of police officers to inventory the contents of a car to safeguard possible valuables and negate the prospect of civil suits against the law enforcement agency for loss or theft of property. Under this rationale, any seizable evidence yielded by the investigation should be admitted.

The counterargument contends that the inventory search is simply not a contemporaneous search and that inventories are unlimited searches for anything that may be discovered. Such searches cannot be sanctioned under "search incident" theory because any danger to the officer's safety or possible destruction of evidence is unlikely in the absence of the arrestee. Lacking this justification, only a search warrant would authorize the search. Moreover, says the California Supreme Court, almost no civil liability attaches to an agency that involuntarily assumes custody of property. Only slight precautionary measures are necessary to avoid civil liability.

The status of impound searches may vary in state and federal jurisdictions and their lawfulness may depend on either of two factors: the reason for the driver's custody, or the basis for the car's custody. In the former case, if the court applies the rule that a search of the car must be for evidence reasonably related to the arrest of the driver or occupant, an officer can determine whether the search of the car would reasonably yield such evidence. Thus, an arrest of a motorist on a traffic warrant would not automatically justify an impound search, because no evidence related to that offense would be found inside the car. If evidence related to the arrest could conceivably be inside the car, the officer must be able to sustain any later (noncontemporaneous) search on one of the theories discussed earlier. In other cases, the custody of the car itself may justify a search of the interior without reference to an arrest—for example, a car impounded as evidence for use in a subsequent forfeiture proceeding against the car for transporting contraband. In such a case, police retain the car as the subject of the crime.

As will be discussed later (chapter 6, Searches without Warrants—Probable Cause to Search a Motor Vehicle), an arrest of a car's occupants for robbery in which the car was used as an instrumentality of the crime would provide probable cause to search the car itself. Probable cause to search the car in custody would remain independent of the arrest.

The Third Requirement: Limited Scope

The rule of contemporaneity applies to searches of houses as well as to those of persons and vehicles. Because searches of dwelling places are considered the most serious invasion of privacy, the courts have insisted that a search of a person's house incidental to arrest can be conducted only if the person is arrested inside the house and the search is made at the same time.

In *Vale* v. *Louisiana,* the U.S. Supreme Court emphasized this rule. Possessing two warrants for the defendant's arrest and having information that he was residing at a specified address, officers proceeded there in an unmarked car and set up a surveillance of the house. "After approximately 15 minutes the officers observed a green 1958 Chevrolet drive up and sound the horn and after backing into a parking place, again blow the horn. At this juncture the defendant, who was well-known to the officers having arrested him twice in the previous month, was seen coming out of the house and walking up to the passenger side of the Chevrolet where he had a close brief conversation with the driver; and after looking up and down the street returned inside of the house. Within a few minutes he reappeared on the porch, and again cautiously looked up and down the street before proceeding to the passenger side of the Chevrolet, then leaned through the window. From this the officers were convinced a narcotics sale had taken place. They returned to their car and immediately drove toward the defendant, and as they reached within approximately three car lengths from the defendant he looked up and, obviously recognizing the officers, turned around, walking quickly toward the house. At the same time the driver of the Chevrolet started to make his get-away when the car was blocked by the police vehicle. The three officers promptly alighted from the car, whereupon two of the officers called to the defendant to stop as he reached the front steps of the house, telling him he was under arrest. The third officer, at the same time, saw the driver of the Chevrolet, whom the officers knew to be a narcotic addict, place something hurriedly in his mouth. Because of the transaction they had just observed they informed the defendant they were going to search the house." The search of a rear bedroom revealed a quantity of narcotics.

"A search may be incident to an arrest only if it is substantially contemporaneous with the arrest and is confined to the *immediate* vicinity of the arrest. If a search of a house is to be upheld as incident to an arrest, that arrest must take place *inside* the house, not somewhere outside—whether two blocks away, twenty feet away, or on the sidewalk near the front steps. Belief, however well founded, that an article sought is concealed in a dwelling house furnishes no justification for a search of that place without a warrant." (*Vale* v. *Louisiana.*)

Suppose that officers delay an arrest to allow a suspect to enter his or her home. Once the suspect is inside, the officers enter, arrest, and search the entire house. The search is indeed conducted at the same time and place as the arrest. Yet the wholesale search of a person's house does not square with other Fourth Amendment principles, and in *Chimel* v. *California,* decided in 1970, the U.S. Supreme Court severely restricted the right of officers to search a house as an incident of the suspect's arrest inside.

To clarify the *Chimel* case, other constitutional principles must be set in context. One of the principal and well-established Fourth Amendment rules was the requirement that a house may never be searched without a warrant, even if there is probable cause to believe seizable evidence is inside. Thus, if the house were unoccupied when the officers entered, no search could be undertaken in the absence of a warrant. If the suspect was arrested several miles from the house, no warrantless search of the suspect's quarters could be justified as an incident of arrest under the "search incident" theory, because there would be no need to avert assault or prevent destruction or loss of evidence. If the house of the arrestee could not be searched if the person were arrested away from his or her quarters, why should the house be subjected to search merely because the suspect was arrested inside? Once the suspect was in custody, no assault or loss of evidence inside the house was likely. The mere accident of an arrest effected inside the house should not expand a right to search that would have been otherwise unlawful had the suspect been arrested outside the house.

In *Chimel* v. *California,* the court applied such reasoning to the following facts: Officers, holding a warrant for the defendant, knew where he worked and where he lived. They chose not to arrest him at his place of business, but instead waited until he came home. After Chimel was inside his house, officers entered, placed him under arrest, and searched the entire house. Incriminating evidence was discovered, and on that evidence Chimel was convicted of burglary.

On his appeal, the U.S. Supreme Court reviewed past decisions that had seemingly authorized the search of an entire house as an incident of the defendant's arrest. The Court modified the rule of contemporaneity by deciding that henceforth the search of a house incidental to the arrest of an occupant would be limited in its scope. The Court said: "When an arrest is made, it is reasonable for the arresting officer to search the person arrested in order to remove any weapons that the latter might seek to use in order to resist arrest or effect his escape. Otherwise, the officer's safety might well be endangered, and the arrest itself frustrated. In addition, it is entirely reasonable for the arresting officer to search for and seize any evidence on the arrestee's person in order to prevent its concealment or destruction. And the area into which an arrestee might reach in order to grab a weapon or evidentiary items must, of course, be governed by a like rule. A gun on a table or in a drawer in front of one who is arrested can be as dangerous to the arresting officer as one concealed in the clothing of the person arrested. *There is ample justification, therefore, for a search of the arrestee's person and the area 'within his immediate control'—construing that phrase to mean the area from within which he might gain possession of a weapon or destructible evidence.*

"*There is no comparable justification, however, for routinely searching rooms other than that in which an arrest occurs—or, for that matter, for searching through all the desk drawers or other closed or concealed areas in that room itself.* Such searches, in the absence of well-recognized exceptions, may be made only under the authority of a search warrant. The 'adherence to judicial processes' mandated by the Fourth Amendment requires no less."

The *Chimel* case thus places a third limitation on a warrantless search incidental to a lawful arrest: the search must be limited to the area under the immediate control of the defendant. What are the boundaries of this term? Consider this example: The defendant was lawfully arrested while sleeping on a bed in her home. "The officer then directed defendant to remove herself from the bed; and, without having to move any bedding or clothing, he looked under the bed with his flashlight and saw a brown paper sack. The sack was open, and he observed a small piece of cellophane sticking out of it. As a qualified expert on the packaging and use of benzedrine, he believed that the bag might contain dangerous drugs. He thereupon removed the bag and discovered that it contained benzedrine tablets. He then placed defendant under arrest.

"Even under the restrictions imposed by *Chimel,* however, the officer's search did not exceed the permissible scope. Under the *Chimel* rule it is entirely reasonable for the arresting officer to search for and seize any evidence . . . [within] the area into which an arrestee might reach in order to grab . . . evidentiary items. . . . When the defendant was sitting on the bed, the area under it was within 'the area into which [she] might [have] reached in order to grab . . . evidentiary items.'" (*People* v. *King.*)

Under the *Chimel* rule, a thorough search of a house as an incident of an arrest may only be conducted under the authority of a search warrant. The Court in *Chimel* also harmonized their rule governing the scope of a search incidental to an arrest with rules affecting other kinds of searches. The Court said that in analyzing searches and seizures generally, the inquiry should be twofold: (1) Is there a reasonable basis for the search? and (2) If so, is the scope of that search reasonably related to the reason for the initial intrusion? This rule governs the search of a person and the person's car and house. Thus, if there is a reasonable basis for stopping a person, the frisk is related to the original detention because of the need to neutralize potential danger. The scope of the search, that is, a limited pat-down, reasonably relates to that end. Similarly, any search of an automobile will be measured by the reasons for the original detention. If the original detention was for a traffic violation, no search of the car would be reasonably related to the traffic offense. If some other offense is discovered after the stop, the scope of any search must be reasonably related to such offense. And finally, a search of the house itself would exceed the scope of a search incident to arrest of the suspect inside—for whatever offense—because custody would foreclose any danger to the officer or destruction of evidence. A full search of the person—at least for a felony arrest—would be authorized whether an arrest was made of a pedestrian, a motorist, or a household occupant. Beyond that, a warrant might be necessary.

The full implications of the *Chimel* decision remain to be explored. If seizable evidence is seen in plain view inside the house where officers have made an arrest, the object may be seized under the "plain view" doctrine (see chapter 3, Search). A more difficult question arises when officers enter rooms other than where the arrest is made and observe evidence in plain view. If the officers had some basis for being in an adjoining room—perhaps because of the suspect's flight or because there was a reasonable basis to believe confederates were present—any evidence in plain view could lawfully be seized. If curiosity was the officers' only object, the courts would probably reach the opposite result. In some cases the kind of crime arrested for may define the area into which officers might enter. For example: "Police officers were told by an informant that defendant, his mistress and others were engaged in large scale dealings in heroin. They arranged with the informant to purchase an ounce of heroin from defendant. After that transaction, defendant departed for his home and the informant returned to the police officers, gave them a condom of heroin that he claimed he had received from defendant, told them of his conversations with defendant, including the information that defendant had gone home to await the arrival of some potential buyers.

"The officers then proceeded to defendant's home and arrested him in the living room of the house. After the arrest, one officer went into the kitchen, where he observed a large quantity of heroin, together with other supplies and equipment commonly used to package heroin for sale. A search of the house for other occupants was unavailing. The defendant contended that the search of the kitchen exceeded the allowed scope of *Chimel.*

"In this case, the officer had a right to enter the kitchen to look for possible confederates of the defendant. The informant had told the officers that defendant was living with a woman, that other persons frequented the apartment, and that a buyer was expected momentarily—in fact that defendant had gone home to meet that buyer. Even if the sale by the defendant to the informant was not sufficient corroboration to make him thereafter a 'reliable' informant, it is clear that the officers had information as to other persons which it was their right, and their duty, to follow up. Having arrested defendant, it was not unreasonable for them to walk through the house to see if others were there and, if found, at least to interrogate them. To walk through an open doorway, in pursuit of such an investigation, is not the kind of excessive invasion of privacy that *Chimel* is designed to prevent; it is merely basic police investigation of information received. If the officer lawfully entered the kitchen, his observations thereafter were not a 'search' within the definition of the term." (*Guevara* v. *Superior Court*).

The courts, however, are likely to scrutinize entry of adjacent rooms. In order for officers to avail themselves of the "plain view" theory, they must establish their right to have a view. The courts would not approve entry and search of rooms adjoining the arrest in the absence of an articulable reason for the officer to enter those rooms.

Although the Supreme Court in *Chimel* attempted to define the area that could be searched incidental to an arrest inside a dwelling place, the Court left the door open for a flexible approach to circumstances that present themselves to an officer at the time of an arrest. Part of that determination depends on who the suspect is and what crime the person has committed. And more latitude will be allowed depending on the nature of the evidence seized. If there is a reasonable basis for believing that guns are present on the premises, officers will be allowed a wider area of discretion than if marijuana is involved. In most arrests, the officers' attempt to maximize their safety, and an explanation of those steps, will satisfy the Court that the officers were acting reasonably.

The "search incident" theory was one of the first exceptions carved out of the general rule requiring that all searches be conducted pursuant to warrant. The twin needs—officer safety and preserving evidence—were apparent. But the right to search incident to an arrest was always an exception to the general rule. As time passed, however, the exception threatened to swallow the rule. For example, an "arrest" for a traffic citation would theoretically allow an "incidental search" of the person and the car. Thus, the rule requiring a search to be reasonably related to the arrest emerged. Another example: If the defendant was arrested in Miami, the person's car could theoretically be searched in Tampa for evidence reasonably related to the arrest. Thus the rule emerged requiring searches to be not only for evidence reasonably related to the arrest, but also contemporaneous. Finally, *Chimel* requires the search to be limited to the area under the arrestee's control.

All these apparent restrictions on searching authority relate directly back to the rule prohibiting searches without a warrant. What had happened was that the arrest was invoked as justification for a search without a warrant. But *Chimel* clearly reaffirms the old rule requiring searches to be conducted pursuant to warrant. An arrest cannot bootstrap itself to permit an otherwise unreasonable search. The courts will no longer assume that an arrest authorizes an automatic search. The nature of the seizure will delineate searching authority.

Another method of analyzing the search-incident-to-arrest theory: The arrest, whether traffic stop, detention for investigation of criminal activity, misdemeanor, or felony, confers on the officer a "right to search." Once the "right to search" is established, the extent, or scope, of that right must be determined. If the officer establishes the right to arrest, he or she correspondingly establishes the right to search. But the kind of arrest effected will mark the boundaries of the search. The scope of the search must bear some reasonable relationship to the reason for the seizure. Nowhere is this principle better illustrated than in stop and frisk. The temporary detention of a person (the right to seize) authorizes only a search that is limited in scope, for example, the removal of weapons.

CASES AND MATERIALS

Chimel v. *California*, 395 U.S. 752, 89 S. Ct. 2034, 23 L. Ed. 2d 685.

Guevara v. *Superior Court*, 7 Cal. App. 3d 531, 86 Cal. R. 657.

Mozzetti v. *Superior Court,* 4 C. 3d 699, 484 P. 2d 84 (impound searches).

People v. *Block,* 6 C. 3d 239, 499 P. 2d 961 (house).

People v. *King,* 5 C. 3d 458, 487 P. 2d 1082.

People v. *Superior Court* (Kiefer), 3 C. 3d 807, 478 P. 2d 499.

Preston v. *United States,* 376 U.S. 364, 84 S. Ct. 881, 11 L. Ed. 2d 777.

South Dakota v. *Opperman,* 49 L. Ed. 2d 1000.

Stoner v. *California,* 376 U.S. 483, 84 S. Ct. 889, 11 L. Ed. 2d 856.

United States v. *Edwards,* 415 U.S. 800, 39 L. Ed. 2d 771, 94 S. Ct. 1234.

Vale v. *Louisiana,* 399 U.S. 30, 90 S. Ct. 1969, 26 L. Ed. 2d 409.

1. Around 11 P.M., officers observed a female, who appeared to be a minor, walking slowly on a city street in an area frequented by prostitutes. One of the officers suspected this person of being a prostitute and described her walk as a "prostitute walk" or "prostitute stroll." The officers drove around the block and, on seeing her again, stopped and questioned her. They ascertained that her name was Nancy C. and that she was sixteen. She indicated to the officers that she was coming from a nearby club—which does not admit persons under twenty-one—and she had been staying with someone who was known to one of the officers as a prostitute. Finally, she said she was on her way to the bus depot to meet a friend. The minor was arrested for violation of a local curfew ordinance and was booked at city jail. During the booking, her purse was searched, and a bag appearing to contain marijuana was discovered. Will this search be reasonable as an incident of the minor's arrest for violation of a county ordinance? (*In re Nancy C.,* 28 Cal. App. 3d 747, 105 Cal. R. 113.)

2. The defendant is arrested for being drunk in a public place. A cursory search reveals no weapons, and the officer does not believe the arrestee is armed or dangerous. Instead of confining him to the city jail, the officer transports the inebriate to a detoxification facility authorized under a state statute. On arrival, a thorough search of his person reveals contraband. At trial, the defendant contends that any search of his person prior to commitment in a civil facility is unlawful, or, in the alternative, even if the search is reasonably related to the need for security in a facility, any evidence secured from his person should not be admitted in a subsequent criminal trial.

What should be the result? (*People* v. *Superior Court* [Colon], 29 Cal. App. 3d 397, 105 Cal. R. 695.)

3. The defendant sold heroin to a police informant in the presence of a deputy sheriff in the defendant's car in a parking lot. Two weeks later, two officers assigned to the narcotics bureau went to the defendant's residence to serve a warrant for the defendant's arrest on the charge of selling heroin relating to the sale. The officers entered the house and proceeded to the front room, where the defendant was arrested. The officers then searched defendant's apartment and found a red balloon containing heroin in a light fixture on a bedroom wall.

Assuming this search was properly incident to the arrest, was it lawful? What evidence, if discovered, would be reasonably related to the offense of sale committed two weeks earlier?

4. Officers lawfully arrested several suspects inside a house for possession of alcohol. One officer observed that at least four of the six suspects had dilated eyes and pupils and an odor of marijuana upon their breath. "We went upstairs 'to see if there were any other people in the house.' He testified that 'because of the number of defendants in the house, I believed there was a possibility of more defendants' upstairs. The house was 'quite large,' containing three or possibly four bedrooms. Lights were turned on to illuminate the stairs leading to the second floor and the upstairs hallway. On the second floor, he looked in one bedroom, a bathroom, and then a second bedroom. The light in the second bedroom was off and the door partially open. He turned on the light, looked behind the door to see if anyone was hiding there, and then surveyed the room. He then observed a clear plastic vial lying in plain sight on the table containing marijuana.

"Was the search of the upstairs lawful?" (*People* v. *Block,* 6 C. 3d 239, 499 P. 2d 961.)

5. Officers contacted the defendant, who, in an inebriated state, informed them his car had just been involved in an accident. The car was discovered in a severely damaged condition just off the roadway. After towing the car away to a private garage, officers drove the defendant to the police station and placed him under arrest for driving under the influence of alcohol.

Upon learning the defendant was a police officer, the arresting officer attempted to locate his service revolver, which they believed he kept in his possession. One officer returned to the yard where the disabled car had been towed and searched the interior of the car and glove compartment. Unsuccessful in his quest, he unlocked the trunk and discovered evidence of a homicide. The evidence revealed that the arrest and search took place in a rural community and no facilities were available to guard the vehicle from intrusion by others. The officer further testified that he searched the car only to locate a potential lethal weapon.

The driver's custody was based upon an arrest for driving under the influence of alcohol, but the search cannot be sustained as incident to the arrest because it was conducted at a time and place remote from the arrest. Because the homicide was unknown to the officer prior to the search, no independent probable cause existed to search the vehicle. What reasons, if any, make this search reasonable? *Cady* v. *Dombrowski,* 414 U.S. 218, 38 L. Ed. 2d 427, 94 S. Ct. 467. See also *Gustafson* v. *Florida,* 414 U.S. 260, 38 L. Ed. 2d 456, 94 S. Ct. 488; *United States* v. *Robinson,* 414 U.S. 216, 38 L. Ed. 2d 415, 94 S. Ct. 460.

5 Consent Searches

Chapter Objectives

After reading this chapter, you will be able to:

1. Explain how consent searches are "reasonable" within the meaning of the Fourth Amendment.

2. Define the requirement of voluntariness in securing consent.

3. Distinguish between the actual and apparent authority of a party to consent.

The courts have held that a constitutional right may be surrendered if it is surrendered knowingly and voluntarily. The Fourth Amendment is no exception to this rule, and officers may request consent to search a person, a car, or a dwelling place. Officers do not have the right to enter or search anyone's home in the absence of probable cause to arrest, an arrest warrant, a search warrant, or some evidence of an emergency, but they can request permission to enter a car or a dwelling place. Because there is no "right" to conduct a consent search, the lawfulness of the ensuing search depends on the decision of the person whose consent is sought. Before approving a consent search, the court will examine the circumstances in which consent was granted.

Questions of Consent

The initial inquiry is into the fact of consent itself. The consenting party must expressly or impliedly consent to the search. In all cases, this issue will become a matter for the trial court to determine. Typically the officer will testify that he or she asked for and received consent; the defendant will deny it. The court must determine where the truth lies. Although it is not essential, the case is clearly stronger if the consenting party expressly authorizes the search than if the prosecution must rely on consent implied from the circumstances. A householder who retreats silently from an open door when confronted by officers may be either inviting entry or merely acquiescing to a display of authority.

The general rule is that the validity of a consent search depends on all the facts and circumstances of the case. The contours of such a rule are obviously imprecise. The officer must establish that the defendant in fact consented and that the consent was voluntary, and these elements must be proved by the prosecutor. The court will review numerous factors: the time of day, the location, the number of officers, the number of occupants at the house, the language and tone of the request, the nature of the response, whether the defendant was in custody or not at the time the consent was requested, whether there was any detention prior to the request, and whether any false or misleading statements were made by the officer. These are the facts and circumstances relevant to a determination of voluntariness that the prosecution must consider in proving consent.

Involuntary Consent

Officers arrested the defendant (with adequate probable cause) on the street. The officers testified that they asked him if he had any more narcotics at his house and that the defendant said he did not. "I asked him if we could look, and he asked me if I had a search warrant. I stated I did not have a search warrant, and I would not need one if he would give me consent, at which time he gave me consent. Officers took the defendant with them in their car and started toward his house. The officers asked defendant where he lived, and the defendant said that he lived on Tamarind Street. He was asked if he was sure, and then said 'All right. You guys know where I live.' When they arrived at his house, defendant said, 'I don't live here; I live over here,' and pointed to the house next door. He knocked on the door, and his aunt let him and the officers in. The officers asked defendant's aunt if he lived there and she said, 'No, he lives across the way.'

"The officers took defendant to his house and asked him again if he had any narcotics in the house. The defendant said, 'All right, I will tell you where they are.' He directed the officers to his mother's house on Tamarind Street and told them that there were narcotics on a rafter in the garage. The officers looked and found nothing. They then took defendant back to his house and searched the house in his presence. They discovered a quantity of heroin. . . .

"To protect his right to object to an unreasonable search or seizure a defendant need not forcibly resist an officer's assertion of authority to enter his home or search it or his person, but if he freely consents to an entry or search, or voluntarily produces evidence against himself, his constitutional rights are not violated and any search or taking of evidence pursuant to his consent is not unreasonable. . . . In the present case, the testimony of the officer dispels any inference that might otherwise have been drawn from defendant's words of consent that he freely and voluntarily consented to the search of his home.

"Although not conclusive, a circumstance of particular significance was the defendant's custody at the time of the request for his permission to search, for where he has submitted to arrest, or is in jail, he knows that he is virtually powerless to prevent the search. In the present case, defendant was not only under arrest, but he was handcuffed at all times until he was finally taken to jail several hours after his arrest, and he had no choice but to go wherever the officers took him. He knew that the officers wished to search his home and that if they did so they would find evidence against him. He repeatedly attempted to lead the officers away from his home, and after these efforts failed, he was neither asked to nor did he express his consent to the search of his home. The most that can be inferred is that defendant sought to placate the officers and hoped that by agreeing to the search of another premises, he would forestall the search of his home and the discovery of incriminating evidence. . . . Defendant was under no duty to assist the officers in securing evidence against him. Since the search was not incident to his arrest, he had the right to have a magistrate determine whether there was reasonable cause to search his home and whether a search warrant should therefore issue." (*Castaneda* v. *Superior Court.*)

Another example is as follows: " 'X,' together with three companions, were travelling in an automobile owned by one of them. About 3:30 P.M., an officer observed the automobile going up a hill in the middle lane of a three-lane highway. Because the car was towing a trailer in the wrong lane, the officer signalled 'X' to pull over to the side of the road. 'X' complied.

"The officer walked back to the car and asked 'X' for his driver's license. 'X' answered that he did not have a driver's license or any identification because his wallet had been stolen a short time before. The officer directed him to get out of the automobile and to proceed to the front of the patrol car.

"After ordering 'X' to remain at the patrol car, the officer returned to the car to question its other occupants. He asked them for identification and was apparently satisfied with the identification produced by two of them. The third, a woman, produced a Canadian passport. The officer noticed that her speech 'was a little bit erratic' and thought that 'she was under the influence of something.' He had her step out of the vehicle and proceed to the front of the patrol car. At the same time, he ordered 'X' to return to the car and sit in the driver's seat. The officer asked the woman if she was under the care of a doctor; she replied that she was.

"At this point she searched through her purse for further identification. As she did so the officer saw a gold cigarette case which he thought looked like a wallet.

"He asked her 'if she cared if I looked at it' and she replied in the negative and handed the case to him. He ordered her to open it, looked inside and saw marijuana.

"After arresting her, the officer radioed for assistance. . . .

"The officer went back to the car and advised its three occupants that the woman had been arrested and that he 'was going to check them.' The officer ordered the men to get out of the car so they could be frisked. As he prepared to frisk one occupant, whom he had previously learned to be the owner of the car, the officer asked him 'if he cared if I checked the vehicle and he stated no. . . .' "

Under the left-front bucket seat the officer found marijuana.

As a matter of law, was the consent to the search of the owner's car involuntary? "The circumstances under which consent was given appear from the uncontradicted evidence to be highly coercive. The car which he owned and in which he had been riding, had been stopped by a highway patrol officer who ordered first the driver and then the woman to get out of the vehicle and go with him to the patrol car. The driver was then sent back to the car and ordered to remain in the driver's seat. The woman was detained in the patrol car. For approximately 30 minutes nothing further happened. The owner and his companions were given no explanation for the delay. Later, the officer informed the owner that the woman had been arrested and that the other three occupants of the car were going to be 'checked out.' The officer then ordered the owner to get out of the automobile so that he could be searched and asked whether the owner cared if the officers checked the car. At no time was the owner informed by any of the officers that he could effectively refuse consent." (*People* v. *Superior Court* [Casebeer].)

In both these cases, the officer testified that the person verbalized his consent, that is, the fact of consent was proved, yet in each case other facts and circumstance rebutted the voluntariness of the consent. In the first example, the defendant's conduct implicitly negated his alleged consent. In the second example, the atmosphere in which consent was obtained was highly coercive. Each case illustrates facts that rebut any testimony that the consent was voluntary.

Because the very presence of police officers carries with it an implication of authority, the courts also hold that a consent search cannot be approved if obtained by submission to a display of authority. To many citizens, police officers possess unlimited power that cannot be thwarted. The mere presence of uniformed and armed police officers at a householder's door implies a display of authority difficult to defy. On the highway, the solitary motorist who is detained for a traffic violation nervously confronts the helmeted and armed motor officer. Refusing to grant consent to a search of his or her vehicle may seem foolhardy to most citizens.

If the occupant submits to a display of authority, the consent is involuntary, and any evidence seized is inadmissible. For example, in *Bumper* v. *North Carolina,* officers confronted an elderly woman in her home and informed her that they possessed a search warrant. She told the officers to "go ahead." At trial, no search warrant was offered in evidence, and the prosecution relied on consent. The U.S. Supreme Court held that consent could not be presumed when induced by an apparently false statement. In addition, the officers' assertion of their right to enter based on the authority of the warrant required the occupant to submit. Without proof of the warrant, the search was the unlawful product of an involuntary consent.

Most officers are aware of the need to advise a suspect of the right to counsel and silence before interrogation may begin. Under the *Miranda* decision, the U.S. Supreme Court held that in order for suspects to surrender their right to silence, guaranteed by the Fifth Amendment, and their right to counsel, guaranteed by the Sixth Amendment, they must be informed of those rights. Unless they understand that the Constitution extends these rights to them, they cannot knowingly waive them. Under the Fourth Amendment, however, the U.S. Supreme Court has held that an officer need not inform a person of the right to refuse consent (a right which all citizens enjoy). Failure to advise a person of the right to refuse consent will not void the ensuing search, but it may be relevant in determining whether the defendant's consent was voluntarily given.

Joint Occupancy

A question frequently presented involves a search of premises jointly occupied. For example: Two officers arrested the defendant in an apartment. The officers searched the apartment, but found no narcotics or other contraband. They searched the defendant and found a key and a rent receipt for an apartment, No. 212. The defendant denied knowledge of the receipt. "Having ascertained that apartment No. 212 was on West 87th Street, the officers told defendant they were going to take him there. Defendant then admitted that he had rented the apartment the preceding night. An officer asked the defendant who was in apartment No. 212 and defendant said no one. The officers asked if he had any 'junk' in there and he said no. They asked if they could go down and take a look and the defendant said, 'All right, go ahead.' The officers took the defendant to the apartment and knocked on the door. After some delay the [codefendant] asked who was there. The officers asked defendant to say it was he, but he refused to do so." One of the officers demanded entry, and the codefendant opened the door. The officer testified that she had a hypodermic needle attached to an eye dropper in her left hand. The officers arrested her and searched the apartment. They found heroin.

"The search of the apartment cannot be justified on the ground that defendant consented to it. It is true that one of the officers testified that defendant responded, 'All right, go ahead,' when the officer suggested they go to the apartment and take a look. But his subsequent refusal to assist the officers in gaining access to the apartment establishes that his apparent consent was not voluntarily given. Moreover, even if defendant had voluntarily consented to the search, his consent could not justify the invasion of his joint occupant's privacy that occurred when the officer demanded that the door be opened.''[1] (*People* v. *Shelton.*)

Generally speaking, a cotenant on the premises may admit anyone. If a cotenant freely admits officers to jointly shared quarters, the absent cotenant cannot legally object. Once inside, the cotenant can further consent to a search of jointly shared areas, but not to a search of property belonging exclusively to the other absent tenant. But if both cotenants are on the premises, a consenting cotenant cannot approve of the search of jointly shared areas over the objections of the other cotenant. The consenting cotenant can then only approve the search of property exclusively his or her own. If officers obtain consent to search the quarters of a jointly occupied apartment from the tenant while this person is away from the premises, they cannot enter, unless there is probable cause to arrest, over the objections of a tenant occupying the premises. A cotenant away from the premises implicitly authorizes the occupying tenant to admit or deny anyone entry.

Apparent Authority

The courts have also approved consent searches by those who have apparent authority to consent. For example: The defendant is a guest in a private residence. In the defendant's absence, the homeowner allows the police to search the guest's room, where they find narcotics. When officers act in good faith with the consent and at the request of a homeowner in conducting a search, evidence they obtain cannot be excluded merely because the officers may make a reasonable mistake as to the extent of the owner's authority. Although sometimes criticized, the rule that a search is not unreasonable if made with the consent of a third party whom the police reasonably and in good faith believe has authority to consent to their search has been regularly reaffirmed.

The rule governing searches based on consent by a third party is: A search is not unreasonable if made with the consent of a third party whom the police reasonably and in good faith believe has authority to consent to their search. The operative word in the rule is ''reasonably''; thus, there must be some objective evidence of joint control or access to the places or items to be searched that would indicate that the person authorizing the search has the authority to do so. The good-faith-mistake rule does not apply where the third party makes clear that the property belongs to another.

The good-faith rule also does not apply where the relationship of the third party and the defendant makes clear that the defendant has not authorized the third party to act as his or her agent. Thus, in *Stoner* v. *California,* the Supreme Court, in holding that a room clerk could not consent to the search of a guest's room, and rejecting the ''claim that the search was reasonable because the police, relying upon the night clerk's expressions of consent, had a reasonable basis for the belief that the clerk had authority to consent to the search,'' stated: ''There is nothing in the record to indicate that the police had any basis whatsoever to believe that the night clerk had been authorized by the [occupant of the room] to permit the police to search [his quarters].''

Evidence of apparent authority may emerge from the relationship of the parties (father-son; householder-guest) or from the circumstances of the case. Whether apparent authority exists is a question of fact determined in part on the reasonable good-faith belief of the officers. But some legal relationships preclude any apparent authority of a third party to authorize consent, even though they may possess some evidence of that authority. For example, hotel clerks, motel clerks, or landlords who possess keys to individual living units cannot authorize entry and search. Payment of the rent carries with it the right to exclusive occupancy for the term prescribed and, absent permission to enter by the guest, no entry by others is authorized except in the normal course of housekeeping or maintenance.

Consent searches are legally vulnerable because of the variety of attacks available to the defendant. When officers rely on consent to search, they must realize the legal weaknesses of their position. Only by carefully adhering to the guidelines for obtaining a lawful consent will they enhance their chance for success in court. Courts look critically on consent searches, and many observers predict the day when officers will be denied the right to conduct consent searches without some clear justification for their use.

In determining from all the facts and circumstances whether the consent was valid, the court will not isolate the alleged consent from the context of the situation. If the acts prior to consent are illegal, they taint any further search. For example, if consent is obtained after an arrest that lacks probable cause, the illegal arrest taints the consent and voids it. Officers cannot rescue an unlawful arrest by a subsequent act of consent. The consent depends too heavily on the arrest to be considered truly voluntary. Similar reasoning would be applied to illegal detentions or illegal entries. Any consent secured after these illegal acts cannot be voluntary.

In the case of a dwelling place, consent to enter does not authorize consent to search. The entry must be freely granted, but, once granted, does not automatically bestow any further authority. Once consent to enter has been obtained, the scope of that entry must be reasonably related to the consent bestowed. In most cases, officers are seeking only interviews—not evidence—and consent to entry for that purpose does not include consent to search. The consenting party may not only restrict the scope of consent, but may also withdraw consent at any time.

For example: ''A police officer observed defendant sitting in his car at 2 A.M. and questioned him because of the hour and the area where frequent arrests had been made for burglaries and narcotic violations. The officer had no warrant nor any further information regarding the defendant or his car, other than that it was registered in another name but was not listed as stolen.

Both the defendant and the officer testified that the defendant was cooperative when the defendant was first asked to identify himself. Both testified that the defendant allowed the officer to look around inside the vehicle. The officer then searched the front seat area and the glove compartment. The officer then asked to look in the trunk of the car. There was no key to the trunk and it was not locked. The defendant told the officer that the trunk contained a spare tire, car battery and some tools. The officer testified that he had defendant lift the trunk lid. The defendant testified that the officer opened the trunk and began to examine the contents. Defendant testified that the investigation to this point had taken about 15 minutes and that he was becoming concerned about the delay and harassment of the investigation.

"At this point the defendant asked the officer what he was looking for and told the officer to stop his search because he felt he was being harassed. The officer testified that, in fact, he did not know what he might find, but that he intended to, and did, continue his search despite the defendant's objection. The contraband introduced as evidence in the trial, over appropriate objection by the defendant, was subsequently found concealed under a rag on top of a car battery stored in the trunk."

The court saw no reason why the defendant could not withdraw his consent previously given. (*People* v. *Martinez.*)

CASES AND MATERIALS

Bumper v. *North Carolina,* 391 U.S. 543, 88 S. Ct. 1788, 20 L. Ed. 2d 797.

Castaneda v. *Superior Court,* 59 C. 2d 439, 380 P. 2d 641.

Chapman v. *United States,* 365 U.S. 610, 81 S. Ct. 776, 5 L. Ed. 2d 828.

People v. *Martinez,* 259 Cal. App. 2d Supp. 943, 65 Cal. R. 920.

People v. *Shelton,* 60 C. 2d 740, 388 P. 2d 665.

People v. *Superior Court* (Casebeer), 71 C. 2d 265, 455 P. 2d 146.

People v. *West,* 3 C. 3d 595, 91 Cal. R. 385, 477 P. 2d 409.

Schneckloth v. *Bustamonte,* 412 U.S. 218, 36 L. Ed. 2d 854, 93 S. Ct. 2041.

State v. *Commonwealth,* 246 S.W. 449 (Kentucky).

State v. *Johnson,* 427 P. 2d 705 (Washington).

Stones v. *California,* 376 U.S. 483, 84 S. Ct. 889, 11 L. Ed. 2d 856.

1. Officers are invited into the home by the defendant. While inside, officers question the defendant about a crime and ask if they can "look around." The defendant agrees. One of the officers opens a dresser drawer and discovers evidence of a crime.

Is the defendant's consent to "look around" equivalent to a consent to "search"?

2. Officers stop the defendant's vehicle for commission of a minor traffic violation. Even though the defendant produces satisfactory identification and does not appear to be under the influence of any drug or alcohol, the officer asks whether he may search the vehicle.

Assuming that the defendant is not otherwise suspected of any crime, must the officer have a reasonable basis to request a consent search? In other words, must there be "probable cause" to request that a person consent to a search?

NOTE

1. "The search cannot be justified on the ground that the officers had reasonable cause to arrest the co-defendant before they demanded that she open the door. Although the officers apparently knew that the co-defendant was at the apartment, they did not know that she was also a user or was involved with defendant in the narcotics. Thus, even if the officers had reasonable cause to believe that defendant had narcotics in the apartment, they had no reasonable cause to believe that his possession, if any, was shared with co-defendant. Before they demanded that the door be opened, they knew only that a woman was in an apartment where defendant may have stored narcotics. Such association between a suspect and even a known criminal by itself is not reasonable cause for an arrest and search." (*People* v. *Shelton*.)

6 Searches Without Warrants

Chapter Objectives

After reading this chapter, you will be able to:

1. Explain the rules governing the search of motor vehicles without a warrant.

2. Describe the requirements for a legal search of goods in transit.

3. Discuss emergency as a condition for warrantless searches.

4. Describe the requirements covering probation searches, specialized searches, and searches by private citizens.

Although searches incidental to arrest constitute the vast majority of warrantless searches, there are several other exceptions to the rule that all searches must be conducted under the authority of a search warrant.

Probable Cause to Search a Motor Vehicle

The motor vehicle is a mixed blessing: indispensable to the citizen for business and recreation, yet often essential to the criminal engaged in unlawful enterprise; a source of transportation, yet a weapon of destruction when driven by a drunken driver. For obvious reasons, all state legislatures have heavily regulated the ownership and use of vehicles. Many of the regulations concern theft or damage to vehicles. Other statutes regulate the conduct of the driver.

When a police officer detects a statutory violation involving a vehicle, the detention of the motorist to issue a citation often reveals the commission of a different or more serious criminal offense involving either the driver, the vehicle, or both. In such cases, the arrest and possible search of the persons in the car and the possible search of the car itself involve the constitutional protections of the Fourth Amendment. How have the courts responded?

Note that there is a constitutional distinction between entry of a vehicle and search of a vehicle. In some cases, the officer is not attempting to search, that is, "discover items concealed from view," but is only attempting to verify ownership of the vehicle or perhaps determine the status of a sleeping or possibly injured occupant. If, during a lawful entry, the officer observes seizable evidence in plain view, the courts will not exclude it. If the initial entry is reasonable under all the circumstances and not a subterfuge to search, the officer may escalate the right to search according to the circumstances.

In large part the courts have recognized the automobile's unique characteristic of mobility. In analyzing the search of a person, the courts require that the initial interference with personal freedom be evidenced by probable cause to arrest. For a search of a house, a search warrant is usually required. But in the case of automobiles, the courts have developed the doctrine of "probable cause to search a motor vehicle" without the necessity of an arrest and absent a search warrant. The doctrine of probable cause to search holds that whenever there is probable cause to search a motor vehicle, no arrest or warrant is necessary. This doctrine requires that officers develop probable cause to believe that the car contains stolen property, contraband, evidence or fruits of a crime, or that the car is an instrumentality of the crime itself, for example, the car was used as an instrument of assault or was involved in the negligent injury of a pedestrian.[1] The same standard of probable cause that governs the arrest of a person or the issuance of a search warrant prevails, and officers must comply with the rules of observational probable cause and informational probable cause.

In terms of the circumstances justifying a warrantless search, the Supreme Court in particular has long distinguished between an automobile and a home or an office. In *Carroll* v. *United States,* the issue was the admissibility in evidence of contraband liquor seized in a warrantless search of a car on the highway. After surveying the law from the time of the adoption of the Fourth Amendment onward, the Court held that automobiles and other conveyances may be searched without a warrant in circumstances that would not justify the search without a warrant of a house or an office, provided that there is probable cause to believe that the car contains articles that the officers are entitled to seize. The Court expressed its holding as follows:

"We have made a somewhat extended reference to these [federal] statutes to show that the guaranty of freedom from unreasonable searches and seizures by the Fourth Amendment has been construed, practically since the beginning of the Government, as recognizing a necessary difference between a search of a store, dwelling house or other structure in respect of which a proper official warrant readily may be obtained, and a search of a ship, motor boat, wagon, automobile, for contraband goods, where it is not practicable to secure a warrant because the vehicle can be quickly moved out of the locality or jurisdiction in which the warrant must be sought.

"Having thus established that contraband goods concealed and illegally transported in an automobile or other vehicle may be searched . . . without a warrant, we come now to consider under what circumstances such search may be made. Those lawfully within the country, entitled to use the public highways, have a right to free passage without interruption or search unless there is known to a competent official authorized to search, probable cause for believing that their vehicles are carrying contraband or illegal merchandise. . . . The measure of legality of such a seizure is, therefore, that the seizing officer shall have reasonable or probable cause for believing that the automobile which he stops and searches has contraband liquor therein which is being illegally transported.''

The Court also noted that the search of an automobile on probable cause proceeds on a theory wholly different from that justifying the search incident to an arrest: ''The right to search and the validity of the seizure are not dependent on the right to arrest. They are dependent on the reasonable cause the seizing officer has for belief that the contents of the automobile offend against the law.''

Neither *Carroll* nor other cases decided by the Supreme Court require or suggest that in every conceivable circumstance the search of an automobile, even with probable cause, may be made without the extra protection for privacy that a warrant affords. But the circumstances that furnish probable cause to search a particular auto for particular articles are most often unforeseeable; moreover, the opportunity to search is fleeting since a car is readily movable. Where this is true, as in *Carroll,* if an effective search is to be made at any time, either the search must be made immediately without a warrant or the car itself must be seized and held without a warrant for whatever period is necessary to obtain a warrant for the search.

In enforcing the Fourth Amendment's prohibition against unreasonable searches and seizures, the Court has insisted on probable cause as a minimum requirement for a reasonable search permitted by the Constitution. As a general rule, it has also required the judgment of a magistrate on the probable-cause issue and the issuance of a warrant before a search is made. Only in exigent circumstances will the judgment of the police as to probable cause serve as a sufficient authorization for a search. *Carroll* holds a search warrant unnecessary where there is probable cause to search an automobile stopped on the highway; the car is movable, the occupants are alerted, and the car's contents may never be found again if a warrant must be obtained. Hence an immediate search is constitutionally permissible. Thus, the first issue is whether there is probable cause.

''During a local labor dispute, a car was seen to drive past the home of a nonstriking employee. Shots were fired from the car at or into the home. The occupant of the house was standing in the front yard and fired back at the car with a pistol, and thought his first shot hit the back of the car. He informed the Sheriff by telephone only of the shooting by occupants of the car. Soon after, a deputy sheriff contacted by the Sheriff on his radio and presumably told of the crime, spotted a suspicious car and began following it. The car raced away but was stopped by another policeman notified of a speeding car. The stopped car, which contained the defendant, was taken to jail. While defendant was waiting inside the jail, policemen searched the car. Under the front seat they found an air rifle.

"While the record was not entirely clear, defendant appears to have been arrested for reckless driving. Whether or not a car may constitutionally be searched 'incident' to arrest for a traffic offense, the search here did not take place until defendant was in custody inside the courthouse and the car was parked on the street outside, and under such circumstances a search is too remote in time or place to be incidental to the arrest.

"In this case there is no indication that the police had purported to impound or to hold the car, or that they were authorized by any state law to do so, or that their search of the car was intended to implement the purposes of such custody. Here the police seem to have parked the car near the courthouse merely as a convenience to the owner. The record here did not contain evidence that the Sheriff or deputy sheriff or the officers who assisted in the search had reasonable or probable cause to believe that evidence would be found in defendant's car. The deputy sheriff had not been told that the occupant of the house had identified the car from which shots were fired. He testified: 'All I got is just that it would be an old make model car. Kinda old make model car.'

"The record also contains no suggestion that the occupant of the house told the Sheriff or deputy sheriff or any other law enforcement official that he had fired at the car or that he thought he had hit it with one bullet. As far as this record shows, the deputy knew only that the car he chased as 'an old make model car,' that it speeded up when he chased it, and that it contained a fresh bullet hole. The evidence was insufficient to justify a conclusion that the defendant's car was searched with 'reasonable or probable cause' to believe the search would be fruitful." (*Dyke* v. *Taylor, etc.*)

In determining the lawfulness of a search of a car on probable cause, a variety of fact situations occur and it is useful to categorize them (1) unoccupied vehicles; (2) occupied vehicles; and (3) occupied and abandoned vehicles.

Unoccupied Vehicles

Police began an investigation into the murder of a young girl. "During the ensuing two and a half weeks, the State accumulated a quantity of evidence to support the theory that it was the defendant Coolidge who had killed the girl. The results of the investigation were presented at a meeting among the police officers working on the case. At this meeting, it was decided that there was enough evidence to justify the arrest of defendant on the murder charge and a search of his house and two cars.

"The police arrested defendant in his house. Some time later, the police called a towing company, and about two and a half hours after defendant had been taken into custody his car was towed to the police station. At the time of the arrest the car was parked in the driveway, and although dark had fallen, it was plainly visible both from the street and from inside the house where defendant was actually arrested. The car was searched and vacuumed.

"At defendant's subsequent jury trial on the charge of murder, vacuum sweepings, including particles of gun powder taken from the car, were introduced in evidence against him as part of an attempt by the State to show by microscopic analysis that it was highly probable that the girl murdered had been in defendant's car."

In this case, *Coolidge* v. *New Hampshire.* the Court again reviewed its earlier cases on the search of automobiles based on probable cause. They repeated the constitutional difference between a search of a store, dwelling house, or other structure in which a warrant readily may be obtained for contraband goods, and a search of an automobile, where *it is not practicable to secure a warrant* because the vehicle can be quickly moved out of the locality or jurisidiction in which the warrant must be sought. These exigent circumstances justify the warrantless search of an automobile *stopped on the highway,* where there is probable cause, because the car is movable, the occupants are alerted, and the car's contents may never be found again if a warrant must be obtained. The opportunity to search is fleeting.

"In this case, the police had known for some time of the probable role of the car in the crime. The defendant had been aware that he was a suspect in the murder, but there was no indication that he meant to flee. He had already had ample opportunity to destroy any evidence he thought incriminating. There is no suggestion that, on the night in question, the car was being used for any illegal purpose, and it was regularly parked in the driveway of his house. The opportunity for search was thus hardly 'fleeting.' The objects that the police are assumed to have had probable cause to search for in the car were neither stolen nor contraband nor dangerous.

"When the police arrived at the house to arrest him, two officers were sent to guard the back door while the main party approached from the front. Defendant was arrested inside the house, without resistance of any kind on his part, after he had voluntarily admitted the officers at both front and back doors. There was no way in which he could conceivably have gained access to the automobile after the police arrived on his property.

"The word 'automobile' is not a talisman in whose presence the Fourth Amendment fades away and disappears. There is nothing in this case to invoke the meaning and purpose of the rule—no alerted criminal bent on flight, no fleeting opportunity on an open highway after a hazardous chase, no contraband or stolen goods or weapons, no confederates waiting to move the evidence, not even the inconvenience of a special police detail to guard the immobilized automobile. There is no way this can be made into a case where it is not practicable to secure a warrant, and the 'automobile exception,' despite its label, is simply irrelevant. Here there was probable cause, but no exigent circumstances justified the police in proceeding without a warrant. The later search at the station house was therefore illegal.''

It should be noted that the Coolidge case was subscribed to by only four members of the Supreme Court. The fifth justice concurred in the ruling, but did not concur in the reasoning that, under these circumstances, a warrantless search of an unoccupied car, absent an emergency, is unreasonable. As a consequence, some disagreement exists as to the impact of the decision. For example: Some jurisdictions hold that a car may be seized contemporaneous with an arrest if the car itself is evidence of the crime—as it would be in the case of kidnapping, robbery, or murder—if there is evidence that the car was used as an instrumentality of the crime of murder. This doctrine, coupled with the ''plain view'' rule, allows the officers to seize evidence that comes within their plain view. Thus, if the subject car is observed on the street, that is, in plain view, and there is probable cause to believe that it is the instrumentality of a crime, a seizure of the car would be reasonable without a warrant. Any subsequent search would not be a delayed search because the police are authorized to subject evidence lawfully in their custody to inspection at any time. The search is not an impound search—it is an inspection of evidence.

Occupied Vehicles

If probable cause is established, the doctrine applies whether the initial search is of an occupied car in the street or of a car removed from the street and searched later after the arrest. Yet, the nature of the original custody becomes crucial. If the car was removed from the street after an arrest and searched at the police garage, the validity of the search will be judged by the reasons for the original removal. A car removed from the street after an arrest of the occupants on traffic warrants could not be searched because probable cause to believe that the car contains evidence of a crime is lacking. Even if officers are statutorily authorized to impound vehicles and inventory contents, the results of the inventory may not be admissible unless the inventory search is based on probable cause to search the car independent of inventory.[2] Statutorily, officers may be authorized to inventory the contents of a stored vehicle, but constitutionally speaking, the successful results of such a search may not be admissible in evidence.

''A service station was robbed by two men, each of whom carried and displayed a gun. The robbers took the currency from the cash register; the service station attendant was directed to place the coins in his right-hand glove, which was then taken by the robbers. Two witnesses, who had earlier noticed a blue compact station wagon circling the block in the vicinity of the station, then saw the station wagon speed away from a parking lot close to the station. At the same time, they learned that the station had been robbed. They reported to police, who arrived immediately, that four men were in the station wagon and one was wearing a green sweater. The attendant told the police that one of the men who robbed him was wearing a green sweater and the other was wearing a trench coat. A description of the car and the two robbers was broadcast over the police radio. Within an hour, a light blue compact station wagon answering the description and carrying four men was stopped by the police about two miles from the station. Defendant was one of the men in the station wagon. He was wearing a green sweater and there was a trench coat in the car. The occupants were arrested and the car was driven to the police station. In the course of a thorough search of the car at the station, the police found concealed in a compartment under the dashboard two .38-caliber revolvers and a right-hand glove containing small change.

"The police obviously had probable cause to believe that the robbers, carrying guns and the fruits of the crime, had fled the scene in a light blue compact station wagon which would be carrying four men, one wearing a green sweater and another wearing a trench coat. There was probable cause to arrest the occupants of the station wagon that the officers stopped; just as obviously there was probable cause to search the car for guns and stolen money. Arguably, because of the preference for a magistrate's judgment, only the immobilization of the car should be permitted until a search warrant is obtained; arguably, only the 'lesser' intrusion is permissible until the magistrate authorizes the 'greater.' But which is the 'greater' and which the 'lesser' intrusion is itself a debatable question and the answer may depend on a variety of circumstances. [The Court saw] no difference between on the one hand seizing and holding a car before presenting the probable-cause issue to a magistrate and on the other hand carrying out an immediate search without a warrant. Given probable cause to search, either course is reasonable under the Fourth Amendment." (*Chambers* v. *Maroney.*)

Probable cause to search a motor vehicle allows the officer to detain and search an occupied car even if there is no probable cause to arrest the occupants. In most cases, probable cause to search will be substantially the same probable cause to arrest the occupants—in which case the validity of the search may be sustained on the theory of search incident to arrest. But the added advantage of probable cause to search a motor vehicle arises when officers desire to remove the vehicle to search at a different time and place. Under "search incident" theory, a search at a later time and place is not contemporaneous with the arrest and is therefore unlawful. But the U.S. Supreme Court has held that if the officers had probable cause to search the vehicle at the time the occupants were arrested, that same probable cause continues even after the arrest. The Court held that since the occupants were already arrested and their right of privacy personally invaded, the delayed search of the vehicle in which they were riding at the time of arrest would not be sufficient additional violation of their personal security to require a warrant. But this doctrine applies only when probable cause to search the car existed at the time of arrest. Absent probable cause to search the motor vehicle, any later impound search would be unauthorized without a warrant—except, of course, as to evidence in plain sight.

Developing probable cause to search a motor vehicle can include evidence of the observation of a traffic violation or vehicle equipment violation; or it can rest on a reasonable suspicion that the car or its occupants are involved in criminal activity. Whether the initial stop is statutorily authorized because a misdemeanor has been committed in the officers' presence, or whether a detention for investigation is constitutionally authorized, officers can always request display of the driver's license and evidence of vehicle ownership. The results of this inquiry may be the first step in establishing probable cause. Thereafter, the officers may view the interior of the vehicle as well as the actions of the occupants to determine whether any additional evidence of criminality is present. The conduct and demeanor of the driver and passengers are relevant, and answers to preliminary questions are permitted under the *Miranda* decision. A radio check is also proper. From a combination of circumstances the officers can either build a case for probable cause or dispel the thought of arrest. If they detect the odor of alcohol and ultimately arrest the driver for driving under the influence of it, a search of the car would be authorized as an incident of the arrest. If they detect the odor of marijuana, they could enter and search the car without arrest—based on probable cause to believe the car contains contraband—and the results of this search govern whether or not an arrest is in order.

Despite the rule that a motor vehicle may be searched without a warrant based on probable cause to believe that the car contains evidence of a crime or is of instrumentality of the crime, officers who impound such vehicles for a later search should search as soon after the arrest as possible. An extensive delay in searching may lead the court to ask why a search warrant could not be obtained when time clearly allowed.

Occupied and Abandoned Vehicles

Just as unoccupied or occupied cars may be searched without a warrant, a car occupied and abandoned may also be searched without a warrant. The flight of a suspect from the car cannot frustrate a search of the vehicle as long as probable cause to search the car exists. Cars abandoned after their use as an instrumentality in the commission of a robbery may therefore be entered and searched immediately after discovery, without a warrant, even if there is no pressing emergency or officers are not in hot pursuit—factors that may also justify search of the car without a warrant (see the section entitled Emergency Searches in this chapter).

The Doctrine in Perspective

By treating the automobile as a separate entity, the U.S. Supreme Court has attempted to modify the explicit demands of a warrant required for the search of a house. But the rule that a car may be searched without a warrant based on probable cause to believe the vehicle contains seizable evidence cannot always excuse the requirement of a warrant. The leading case, *Chambers* v. *Maroney,* approving the warrantless search of cars based on probable cause, involved the arrest of its occupants for robbery and a later search at a police facility. Probable cause to search the car as an instrumentality of the crime existed at the time of the arrest of its occupants. Their privacy was already invaded, and an incidental search of the car was not deemed sufficient to justify a warrant. And under well-established rules, the car could be searched for evidence of the robbery at the time and place of arrest. Delaying the search was deemed immaterial when the right to search already existed at the time of arrest.

But in *Coolidge* v. *New Hampshire,* the Court refused to apply the doctrine under almost similar circumstances. The defendant was arrested in his house after a lengthy investigation, and his car, parked nearby, was searched without a warrant. The court held that even if probable cause existed to believe seizable evidence was in the car, a warrant should have been obtained. The car had been subject to investigation for some period of time; at the time of arrest, the car was unoccupied and immobile; and no emergency existed to excuse the warrant. Thus, no justification appears for the initial intrusion without a warrant. If the car had been occupied at the time of the arrest, the result might have been different. Unoccupied cars, therefore, may not always be searched without a warrant absent some other justification or evidence of emergency.

Another unresolved issue affecting the search of vehicles involves the rationale of the *Chimel* decision. Although *Chimel* resolved the scope of a search incident to an arrest effected inside a dwelling place, the rationale could arguably apply to cars. If the scope of a search incidental to arrest was limited to the person of the arrestee and the area within this person's immediate control, why not apply a similar rule to the search of vehicles? In fact, once the driver or passenger has been removed from the vehicle, any possible danger from assault or any loss of evidence is substantially reduced. Perhaps the search of the interior of the car for evidence related to the arrest would be reasonable. But a search of a closed trunk would not necessarily be included.

On balance, the *Chambers* case would probably prevail, that is, once the occupants have been arrested, little significance can be attached to a further invasion of their privacy in searching the trunk. This rule is at least valid when there is probable cause to search the vehicle as a whole at the time of the arrest. If the occupants were arrested for a felony and were merely occupying the vehicle for transportation, the car itself would not necessarily be the intrumentality of the crime.[3] In this case no probable cause to search the car exists independent of the arrest of its occupants. But the arrest itself may authorize a search of the car or the trunk of the car without a warrant, notwithstanding the language of *Chimel.*

Search of Goods in Transit

The doctrine of probable cause to search a motor vehicle without a warrant rests largely on the assumption that the factor of mobility transcends the rule that all searches must be conducted under authority of a warrant. When the Fourth Amendment was adopted, searches of cars were not contemplated, but searches of goods moved in the course of transportation by boat, wagon, or other conveyance were common.[4] Because goods were easily removable before a warrant could be obtained, the U.S. Supreme Court early in constitutional history held that the usual requirement of a warrant to seize contraband goods in transit may be dispensed with as long as probable cause to search the goods exists. Modern transportation methods do not differ, analytically speaking, from colonial travel. But nowhere do Fourth Amendment problems appear more clearly focused than on the issue of warrantless searches of goods in transit.

"An air freight agent testified that defendant brought five cardboard cartons to the freight counter at the airport. Defendant stated he wished to ship the cartons to Seattle; he described the contents as 'personal effects,' and gave the name 'L. McKinnon' as the consignor and 'L. McKinnon' as the consignee.

"The agent had not seen the man before, but suspected that the cartons contained contraband. After defendant left, the agent asked a fellow employee to note the make and license number of defendant's car. He then obtained his supervisor's permission to open one of the cartons for purposes of inspection. In the present of the supervisor and other employees, he slit the tape on one of the cartons and put his hand inside. Beneath some paper he felt brick-shaped packages of what seemed to be soft tobacco or grass. He then lifted the lid of the carton, took out one of the packages, and pinched it open. Upon finding that it contained what he believed to be marijuana, he telephoned the police.

"In response to the call, an officer arrived at the air freight counter 20 or 30 minutes later. He looked at the air bill, then entered a back room where the cartons had been placed. The carton that the agent had inspected stood open on the floor; it contained a large brown plastic bag, which was also open. As the officer approached the carton, he saw inside a number of brick-shaped packages wrapped in red cellophane. Each was 10 to 12 inches long, about 6 inches wide, and 2 to 3 inches thick. The officer formed the opinion that the substance in the packages was marijuana. He proceeded to open one of the packages and verified its contents.

"The officer next learned that a passenger by the name of 'L. McKinnon' had a reservation on a flight due to leave for Seattle within the hour. He obtained from the agent a description of the man who had presented the cartons for shipment, together with the make and license number of his car. Shortly afterward the officer located the car in the parking lot, and arrested defendant as he entered it." (*People* v. *McKinnon.*) The defendant contended that the search by the officer could only be made with a warrant.

To begin with, the U.S. Supreme Court has repeatedly held that if probable cause exists to believe that a search will reveal seizable evidence, a warrant must be obtained—absent an emergency—unless the search is incidental to an arrest. The only other exception to the warrant requirement is a danger of immediate destruction, removal, or concealment of property intended to be seized. This Fourth Amendment protection from unreasonable searches and seizures applies to a search of "effects" as well as searches of houses and cars.[5] Thus, the contents of any container cannot be searched, absent consent, without compliance with the Fourth Amendment.

Cars have been excepted from the warrant requirement because their mobility enables someone to remove seizable evidence before a warrant can be obtained. But suppose that peace officers have probable cause to believe that a locked trunk, consigned for immediate air freight shipment, contains contraband. Can the trunk be searched without a warrant? The trunk and its contents are "effects" within the meaning of the Fourth Amendment. Does its potential removal from the airport dispense with the warrant requirement? At this point, the role of the Fourth Amendment becomes critical. One viewpoint holds that the police alternative is twofold: search the trunk immediately without a warrant, or seize and hold the trunk until they can obtain a warrant. In the automobile search case of *Chambers* v. *Maroney,* the U.S. Supreme Court held that, in these circumstances, there is no constitutional difference between the alternatives facing the police. An immediate search without a warrant, said the court, is no greater an intrusion on the driver's right of privacy than is immobilization of the car until a warrant can be obtained; either course is reasonable under the Fourth Amendment. Under this reasoning, goods consigned to a common carrier for shipment are no less movable than an automobile, and the reasons for the rule permitting a warrantless search of a vehicle on probable cause are equally applicable to the search of goods in transit.

In response, the argument can be made that if indeed "effects" mean anything in the constitutional sense, then warrant protection must be afforded. The mobility of a car or other conveyance is the only distinguishing factor that allows a search without a warrant. Effects are immovable in themselves, and only if the goods are in the course of transportation, that is, in a vehicle or other carrier capable of carrying them beyond the jurisdiction, may the "effects" be searched without a warrant. Manifestly, a trunk consigned for rail or air shipment is not within a vehicle, nor can it move under its own power.

Further, the only other basis for allowing a warrantless search of a vehicle is the arrest of its occupants, which would allow an incidental search. Since the original detention and arrest of the driver is a substantial invasion of his privacy in any event, a search of the vehicle is of little additional significance. But goods consigned for shipment are normally searched in the absence of, and remote from, any arrestee. The arrest, if one occurs, follows the search and is justified by what the search turns up. In this event, the search of the trunk is a classic example of the reason for the Fourth Amendment, that is, probable cause to search requires a warrant, and an arrest cannot justify an incidental search not based on probable cause to arrest someone. Moreover, almost all "effects" are in fact movable, and the Fourth Amendment protection evaporates if the car search theories are applied.

This latter argument probably expresses the most accurate interpretation of the Fourth Amendment, but it fails to consider the element of goods "consigned for transportation." Thus, "effects" on the person, in the car, and in the dwelling place remain personal to the owner and entitled to full Fourth Amendment protection. But if the owner agrees to ship effects on a common carrier, he or she cannot expect the same degree of protection. The mobility of such parcels is substantially equivalent to the mobility of an automobile. If so, no warrant is required for their search as long as probable cause exists.

Emergency Searches

Police work is intimately linked with emergency situations. With the exception of fire fighting, no other job requires as much planning for emergencies as does law enforcement. Because a state of emergency is commonplace in police work, the courts have tailored the rules of arrest and search accordingly. Necessity often justifies an action that would otherwise constitute a trespass, as when the act is prompted by a motive of preserving life or property and reasonably appears to be necessary for that purpose. Emergency entries and searches motivated by such goals need not be judged by usual Fourth Amendment standards. But the Fourth Amendment remains relevant, and the courts have placed boundaries around the doctrine of emergency. The emergency exception must be reasonably related to the situation that confronts the officer. Thus, the tests for emergency entry and search of a vehicle are not necessarily the same as for the entry of a house.

Vehicles: Generally speaking, the driver of an automobile and the automobile itself are entitled to Fourth Amendment protection. An officer who intends to detain a driver or search the car must testify to the reasonableness of these actions. If an officer observes an unoccupied car protruding onto the highway, the decision to enter the car and move it will be motivated by the need to remove a potential safety hazard. Since the officer makes no arrest, and no one can consent, the action can only be justified as an emergency entry. While inside, the officer can make an inspection to determine ownership of the vehicle. If seizable evidence is discovered during the course of this investigation, a warrantless seizure will be lawful. Of course, any search of the car not reasonably related to the safety objective would not be in response to the emergency; rather, it would be merely a general search and, therefore, unreasonable.

Another example of an emergency search of an unoccupied vehicle: Responding to the report of an armed robbery, officers discover the described vehicle shortly after the robbery has occurred. If an officer enters the vehicle, the entry and search would be reasonably related to the emergency situation. Officers are in hot pursuit of a fleeing suspect who has just committed a crime, and the need to identify and locate the suspect under these circumstances clearly creates an emergency that justifies the officer's warrantless entry.

In some cases, officers discover occupants of vehicles whose physical condition clearly warrants investigation. A limited entry of the vehicle to determine whether the occupant is sick or injured is clearly reasonable. Any seizable evidence discovered as a consequence of the entry for that purpose would not be the product of an unreasonable search. A general search for evidence, however, would not be reasonable.

Houses: The warrantless entry into a house in response to an emergency is also reasonable as long as there is some evidence of the emergency. The legal test of entry in a home is stricter than that of entry into a vehicle. Illustrative of this rule is the language of the U.S. Supreme Court in *McDonald* v. *United States:* "The presence of a search warrant serves a high function. Absent some grave emergency, the Fourth Amendment has interposed a magistrate between the citizen and the police. This was not done to shield criminals nor to make the home a safe haven for illegal activities. It was done so that an objective mind could weigh the need to invade the privacy in order to enforce the law. . . . We cannot be true to that constitutional requirement and excuse the absence of a search warrant without a showing by those who seek exemption from the constitutional mandate that the exigencies of the situation made that course imperative."

For example: A murder of a police officer occurred at a local department store. "An officer testified that he arrived at the store within minutes after the shooting and took charge of Mrs. W., one of the suspects involved and, as determined later, defendant's mistress. He explained, 'We were seeking the identity of the man who had accompanied her into the store.' In Mrs. W.'s purse he found her driver's license bearing her address. The officer asked her who lived with her at that address, and she said that Lee did, the man who had come into the store with her (that is, the defendant). The officer then asked her if Lee would go back to that address, and she answered, 'I suppose he will. His clothes are there.' The officer instructed two uniformed policemen to stake out the premises.

"The officer questioned Mrs. W. further, his purpose being 'to attempt to identify the man that shot the officer.' She said she didn't know his real name, but that he had told her to call him 'Jim Snyder.' She gave a physical description of defendant, and the officer caused this description to be broadcast over police radio.

"At the station the officer asked Mrs. W. if she had any pictures of 'this Jim Snyder.' She said there were pictures of him at the house. The officer then asked her if there was anything else in the house to identify 'Jim Snyder,' and she answered there might be 'something in a bag or some bags.'

"The officer then spoke by telephone to other officers and instructed them to pick up the pictures of 'Jim Snyder' at the house and anything else that might aid in identifying him. Being aware, moreover, that the entire shooting incident had arisen out of an attempt by 'Jim Synder' to pass a check of doubtful validity, he told them generally to bring in all identifying evidence in 'a forgery case or shooting case.' In the ensuing search the officers found and removed a photograph of defendant and Mrs. W., a box of .38 caliber ammunition, and other evidence.

"Although 'Jim Snyder' escaped from the scene, the manhunt began immediately. It was reasonable for the police to believe he might stop at his house before continuing his flight, to obtain clothes, money, or ammunition. This belief, in fact, was shared by Mrs. W., who communicated it to the police at that time.

"It was with this kind of danger in mind that officers took reasonable precautions in entering the house. They had received a radio message instructing them to enter that house, and informing them that the suspect had just killed two policemen at the store. Failing to obtain a key from the adjacent house of the landlord, the officer forcibly entered the suspect's residence. With drawn guns the policemen then searched the house for the suspect or 'for any evidence of the suspect's having been there and gone.'

"The law recognizes that fresh pursuit of a fleeing suspect who has committed a grave offense and remains dangerous to life and limb may constitute 'exceptional circumstances' sufficient to justify a search without a warrant. When the police determined the house was vacant, they were not required at that point to abandon their search for 'Jim Snyder' or his true identity. They were not compelled to close their eyes to the contents of the house, and their ensuing search was incidental to the purpose of their entry. While in the house, it was not unreasonable for the officers to look about them for evidence that would identify the suspect, thus far known to them only by one of his several aliases, or that would enable them to pick up his trail." (*People* v. *Smith.*) The evidence obtained by that search was properly admitted.

The emergency exception, however, cannot swallow the rule. At least two conditions must be met: first, officers must present evidence that their entry was motivated by an imminent and substantial threat to life, health, or property; and second, the scope of any search incidental to the emergency must be strictly tied to, and related to, the need for the initial intrusion. By limiting the doctrine of emergency in this way, officers are freed to respond fully to the situation confronting them while simultaneously preserving the citizen's privacy from unjustified invasion.

Emergency searches of the person normally include removal of blood from a suspected intoxicated driver, or an attempt to determine the cause of illness of someone who is either unconscious or unable to respond. In the latter case, a search of the pockets for medicine or other information is reasonable, and if seizable evidence is discovered, the objects are lawfully seized. But in the case of the removal of blood samples, a more difficult problem arises (see chapter 8, Witnesses: Competency, Privilege, and Personal Knowledge).

Probation Searches

Regarded by many as the single most important function of the judiciary, probation is the conditional judicial release of a criminal offender back into society under certain terms and conditions. Failure to comply with these conditions results in the possible revocation of probation and incarceration in jail. Normally the revocation proceedings are instituted if the probationer is arrested for commission of another crime. Can the court go further, though, and impose as a condition of probation that the probationer consent to a search even if the officer lacks probable cause for an arrest?

The issue is whether the court can demand a waiver of Fourth Amendment rights as a condition of probation. Policy issues of the Fourth Amendment emerge again. Probationers who are conditionally released into society may have a reduced expectation of privacy, thereby rendering reasonable certain intrusions by governmental authorities that would otherwise be invalid under traditional constitutional concepts. Moreover, probationary terms can be imposed that reasonably relate to the conditions of release in an attempt to prevent the commission of another crime. Presumably, a probationer subject to search at any time would exercise considerably more caution than if the condition were not imposed. Under these circumstances, waiver of Fourth Amendment rights in advance would be reasonable, depending to some extent on the type of crime involved, but most frequently the condition is imposed on probationers convicted of violating the narcotic laws.

Those who would refuse to approve diminution of Fourth Amendment rights argue that imposing such a condition in no way relates to the objectives of probation. Total denial of Fourth Amendment rights is a serious matter, and, assuming a probationer must accept some dilution of Fourth Amendment protection, any modification of protection against unreasonable searches and seizures should be carefully tailored to the nature of the original offense and not imposed indiscriminately. Law enforcement officers can question or arrest a probationer just as they can anyone else—if adequate grounds exist. The role of the peace officer in the rehabilitative process is marginal, and probationary violations should be the responsibility of the probation officer.

These two divergent theories can be argued plausibly in every state. Some states might require a statute authorizing such a procedure; in others the court could impose the condition as an exercise of judicial authority. If a state does sanction a probationary search, the danger of harassment is ever present. Use of the probationary search should be carefully exercised.

Specialized Searches

Because the Fourth Amendment protects people—not places—from unreasonable searches and seizures, the scope of constitutional protection cannot be judged solely by the area in which a search takes place. For obvious reasons, however, one cannot discuss search and seizure without reference to places, and in some cases the place will affect searching authority. The Fourth Amendment is a guarantee of personal security that follows citizens no matter where they travel. The degree of protection, or privacy, to which they are entitled varies, however, as they move from place to place. Searches of houses are measured by the same rules as are searches of vehicles, but their application differs according to the amount of privacy expected in each of these places. But the vehicle is not talismanic, and Fourth Amendment protection does not disappear merely because a car is involved. Yet certain places have been singled out for special Fourth Amendment treatment because of their unique characteristics.

School Searches

Because children and young people depend heavily on their parents and others for most of their needs, the law recognizes this unique relationship in many ways. In the context of the Fourth Amendment, however, the courts have generally regarded parents as supervisors of their children who are empowered to make decisions on their behalf. For example, parents are authorized to consent to a search of quarters occupied by their son or daughter as long as there is evidence that the child has not established an independent status as an adult.[6]

When a minor child attends school, courts still hold the school to accountability for the child's safety and welfare. Standing in the place of parents, though, the schools also exercise similar parental powers over the child as student. Certainly this power extends to students at the elementary and high school level and, to some extent, at college and university campuses.

In a typical case, school officials will be informed that a student is in possession of contraband or that the contraband is concealed in the student's locker. If school officials attempt to search the student's person, they may fear possible resistance or violence and request police assistance. If the police search reveals contraband, the student will argue insufficient probable cause for the arrest, calling into question the entire range of law on probable cause.

The court must determine whether to apply the usual rules of search and seizure, or whether to subordinate a full application of Fourth Amendment principles to the need for the school to maintain discipline. Alternatively, the court might conclude that the purpose of the search was not police-initiated; their assistance was requested to prevent a possible eruption of violence in the school office. In this case, the search would be classified as a citizen search, not within the scope of the Fourth Amendment (see Citizen Arrest and Search, this chapter). If school officials were informed that contraband was concealed in a locker, the validity of their search would be tested by a similar analysis, although school officials could argue that school lockers are provided only for the convenience of students, and that although school property was made available to the students, the school had authority to consent to their search.

Increasingly vocal demands for student rights might persuade some courts to extend Fourth Amendment protection. Yet the special nature of a school-student relationship argues strongly for the continued flexible use of searching authority of students and their "effects" as long as the student is an enrolled pupil and on school property.

Border Searches

Responsibility for preventing the unauthorized entry of aliens, contraband, stolen property, and foreign goods in the United States is vested in the federal government, and state laws do not control these areas. Border detention and search of people and automobiles is of the widest possible scope, although probable cause is still a factor. Strip searches, which involve substantial invasions of privacy, are allowable as long as there is some suggestion that such a search is necessary. A search may even be conducted inland and at some distance from the border, if the government can establish that seized items were carried across the border within a reasonable time before the actual search took place. But searches for aliens remote from the borders (or functional equivalents of the border) cannot be indiscriminate. Probable cause still remains a factor in evaluating the lawfulness of the detention. At a minimum, officers must offer evidence of probable cause to believe the car contained aliens or at least probable cause to believe the car made a border crossing: *Condrado Almeida-Sanchez* v. *United States,* 413 U.S. 266, 37 L. Ed. 2d 596, 93 S. Ct. 2535.

Citizen Arrest and Search

The authority of a private citizen to arrest is usually defined by statute, but usually this person's power to arrest is narrower than that of a peace officer. The validity of arrests, which can be made for misdemeanors committed in a citizen's presence or felonies based on probable cause, can be tested by the same theories that are applied to peace officers. Perhaps the only difficult question is the power of the citizen to delegate arresting authority when the peace officer arrives. Other arrest issues involving citizens usually emerge from policy decisions adopted by all police departments. Different questions do arise when a police agency requires that a citizen adopt certain procedures before the law enforcement agency takes custody of the arrestee. Frequently the civil aspects of a case supersede any question of criminal responsibility. Because the practice varies widely, no general rules can be stated.

On the other hand, a search by a private citizen involves a more serious invasion of the right of privacy, and questions have arisen as to the power of a citizen to search. In *Burdeau* v. *McDowell,* decided by the U.S. Supreme Court in 1921, the Court held that the Fourth Amendment prohibited only governmental action, that is, state action, and could not be applied to searches by private individuals. Thus, if the citizen search was unreasonable within the meaning of the Fourth Amendment, the exclusionary rule will not be invoked, and any seized evidence will be admitted in a subsequent criminal prosecution. Because the exclusionary rule exists to deter unlawful acts by state and federal officials, the purpose of the rule is not served by applying it to those who do not regularly enforce the law and whose conduct is not likely to be repeated.

The general rule allowing citizen searches without reference to the Fourth Amendment has some limitations. If a state statute defines the searching authority of a citizen, a state court could apply the stricter provisions of the statute to prevent searches that would otherwise be lawful under the Fourth Amendment. Nothing prevents a state from imposing a stricter standard of search and seizure than that required by the Fourth Amendment. Thus a search incidental to a citizen arrest might be limited by statute to authorize only the removal of weapons, not evidence.

Second, any search by a private citizen must have been instigated on personal initiative in order to come within the general rule allowing such searches without reference to the Fourth Amendment. If the citizen acts as an agent of the police to carry out their directions, any search would be judged by standards applicable to governmental searches. A similar result would follow if the citizen and police were acting jointly. Because the line between agency, or some form of joint operation, may not always be drawn clearly, the court may impose a duty on the police to prevent unlawful searches by private citizens, rather than allow officers to stand idly by and tacitly consent to a search they could not conduct themselves.

This latter rule has emerged in recognition of widespread cooperation between police departments and private investigative agencies whose sole function is the investigation, detection, and apprehension of people suspected of committing crimes, usually against large commercial companies. Private security agencies differ widely in objectives, ranging from in-house security personnel employed by large department stores to nationwide detective firms. In the former category, personnel are employed to prevent the theft of goods from the store; in the latter case, personnel are hired to locate and apprehend those suspected of committing theft or fraud from the client. Because the conduct of these agencies closely resembles conventional law enforcement, the courts may reexamine the rules that allow these full-time investigative officials to escape the restrictions of the Fourth Amendment. And closely allied to this issue is the scope of arrest and search authority held by a regularly salaried peace officer who works off-duty on an investigative assignment for a private employer. Serious Fourth Amendment issues arise when the officer merely removes the police uniform in order to engage in a slightly different type of police work.

CASES AND MATERIALS

1. The guest of a hotel desposited a package with the hotel clerk for safekeeping. When the package was not requested by the guest for several days, the clerk opened it. Inside he found a loaded revolver. The police were contacted and, subsequently, when the guest returned and claimed his package, he was arrested for carrying a loaded firearm in a public place. The search of the package by the officer revealed a gun.

Assuming that the officer had sufficient probable cause to search the bag, was a warrant required? Is the package deposited for safekeeping in a hotel analogous to the carton consigned for shipment to a common carrier?

2. The sudden increase of skyjacking led the U.S. Congress to enact heavy penalties for the commission of this crime. In an effort to focus on deterrence, a

federal task force developed a preflight apprehension system, which consists of the following features:

a) Notice to the Public.

Signs in English and Spanish are posted at the boarding gates where passengers' tickets are checked, reading as follows:

AIRCRAFT HIJACKING IS A FEDERAL CRIME
PUNISHABLE BY DEATH

CARRYING CONCEALED WEAPONS ABOARD
AIRCRAFT IS PUNISHABLE BY PRISON
SENTENCES & FINES

PASSENGERS AND BAGGAGE
SUBJECT TO SEARCH

These signs are eleven by fourteen inches with half-inch-high letters. Warnings of the same or larger dimensions are posted conspicuously at other parts of the air terminal.

While probably not required to give notice of the applicable law and penalties, these signs fill that function. They serve to deter and to reduce the possibility of embarrassment should a passenger's boarding progress be interrupted.

b) Profile.

If a passenger meets a prescribed "profile," airline employees focus on him. The details of the profile and its use are set out below.

c) Magnetometer.

A magnetometer is installed in the passageway leading to the plane so that all passengers must pass through it. It is set to flash a warning light when metal equal to or greater than an average .25-caliber gun in magnetic force deflecting power is carried by. This device is described in more detail below.

d) Interview by Airlines Personnel.

A person who triggers the magnetometer and meets the profile requirements is "interviewed" by airlines personnel. If he provides satisfactory identification, he is permitted to proceed unimpeded. Otherwise he is designated a "selectee" and is denied boarding until a deputy United States Marshal is summoned.

e) Interview by Marshal.

The Marshal again requests identification of those designated as selectees. If a person furnishes satisfactory identification, it is suggested that he go through the magnetometer once more. Before walking through, he is asked if he has any metal on his person or in any baggage he is carrying. If he replies in the negative and still sets off the magnetometer, he is requested to submit to a "voluntary" search. It is explained that this search is part of an attempt by the government to prevent hijacking.

f) Frisk.

The Marshal pats down the external clothing of the subject in order to discover whether he is carrying any weapons. Depending on what is found as a result of the frisk, boarding is permitted or the person is detained.

The program is designed to speed passengers who are unlikely to present danger and to isolate, with the least possible discomfiture or delay, those presenting a substantial probability of danger. At each successive screening stage, an attempt is made to permit as many as possible to complete boarding.

While no single screening technique can by itself completely protect the flying public—without creating an objectionable level of disturbance and inconvenience—probabilities are increased by combining several approaches, thus sufficiently reducing the size of the population that must ultimately be physically interfered with to a practicable and socially acceptable level.

Obviously, the use of the magnetometer and subsequent frisk for weapons raises Fourth Amendment issues. In the usual cases of stop and frisk on the street, the officer must observe some unusual activity relating to crime and inconsistent with innocent activity. If the officer's observations justify detention, the frisk is justified only if there is some reasonable basis to believe that the person whom the officer is confronting is armed and dangerous.

Assuming now that the act of a person passing through the magnetic device designed to detect the presence of metal on boarding aircraft passengers is not "detention," what occurs when the magnetometer reacts positively? For Fourth Amendment purposes, when some governmental agent detains the passenger to determine whether he is carrying a prohibited metal object, the agent will subject the passenger to a limited search—a frisk—for weapons. There is no objective evidence, however, that the person detained poses any danger to the officer absent any testimony by the officer that he or she believed the person was armed or dangerous. And if the frisk reveals a hard object, may the officer conduct a second search to remove it? If the search reveals no weapons but, rather, a closed metal container, may the officer open (that is, search) it without probable cause? If the officer feels a possibly dangerous object on a person frisked on the street, the officer is justified in removing it. But once the officer is satisfied that the object is not lethal, he or she cannot open it. Can the airport security officer be given more latitude?

Finally, suppose that the officer removes contraband, instead of a weapon, from the passenger. Should such evidence be admitted or should it be excluded, even though the initial search was lawful?

For a discussion of these problems see: *United States* v. *Lopez,* 328 F. Supp. 1077; *United States* v. *Epperson,* 454 F. 2d 769; *United States* v. *Lindsey,* 451 F. 2d 701; and *People* v. *Lacey,* 30 Cal. App. 3d 170, 105 Cal. R. 102.

3. Mrs. K. was the owner of a building containing two flats. She occupied the downstairs unit; the defendant rented the upstairs unit where she lived with her daughter, who was approximately six years old.

"Mrs. K. returned from a shopping trip and heard defendant's daughter crying, and saw the girl sitting on the steps outside the upstairs flat. The girl told Mrs. K. she had hurt her knee while dancing, but no injury could be seen. She also told Mrs. K. she was alone in her apartment, and did not want to stay there because she was 'lonesome.' Mrs. K. took the girl into her own flat, consoled her, and gave her some food. After about an hour, however, Mrs. K. decided she could not continue to assume responsibility for the girl, and therefore called the police.

"An officer came in response to the call, and questioned the girl for 10 or 15 minutes. He learned she had been left alone in her apartment, had apparently fallen down and begun crying, and had been taken in by Mrs. K.

"According to his testimony, the officer then decided to ascertain whether the girl's mother had returned home in the interim. Accompanied by Mrs. K., he went upstairs and knocked on defendant's door, announcing his identification. There was no response. He nevertheless directed Mrs. K. to unlock the door with her key. He stepped inside and called defendant's name. Again there was no response. Yet the officer 'continued to go through the apartment,' entering each room in turn. On a nightstand in the bedroom he found a jar containing marijuana, and additional marijuana on a newspaper on the dresser.

"The officer looked through the rest of the flat, then confiscated the marijuana and returned downstairs. When the defendant arrived he placed her under arrest." (*People* v. *Smith,* 7 C. 3d 282, 101 Cal. R. 893, 496 P. 2d 1261.

Was there an emergency, and, if so, did the officer's act in entering and seeking the mother exceed the scope of an emergency entry?

4. An officer went to the defendant's home and found the latter's wife slumped in a chair with blood on her face, hands, and clothing. Defendant volunteered that "she fell down" and that "she hemorrhaged." The defendant was taken into custody, but no charges were filed. On the following day, the police made a complete and thorough search of the entire house and basement and found the murder weapon, a whiskey bottle, concealed under paper and trash in a barrel in the garage. (*State* v. *Chapman,* 250 A. 2d 203.)

Was this search lawful?

5. In the following two examples, the court came to different conclusions on whether a search was reasonable. Can you see a distinction?

a) Burglars broke into a medical center and stole money, stamps, retail sales items, a radio, hypodermic needles, barbiturates, and amphetamines. The officers developed probable cause to arrest the defendant for the burglary. The defendant had also registered as a narcotics offender and was on probation for the possession of marijuana. The officers noted that one of the conditions of the defendant's probation required that he "submit his person, place of residence, vehicle, to search and seizure at any time of the day or night, with or without a search warrant, whenever requested to do so by the Probation Officer or any law enforcement officer."

The officers went to the defendant's residence and saw his car parked in front. An officer knocked on the door of the house, identified himself, and announced he wanted to search the apartment. When defendant opened the door, the officer informed him that he had reason to believe that the defendant had participated in a burglary and that he was subject to search and seizure by court order as a condition of probation. The defendant admitted he was subject to such a condition. Thereupon, the officers entered the house, searched, and found evidence of the burglary.

b) The defendant, in the company of another young woman, was stopped by an officer for a speeding violation and for driving with one headlight only. When asked for identification, she produced a driver's license. Then, as the officer testified: "A. When I received the driver's license from the young lady, I went back to the radio car and ran a warrant check, and while I was waiting for the warrant check, I issued a citation for speeding. Q. What was the result of the warrant check? A. I was advised by radio that there were no outstanding warrants; however, the subject had a prior arrest for sales of dangerous drugs and that she was on probation and that the stipulation of the probation was that she was open to search and seizure.

"The officer returned to defendant's car, requested her to step out, and inquired if she had been previously arrested. She replied she had. He then asked if she were 'open to search and seizure,' and when she answered that so far as she knew she still was, he said he was going to search the vehicle and her handbag. Inside her handbag he found a change purse containing contraband." (*People* v. *Bremmer,* 30 Cal. App. 3d 1058.)

Would this search be lawful?

Motor Vehicles

Cardwell v. *Lewis,* 417 U.S. 583, 41 L. Ed. 2d 325, 94 S. Ct. 2464.

Chambers v. *Maroney,* 399 U.S. 42, 90 S. Ct. 1975, 26 L. Ed. 2d 419.

Coolidge v. *New Hampshire,* 403 U.S. 443, 91 S. Ct. 2022, 29 L. Ed. 2d 564.

Johnson v. *State,* 238 Md. 528, 209 A. 2d 765 (Maryland).

People v. *Teale,* 70 C. 2d 497, 450 P. 2d 564.

Texas v. *White,* 423 U.S. 67, 46 L. Ed. 2d 209.

Emergency

McDonald v. *United States,* 335, U.S. 451, 69 S. Ct. 191, 93 L. Ed. 153.

People v. *Smith,* 63 C. 2d 779, 409 P. 2d 222.

Schmerber v. *United States,* 384 U.S. 757, 86 S. Ct. 1826, 16 L. Ed. 2d 908.

Warden v. *Hayden,* 387 U.S. 294, 87 S. Ct. 1642, 18 L. Ed. 2d 782.

Goods in Transit

People v. *McKinnon,* 7 C. 3d 899, 103 Cal. R. 897.

Parole and Probation Searches

People v. *Kanos,* 14 Cal. App. 3d 642, 92 Cal. R. 613 (n. 3).

People v. *Mason,* 5 C. 3d 759, 97 Cal. R. 302.

Student Searches

In re Thomas G., 11 Cal. App. 3d 1193, 90 Cal. R. 361.

People v. *Jackson,* 65 M. 2d 909, 319 NYS 2d 731 (New York).

See articles collected in *People* v. *Lanthier,* 5 C. 3d 751 (n. 3), 488 P. 2d 625.

"The Fourth Amendment and High School Students," 6 *Willamette Law Journal,* 567.

Citizen Searches

Burdeau v. *McDowell,* 256 U.S. 465, 41 S. Ct. 574, 65 L. Ed. 1048.

Stapleton v. *Superior Court,* 70 C. 2d 97 (n. 2), 447 P. 2d 967.

NOTES

1. Classification of the crime may be important. If the crime were a misdemeanor, officers might need an arrest warrant for the driver because the crime was not committed in their presence. But a warrant would not be required for the seizure and search of the car.

2. The California Supreme Court has held that peace officers who become involuntary recipients of vehicles need only exercise a slight amount of care to immunize their department from charges of negligence.

3. In burglary, for example, the crime is complete when the burglar enters the dwelling place with the requisite criminal intent. Transporting the stolen property is only incidental. In robbery, however, transportation of the goods is usually a part of the crime, and the crime is not complete until the goods are reasonably secure in the thief's custody.

4. But not first-class mail, which is afforded greater protection; *United States* v. *Van Leuween,* 397 U.S. 249, 90 S. Ct. 1029, 25 L. Ed. 2d 282.

5. "The right of the people to be secure in their persons, houses, papers, and effects against unreasonable searches and seizures, shall not be violated. . . ."

6. For example, if the minor were eighteen and could prove he was fully employed, paid room, board, and laundry costs to his parents, owned his own car, and in no way depended financially on his parents, his independent status might not allow his parents, with whom he lived, to authorize consent any more than if he were a tenant.

7 Courtroom Procedure and Types of Evidence

Chapter Objectives

After reading this chapter, you will be able to:

1. Describe the basic procedure of criminal trials, including the roles of the prosecution and the defense.

2. Explain the role of evidence in proving the elements of a crime.

3. Identify relevant evidence and material evidence.

Courtroom Procedure

Rules of evidence do not exist in a vacuum; they are important only in the context of a trial. Most trials follow a basic pattern. After the jury has been selected, the prosecutor orally summarizes for them the evidence that the prosecution intends to offer in support of the charge. This opening statement is not evidence, and the jurors are so instructed. Thereafter, the prosecutor presents witnesses and evidence as part of the "case in chief," which is the basic evidence needed to prove the commission of the crime charged. The prosecutor solicits answers to questions as part of the direct examination. Normally, the prosecutor will ask questions that will elicit only favorable responses during direct examination in an attempt to create a good impression of the witness with the jury. But prosecutors sometimes ask questions which damage their own case in order to blunt the effectiveness of such questions during cross-examination.

When the prosecutor concludes the direct examination of a witness, the defense cross-examines. During cross-examination, the defense attorney attempts to determine the extent of the witness's ability to recall the facts accurately. This is accomplished by questioning the witness's opportunity to observe any conduct he or she testified to having seen, by ascertaining any bias the witness may harbor against the defendant, and by attempting to contradict the witness's testimony by asking about statements he or she made prior to trial which are inconsistent with the present testimony. The defense attorney will attempt to demonstrate that the witness's testimony is inaccurate, incomplete, untruthful, or improperly motivated.

When the defense concludes cross-examination of the witness, the prosecution is entitled to redirect examination. During redirect examination, the prosecutor attempts to clarify any ambiguities created by cross-examination and to otherwise strengthen the testimony of the witness. If necessary, recross-examination will be allowed. This pattern of examination and cross-examination applies to all subsequent witnesses.

In addition to the testimony of witnesses who directly observed certain events, the prosecutor may offer ''expert witnesses''—specialists in areas such as ballistics, handwriting, and psychiatry. If witnesses qualify as experts because of academic background, training, or experience, their opinions may be received in evidence and the jury may consider their veiws.[1] This is an exception to the general rule that witnesses may not testify to their conclusions about a case.

Exhibits play an equally important role in criminal cases. Because an exhibit is tangible evidence which a jury can see and examine, its importance cannot be overestimated. Oral testimony describing a dead body cannot substitute for a color photograph of the corpse. Similarly, photographs of an injured assault victim illustrate the severity of the wounds beyond any statement by the witness. Knives, guns, bullets and similar weapons graphically portray what the witness cannot.

But exhibits do not speak for themselves. Each exhibit must be identified by a witness who saw it or seized it. The prosecution must ''lay a foundation'' for every exhibit by tracing its history from the initial seizure to the presentation of the exhibit in court. This chain of evidence requires witnesses to record the seizure and subsequent disposition of any exhibit until it is identified in court.

At the conclusion of the prosecution's case, the defendant offers his or her evidence in the same way. When all the witnesses have testified and the exhibits have been received in evidence, each attorney summarizes the evidence to the jury. After these ''closing statements,'' the judge provides the jury with statements of law which jurors must apply to the facts. Included in these instructions are a definition of the elements of the crime, the kinds of evidence which establish whether the crime was committed (that is, direct evidence or circumstantial evidence, which will be discussed later), the manner in which the jury may evaluate the testimony of the witnesses, the presumption of innocence which attaches to the defendant, and the burden of proof imposed on the prosecution. The jury then retires to deliberate.

Officers are often uninformed about jury instructions. Yet every case must be evaluated against the instructions which the judge provides the jury. In this volume, jury instructions will be included to enable the officer to obtain insight into the goal the prosecutor must achieve.

Because the law presumes the defendant innocent of the charge, and the jury is so instructed, the burden is on the prosecution to establish the defendant's guilt beyond a reasonable doubt. Although the term "reasonable doubt" is necessarily vague, it may be defined as follows: It is not a mere *possible* doubt, because everything relating to human affairs and depending on moral evidence is open to some possible or imaginary doubt. It is that stage of the case which, after the entire comparison and consideration of all the evidence, leaves the minds of the jurors in such a condition that they cannot say they feel an abiding conviction, to a moral certainty, of the truth of the charge. The entire thrust of the prosecution's case in chief is to present evidence to overcome the presumption of innocence and to establish guilt beyond a reasonable doubt.

Defendants attempt to question the validity of all evidence offered by the prosecution in the State's case in chief. Defendants may elect to present evidence in their own behalf as part of their "case in chief," or they may elect to present no evidence and rest solely on the prosecution's evidence. Defendants need not prove themselves innocent—the burden of proof is always on the state. If a defendant chooses not to testify, the jury will be instructed as follows: "It is a constitutional right of a defendant in a criminal trial that he may not be compelled to testify. You must not draw any inference of guilt from the fact that he does not testify, nor should this fact be discussed by you or enter into your deliberations in any way. In deciding whether or not to testify, the defendant may choose to rely on the state of the evidence and upon the failure, if any, of the People to prove every essential element of the charge against him, and no lack of testimony on defendant's part will supply a failure of proof by the People so as to support a finding against him on any such essential element." (California Jury Instructions.)

During the course of the trial, disputes will arise over the admissibility of evidence. At this point the rules of evidence become crucial. The party offering the evidence must convince the court that the evidence offered is admissible. If the court excludes important evidence from the prosecution case, the success of the prosecution may be gravely jeopardized, and the State usually has no right of appeal. If additional admissible evidence can be obtained, the prosecution may be able to rescue its case. Knowing the rules of evidence in advance, however, can save costly and sometimes fatal mistakes.

Although beyond the scope of these materials, the importance of correctly preserving the crime scene and collecting the evidence must be mentioned. Cases have been lost or severely impaired because officers allowed opportunities for a defense challenge that evidence had been carelessly collected, improperly marked, incorrectly tagged, obtained by a witness who was not present at the time, or not properly stored to prevent interference prior to trial. Objections such as these can be avoided if officers follow careful investigation policy and write accurate reports. No officer can afford to prevent a court from considering relevant evidence merely because the investigation was inept.

Relevant and Material Evidence

Persons charged with the commission of a crime must be informed of the charges filed against them in order that they may be advised of the acts which they allegedly have committed. Regardless of the gravity of the crime, this fundamental principle of fairness is essential to the American trial system. In most criminal cases, the defendant is charged in the language of the statute which he or she allegedly violated, as supplemented by any additional facts that the court determines are essential to enable the defendant to prepare the defense adequately. These charges, sometimes called the "pleadings," frame the issues of the case and relate subsequently to the evidence which may be admitted to substantiate the charge or to disprove it.

A representative criminal case would involve one "count," that is, an allegation of a criminal act against a single defendant. When the number of counts increases or the number of defendants alleged to have committed one or more of the acts increases, this is called "joinder," and in such cases the evidentiary problems become more difficult. The legal issues involving joinder of offenses and joinder of defendants vary from state to state, and largely become the responsibility of the prosecutor to determine. Once the decision has been made to try multiple defendants on multiple counts, the officer must be alert to special rules of evidence affecting the trial. These rules will be discussed in context in later chapters.

Because of the rule requiring that the defendant be adequately informed of the acts he or she is alleged to have committed, the prosecution will be limited in presenting only evidence which is "material" and "relevant" to the charge. These two terms are frequently used interchangeably, but each has a different meaning. Evidence is *material* only if it relates to the charges filed against the defendant. Evidence cannot be received unless it bears some reasonable relationship to the charge. On the other hand, *relevant* evidence is a term which applies to individual items of evidence as they relate to substantiating the charges alleged. For example: A witness testifies that she returned to her house and discovered a broken window. Inside the house she observed that the rooms were in disarray and that numerous items were missing, including a watch inscribed with her initials, a television set, and a distinctive CB radio. This testimony relates to and establishes the crime of burglary, and is *material* to the charge. The defendant was arrested later, and each of the missing items was found in his possession. This evidence is *relevant* to prove the defendant's connection with the theft.

Most criminal complaints allege that the defendant committed a specific act with a "criminal" intent, that is, the crime was an intentional act, knowingly and unlawfully committed. Depending upon the specific crime, the prosecutor must introduce items of evidence which establish the commission of the wrongful act by the defendant, and must establish that the defendant committed the act knowingly and intentionally. Each item of evidence must be relevant to proving the act as well as the intent of the defendant, and must be material only to that crime.

Once the distinction between relevant evidence and material evidence has been made, the officer knows that all evidence collected in the investigation must relate to the issues framed by the pleadings and to each item of evidence which will be offered. In many routine investigations, the officer may not know in advance what charge will eventually be lodged. But as the investigation sharpens focus, the evidence the officer needs will become more apparent and relevancy and materiality will emerge as significant factors.

The officer must classify the relevant and material evidence into two major categories: direct evidence and circumstantial evidence. One court has defined the distinction between these two types of evidence as follows: "Direct evidence is that which is applied to the fact to be proved, immediately and directly, and without the aid of any intervening fact or process: as where, on a trial for murder, a witness positively testifies he saw the accused inflict the mortal wound, or administer the poison. Circumstantial evidence is that which is applied to the principal fact indirectly, or through the medium of other facts, from which the principal fact is inferred. . . . It has been said that circumstantial evidence, as distinguished from direct evidence, is testimony not based on actual personal knowledge or observation of the facts in controversy, but of other facts from which deductions are drawn, showing indirectly the facts sought to be proved." (*People* v. *Goldstein.*)

Because many criminal acts are committed secretly, without witnesses, the prosecution sometimes must attempt to prove the crime indirectly rather than directly. Or, put another way, the prosecutor will offer evidence of facts from which an inference of other facts may be drawn. This "circumstantial evidence" often meets objection from the defendant on the ground that such facts, from which other facts may be inferred, are not relevant to establish an "item of proof"—that is, a fact necessary to prove the crime charged against the defendant. In admitting such evidence, the court is granted wide discretion in determining if the offered evidence is too remote to be relevant or if other factors outweigh the desirability of admitting such evidence.

Evidence, whether direct or circumstantial, may be offered to prove that a crime was in fact committed *and* that the defendant committed the criminal act. For example: Burglary is an unlawful entry into a dwelling place (or other structure) committed by a person who intends to commit theft or some other felony as designated by statute. If the prosecution establishes the unlawful entry but cannot prove the wrongful intent, the crime of burglary is not committed. To show the unlawful intent, the prosecution may offer a witness who observed damage to his or her doors or windows, saw the contents of the house in disarray, and determined the absence of personal property from inside the house. Even though no one directly observed anyone enter the house or remove the items, the jury may draw the inference from the circumstances that someone entered without permission and unlawfully took personal property. The unlawful act—entry—and the wrongful intent—entry plus loss of property—establish the crime of burglary circumstantially.

Assuming that the crime of burglary has been proved, the prosecution must then link the defendant to this unlawful act. This link can be forged circumstantially as well as directly. In attempting to connect the defendant—that is, to identify the defendant with the commission of the crime—the prosecution may offer the following kinds of circumstantial evidence: (1) proof of similar crimes committed by the defendant to show a common plan or design, or (2) proof of motive.

Often this evidence may be established by proof that the defendant committed other crimes which identify him or her as the culprit in the current trial. Are these other crimes relevant and material? Each state varies in its interpretation of relevancy of other crimes to establish the defendant's identity. The judge must determine whether evidence of other crimes may cause the jury to react to the previous criminal history of the defendant rather than to the present case. The test is whether the commission of another crime logically tends to prove a material—that is, important—element in the People's case.

The materiality of the evidence to the issues and the relevancy of items as evidence towards establishing proof of those issues are the basic steps in evaluating the admissibility of evidence. But not all evidence is admissible, even if it meets these tests. The law excludes even relevant and material evidence under several well-recognized exceptions which are based upon a policy of the law which serves other interests. For example, under the exclusionary rules implementing the Fourth Amendment's prohibition against unreasonable search and seizure, even relevant and material evidence seized in violation of the Fourth Amendment is excluded on the ground that such a remedy is the only effective device to implement the intent of the amendment. Similarly, voluntary confessions are excluded under the Fifth Amendment to the U.S. Constitution unless there is testimony that the accused was informed of his or her right to counsel and silence prior to making a confession.

Relevant evidence may also be excluded because it is of doubtful value to the issues or too remote for the jury to consider properly. Evidence is inadmissible if its introduction would unfairly prejudice one of several defendants. Evidence also may be excluded because its truthfulness is too questionable (hearsay) or because it is based upon a witness's opinion rather than upon fact. Evidence is inadmissible if a statement is confidential or privileged, or if the witness is not competent to testify. Evidence may also be questionable because the original item of evidence—that is, a document, such as a contract—is not offered.

Not all evidence obtained in the course of a police investigation is collected with the expectation of a subsequent trial. But if a trial does occur, the officer must know whether the evidence will be admissible before considering the weight of such evidence. Witnesses are the key to most criminal cases, and their role will be studied next.

CASES AND MATERIALS

People v. *Goldstein,* 139 Cal. 2d 146, 293 P. 2d 495.

NOTES

1. A jury would be instructed as follows: ''In determining the weight to be given to the opinion of any expert who has testified in this case, you should consider the qualifications and credibility of such expert and the reasons given for his opinion.

   ''If there was any conflict in the testimony of expert witnesses, you should consider their relative qualifications and credibility in weighing the opinion of one expert against that of another, as well as the reasons given for each opinion and the facts upon which it was based.

   ''You are not bound to accept an expert opinion as conclusive, but should give to it the weight, if any, to which you find it to be entitled.'' (California Jury Instructions.)

8 Witnesses: Competency, Privilege, and Personal Knowledge

Chapter Objectives

After reading this chapter, you will be able to:

1. Explain why witnesses are the key to all criminal cases.

2. State the general rule for competency.

3. Explain the law of privilege and its application to various categories of witnesses.

4. Discuss the ways the privilege against self-incrimination can be applied to blood, breath, and urine samples; field sobriety tests; voice and handwriting samples, lineups; and choking cases.

5. Describe the requirement of personal knowledge.

Witnesses

Witnesses are the lifeblood of every criminal case. They range in character from reputable bank officers to hopelessly incurable drug addicts. For most witnesses in criminal cases, the courtroom is a novel and unsettling experience. Accustomed to the unrealistic world of television trials, civilians are astonished at the vast, bustling, and confusing aura of an urban courtroom. For the inexperienced, the shy, and the nervous, the prospect of being called in open court to publicly relate their testimony demands fortitude. Because trials are routine for peace officers and prosecutors, they may overlook their witnesses' apprehension. Aside from personal assurances which should be given by the officer, much can be done to strengthen the confidence of the witness. We will examine such methods shortly.

Following the commission of a crime, officers routinely attempt to interview all witnesses as soon as possible. If the crime involves violence, witnesses may still be in shock, or excited by the event. Witnesses who are friends, relatives, or spouses of victims may be overwhelmed by the tragedy of the crime. Police manuals and departmental policy are relevant here in suggesting ways to calm and reassure emotional witnesses.

Although the trauma of the original crime may have been evident at the time, at the courtroom trial several months later the emotional level of the witnesses will be substantially reduced. The prosecutor will never be able to recreate the violence and hysteria of the crime scene. Moreover, trials are intentionally designed to operate calmly and without resort to drama, even though the crime itself may have been dramatic. The courtroom provides a neutral forum for all parties to present evidence logically and dispassionately. Yet a trial cannot be a sterile event. The officer must be able to assist the prosecutor in duplicating the events in question so that the jury may obtain an accurate impression of the crime. The prosecutor should not be limited to a dry, unemotional repetition of testimony; instead, he or she should vividly impress the jury with strong and convincing evidence.

The officer's main responsibility in interviewing the witness is twofold. First, the officer must obtain an accurate statement of the events the witness saw, heard, or smelled. Only the witness's personal knowledge is important at the trial; the witness will not be able to testify concerning what someone else said that they saw or heard. In some cases, the latter source of information may be valuable for the investigation of the crime, but it will always be inadmissible in court. Second, the officer must obtain as much independent evidence of the crime as possible through the use of photographs, moving pictures, videotapes, physical evidence, or documentary evidence. Photographs capture a story much better than any witness. And when they have been introduced in evidence, exhibits can be viewed by the jury during their deliberations; witnesses, on the other hand, cannot be brought into the jury room.

During the investigation of a crime, the officer will subjectively evaluate the potential credibility of a witness basing the final conclusion on numerous intangible factors such as intelligence, ability to articulate, opportunity to observe, presence or absence of stress at the time of observations, state of sobriety, and similar factors. This same analysis will be repeated later when the jury listens to the witness's testimony. Jurors will ask the same questions as did the officer; in particular, they will ask themselves if the witness inspires belief.

In writing a crime report, officers must note carefully what witnesses say and must record this accurately. Officers should read what they have written to witnesses to be sure they concur. Officers should not lead witnesses, but should let them tell their own story as much as possible.

Later, officers may use these witness statements for trial purposes. At trial, witnesses can read their statements before giving testimony to refresh their recollection of details. At this time, witnesses may also correct any errors or omissions in the report. Such information can help prosecutors avoid damaging cross-examination, since witnesses can then be asked on direct examination about any discrepancies in their statements in order to clarify them. The use of a police crime report which is carelessly written can be a sword in the hands of a skilled lawyer against even the most honest witness.

Officers need to answer several preliminary questions before they can be assured that a person they interview can testify as a witness. Officers should ask themselves: if the witness is *competent* to testify; if the witness can assert any *privilege* at trial not to testify; and if the witness has *personal knowledge* of the facts related?

On the following pages, these preliminary questions will be examined in greater detail.

Competency

The general rule for competency is as follows: *Every person is qualified to be a witness unless he is incapable of expressing himself concerning the matter so as to be understood or incapable of understanding the duty of a witness to tell the truth.*

In early English law, certain witnesses were deemed incompetent to testify because they were parties to the case, that is, litigants, or had a financial interest in the outcome of the litigation. Modern legal theory has abandoned many of these restrictions, and now, as long as witnesses have personal knowledge of the facts, they may be disqualified only if they are incapable of understanding their duty to tell the truth or if they are incapable of expressing themselves. These restrictions usually apply to children or to those who have mental defects.

Children are frequently called as witnesses in child molestation cases as victims of the crime. Because the crime itself is a source of acute embarrassment to them, they often testify reluctantly, and only with considerable leading by the prosecutor. Yet children are often the only witnesses to the crime, and corroboration of their testimony is rare. Careful questioning of children by officers during pre-trial interviews can alert prosecutors to the kind of witnesses they can expect. Although the ultimate issue in a trial will be the *credibility,* or believability, of the witness, the first issue is the child's ability to pass the legal test of competency, that is, to express him- or herself and to understand the need to tell the truth. Depending on the court, either party or the judge may question the child-witness to determine competency. The court may also allow cross-examination by either party.[1]

Witnesses are considered competent to testify even if they cannot speak English. In such cases, interpreters will be appointed by the court to translate. By alerting the prosecutor to the need for an interpreter in advance of trial, the officer can facilitate the witness's court appearance.

Privileges

If there is no evidence of incompetency, all persons must respond to a demand for their appearance in court to testify as a witness. But witnesses may invoke a "privilege" not to testify, even if they are able to testify to relevant and material evidence. Privileges, therefore, *exempt* a witness from testifying. These privileges are granted for reasons of public policy unrelated to the reliability of the information involved. A privilege is granted because it is considered more important to keep certain information confidential than it is to require disclosure of all the information relevant to the issues in a pending proceeding.[2]

Privileges exempting a witness from testifying may be of two kinds: absolute or conditional. An absolute privilege admits of no exceptions, and, if the witness claims the privilege not to testify to the protected information, the evidence cannot be received. A conditional privilege may be claimed by a witness, but will not be honored unless the reason for secrecy outweighs the necessity for disclosure in the interests of justice. Usually the "official information privilege" and the "privilege not to disclose the identity of an informant," which will be discussed later in this chapter, are conditional privileges. Privileges, however, may be waived by the holder of the privilege if done in accordance with local statutes.

Although some variance exists among the states, several generally recognized privileges are available to a witness. Some of these privileges occur only rarely in criminal cases, while others are of major importance.

The Attorney-Client Privilege

The general rule for the attorney-client privilege is as follows: *A client, whether or not a party, has a privilege to refuse to disclose, and to prevent another from disclosing, a confidential communication between client and lawyer if the privilege is claimed by either the attorney or the client.*

To assure this absolute confidentiality, local statutes may also prohibit other persons—including eavesdroppers—from disclosing the contents of the communication. Electronic eavesdropping between attorney and client can, therefore, be prohibited, and in some cases, the eavesdropping party may be subject to prosecution.[3]

In criminal cases, an accused usually consults with an attorney only after arrest, or whenever the case is under active official investigation. These communications are confidential, and neither the attorney nor the client can be compelled to disclose their contents in a subsequent criminal trial. Prosecutors are fully cognizant of this rule and cannot compel disclosure of confidential communications. The attorney-client privilege seldom arises in criminal cases. (Note, however, that the attorney-client privilege does not prohibit officers from overhearing conversations between *suspects* in custody when the attorney is not present. This subject is discussed in chapter 10, Hearsay.)

The Physician-Patient Privilege

The general rule for the physician-patient privilege is as follows: *A patient, whether or not a party, has a privilege to refuse to disclose, and to prevent another from disclosing, a confidential communication between patient and physician if the privilege is claimed.*

Because this privilege is usually inapplicable in criminal proceedings, no discussion is required. Note, however, that the pyschotherapist-patient privilege discussed in the next section may apply.

The Psychotherapist-Patient Privilege

The general rule for the psychotherapist-patient privilege is as follows: *A patient, whether or not a party to the case, has a privilege to refuse to disclose, and to prevent another from disclosing, a confidential communication between patient and psychotherapist if the privilege is claimed.*

The psychotherapist-patient privilege authorizes a person who holds the privilege (usually the patient) to refuse disclosure of confidential communications between the psychotherapist and the patient. In criminal cases, defense counsel may request that the court appoint a psychotherapist in advance of the trial to examine the defendant in order to determine whether to enter a plea of not guilty by reason of insanity. Or, in homicide cases, among others, the defendant's state of mind frequently will be relevant and the psychiatric examination may provide evidence relevant to the issue of premeditation, malice, or intent. Cases alleging sexual misconduct may also put the defendant's state of mind—and, in some cases, that of the victim—in issue. Because the appointment of psychiatrists to examine the defendant is made by the court after the defendant has been arrested and judicial proceedings commence, officers are usually not involved in the exercise of the privilege.

The Husband-Wife Privilege

The general rule for the husband-wife privilege is as follows: *A married person has a privilege not to testify against his spouse in any proceeding.*

Most jurisdictions recognize that compelling one spouse to testify against the other during a trial tends to disrupt the marital relationship or to enlarge existing differences between the couple. (*Hawkins* v. *United States*.) To reduce this possibility, the law permits either spouse to refuse to testify against the other when one of the spouses is a party to the proceeding. Thus, a married person has a privilege not to testify as a witness against his or her spouse if the spouse is a defendant in a criminal case. Of course, the witness-spouse may waive the privilege and testify. Moreover, the privilege expires and may not be claimed if the parties are divorced or if the marriage is annulled. Because not all states apply this rule, local statutes must be consulted.[5]

Even if a state has the husband-wife privilege, the privilege does not apply if the defendant has committed a crime against the witness-spouse or their child, and either may testify against the defendant. Most criminal investigations which involve crimes against the spouse present no privilege problems for the investigator because the injured spouse can testify against the defendant. Oftentimes, however, the spouse who caused the arrest of the defendant spouse refuses to testify because the parties have become reconciled or because of fear. Or, if the spouse does testify, the witness's hostility will frequently be apparent to the jury. In cases involving violence, photographs of any injuries inflicted on the spouse will corroborate the testimony of the witness.

The Confidential Marital Communications Privilege

The general rule for confidential marital communications is as follows: *A spouse has a privilege, during the marital relationship and afterwards, to refuse to disclose, and prevent another from disclosing, a communication made in confidence between him and the other spouse while they were husband and wife.*

Closely related to the previous marital privilege is the privilege of a spouse to refuse to testify about confidential communications between the spouses which occurred during marriage. The privilege may be invoked at trial by one of the spouses on his or her own behalf to prevent the other spouse from testifying. This privilege is broader than the privilege not to testify against a spouse, because one spouse can prevent the other from disclosing confidential communications exchanged during marriage. In the husband-wife witness privilege, the privilege belongs to the witness only. In addition, the privilege not to disclose marital communications remains even after the marriage is dissolved or annulled. (*Blau* v. *United States*.)

Like the husband-wife privilege, the privilege against disclosing confidential communications during marriage does not apply in a criminal proceeding in which the defendant spouse has committed a crime against the witness spouse or a child of the marriage. Note also that the law may require a *valid* marriage before either privilege may be invoked. "Common-law" relationships probably do not qualify.

Investigating officers should be alert to certain threshold questions which should be answered if a spouse is subpoenaed as a witness:

1. Is the witness-spouse lawfully married to the defendant? An invalid marriage, or no marriage, prevents the witness from claiming either privilege.

2. Is the defendant charged with committing a crime against his or her spouse or their child? If so, neither privilege applies.

3. If the witness-spouse is subpoenaed, will the witness claim the privilege not to testify against the defendant-spouse?

4. If the witness-spouse is subpoenaed and is willing to testify, does the expected testimony consist of any communication (verbal or written) between the spouses during their marriage?

5. If the witness is willing to testify, was this communication "confidential," that is, a private conversation? If the conversation took place in public, or in circumstances where privacy could not reasonably be expected, the communication will not be confidential and the privilege is unavailable.

The Clergyman-Penitent Privilege

The general rule governing the clergyman-penitent privilege is as follows: *A penitent, whether or not a party to the case, has a privilege to refuse to disclose, and to prevent another from disclosing, a penitenial communication if he claims the privilege.*[6]

This privilege occurs rarely in criminal cases. Note that only "communications" that are received in confidence are protected from disclosure. Priests or ministers of religious denominations who are victims of crime can testify freely.[7]

The Official Information Privilege

The general rule governing the official information privilege is as follows: *A public entity has a privilege to refuse to disclose official information, and to prevent another from disclosing such information, if the privilege is claimed by a person authorized by the public entity to do so; and*

Disclosure is forbidden by an act of the Congress of the United States or a statute of this state; or

Disclosure of the information is against the public interest because there is a necessity for preserving the confidentiality of the information that outweighs the necessity for disclosure in the interest of justice. In determining whether disclosure of the information is against the public interest, the interest of the public entity as a party in the outcome of the proceeding may not be considered.[8]

"Official information" means information acquired in confidence by a public employee in the course of his or her duty and not open, or officially disclosed, to the public prior to the time the claim of privilege is made. The official information privilege, historically acknowledged as a means to prevent disclosure of military, diplomatic, or state secrets, is a conditional privilege; that is, the communications are protected only if the interest in secrecy outweighs the necessity for disclosure in the interest of justice. (*United States* v. *Reynolds*.) State statutes have expanded the privilege to permit the government to withhold conversations concerning minor government secrets. This expanded protection encourages citizens to provide information to the government without fear of disclosure.

Despite this governmental privilege, defendants in criminal cases may seek disclosure of official records to establish a defense to the charge filed against them. For example, if a defendant is charged with resisting arrest, or battery on a peace officer, he or she may seek to defend on the grounds that the arresting officer applied unreasonable or excessive force in effecting the arrest. In support of this claim, the defendant attempts to prove that the officer-witness has a character trait of force and violence. Evidence in support of this claim may be obtained from others who have complained to the agency employing the officer about his or her use of force and violence, as records of such complaints are usually maintained in the personnel files of the department. These records qualify as official information, and the prosecution may attempt to assert the official information privilege on behalf of the agency if the defendant subpoenas the files or requests a court order for disclosure.

Because the privilege to refuse disclosure of such information is a conditional privilege, the court must determine whether the need for "preserving confidentiality outweighs the necessity for disclosure in the interest of justice." Fairness to the defendant requires that the prosecution cannot commence criminal proceedings and then invoke its governmental privilege to deprive the accused of anything which might be material to his or her defense. (*Jencks* v. *United States*.)

Thus, the trial court must determine what records, if any, are to be disclosed and to what extent disclosure is required. The U.S. Supreme Court has said: First, the government's claim of privilege is not conclusive; it is subject to judicial inquiry but without forcing public disclosure of the very material the privilege is designed to protect. Second, the litigant must make a showing of necessity which will determine how far the court will probe in satisfying itself that the government's claim of necessity may be minimized if the government offers an "available alternative" which would permit the litigant to make out his case without forcing a showdown on the claim of privilege. (*United States* v. *Reynolds*.)

The method of reconciling conflicting interests between prosecution and defense varies. In some jurisdictions, the court reviews the evidence sought by the defendant in chambers and attempts to determine whether the privileged information may be disclosed. Because this procedure is conducted in the absence of defense counsel, the court lacks the benefit of an adversary hearing. The U.S. Supreme Court has said that the practice of producing government documents to the trial judge for determination of relevancy and materiality without hearing the accused is unsatisfactory, not for lack of confidence in the integrity of the trial judge or government counsel, but because such a hearing is inadequate to safeguard the defendant's rights.[9]

If the governmental privilege is invoked by the prosecution and the court rules that the interest in confidentiality is outweighed by the necessity of disclosure, the court can either dismiss the case against the defendant, strike the testimony of the witness, or make some other order adverse to the prosecution. The State cannot be compelled to divulge the privileged information to the defendant in court, but a penalty is imposed on the prosecution as a consequence of its exercise of the privilege.

The Identity of Informant Privilege

The general rule governing the identity of informant privilege is as follows: *A public entity has a privilege to refuse to disclose the identity of a person who has furnished information purporting to disclose a violation of a law of the United States or of this state or a public entity in this state, and to prevent another from disclosing such identity, if the privilege is claimed by a person authorized by the public entity to do so and:*

> (1) *Disclosure is forbidden by an act of the Congress of the United States or a statute of this state; or*
>
> (2) *Disclosure of the identity of the informer is against the public interest because there is a necessity for preserving the confidentiality of his identity that outweighs the necessity for disclosure in the interest of justice; but no privilege may be claimed under this paragraph if any person authorized to do so has consented that the identity of the informer be disclosed in the proceeding. In determining whether disclosure of the identity of the informer is against the public interest, the interest of the public entity as a party in the outcome of the proceeding may not be considered.*[10]

The most frequent application of the informer's privilege occurs in narcotic cases, although the privilege may apply to all crimes. The prosecution attempts to invoke the privilege, which is conditional, in order to conceal the identity of an informant who has furnished officers with information resulting in an arrest or search or who is a witness on the issue of guilt or innocence. The prosecution will usually assert that any disclosure of the informant's identity would subject this person to harassment, injury, or possibly death. Yet if an arrest or search is based on information related to the officer by an informant, the defendant may attempt to learn the name of that person in order to test the lawfulness of the arrest or search. Or the defendant may seek disclosure in order to establish a defense such as entrapment, lack of knowledge that the contraband was in his or her possession, and/or lack of knowledge that the substance was a narcotic. The defendant may also seek disclosure in order to demonstrate that someone "planted" the evidence on the premises or to interview the informant to determine the truthfulness of his or her statements. This conflict between prosecution and defense requires that the court determine whether the interest in confidentiality outweighs the necessity for disclosure. To resolve the conflict, the court may conduct an evidentiary hearing, either in court or in chambers, to determine whether the prosecution may properly invoke the privilege. If the court sustains the prosecution's objection to disclosure and rules that the informant not be identified, the defendant must abide by this decision, but may appeal later to a higher court. If the court rules that disclosure is required, the prosecution must disclose the identity of the informant or incur a dismissal.[11]

In making this determination, the court must evaluate the issues that are discussed below.

Informant Defined Initially, the court must determine whether the person who has supplied information to law enforcement is an "informant." An informant is a person who regularly supplies information to a law enforcement agency, or who is compensated for furnishing information, or who serves as an active agent of the police. "Compensation" may be cash, but may also consist of promises of immunity or of lesser charges of punishment. (*Eleazer* v. *Supreme Court.*) "But one who simply points the finger of suspicion at a person who has violated the law is not an informant. He puts the wheels in motion which cause the defendant to be suspected and perhaps arrested, but he plays no part in the criminal act with which the defendant is charged." (*People* v. *Lawrence.*) If the court finds that the person who provided the information served only to focus official attention on a suspect, his or her identity need not be disclosed. If the person's role leading to the arrest and prosecution of a suspect is more substantial, then disclosure may be required. Assuming the court finds the person is an informant within the meaning of the definition, the prosecution moves to the next issue.

Disclosure on the Validity of the Arrest A distinction has arisen between disclosure of informants sought on the issue of the legality of the arrest on the one hand, and disclosure on the issue of the defendant's guilt on the other. For example: An informant relates that the defendant is concealing contraband at a specific address. After a preliminary investigation corroborates the information, officers execute an arrest warrant for the defendant at his premises and discover seizable evidence. The defendant, who is arrested on the premises, is charged with possession of contraband. At the trial, he seeks disclosure of the informant. Two issues emerge. First, is the arrest lawful under the Fourth Amendment to the United States Constitution, which requires that all arrests be based on probable cause?[12] (See chapter 2,

Arrest.) Second, is the informant an important witness on the issue of the defendant's guilt?

The Fourth Amendment to the U.S. Constitution provides that: "The right of the people to be secure in their persons, houses, papers, and effects, against unreasonable searches and seizures, shall not be violated and no warrants shall issue, but upon probable cause, . . . and particularly describing the place to be searched, and the persons or things to be seized."[13]

As stated in chapter 2, the Supreme Court has interpreted this constitutional provision to require that all arrests, that is, "seizures," be based on probable cause. The Court ruled as follows: "Reasonable or probable cause for an arrest has been the subject of much judicial scrutiny and decision. There is no exact formula for the determination of reasonableness. Each case must be decided on its own facts and circumstances and on the total atmosphere of the case. Reasonable cause has been generally defined to be such a state of facts as would lead a man of ordinary care and prudence to believe and conscientiously entertain an honest and strong suspicion that the person is guilty of a crime. Probable cause has also been defined as having more evidence for than against; supported by evidence which inclines the mind to believe, but leaves some room for doubt. It is not limited to evidence that would be admissible at the trial on the issue of guilt. The test is not whether the evidence upon which the officer acts in making the arrest is sufficient to convict but only whether the person should stand trial." (*Beck* v. *Ohio*.)

Thus, in order for an arrest to be "reasonable" within the meaning of the Fourth Amendment, the officer must have "probable cause" to arrest the defendant. Probable cause may be established by a statement from another person—the informant—to the officer that the arrestee is currently engaged in criminal conduct or in possession of seizable evidence. Although such a statement may not be used at the trial on the issue of the defendant's guilt—since such out-of-court unsworn statements are hearsay and otherwise inadmissible—officers may rely on such statements to arrest. In other words, probable cause may be established by hearsay.[14] Such hearsay, however, qualifies as probable cause only if the person is reliable and has personal knowledge of the facts he or she relates. In most cases the source of that hearsay statement is an informant.

A hearing on the issue of probable cause for the arrest, usually precedes the trial on the issue of guilt or innocence. At this hearing, the defendant may demand the name of the informant from the officer-witness. The defendant may seek to challenge the testimony of the officer that the informant is reliable and may challenge the officer's testimony that the informant's statement was based on personal knowledge. Because "reliability" is a conclusion of the witness, the officer may be asked to state the basis for his or her opinion. "Reliability" of an informant is often based upon previous statements by the informant to the officer which have led to other arrests, searches, or prosecutions in the past. If the officer must reveal the names and cases which were initiated earlier upon information received from the informant, the defendant may be able to establish the identity of the informant circumstantially. Yet the officer cannot be permitted to foreclose cross-examination of his or her opinion that the informant is a reliable person by refusing to answer questions about past experiences with the informant.

Moreover, even if the defendant cannot learn the informant's identity through this approach, he or she may be able to do so indirectly by asking the officer-witness whether the informant spoke from "personal knowledge." In order for a hearsay statement from an informant to qualify as probable cause, the informant must have obtained the information directly from what he or she saw or heard. The informant cannot repeat to the officer what another person said about the defendant—such a statement would be double hearsay. Because the informant must have "personal knowledge" of the facts related to the officer, the defendant can learn through cross-examination of the officer-witness when and where the informant made observations of the defendant's criminal conduct or possession of seizable evidence. Necessarily, the informant must have observed the defendant's criminal activity recently, that is, at least within the last three or four weeks. By a process of elimination, the defendant can narrow the focus substantially.

The requirement of personal knowledge demands that the informant saw the seizable evidence or heard incriminating evidence. As a result, the informant now becomes an eyewitness to the crime. Under these circumstances, the informant is now a *material* witness, that is, a witness who may be called to testify to the crime itself—and, as we will see shortly—a material witness must always be disclosed on the issue of guilt. For these reasons, therefore, concealing the identity of the informant on the lawfulness of the arrest does not assure the informant's anonymity at the time of trial.

Disclosure on the Validity of the Search Just as the Fourth Amendment requires that all "seizures" be based upon probable cause, all "searches" must also be supported by evidence of probable cause. Hearsay statements from an informant may be used to establish probable cause to search as long as the twin requirements of a reliable informant and the informant's personal knowledge are present. Thus, an informant's statement to an officer may qualify either as probable cause to arrest, or seize, the defendant or as probable cause to search a dwelling place or vehicle pursuant to a search warrant.[15]

In conformance to judicial interpretation of the Fourth Amendment, all searches must be conducted under the authority of a search warrant unless an exception to the warrant requirement exists. Three major exceptions to the warrant requirement are: searches incidental to a lawful arrest, searches incidental to an emergency, and searches consented to by persons authorized to consent. Informants are usually not involved in searches without a warrant unless their information contributes to probable cause to arrest, which in turn justifies an incidental search. But informants do play a major role in cases involving searches conducted pursuant to a search warrant. Before the court can issue a search warrant, the magistrate must find probable cause to search the described premises or vehicle. The probable cause is outlined in an affidavit prepared by the officer, or prosecutor, detailing the information the officer has received concerning the premises or vehicle to be searched. If the source of the information is an informant, the officer repeats the substance of their conversation in the affidavit. If the warrant is successfully executed and the suspect is arrested, the defendant will seek to cross-examine the officer at trial concerning the identity of the informant. Although the officer may be able to conceal the identity of the informant on the issue of the validity of the search, he or she may not be able to assert the privilege successfully on the issue of guilt for the same reasons outlined in the section concerning the validity of the arrest.

Disclosure on the Issue of Guilt The court has ruled that: ''The governmental privilege to conceal the identity of the informant must yield whenever it is shown that the informant whose identity is sought is a material witness for the defense and nondisclosure would deprive the defendant of a fair trial. Only after it is first determined the informant is not a material witness to the guilt or innocence of the accused can disclosure be denied.'' (*People* v. *Garcia.*)

For example: At the request of narcotic investigators, an informant arranges to purchase a quantity of heroin from a suspect. After searching the informant, one of the officers conceals himself in the trunk of the informant's automobile. The informant drives the car to a prearranged location and meets the suspect, who immediately enters the car. The officer, hiding in the trunk, overhears the conversation between the informant and the suspect. The suspect agrees to sell heroin to the informant, leaves the car, and returns shortly to consummate the sale. After the exchange of money and heroin between the informant and the suspect, the officer signals to his partner. Officers arrest the suspect, confiscate the money, and later charge the suspect with sale of heroin.

At the trial, the government offers only the testimony of the agent who overheard the conversation. The defendant demands the name of the informant. Under these facts, the informant who directly participated in the sale is a ''material witness'' on the issue of guilt. This informant did more than focus attention on a suspect who was subsequently arrested; he was an active agent of law enforcement who participated in the crime itself. The informant was the only eyewitness participant to the sale, and only he could offer direct testimony about the sale. Neither of the officers could testify to a direct observation of the sale; all they heard was the conversation. The U.S. Supreme Court has written: A further limitation on the applicability of the (informer's) privilege arises from the fundamental requirements of fairness [under the Due Process Clause of the U.S. Constitution]. Where the disclosure of an informer's identity, or of the contents of his communication, is relevant and helpful to the defense of an accused or is essential to a fair determination of a cause, the privilege must give way. We believe that no fixed rule with respect to disclosure is justifiable. The problem is one that calls for balancing the public interest in protecting the flow of information against the individual's right to prepare his defense. Whether a proper balance renders nondisclosure erroneous must depend on the particular circumstances of each case, taking into consideration the crime charged, the possible defenses, the possible significance of the informer's testimony, and other relevant factors."[16]

This balancing test can be illustrated by examples of the role an informant plays in the arrest and prosecution of a suspect. Whether the informant is or is not a "material witness" depends upon at least three factors: first, the elements of the offense charged against the defendant; second, the nature of the defense to the charge; and third, the identity of the person who allegedly sold or possessed the contraband. The informant's privilege arises most often in drug and narcotic prosecutions. For example: An officer testifies that the informant introduced him to the defendant. At that time, the officer and the defendant agreed upon a purchase price for exchange of narcotics. All three drove to an apartment where the defendant admitted them with a key. Inside, the defendant removed a large paper sack from the closet. He then withdrew a quantity of narcotics from the sack and handed them to the officer in exchange for cash. The informant, who had been present throughout the sale, then left the apartment with the officer; shortly thereafter, other officers entered the apartment, arrested the defendant, and seized a large quantity of drugs and narcotics in plain sight. The defendant is charged in count one of a criminal complaint with sale of narcotics and in count two with possession of narcotics and drugs. Must the informant be disclosed?

On the first count, charging sale of narcotics, the informant was an eyewitness-participant, and his identity must be disclosed even though the officer was also present and testified to the fact of sale and possession. But on the second count, charging possession, the elements of the charge are dominion and control of the narcotics as well as knowledge of their narcotic content. Because the defendant admitted the informant and the officer into his apartment, the court can infer that he was an occupant of the apartment or at least a person entrusted with access—that is, he had control of the premises. The large quantity of narcotics observed in plain sight and subsequently seized by the police corroborated the defendant's knowledge of their narcotic content. Under these circumstances, disclosure of the informant's identity would not be required on the possession count.

The mere presence of the defendant inside a dwelling at the time officers search and discover contraband, however, does not prevent disclosure of the informant's identity. For example, an informant reports that X is currently living at a specific apartment and selling narcotics regularly from the apartment. The informant reports that the narcotics are stored under a mattress in the bedroom. The informant further reports that numerous visitors enter the apartment, including himself. Officers execute a search warrant, and find the defendant sleeping on a mattress in the bedroom. Under the mattress, officers find a large quantity of narcotics, and they arrest the defendant. No narcotics, however, are found on the defendant's person. X is absent, but returns later and is also arrested.

The defendant is prosecuted for possession of the narcotics, and he seeks disclosure of the informant who supplied officers with the information. Because the narcotics were seized from underneath the mattress on which he was sleeping, his close proximity to the contraband might support an inference that he had dominion and control over the evidence. But if the elements of possession of narcotics also include evidence of a person's knowledge of the narcotic content of a substance, the defendant can maintain that he lacked knowledge of the presence of the drug because he was only a visitor. The informant did not identify the defendant as a resident of the apartment, and a search of the defendant's person yielded no narcotics. The defendant would not necessarily be required to inspect the apartment—particularly the area under a mattress on the floor—for the presence of contraband. Arguably, the defendant would be granted disclosure to establish from the informant his lack of knowledge that the evidence seized was in fact a narcotic substance.

Although the defendant's presence in the dwelling at the time of the arrest and search may reduce some of the reasons for disclosure, this factor does not foreclose attempts to discover the identity of the informant, even under highly incriminating circumstances. An example will illustrate this point. An informant reports that the defendant is in possession of dangerous drugs at her apartment. The informant's knoweldge is based on his observations one day earlier. Officers drive to the location, knock, and identify themselves. Upon hearing sounds suggesting flight by the occupants, the officers enter and arrest numerous persons in the apartment, including the defendant. No dangerous drugs are found, although officers seize a quantity of marijuana concealed in a desk drawer. After her arrest, the defendant admits she lives in the apartment.

At her trial, the defendant testifies she had been in jail from the time the informant stated he had observed the dangerous drugs inside the apartment until shortly before her rearrest on the current charge of possession of marijuana; that she lived with several other occupants at the apartment, some of whom were arrested at the same time; and that she lacked dominion and control of the marijuana found in the desk drawer.

Under these circumstances, disclosure would be required. The informant reported that the defendant possessed dangerous drugs, yet none were found. The defendant testified that she had been in custody on another charge at or about the time the informant stated she was in possession of dangerous drugs, and her statement can be verified by jail records. The presence of co-occupants at the time of the search suggests that someone else who lived on the premises had access to the drawers which concealed the marijuana, and that the defendant was unaware of the presence of contraband. Or, alternatively, even though she might have been aware of the presence of marijuana, she exercised no dominion and control over it.

Even if a defendant is the sole occupant of the room where contraband is seized, he or she may still request that the informant be disclosed. Consider the following example. Officers testify that an informant told them the defendant was in possession of marijuana at his apartment. The officers arrived at the location and the defendant admitted them inside. They found a quantity of marijuana inside a large shopping bag in the corner of the defendant's apartment, but the defendant denied knowledge of the marijuana in the bag. At his trial, the defendant testifies that he drove a man home from a bar where they had met, and that the man brought the bag into the apartment and left it in the corner. The next morning the man left, saying that he would return late in the day to pick up the bag; but before the man returned, the officers entered the defendant's apartment and seized the bag. The defendant testified that he was unaware of the contents of the bag, and that no one else had entered the apartment during the stranger's absence.

In this case the defendant was arrested while alone in an apartment solely occupied by him. Marijuana was found in his immediate presence in an unconcealed area of the apartment. The inference that he had dominion and control of the bag and its contents, as well as knowledge of the contents, is rebutted by his testimony that someone else left the marijuana in his apartment. Because the defendant testified that no one else entered the apartment after the stranger deposited his bag and left, an inference could be drawn that the stranger was the informant and that he had either "planted" the marijuana or intended to entrap the defendant. In this case, disclosure would be required.

In narcotic possession cases, the prosecutor may establish the elements of dominion and control, or knowledge of contraband either by means of direct or circumstantial evidence. For example: Officers receive information from a reliable informant that the defendant is currently packaging narcotics for sale at his residence, the informant having just left the premises. The officers obtain a search warrant upon presentation of an affidavit to a magistrate alleging these facts. In executing the search warrant, officers force entry and observe the defendant attempting to destroy narcotics by flushing them down the toilet. Narcotics are seized from his person, and the defendant is apparently under the influence of a narcotic. Under these facts, the defendant probably could not successfully compel disclosure of the informant's identity because the direct evidence of his possession of narcotics is so overwhelming.

In those cases where the defendant is arrested and unprescribed narcotics are seized from his or her person (*People* v. *Acuna*), or the defendant attempts to conceal or discard them, the direct evidence of possession is usually sufficient to convict without disclosing the informant whose information led to the arrest. But if circumstantial evidence is relied on, the informant's identity may become relevant. For example: Officers receive information that X is selling dangerous drugs from a specific location. The informant states that X lives at that location and carries the drugs in a brown suitcase. Upon obtaining a search warrant, officers enter the apartment and observe X and the defendant seated on a couch. In front of X is a closed brown suitcase; in front of the defendant lies a blue sports bag. Each bag contains a quantity of dangerous drugs, but the defendant produces a prescription for the drugs found in the blue bag.

X and the defendant are tried for joint possession of the drugs in the brown suitcase. No direct evidence of possession is offered; that is, the officer did not see the defendant in actual possession of the brown suitcase. The inference of possession can only be drawn circumstantially. At the trial, the defendant asks for disclosure of the informant to assist him in establishing the fact that he lacked knowledge of the contents of the suitcase. Even if the defendant's close proximity to the suitcase might suggest that he exercised dominion and control jointly with X, no inference can be drawn that he knew the closed brown suitcase contained contraband. His own possession of prescribed drugs suggests that he lacks a need for contraband drugs. Under these circumstances, the informant might testify that he never saw the defendant in X's apartment; or, even if the informant had seen the defendant previously, that the defendant was unaware of any drug possession or sales by X; or that the informant had never seen the defendant in possession of the brown suitcase. Disclosure would probably be required.

Extent of Disclosure of Identity Because the defendant can submit a variety of reasons to support a demand for disclosure of the informant's identity, the governmental privilege to refuse disclosure of an informant frequently must yield. But in some cases, disclosure of "identity" has been so useless to the defendant that the information is meaningless. For example: At a preliminary hearing, the officer testified that he saw the defendant sell narcotics to an informant known as "Spider." The defendant moved for discovery of the informant's identity, and the officer disclosed the informant's name as Larry Stine. The officer also furnished a physical description of the informant, a photograph, a police information sheet, and three arrest reports. The officer testified that Larry Stine had participated in about twenty narcotics purchases and was paid in cash for his services. Stine had stopped working for the police about three or four weeks before the discovery hearing. The officer had made no effort to secure an address from Stine, and he had no idea where Stine could be located. The following exchange took place at the hearing:

Defense: You don't have any records on him as far as where he lives, social security number, any of these types of information.
Officer: His address is ''transient'' on the arrest reports.
Defense: Do you know where Mr. [Stine] presently is?
Officer: No, sir.
Defense: Do you have any idea where he can be located?
Officer: No, sir.
Defense: How would Stine and you meet each time you would go out to try to make these purchases? Where would you meet?
Officer: Larry [Stine] would call up and say that he was at such and such a location, and we would go meet him there.
Defense: Now it's your position that neither you nor anybody in your office can locate this Larry or Spider so he can come in and testify in court next week?
Officer: Not unless he calls me. . . .
Defense: [by the deputy district attorney] Officer, during the period of time that Mr. [Stine] was working for the police department, did you make any efforts to secure from [him] his address or telephone number or other information, and if you did, what results did you have?
Officer: I did not.
Defense: Do you know if your partner did?
Officer: I think at one time he might have had a phone number where he could be reached, but to the best of my knowledge Larry [Stine] moved from the location a short time later.
Defense: What I'm trying to get at is, was it a situation wherein you already said he could call you?
Officer: That's correct.
Defense: What was the reason for that . . .?
Officer: It was to keep Larry [Stine] from having any fear that the police department was trying to arrest him or to put any pressure on him . . . he didn't want me to know where he lived. The first time I met him, I met him on a street corner.
Defense: Did you ask him?
Officer: No sir, I did not . . . he'd be reluctant to give me any information if I'd pry into his personal affairs.
Defense: Do you find this to be the usual procedure with this type of informant?
Officer: Yes, sir. (*Eleazer* v. *Supreme Court.*)

Even though the officer disclosed the identity of the informant, the intentional failure to learn more details about the informant prevented the defendant from obtaining useful information. However praiseworthy the motives of an officer who uses such methods, the defendant's right to a fair trial must prevail. The California Supreme Court fashioned this rule in response to this problem:

"Although originally the duty to disclose the identity of a material witness required only that the prosecution reveal information actually in its possession, we have extended the prosecution's obligation and required, in addition, reasonable steps to locate or obtain information about such informants. If through police tactics or happenstance (an) informer becomes a material witness, the police should make such inquiries and arrangements as are reasonably necessary to enable the prosecution and defense to locate him. We recognize the futility of a rule requiring disclosure of the information which the police know about a material witness informer without a further requirement that the police make efforts to obtain information useful in locating the informer as well. We noted, however, that due process requires only that the police and the district attorney undertake reasonable efforts in good faith to locate the informer so that either party or the court itself could, if it so desired, subpoena him as a witness.

The efforts required will vary, of course, depending on the case: "If the informer has a regular abode and place of employment, simply obtaining his address and telephone number may suffice; if he is transient, or conceals his address, the law enforcement agency probably should make some arrangements for maintaining close communication with him."

Even if officers record sufficient information to enable the court to subpoena an informant, the prosecution can still be held responsible for his or her absence. For example: "A deputy sheriff assigned to the narcotics detail, and one Robert Stough, a confidential informant, were seated in a cafe when the defendant entered. The officer testified that after Stough spoke to the defendant, the latter joined Stough and the officer in the restroom, where the defendant stated . . . that a gram of 'junk' would cost $17.00, . . . [and] that the money should be paid to the defendant who would return with the 'junk' to the officer. The officer gave the defendant $17. The defendant left and after five or ten minutes he returned and delivered a package which, upon later analysis, was found to contain heroin. . . .

"The defendant was first arrested for the alleged violation, without a warrant, by a police officer who had taken no part in the foregoing transaction. No charges were filed against the defendant at that time, and he was released after being held for 51 hours. Thereafter charges were refiled against the defendant, and he was rearrested and brought to trial. . . .

"The prosecution, in an attempt to explain the circumstances of the defendant's arrests, produced a police officer who testified that the defendant was released because it would be necessary to divulge the identity of the informant if they proceeded to trial, that Stough (the informant) had been intimidated and did not wish to be identified, and that it was established policy not to prosecute in these circumstances. This witness was informed, however, that after the defendant's release Stough had left the state. That being the case, and it appearing that Stough might then be identified without subjecting him to reprisals, the accused was rearrested and brought to trial. . . ."

The court said: "The frankness of the prosecution witnesses in admitting that they first arrested, then released and rearrested the defendant in order to avoid the necessity of identifying the informer Stough at the time when the defendant could have procured Stough's attendance at the trial and have elicited testimony from him, would seem to point unerringly to the conclusion that the State sought to circumvent, if not to stultify, the reason for the rule requiring disclosure. The procedure resorted to . . . manifestly denied the defendant a fair trial just as effectively as if the informer had never been identified." (*People* v. *Kiihoa.*)

Because of a desire to maintain the anonymity of their informants, officers usually attempt to avoid involving the informant with an exchange of narcotics. For example: An undercover officer testified that he and another man met the defendant. The officer's companion asked the defendant about getting some "stuff." They went into the restroom; the officer followed them and saw defendant give his companion a balloon in exchange for $12.00. The latter handed the balloon to the officer.

The officer further testified that two days later he met the defendant alone on the sidewalk in front of a food market and asked the defendant to sell him "a half." The defendant agreed, and they went into the market, where the officer gave the defendant $12.00 in exchange for two pieces of balloon. The officer also testified that on a third occasion he again met the defendant alone on the street and bought from him a $5.00 balloon. Expert testimony established that all the balloons contained heroin.

The officer was the only witness for the prosecution. He testified that the person who accompanied him on the first sale was a confidential informer and claimed the privilege of withholding his name. He also testified that the informer was not present at the later sales and that they were not prearranged.

In view of the unidentified informer's participation in the first sale, the prosecution sought dismissal of count one (the first sale). With respect to counts two and three, the defendant's counsel sought on cross-examination to ascertain the informer's identity. In his testimony, the defendant denied both that he had sold narcotics and that he had ever seen the officer before the trial. The officer testified that he had not known the defendant before the first sale of heroin to the informer. The Grand Jury proceedings at which the officer had earlier identified the defendant as the seller did not take place until some three weeks after the last sale, and the defendant was not arrested until three months later. Under these circumstances, the informer was a material witness on the issue of defendant's guilt on *all three* counts. Had he contradicted the officer's identification of the defendant with respect to the first sale, his testimony would have been a highly significant factor in discrediting the identification with respect to the later transactions. (*People* v. *Durazo*.)

The courts have stated that the privilege to conceal the identity of an informant must yield because the Due Process Clause of the Constitution requires that every defendant be accorded a fair trial, and a fair trial cannot occur in the absence of a material witness on the issue of the defendant's guilt if the absence of that witness is attributable to the prosecution. No statutory privilege may prevail over the constitutional command. Moreover, other constitutional requirements must be considered when informants are involved in arrest and prosecution of suspects. The Sixth Amendment to the U.S. Constitution demands that defendants be allowed to confront and cross-examine their accusers. The Fourth Amendment protects defendants against unreasonable invasions of their privacy, a right defendants will assert when undercover police officers or informants enter their homes to purchase contraband, when police officers monitor their conversations with informants, or when such conversations are recorded. If undercover officers solicit incriminating statements from defendants, they may assert that they were unaware of their constitutional rights under the Fifth Amendment to counsel and silence. These objections are discussed in the section in chapter 11, the *Miranda* Decision.

The Privilege Against Self-Incrimination

The general rule governing the privilege against self-incrimination is as follows: *No person . . . shall be compelled in any criminal case to be a witness against himself.*[17]

Although all the privileges previously discussed are statutory, the privilege against self-incrimination is based upon the Fifth Amendment to the U.S. Constitution. Regardless of local statutes, the scope of the privilege against self-incrimination is essentially a federal question and is interpreted by U.S. Supreme Court opinions. Many state courts also interpret this constitutional language, but their decisions are governed by opinions decided by the U.S. Supreme Court.

As interpreted by these court decisions, the privilege against self-incrimination embodies two distinct privileges: (1) the privilege of the *accused* not to be called as a witness, and (2) the privilege of *any witness* not to answer any questions which will tend to be self-incriminating. Although these two privileges apply to different fact situations, the policy underlying the privilege is the same: Persons should not be required to convict themselves by their own admission. The Fifth Amendment reflects the experience of those who drafted the Constitution—people who were not unfamiliar with the tactics of the Star Chamber and the Spanish Inquisition. Confessions wrung from the rack and screw were despised and feared by colonial New England. To prohibit the new government of the United States from resorting to such tactics, the Constitution's framers drafted the Fifth Amendment as a limitation on the government's power. The Fifth Amendment is a restatement of the conviction that our system of government is accusatorial, not inquisitorial. The responsibility for proving the guilt of the accused should lie with the State, and the accused should bear no burden in establishing his or her own guilt, nor may the accused's confession substitute for independent proof of guilt.[18] The U.S. Supreme Court summed up the philosophy of the Fifth Amendment as follows: "It reflects many of our fundamental values and most noble aspirations; our unwillingness to subject those suspected of crime to the cruel trilemma of self-accusation, perjury or contempt; our preference for an accusatorial rather than an inquisitorial system of criminal justice; our fear that self-incriminating statements will be elicited by inhumane treatment and abuses; our sense of fair play which dictates 'a fair state-individual balance by requiring the government to leave the individual alone until good cause is shown for disturbing him and by requiring the government in its contest with the individual to shoulder the entire load' . . .; our respect for the inviolability of the human personality and of the right of each individual 'to a private enclave where he may lead a private life,' . . . our distrust of self-deprecatory statements; and our realization that the privilege, while sometimes 'a shelter to the guilty,' is often 'a protection to the innocent.'"[19]

For law enforcement officers, the privilege is most frequently encountered prior to taking statements. A warning to those accused that they have the right to remain silent and that anything they say may be used against them constitutes advice of the right not to answer questions and not to incriminate oneself. Although originally the Fifth Amendment was applied only in the context of a trial, court decisions have required that officers advise suspects of their Fifth Amendment rights in the field or at the police station, well in advance of any judicial proceedings. The U.S. Supreme Court has held that such advice must be given to inform a person adequately of the right not to answer questions if the accused so desires. In that context, the Fifth Amendment is applicable in this section, but the privilege will be treated more fully in chapter 11, The *Miranda* Decision. Although the Fifth Amendment applies to grand jury investigations, legislative hearings, and discharge of public employees who invoke the Fifth Amendment (*United*

States v. *Wade*), this section discusses the Fifth Amendment as it is applicable to familiar daily law enforcement work.

The Privilege of the Accused Not To Be a Witness

The privilege against self-incrimination protects only against *testimony* which is *compelled:* that is, the defendant cannot be compelled to give oral testimony or produce documents. (*Kastigar* v. *United States.*) The privilege does not extend, however, to "real or physical" evidence derived from an accused. Each of these limitations, therefore, allows the reception of nontestimonial evidence, even if obtained under a degree of compulsion. "Testimonial evidence" has been interpreted to include oral statements obtained from the accused prior to trial. But nontestimonial evidence taken from the person of the defendant may be admissible even if the defendant must actively cooperate. What kinds of evidence obtained from the person of the accused can be obtained without violating the privilege against self-incrimination? The difference between testimonial evidence—evidence protected by the privilege—and nontestimonial evidence is critical. Evidence obtained in violation of the privilege will be excluded at trial.

Blood Samples The use of blood, breath, or urine samples is most often associated with criminal prosecution for driving under the influence of alcohol or drugs. Generally speaking, arresting officers obtain a sample of the defendant's blood (extracted by a person with medical training) which is later analyzed for alcoholic content by laboratory personnel. The results of this test is then offered in evidence at trial to establish the defendant's degree of sobriety.

In addition, many state legislatures have passed "implied consent" laws in an attempt to curb the drinking driver. Such statutes usually provide that the driver of a motor vehicle on a public highway is deemed to have consented to provide a sample of blood, breath, or urine if detained while driving a motor vehicle and assuming that probable cause exists to arrest this person for driving under the influence of drugs or alcohol. (See chapter 13, Driving Under the Influence Prosecutions.) These statutes, which usually provide that the arrestee's driving privilege will be suspended or revoked upon refusal to submit to the test, should not be confused with criminal prosecution for driving under the influence of alcohol or drugs. "Implied consent" statutes implement an administrative remedy to remove driving privileges, but only indirectly do they affect the criminal prosecution.

The general rule for blood samples is as follows: *The privilege against self-incrimination protects an accused only from being compelled to testify against himself, or otherwise provide the state with evidence of a testimonial or communicative nature, and the withdrawal of a blood sample and use of the analysis does not involve compulsion to these ends.*

This rule was announced by the U.S. Supreme Court in *Schmerber* v. *California*. In *Schmerber,* the defendant had been arrested for driving under the influence of alcohol and was taken to a hospital to receive treatment for injuries suffered in an accident involving the automobile he apparently had been driving. At the direction of a police officer, a blood sample was withdrawn from the defendant by a physician at the hospital. Subsequent analysis of the blood evidenced a high alcoholic content, and this evidence was introduced at the trial over the defendant's objection. The U.S. Supreme Court said: "Not even a shadow of testimonial compulsion upon or enforced communication by the accused was involved either in the extraction or in the chemical analysis [of the blood]. The arrestee's testimonial capacities were in no way implicated; indeed, his participation, except as a donor, was irrelevant to the results of the test, which depend on chemical analysis and on that alone. Since the blood test evidence, although an incriminating product of compulsion, was neither [defendant's] testimony nor evidence relating to some communicative act or writing by [him], it was not inadmissible on privilege grounds."

Analysis of a blood sample may also be valuable in a homicide investigation, both in providing a sample of the defendant's blood for comparison with blood types found at the scene of a homicide, and in refuting testimony by the defendant at the trial that he or she was under the influence of alcohol or drugs at the time of the crime.

Although removal of a blood sample does not violate the privilege against self-incrimination under the Fifth Amendment, another constitutional limitation on the admissibility of this evidence must also be considered. The Fourth Amendment to the U.S. Constitution provides that: "The right of the people to be secure in their persons, houses, papers and effects against unreasonable searches and seizures shall not be violated and no warrants shall issue, but upon probable cause . . . particularly describing the place to be searched and the things or persons to be seized."

Does the insertion of a needle into the arm of an arrestee constitute a "search" within the meaning of the Fourth Amendment? If so, may the search be conducted without a warrant? In *Schmerber,* the Court said the removal of a blood sample was a "search," but that such a search was reasonable within the meaning of the Fourth Amendment. Moreover, said the Court, no warrant was required because of the emergency confronting the officers. The evidence, that is, alcohol in the blood stream, disappears or diminishes in time. A warrant, therefore, is impractical. Thus, if officers arrest a suspect immediately after the commission of a crime and the suspect appears to be under the influence of alcohol, a blood sample can be removed without violating either the Fourth or Fifth Amendments. But if the blood is needed solely to compare for blood type, no emergency exists because the evidence will not disappear. Under these circumstances, officers probably need a search warrant to remove a sample of the accused's blood in order to comply with the Fourth Amendment, even though no Fifth Amendment principle is involved.[20]

Breath Samples As an alternative to the blood test, many states have adopted the use of breathalyzer or, more recently, a gas chromatograph intoximeter.[21] Generally speaking, these instruments record the presence of alcohol in the human body by measuring deep lung air expelled into the machine by the person taking the test. The defendant is asked to breathe air as deeply as possible into a tube which is inserted into the mouth. The air passes into the machine, activates another portion of the instrument which holds an ampoule containing certain chemical ingredients, and this ampoule records electronically the alcoholic content of the defendant's blood. The percentage of alcohol is then printed out on a chart, which is available as evidence at the trial.

In most states, any person whose reading exceeds .10 blood alcohol (weight of alcohol in the defendant's blood) is presumed to be under the influence of alcohol.[22] The prosecutor may offer this evidence as corroboration that the defendant drove a motor vehicle under the influence of alcohol. But do the test and the results constitute a violation of the defendant's privilege not to give evidence against him- or herself?

There is a distinction between removing a sample of blood from arrestees and capturing a sample of breath. In the former process, the sample may be removed from defendants passively; in the latter, however, defendants must cooperate by expelling a sample of breath on demand, thereby actively providing evidence which may incriminate them. The California Supreme Court rejected any distinction between blood and breath tests and, in holding that no constitutional privilege was infringed, said: "It has been urged that the privilege reflects an ultimate sense of fairness that prohibits the state from demanding assistance of any kind from an individual in penal proceedings taken against him. The privilege includes no such prohibition. Criminal proceedings are replete with instances where at least passive cooperation of an accused may be constitutionally required." (*People* v. *Ellis.*)

Moreover, said the court in a later case: "We note that the physical and psychological disturbance of the individual involved in obtaining a breath sample is apt to be significantly less than that involved in extracting a blood sample, . . . and that the blood alcohol test and the breath test for alcoholic absorption are alternate means for determining the percentage of alcohol in the blood. The value of such objective scientific data of intoxication to supplement the fallible observations by humans of behavior seemingly symptomatic of intoxication cannot be disputed. In a day when excessive loss of life and property is caused by inebriated drivers, an imperative need exists for a fair, efficient, and accurate system of detection, enforcement and, hence, prevention." (*People* v. *Sudduth.*)

Not all states admit the results of the breath analysis if the defendant asserts the privilege against self-incrimination. The answer reached by other courts may be ascribed to the presence or absence of an underlying constitutional or statutory right to refuse to produce the physical evidence sought. States that recognize a right to refuse to take such tests exclude evidence of a refusal. States that recognize no right to refuse allow testimony and comment on the refusal.[23]

Urine Samples On reasoning similar to that which admits evidence of the alcoholic content of blood or breath, a urine sample may also be obtained and subsequently analyzed to determine the presence of alcohol in the body. The privilege against self-incrimination is not infringed upon when the defendant provides real or physical evidence, even if such evidence intends to incriminate this person.[24]

Field Sobriety Tests The analysis of a blood, breath, or urine specimen is a scientific measurement of the amount of alcohol in a person's body. The sample is usually obtained, however, after the officers have formed the opinion that a person is under the influence of alcohol. In addition to observing the manner of driving, officers look for other symptoms of intoxication such as bloodshot eyes, thick speech, and slow and deliberate body movements.[25] To corroborate such an opinion, officers may request that drivers walk heel-to-toe on an imaginary line, press their fingers to their noses, and perform other tests of balance and coordination (see Chapter 13, Driving Under the Influence Prosecutions). Do these tests violate the privilege against self-incrimination?

The general rule governing field sobriety tests is as follows: *Evidence obtained by an officer in observing the defendant perform the simple physical exercises required in a field sobriety test does not fall within the protection of the privilege against self-incrimination and is admissible in court. Such tests do not require any "communication," and are considered physical evidence. (Whalen* v. *Municipal Court.)*

Voice Samples Voice samples are often used as a means of identifying suspects. For example: The victim of an assault testifies that while she was waiting for a bus the defendant attempted to attack her. When she rebuffed him, he threatened to use his knife. She saw no knife, but fled, screaming. The defendant ran beside her, repeatedly whispering, "Walk, don't run." When a newsboy appeared on the otherwise deserted street, the defendant disappeared.

The defendant was arrested later and taken to the police department, where the victim tentatively identified him in a lineup as her assailant. The victim also indicated that she could identify her assailant's voice. She was placed in a room next to the interrogation room and the defendant was asked to repeat phrases recited by the police. When he complied, the victim positively identified him. May the defendant exclude such evidence on grounds that the compelled phrase repeated by him violated his privilege against self-incrimination?

The general rule governing voice samples is as follows: *The results of a voice identification test fall within the category of real or physical evidence and do not violate the privilege against self-incrimination. (Gilbert* v. *California.)*

"In such a test, the speaker is asked not to communicate ideas or knowledge of facts, but to engage in the physiological processes necessary to produce a series of articulated sounds, the verbal meanings of which are unimportant. The sounds alone are elicited for identification purposes through characteristics such as pitch, tone, intonation, accent, and word stress. The speech patterns of individuals are distinctive physical characteristics that serve to identify them just as do other physical characteristics such as color of eyes, hair, and skin, physical build and fingerprints.

"Voice identification testimony is the product of an observable physical characteristic made by an independent witness. It is the very type of objective factual evidence, independent of information communicated by the accused, that the privilege encourages police to seek. Moreover, independent identification testimony, unlike testimonial evidence derived from the accused, raises no question of reliance on the veracity of the accused. Any attempt by a suspect to disguise his voice is apt to be detected readily by those persons present who can compare the sample with his normal voice. Furthermore, there is no risk that one could be coerced into falsely accusing himself. It is difficult to imagine how a suspect could be induced to impersonate an unknown voice to incriminate himself. . . .

"A suspect asked to speak for voice identification is not subjected to the same psychological pressures said to be generated by a demand for testimony. It is no more unfair to ask a suspect to speak for voice identification than to ask him to appear in a lineup for visual identification. The psychological pressures are reduced to the same degree, through a limitation of alternatives. Deceit is improbable; the simple choice for a guilty person is between conduct likely to expose incriminating evidence and inferences as to guilt likely to flow from a successful refusal to participate." (*People* v. *Ellis.*)

If the defendant was arrested and questioned, officers will advise him prior to questioning that he has a right to remain silent and anything he says may be used against him. This warning is a restatement of the Fifth Amendment privilege that the defendant need not incriminate himself by his statements. If thereafter the defendant is asked to speak several words for "voice identification," as distinct from incriminating himself by verbal admissions, "he may well contend that he need not speak because of his desire to remain silent; that the warning does not distinguish between speech in terms of communication and speech for voice identification; between a refusal to speak free from sanctions and refusal to speak from which adverse inferences could be drawn. The usual Fifth Amendment warning that a suspect has a right to remain silent creates this problem, for if taken literally it includes the right not to speak at all. After having given such a warning, if the police direct a defendant to speak for voice identification and he refuses, they must, as a prerequisite to the use of the defendant's refusal to speak as evidence of consciousness of guilt, advise him that the right to remain silent does not include the right to refuse to participate in such a test." (*People* v. *Ellis*.)

Handwriting Samples In certain types of prosecutions, a suspect's handwriting is a useful means of identification. For example: The defendant is arrested for forgery and the officer asks him to provide a sample of his handwriting for analysis by an expert witness. At the trial, the witness testifies that he compared the handwriting on the forged check with that supplied by the defendant, and, in the expert's opinion, they are identical. Can the defendant object to the introduction of the sample of his handwriting—which he furnished at police request—on the grounds that his privilege against self-incrimination was violated?

The general rule governing handwriting samples is as follows: *Handwriting samples are not protected by the privilege against self-incrimination. (Gilbert* v. *California.)*

As noted earlier, not every aid that a suspect or defendant is required to give the prosecution violates the privilege against self-incrimination. Yet handwriting samples do differ from other examples of evidence discussed in two respects. First, defendants are required to provide evidence which is not in existence, and must therefore create the evidence themselves. And second, although under the Fifth Amendment suspects can never be compelled to provide documents which might tend to incriminate them, the police request for a handwriting sample closely resembles compulsion to provide a document to be used against the defendant. Note also that the written name, or exemplar, closely parallels a written statement, and statements are clearly protected by the privilege against self-incrimination. Although not all courts agree, most hold that the exemplar represents evidence of identity—albeit through the testimony of an expert—and that one's handwriting can identify a person almost as surely as visual identification. Thus, handwriting samples of the defendant may be sought without violating the Fifth Amendment privilege.[26]

Fingerprints Fingerprints are "real or physical evidence" and do not fall within the privilege against self-incrimination. (*United States* v. *Kelly*.)

Hair Samples Removal of a sample of hair while the defendant is in custody constitutes real or physical evidence and does not violate the privilege against self-incrimination as long as no unreasonable force is applied. (*Grimes* v. *United States.*) Good practice suggests requesting that the defendant massage his or her head and comb it over a sheet of paper with a new comb provided by the officer.

Identification by Means of Clothing The victim of a crime may attempt to identify a person in a variety of ways: by voice, by facial features, by gait, by stance, by facial hair, by eyeglasses, or by distinctive physical characteristics. In some cases, the ability to identify a person may be improved if the arrestee wears clothes identical to those described by the victim at the scene of the crime. Officers may request that a suspect remove the clothes provided by jail authorities and don his or her original clothing to determine if the victim can identify the arrestee. The privilege against self-incrimination does not protect a suspect against such a request. If the victim identifies the defendant dressed in the original clothes, the testimony is admissible. (*Gilbert* v. *California.*)

Lineups Not infrequently, investigating officers compose a lineup of several people to determine if the victim can identify someone in the line. An arrestee has no right to refuse to participate in a lineup and may be compelled to do so. During the lineup, the suspect may be asked to assume a certain stance, to repeat a gesture, to turn and walk, or to speak several words. None of these acts are testimonial evidence and, consequently, they do not violate the privilege against self-incrimination. (*Gilbert* v. *California.*)

Refusal to Submit to Requests for Physical Evidence

The U.S. Supreme Court has held that, in order to fully protect the defendant's privilege against self-incrimination, the prosecution may not introduce evidence that the defendant refused to answer questions asked by police officers at the time of arrest. Silence or denials by an accused in the face of police questioning cannot be introduced at the trial as an admission of guilt or as evidence of consciousness of guilt. To introduce such evidence would improperly allow adverse inferences to be drawn from the defendant's rightful exercise of the Fifth Amendment right to remain silent.[27]

However, if the evidence offered is "real or physical" evidence, and therefore not included within the privilege against self-incrimination, evidence of a refusal may be admitted. Under this interpretation of the Fifth Amendment, if the defendant refused to submit to a blood, breath, or urine test, or refused to submit to any of the other requests for "real or physical" evidence, such refusal is circumstantial evidence of consciousness of guilt, and its admission does not violate the privilege. As expressed by one court: "Although conduct indicating consciousness of guilt is often described as an 'admission by conduct,' such nomenclature should not obscure the fact that guilty conduct is not a testimonial statement of guilt. It is therefore not protected by the Fifth Amendment. By acting like a guilty person, a man does not testify to his guilt but merely exposes himself to the drawing of inferences from circumstantial evidence of his state of mind. . . . Evidence of the refusal is not only probative; its admission operates to induce suspects to cooperate with law enforcement officials. . . . Without exception, none of the reasons that support the privilege lends support to a rule that would exclude probative evidence obtained from an accused's effort to conceal non-privileged evidence." (*People* v. *Ellis*.)

Except in cases involving voice identification, investigating officers can prepare suitable forms, often with the help of prosecutors, to advise arrestees that they have no right to refuse to submit a sample of "real or physical evidence," and that a refusal to submit may be used as evidence against them in a further criminal proceeding. Note, however, that suspects do have a right to refuse to answer questions which will elicit statements from them, and such refusal will not be admissible in court. Only the voice identification issue poses a problem in that respect.

Compulsion to Provide Real or Physical Evidence

As noted earlier, a suspect under arrest has no right to refuse to provide real or physical evidence, because such evidence is not protected by the Fifth Amendment. When a suspect does refuse to comply with a request for such evidence, officers have two alternatives: they may respect the request and not require submission for the purpose of obtaining a sample of real or physical evidence, or they may compel the defendant to submit by force. Although the application of force to secure real or physical evidence may not violate the privilege against self-incrimination, another constitutional limitation on the admissibility of evidence, the Due Process Clause, may prevent the use of brutality.

For example: A deputy sheriff testified that he and two other deputies entered the defendant's bedroom after having forced the bedroom door open. The defendant was inside. "Two capsules, which were wrapped in cellophane, were on a small table therein. [One of the deputies] stated to the defendant, 'Whose stuff is this?' Defendant then grabbed the capsules and put them in his mouth. [The deputy] testified that at that moment the other deputies jumped upon the defendant, grabbed him by the throat, and began to squeeze his throat in an effort to eject the capsules from his mouth; that force was applied to this throat; . . . that [the deputy] put his fingers in the defendant's mouth; and they put handcuffs on the defendant while he was in the room. [The deputy] then took the defendant to a hospital and into the operating room there. A doctor's assistant strapped the handcuffed defendant to the operating table. . . . A doctor placed an empty pail by the defendant, placed 'a tube down the defendant's throat,' and released a white chemical solution into the tube and into the defendant's stomach. The defendant vomited into the pail, and two capsules in cellophane floated in the pail. The deputy took the capsules from the pail and delivered them to a chemist in the sheriff's office.'' (*People* v. *Rochin.*) The chemist testified that the contents of the capsules contained a residue of contraband.

In the landmark case of *Rochin* v. *California,* The U.S. Supreme Court said: ''To attempt in this case to distinguish 'real evidence' from 'verbal evidence' is to ignore the reasons for excluding coerced confessions. Use of involuntary verbal confessions in state criminal trials is constitutionally obnoxious not only because of their unreliability. They are inadmissible under the Due Process Clause of the Fourteenth Amendment to the United States Constitution, even though statements contained in them may be independently true. Coerced confessions offend the community's sense of fair play and decency. So here, to sanction the brutal conduct which naturally enough was condemned by a court whose judgment is before us, would be to afford brutality the cloak of law. Nothing would be more calculated to discredit law and thereby to brutalize the temper of a society.''

Thus, even though officers may compel the defendant to provide real or physical evidence, the *Rochin* case limits the application of force which may be used on a suspect as a matter of due process under the Due Process Clause. Evidence seized in a brutal manner from an arrestee will be excluded from evidence and will be inadmissible against the defendant. The application of this due process limitation varies, but common illustrations will be examined on the following pages.

Choking Cases Because of the ease with which narcotics and drugs may be concealed, destroyed, or discarded, officers must move quickly and decisively in apprehending those suspected of possessing narcotic contraband. The most frequent response by such suspects to the approach of officers is to insert the drugs quickly into the mouth and swallow the materials. In *Rochin,* the officers attempted to retrieve the swallowed evidence after the fact. Because of the obvious difficulties of this technique, officers frequently attempt to prevent a suspect from swallowing the contraband by means of choking.

But the courts have condemned the use of choking to secure evidence. Choking a person to extract evidence from the mouth violates due process. Nor does it seem to make any difference how hard the person is choked or for how long. One case says, ''The question, however, is not how hard an officer may choke a suspect to obtain evidence but whether he may choke him at all.'' (*People* v. *Martinez.*) Under this rule, a choke hold that may stop the blood flow to the head so that the person passes out was said to be illegal.

A suspect has no constitutional right to destroy evidence, and a police officer does not have to stand idly by while contraband is disposed of. Not every display of force by an officer is unreasonable. That the suspect physically resists or does not consent is not enough, in and of itself, to create or constitute illegality on the part of officers. As one case put it, the courts are "concerned with condemning the excessive force executed upon the individual rather than making the 'mouth' a sacred orifice into which contraband may be placed and thereafter disposed of in leisurely fashion. Although we agree that physical evidence, like verbal confessions, may not be 'tortured' from the lips of the accused, it does not follow that merely because a suspect has placed a substance behind his lips, he necessarily is entitled to cry 'sanctuary' when an officer of the law, under appropriate circumstances, directs him to surrender it." (*People* v. *Bass.*)

It is proper to order a suspect to spit out the substance, and it is proper for an officer to put an arm around the defendant's neck and tell him or her to spit it out, since if a suspect spits out the narcotic voluntarily, the evidence will not be excluded.

Although the cases condemn choking, a variety of holds in the neck area have been permitted. In general, what seems to be allowed is a hold which prevents swallowing but permits breathing. In one case, the officer pressed the suspect's head forward and downward, to the end that he could not swallow. In another case, officers placed their fingers over the defendant's Adam's apple to prevent swallowing. In still another case, the officer placed his hand on the defendant's throat, pushed sideways on the neck with his thumb, and told the suspect to spit—which he did almost immediately.

The officer who uses an ingenious hold to "prevent swallowing" runs a risk. He or she must convince the judge that limited force was used, and the judge may reconcile any doubts in favor of the defendant's story. The line the courts have drawn may not be a clear one, and officers who become involved in activity in the neck area may open themselves to a risk that the wrong label will be put upon their actions. Thus, officers who use an "approved" technique could well find themselves losing a case in spite of this.

Because the case will be decided in court, the nature of the officer's testimony, as well as that of the officer's conduct in the field, will influence the outcome. It is not enough to act properly when seizing the evidence. It is important to duplicate in court, accurately and fully, what occurred at the time of arrest to enable the trier of fact to determine the validity of the police conduct.

As mentioned earlier, police officers may act properly in the field by holding a defendant's neck and telling the person to spit out evidence. If, however, officers testify in court that they "choked" a defendant, they may lose the case. Obviously the word "choked" should not be employed unless there really was choking. Officers can help to remove the specter of choking by describing the defendant's ability to breathe and speak while the hold was being applied, and by testifying to the duration of the hold. Officers can also describe the degree of force used by the suspect—that is, what the suspect was doing to the officer. If possible, officers should also try to make clear that they were not unduly aggressive and did not use force more than they had to.

Blood Samples Even though removal of a blood sample does not violate the privilege against self-incrimination, does the Due Process Clause prohibit such conduct? In *Breithaupt* v. *Abram,* the defendant was charged with involuntary manslaughter. Evidence was introduced which established that his car had struck another vehicle, killing one of the occupants. The defendant was rendered unconscious and taken to a hospital where a doctor removed a blood sample; analysis of the blood established that the defendant had been driving under the influence of alcohol at the time of the accident. In rejecting the defendant's contention that the removal of a blood sample constituted a violation of the *Rochin* rule of due process, the U.S. Supreme Court said: ''Basically the distinction rests on the fact that there is nothing 'brutal' or 'offensive' in the taking of a sample of blood when done, as in this case, under the protective eye of a physician. To be sure, the driver here was unconscious when the blood was taken, but the absence of conscious consent, without more, does not necessarily render the taking a violation of a constitutional right; and certainly the test as administered here would not be considered offensive by even the most delicate. Furthermore, due process is not measured by the yardstick of personal reaction or the [repugnance] of the mot sensitive person, but by that whole community sense of 'decency and fairness' that has been woven by common experience into the fabric of acceptable conduct. It is on this bedrock that this Court has established the concept of due process.'' But the Court added: ''This is not to say that the indiscriminate taking of blood under different conditions, or by those not competent to do so may not amount to such 'brutality' as would come under the *Rochin* rule.''

Whether the sample was removed from a conscious or unconscious person is immaterial. The U.S. Supreme Court later reaffirmed its original opinion that removal of a blood sample in a medically approved manner does not violate due process. (*Schmerber* v. *California.*)

Although the phrase ''the use of *unreasonable* force and violence to obtain a blood sample'' is necessarily vague, some boundaries can be outlined. For example: Officers arrested the defendant for driving under the influence of alcohol and transported him to the hospital. After arriving at the hospital, the defendant refused to provide a blood sample. The following testimony by the officer ensued:

Q: (By the deputy district attorney) What did you do? Then what happened?

A: We took hold of the defendant's arms, attempted to place him on the bed, were unsuccessful, fell to the floor, and he was then placed on the floor, face down—mostly face down, and I held his right arm up and [the doctor] drew the sample.

Q: And he drew it from the right arm?

A: As I recall, it was the inside of the right arm.

Q: All right, and where was your fellow officer while you were doing all this?

A: He was assisting me in placing [the defendant] on the floor.

Q: Did [your partner] have hold of any portion of [defendant's] body at this time?

A: As I recall, he had a hold of his other arm and was across his legs, or slightly under his legs, actually.

Q: And, how did you have his right arm, and hold him in position for the doctor—could you describe, or tell us?

A: I had him face down with his right arm tilted back—brought back up and turned to the inside—palm toward the back of his head—the palm of his hand toward the back of his head . . .

Further elaboration of the means used to take the blood was obtained upon cross-examination as follows:

Q: Each of you had one arm, initially?

A: Initially, we grabbed his arms as he sat in the chair, then we put his arm over the—a little table, for the Doctor to work on, and he—he started to submit. At that point the Doctor approached him, and he withdrew his arm, but he didn't initially withdraw his arm. I don't recall whether or not the Doctor actually got the needle in at that point, but he started to submit and then he again refused. We then placed him on the ground and held him physically while the Doctor withdrew the sample.

Q: Now you say "placed him on the ground." You in fact twisted his arms and knocked him to the floor?

A: We didn't twist his arms and knock him to the floor, but we did have a hold of his arms and we did go to the floor. But it wasn't a knocking motion on his part; we fell . . .

Q: All right. And then you indicated he was mostly—mostly prone—mostly on his face?

A: Yes, Sir.

Q: On the floor?

A: Yes, Sir.

Q: And you twisted, you think it was his right arm?

A: I believe so.

Q: Behind his back?

A: I believe so.

Q: And you think the Doctor took the blood from the—for want of a better term, the interior of the elbow, or near the elbow?

A: In that vicinity, yes, sir . . .

Q: . . . At the time that you were holding his arm behind his back, were you in a kneeling position on the floor, or a sitting position, or what?
A: I was crouched.
Q: You were crouched?
A: I was crouched.
Q: On your feet—were you kneeling on him, by any chance? Did you have your body on [the defendant].
A: Yeah—yeah. I have some recollection, but I don't recall specifically. . . .
Q: But you were—what direction were you facing? Were you watching . . .
A: Facing [defendant] and watching his head. (*People* v. *Kraft.*)

Was such force reasonable? Courts could differ on whether the officers acted with unwarranted force or whether the force was reasonable because of the defendant's belligerence and resistance to the test. From the prosecutor's standpoint, the actual results of the chemical test are very helpful in evaluating the strength of the prosecution case. Yet a *refusal* to take a test is also admissible as evidence and the prosecutor can comment on that refusal as evidence of a consciousness of guilt.

Rectal Searches The courts have recognized that persons who deal in narcotics will attempt to conceal them in body cavities such as the rectum. In California, a rectal examination conducted in a medically approved manner by a doctor has been sustained by the court. Several federal cases allow such a search at the border if there is a clear indication that the person may have narcotics secreted in this manner.

Emetics The leading U.S. Supreme Court case on brutality, *Rochin,* relied in part for the finding of illegality on the fact that stomach pumping—the forcible extraction of stomach contents—occurred. But stomach contents can also be extracted by the use of emetics, which induce involuntary regurgitation. For example: "On March 10, 1972, a field supervisor for the California Bureau of Narcotic Enforcement, acting on knowledge gained from two confidential informants and from observations made by himself and by other agents, procured a warrant authorizing the search of the residence of defendant and her husband, their vehicles and their persons.

"On the morning of March 15, 1972, an agent who was participating in the search observed defendant enter one of the cars described in the warrant. . . . [The agent] maneuvered his vehicle in front of defendant's car and . . . approached the defendant's automobile. Defendant looked directly at [him] and immediately thereafter put her car in reverse and accelerated backwards. [The agent] observed the defendant reach down with her right hand toward the seat of the automobile and, when the hand reappeared, rapidly placed two balloons in her mouth and swallow them. As defendant's car continued backwards, [he] saw the defendant make two more quick hand movements, each time apparently placing more objects into her mouth.

"Defendant was apprehended a short distance away by other agents. After a struggle, she was removed from her car, handcuffed and advised of her constitutional rights. She was driven to her residence where the agents conducted a search of the house. Approximately 20 minutes later she was transported to a local hospital for the purpose of retrieving through medical methods the objects which [the agent] had observed defendant swallowing.

"At the hospital [the agent] exhibited the search warrant to the attending physician of the emergency section, told the latter that the warrant authorized a search of defendant's person, and requested that the stomach be pumped. The doctor ordered two nurses to prepare an emetic solution known as Syrup of Ipecac. After defendant refused to drink the liquid, she was forced to her back on a table and the two nurses prepared to strap her down. Defendant, whose hands were handcuffed behind her back, strenuously resisted and a struggle ensued. The nurses eventually put a strap across her chest and knees. Defendant continued to kick and struggle.

"Because of anticipated difficulty in forcing defendant to swallow the liquid, the nurses inserted a rubber tube through one of defendant's nostrils and down into her esophagus, planning to use the tube to administer the emetic directly into defendant's stomach. Defendant's continued physical resistance, however, caused the tube to move about and prevented the nurses from administering the liquid. After about five minutes of repeated but unsuccessful attempts, defendant said that the tube was 'too painful' and agreed to drink the emetic. Shortly thereafter she regurgitated seven multicolored balloons which later proved to contain heroin. She continued vomiting for approximately 10 minutes and remained nauseous for approximately an additional quarter of an hour.

"It was stipulated by counsel that if the attending physician was called to testify he would state that he ordered the emetic because of the warrant which he understood authorized the search and that absent a search warrant he would not force a patient to regurgitate over objections." (*People* v. *Bracamonte*.)

Because the evidence was physical rather than verbal, the defendant could not invoke the Fifth Amendment privilege against self-incrimination. But the intrusion into the human body is a "search" within the meaning of the Fourth Amendment and as such must be supported by probable cause. The warrant in this case did not command a search of the "inside" of the person; therefore, the search could not be sustained on that ground. A warrantless search could only be lawful if an emergency existed, that is, in order to save the defendant's life. Absent any testimony by a doctor that an emetic was necessary to save the defendant's life, no emergency existed. Nor could the search be incidental to a lawful arrest unless there was a clear indication that the evidence would disappear or be destroyed. "Thus, not only must there be more than probable cause to believe that contraband will be found inside the body, but to justify a search incident to a lawful arrest, there must also be the need to prevent the arrested person from obtaining a weapon or destroying evidence. Here, although there was a 'clear indication' that the defendant probably swallowed balloons of heroin, unlike the blood-alcohol cases where 'the rapid dissipation of the alcohol would make the delay involved in obtaining a search warrant unnecessary and unjustifiable,' there was no substantial reason to believe that evidence would be destroyed. 'The testimony further disclosed that objects such as that swallowed by defendant may pass completely through the digestive tract, by the ordinary processes of nature, without causing any ill effects. The rubber container would effectively prevent the contents from being absorbed into the system.' It thus appears that defendant in the instant case easily could have been transported to jail and placed in an isolation cell and kept under proper surveillance.

"We are mindful of the Supreme Court's warning in *Schmerber* that '(t)he integrity of an individual's person is a cherished value of our society. That we today hold that the Constitution does not forbid the States minor intrusions into an individual's body under stringently limited conditions in no way indicates that it permits more substantial intrusions, or intrusions under other conditions. We cannot but conclude that the forceful placing of a tube into the nostrils and down the esophagus of defendant which by reason of the pain inflicted upon her coerced her to agree to swallow the emetic, and the consequent regurgitation were more than a 'minor intrusion into an individual's body' and that the high statistical probability that the balloons would 'pass through' constituted a condition other than the emergency situation in *Schmerber*." (*People* v. *Bracamonte*.)

As we have seen, brutal conduct is forbidden under the Due Process Clause of the Fourteenth Amendment, as well as under the search and seizure provisions of the Fourth Amendment. The following strict conditions are necessary to justify removal of contraband from inside the body:

1. A lawful arrest;

2. More than probable cause to believe contraband will be found inside the body;

3. A substantial reason to believe the evidence will be destroyed; or,

4. An emergency: defined as a hazard posing potential or serious injury to the defendant's life; or,

5. Consent freely given; or,

6. A search warrant, supported by more than probable cause to believe that contraband is present inside the body and reciting:
a. A need to prevent the destruction of evidence;

b. An order commanding the test be performed by a physician under medically approved conditions;
c. No reasonable alternative to the use of the emetic.

The Requirement of Personal Knowledge

Assuming that a witness is competent to testify and that no privilege is likely to be invoked to prevent the testimony, the prosecution must also establish that the witness had personal knowledge of the facts which he or she will relate. The witness must have a present recollection of an impression derived from the exercise of his or her own senses. Even if a witness testifies to seeing a particular event or hearing a distinctive sound, numerous questions will be asked on cross-examination to test the strength of the recollection. Questions which may be asked are: whether the witness observed the act from start to finish, or observed only part of the act; the location of the witness at the time of the observation; any obstruction which might have impaired vision; whether the observation was made while the witness was standing still or moving; whether the witness was under any stress at the time of the observation; whether he or she was a victim of the crime or a witness; and the ability to recall the presence or absence of others in the area. But in any event, the witness must testify to what he or she observed rather than to the observations of another person.

A witness must also testify to facts and avoid conclusions and opinions. If an officer testifies that the "defendant saw me and started to run," he is concluding that the defendant in fact saw and recognized him. Although such a conclusion may be entirely valid, the laws of evidence require that a witness testify to facts—not opinions or conclusions. Correctly stated, the testimony should be: "The defendant looked in my direction, our eyes appeared to make contact, he turned immediately and ran." These are facts—not conclusions.

The law does allow some witnesses to testify to opinions and conclusions. A witness with special training, education, and expertise may express an opinion on the significance of certain evidence. As stated by one court: "The decisive consideration in determining the admissibility of expert opinion evidence is whether the subject of inquiry is one of such common knowledge that men of ordinary education could reach a conclusion as intelligently as the witness or whether, on the other hand, the matter is sufficiently beyond common experience that the opinion of an expert would assist the trier of fact." (*People* v. *Jenkins.*)

"The chief value of an expert's testimony rests upon the material from which his opinion is fashioned and the reasoning behind which he progresses from the material to his conclusion. . . . It does not lie in his mere expression of conclusion." (*Carter* v. *United States.*)

Expert testimony is most frequently used in the following:

1. Driving under the influence of alcohol offenses: Chemist's testimony that a person is under the influence of alcohol, with a specific blood alcohol level.

2. Narcotics offenses: Officer's testimony that the material seized was marijuana, heroin, cocaine, etc.

3. Narcotics offenses: Officer's testimony that the defendant was under the influence of an opiate.

4. Narcotics offenses: Officer's testimony that the material seized was possessed for the purpose of sale (a more serious offense than mere possession).

5. Narcotics offenses: Chemist's testimony that the material examined by him or her was heroin, cocaine, etc.

6. Homicide prosecutions: Coroner's testimony concerning the cause of death.

7. Homicide prosecutions: Testimony by a psychiatrist concerning the defendant's sanity.

8. Arson prosecutions: Expert's testimony concerning the cause of the fire.

9. Weapons cases: Expert's testimony concerning the operability of the weapon and the result of ballistics tests to determine whether shells were fired from a particular weapon.

10. Writings: The testimony of a witness comparing a known sample of handwriting with an unknown sample.

11. Fingerprints: Testimony by a witness comparing a known sample with an unknown sample.

12. Burglary prosecutions: Officer's testimony that certain tools are used for burglary.

13. Bookmaking cases: Opinion by a witness as to the significance of certain letters, numbers, or symbols indicating a gambling operation.

14. Rape cases: Testimony by a medical doctor concerning injuries to the person and the presence or absence of sperm in the victim.

15. Voice identification: Opinion by a witness comparing a known sample with an unknown sample (not yet accepted in some states).

CASES AND MATERIALS

Beck v. *Ohio* (1964), 379 U.S. 89, 85 S. Ct. 223, 13 L. Ed. 2d 142.

Blau v. *United States* (1951), 340 U.S. 332, 71 S. Ct. 301, 95 L. Ed. 306.

Breithaupt v. *Abram,* 352 U.S. 432, 77 S. Ct. 408, 1 L. Ed. 2d 448.

Carter v. *United States,* 252 F. 2d 608.

Eleazer v. *Supreme Court,* 1 C. 3d 847, 83 Cal. R. 586, 464 P. 2d 42.

Frye v. *United States,* 293 F. 1013.

Gilbert v. *California* (1967), 388 U.S. 263, 87 S. Ct. 1826, 18 L. Ed. 2d 1178.

Grimes v. *United States,* 405 F. 2d 477.

Hawkins v. *United States* (1958), 358 U.S. 74, 79 S. Ct. 136, 3 L. Ed. 2d 125.

Jencks v. *United States* (1957), 353 U.S. 657, 1. L. Ed. 2d 1103, 77 S. Ct. 1007.

Kastigar v. *United States* (1972), 406 U.S. 441, 92 S. Ct. 1653, 32 L. Ed. 2d 212.

People v. *Acuna,* 35 Cal. App. 3d 987, 111 Cal. R. 878.

People v. *Allen,* 41 Cal. App. 3d 196, 115 Cal. R. 839.

People v. *Bass,* 214 C. 2d 742, 29 Cal. R. 778.

People v. *Bracamonte,* 15 C. 3d 394, 124 Cal. R. 528, 540 P. 2d 624.

People v. *Durazo,* 52 C. 2d 354, 340 P. 2d 594.

People v. *Ellis,* 65 C. 2d 529, 55 Cal. R. 385, 421 P. 2d 393.

People v. *Garcia,* 67 C. 2d 830, 64 Cal. R. 110, 484 P. 2d 366.

People v. *Jenkins,* 13 C. 3d 749, 119 Cal. R. 705, 532 P. 2d 857.

People v. *Kiihoa,* 53 C. 2d 748, 3 Cal. R. 1, 349 P. 2d 673.

People v. *Kraft,* 3 Cal. App. 3d 890, 84 Cal. R. 280.

Peeple v. *Lawrence,* 149 Cal. App. 2d 435, 308 P. 2d 821.

People v. *Martinez,* 130 Cal. App. 2d 54, 278 P. 2d 26.

People v. *Rochin,* 101 Cal App. 2d 140, 225 P. 2d 1.

People v. *Smith,* 13 C. 3d 897, 91 Cal. R. 786.

People v. *Sudduth,* 65 C. 2d 543, 55 Cal. R. 393, 421 P. 2d 401.

People v. *Superior Court* [Biggs], 19 Cal. App. 3d 522, 97 Cal. R. 118.

People v. *Williams,* 71 C. 2d 614, 79 Cal. R. 65, 465 P. 2d 633.

Rochin v. *California,* 342 U.S. 165, 96 L. Ed. 154, 72 S. Ct. 205.

Schmerber v. *California,* 384 U.S. 757, 16 L. Ed. 2d 908, 86 S. Ct. 1826.

United States v. *Kelly,* 55 F. 2d 67.

United States v. *Reynolds* (1953), 235 U.S. 1, 73 S. Ct. 528, 97 L. Ed. 727.

United States v. *Sample,* 378 Fed. Supp. 43.

United States v. *Wade* (1967), 388 U.S. 218, 87 S. Ct. 1926, 18 L. Ed. 2d 1149.

Whalen v. *Municipal Court,* 274 Cal. App. 2d 813, 79 Cal. R. 508.

Worley v. *State,* 263 So. 2d 613 (Florida).

1. The defendant was arrested and charged with possession of marijuana. While in custody, he telephoned his wife and made incriminating statements to her over the telephone. Unknown to the defendant, police officers monitored and recorded the conversation. Can this tape recording be played to the jury?

(a) Can the defendant object to introducing the conversation because of the privilege preventing disclosure of communications during marriage? Who holds the privilege?

(b) Was the conversation held in confidence? If a police officer stood in the defendant's immediate presence, would such fact evidence a waiver of the privilege?

(c) If either of the parties was aware that the conversation was being monitored, would this fact indicate a waiver of the privilege?

(d) Can the defendant reasonably expect a right of privacy for "confidential" marital communications in jail?

(e) Can the prosecutor call the defendant's wife as a witness to establish the validity of the marriage and require that she present evidence thereof before she can claim the privilege?

(f) Does monitoring and taping the telephone conversation by state police officers violate the provisions of the federal law prohibiting wiretapping? Material relevant to this issue is provided below.

Omnibus Crime Control and Safe Streets Act, 18 U.S. Code, Sections 2510 and 2520.

Section 2511 provides in subdivision (1): "Except as otherwise specifically provided in this chapter any person who—(a) willfully intercepts . . . any wire or oral communication; (b) willfully uses . . . any electronic, mechanical, or other device to intercept any oral communication . . . (c) willfully discloses . . . to any other person the contents of any wire or oral communication, knowing or having reason to know that the information was obtained through the interception of a wire or oral communication in violation of this subsection; or (d) willfully uses . . . the contents of any wire or oral communication, knowing or having reason to know that the information was obtained through the interception of a wire or oral communication in violation of this subsection; shall be fined not more than $10,000 or imprisoned not more than five years, or both."

In the Senate Report on the Omnibus Crime Control and Safe Streets Act of 1968 (Senate Committee on the Judiciary, Omnibus Crime Control and Safe Streets Act of 1968, Sen. Rep. No. 1097, 90th Cong., Second Sess. (1968) [hereinafter cited as Senate Report]) section 2511 was explained in part as follows: "Section 2511 of the new chapter prohibits, except as otherwise specifically provided in the chapter itself, the interception and disclosure of all wire or oral communications. Paragraph (1) sets out several prohibitions. Subparagraph (a) prohibits the interception itself. This eliminates the requirement under existing law that an 'interception' and a 'divulgence' must take place.'' See *Massicot* v. *United States,* 254 F. 2d 58; *Benanti* v. *United States* (1957), 355 U.S. 96, 2 L. Ed. 2d 126, 78 S. Ct. 1550.

Subparagraph (a) establishes a blanket prohibition against the interception of any wire communication. Since the facilities used to transmit wire communications form part of the interstate or foreign communications network, Congress has plenary power under the commerce clause to prohibit all interceptions of such communications, whether by wiretapping or otherwise. See *Weiss* v. *United States* (1939), 308 U.S. 321, 84 L. Ed. 298, 60 S. Ct. 269.

In the Senate Report, ''wire communication'' was defined ''to include all communications carried by a common carrier, in whole or in part, through our Nation's communications network.'' The coverage is intended to be comprehensive. (Sen. Rep., p. 89.)

Section 2515 provides: ''Whenever any wire or oral communication has been intercepted, no part of the contents of such communication and no evidence derived therefrom may be received in evidence in any trial, hearing, or other proceeding in or before any court, grand jury, department, officer, agency, regulatory body, legislative committee, or other authority of the United States, a State, or a political subdivision thereof if the disclosure of that information would be in violation of this chapter.'' (See also Sen. Rep., p. 96.)

2. The defendant was arrested and charged with murder, and following this, his wife visited him in the jail during visitor hours. The detective in charge of the investigation, whose office was in the same building, led the wife to his office to visit with the defendant. Leaving the husband and wife alone, the detective left the room and closed the door. He began to secretly monitor and tape-record the conversation between the husband and wife. At the trial, the prosecutor offers the tape recording of the conversation, which includes incriminating statements.

(a) Has the detective provided a place where, by his conduct in withdrawing from his own office and leaving the parties alone together, they could reasonably expect their communications would be ''confidential''?

(b) Could the defendant object on the grounds that the ''search''—recording the conversation—violated his rights of privacy, as protected by the Fourth Amendment? (*Lanza* v. *New York* 370 U.S. 139, 8 L. Ed. 2d 384, 82 S. Ct. 1218; *North* v. *Superior Court,* 8 C. 3d 301, 104 Cal. R. 833, 502 P. 2d 1305.)

3. In a burglary prosecution, the People call the defendant's wife as a witness to testify that she saw the defendant hiding undetermined items under the house, and that the defendant returned to the house and handed her jewelry which later was identified as stolen. The defendant told her he had just hidden jewelry under the house and that the jewelry he had given her earlier was stolen. The communications were confidential and between husband and wife during the course of a valid marriage. Can the wife testify to her observation of the husband-defendant's conduct as well as to receiving the jewelry itself from the defendant? (*People* v. *Bradford,* 70 C. 2d 333, 74 Cal. R. 726, 450 P. 2d 46.)

4. Defendant is charged with forgery and the prosecutor seeks to link him to the crime by proving that the defendant's wife had cashed the check. The wife, through counsel, informs the court that she will exercise her privilege not to testify against her husband and asks the court to quash the subpoena compelling her appearance. The prosecution contends that the privilege must in fact be exercised before the court can rule on the privilege. The court agrees, the witness is subpoenaed, and she is sworn as a witness and exercises her privilege. She is excused, and a prosecution witness then identifies the wife as the person who cashed the check. Without the wife's compelled presence in court, the witness could not have identified her, thereby linking the defendant to the crime. Is this procedure a violation of the marital privilege? (*People* v. *Villarino,* 7 Cal. App. 3d 56, 86 Cal. R. 338.)

5. "A hardtop sports car, travelling at high speed, crossed the double line and struck another car head on. Occupants of the sports car were defendant, his four-year-old son, and X, who owned the car. The boy and X were thrown from the car by the impact. When the car came to rest, defendant was unconscious. The upper portion of his body was hanging outside the car on the right (the driver's seat was on the left), but his feet were wedged between the gear shift lever and the seat. A pair of sunglasses lay on the pavement beneath his head. Defendant and X were seriously injured, and the latter died in the hospital to which he was taken from the scene. A motorist who had seen the sports car before the accident identified the driver as wearing sunglasses and a distinctive shirt matching that seen on defendant immediately after the collision. Two doctors testified that X's injuries were consistent with his having been thrown against the steering wheel, and those of defendant of the type which would be sustained by the passenger. But another physician expressed a contrary opinion."

Samples of blood were taken from both the defendant and X shortly after the accident, although officers could not establish at that time who was the driver of the car. By subsequent investigation, the prosecution was able to establish that the defendant was driving. Can the defendant object to the admissibility of the results of the blood sample (which showed a high alcoholic content in his blood) on the ground that he had not been arrested at the time of the accident? (*People* v. *Bustons,* 247 Cal. App. 2d 422, 55 Cal. R. 603.)

6. For other cases involving compulsion to submit to physical evidence, see: *People* v. *Matteson,* 61 C. 2d 466, 39 Cal. R. 1, 393, P. 2d 161; *Blefare* v. *United States,* 362 F. 2d 870 (Emetic). For a case holding that forcibly obtaining a breath sample does not violate the privilege against self-incrimination, see: *State* v. *Berg,* 76 Ariz. 96, 259 P. 2d 261.

7. In prosecutions for resisting arrest or assault on a police officer, the defendant may attempt to locate the names of persons who have complained to the police department about the arresting officer's use of force and violence against them on previous occasions. Most police departments conduct investigations of citizen complaints against their personnel and keep records of interviews with concerned parties.

Can the prosecution assert a privilege held by a police agency not to disclose the results of an internal investigation of their own department? If not, would the evidence sought be admissible to attack the credibility of the officer-victim? Would the evidence be admissible as independent evidence of the officer's character traits of force and violence? Is such evidence limited to opinion testimony, or may specific acts of misconduct be established? See *Pitchess* v. *Superior Court,* 11 C. 3d 531, 113 Cal. R. 897, 522 P. 2d 305.

8. Motor vehicles are identified by license number, registration number, and vehicle identification number (VIN). A VIN number is normally attached to the door post of the vehicle and enables officers to identify the owner if the license plates are missing and no registration is found in the vehicle. Although these VIN numbers can be removed, a second VIN number is stamped at a secret location on the vehicle. Auto theft investigators are familiar with the location of the number, but the general public is not.

In a trial for grand theft auto, the defendant asks the officer-witness for the location of the secret VIN number to establish registration of the vehicle. The witness refuses to disclose the location, claiming the need for secrecy to facilitate auto theft investigations. Is the official information privilege properly invoked? (*In Re David W.,* 62 Cal. App. 3d 840.)

9. Some enforcement agencies use an intoxilyzer to determine blood alcohol. The subject's breath is captured in a metal chamber, and infrared energy of fixed intensity and wave length is passed through the chamber from one side to a photoelectric cell on the other side. Alcohol absorbs light of the fixed wave length. The device computes the loss of energy, translates the result in terms of the grams of alcohol per 100 milliliters of blood, and prints the result upon a card. In the prescribed operation of the device, clear air is first tested, then the breath of the subject. The chamber is then purged by blowing clear air through it, the clear air is tested, and all three results appear upon the printout card. The two tests of clear air constitute a test of the machine, and should show zero alcohol content. It is apparent that no test result, save the printout card, is available for preservation.

If no sample can be preserved for later retesting, is the defendant's right to a fair trial impaired? (*United States* v. *Bryant,* 439 F. 2d 642.)

NOTES

1. A sample examination can be found in *People* v. *McIntyre,* 256 Cal. App. 2d 894, 64 Cal. R. 530.
2. California Evidence Code, Section 910.
3. Uniform Rules of Evidence, Rule 26(1)(c); California Penal Code Section 636: "Every person who, without permission from all parties to the conversation, eavesdrops on or records by means of an electronic or other device, a conversation or any portion thereof, between a person who is in the physical custody of a law enforcement officer or other public officer, or who is on the property of a law enforcement agency or other public agency, and such person's attorney, religious advisor, or licensed physician, is guilty of a felony; provided, however, the provisions of this section shall not apply to any employee of a public utility engaged in the business of providing service and facilities for

telephone or telegraph communications while engaged in the construction, maintenance, conduct, or operation of the services or facilities of such public utility who listens in to such conversations for the limited purpose of testing or servicing such equipment.''

4. California Evidence Code, Section 994.
5. Uniform Rules of Evidence, Rule 215(a).
6. Uniform Rules of Evidence, Rule 29.
7. Evidence Code, Section 1032.
8. California Evidence Code, Section 1040.
9. *Jencks* v. *United States,* 350 U.S. 980, 76 S. Ct. 467, 100 L. Ed. 849; *Alderman* v. *United States* (1969), 394 U.S. 165, 22 L. Ed. 2d 176, 89 S. Ct. 961. For a statutory *in camera* (in chambers) proceeding, see Evidence Code, Section 915: ''(a) . . . The presiding officer may not require disclosure of information claimed to be privileged in order to rule on the claim of privilege. (b) When a court is ruling on a claim of privilege (official information or identity of informer) . . . and is unable to do so without requiring disclosure of the information claimed to be privileged, the court may require the person from whom disclosure is sought or the person authorized to claim the privilege, or both, to disclose the information in chambers out of the presence and hearing of all persons except the person authorized to claim the privilege and such other persons as the person authorized to claim the privilege is willing to have present. If the judge determines that the information is privileged, neither he nor any other person may ever disclose, without the consent of a person authorized to permit disclosure, what was disclosed in the course of the proceedings in chambers.''
10. California Evidence Code, Section 1041.
11. Evidence Code, Section 1042(d): ''When, in any such criminal proceeding, a party demands disclosure of the identity of the informant on the ground the informant is a material witness on the issue of guilt, the court shall conduct a hearing at which all parties may present evidence on the issue of disclosure. Such hearing shall be conducted outside the presence of the jury, if any. During the hearing, if the privilege . . . is claimed by a person authorized to do so or if a person who is authorized to claim such privilege refuses to answer any question on the ground that the answer would tend to disclose the identity of the informant, the prosecuting attorney may request that the court hold an *in camera* hearing. If such a request is made, the court shall hold such a hearing outside the presence of the defendant and his counsel. At the *in camera* hearing, the prosecution may offer evidence which would tend to disclose or which discloses the identity of the informant to aid the court in its determination whether there is a reasonable possibility that nondisclosure might deprive the defendant of a fair trial. A reporter shall be present at the *in camera* hearing. Any transcription of the proceedings at the *in camera* hearing, as well as any physical evidence presented at the hearing, shall be ordered sealed by the court, and only a court may have access to its contents. The court shall not order disclosure, nor strike the testimony of the witness who invokes the privilege, nor dismiss the criminal proceeding, if the party offering the witness refuses to disclose the identity of the informant, unless, based upon the evidence presented at the hearing held in the presence of the defendant and his counsel and the evidence presented at the *in*

camera hearing, the court concludes that there is a reasonable possibility that nondisclosure might deprive the defendant of a fair trial."

12. Evidence Code, Section 1042 (c): ". . . in any preliminary hearing, criminal trial, or other criminal proceeding, any otherwise admissible evidence of information communicated to a peace officer by a confidential informant, who is not a material witness to the guilt or innocence of the accused of the offense charged, is admissible on the issue of reasonable cause to make an arrest or search without requiring that the name or identity of the informant be disclosed if the judge or magistrate is satisfied, based upon evidence produced in open court, out of the presence of the jury, that such information was received from a reliable informant and in his discretion does not require such disclosure." See *McCray* v. *Illinois* (1967), 386 U.S. 300, 87 S. Ct. 1056, 18 L. Ed. 2d 62.

13. The Fourth Amendment applies to state and federal law enforcement officers; See *Ker* v. *California* (1963), 374 U.S. 23, 83 S. Ct. 1623, 10 L. Ed. 2d 726.

14. Hearsay evidence is also admissible to detain a person without necessarily effecting an arrest: *Draper* v. *United States* (1959), 358 U.S. 307, 79 S. Ct. 329, L. Ed. 2d 327; *Adams* v. *Williams,* 407 U.S. 143, 32 L. Ed. 2d 612, 92 S. Ct. 1921.

15. The search of a vehicle need not necessarily be undertaken pursuant to a search warrant; *Chambers* v. *Maroney* (1970), 399 U.S. 41, 90 S. Ct. 1975, 20 L. Ed. 2d 419. But a warrantless search of a vehicle must still be supported by probable cause unless the search is incidental to the arrest of the occupants; *Dyke* v. *Taylor Implement Manufacturing Co.* (1968), 391 U.S. 216, 88 S. Ct. 1472, 20 L. Ed. 2d 538.

16. *Roviaro* v. *United States* (1957), 252 U.S. 53, 77 S. Ct. 623, 1 L. Ed. 2d 639. A similar rule would apply if the informant telephoned the defendant and the officers overheard the conversation; *People* v. *McShann,* 50 C. 2d 802, 330 P. 2d 33.

17. U.S. Constitution, Amendment V.

18. Other constitutional and statutory provisions supplement the constitutional command: The defendant is presumed innocent; the defendant must be proven guilty beyond a reasonable doubt; he or she may not be convicted upon evidence seized unlawfully; and all witnesses must submit to cross-examination.

19. *Murphy* v. *Waterfront Commissioner* (1964), 378 U.S. 52, 84 S. Ct. 1594, 12 L. Ed. 2d 678. A related view of the individual interest protected by the privilege focuses on the right of "privacy." *United States* v. *Grunewald* (2d Cir. 1956), 233 F. 2d 556, 581-582 (Frank, J., dissenting) revd. 353 U.S. 391, 77 S. Ct. 963, 1 L. Ed. 2d 931; Ratner, "Consequences of Exercising the Privilege Against Self-Incrimination" (1957) 24 U. Chi. L. Rev. 472, 488-489. The Fifth Amendment right of privacy protects at least uncommunicated thoughts and has been extended to preclude compelled production of private papers and documents; *Boyd* v. *United States* (1886), 116 U.S. 616, 6 S. Ct. 524, 29 L. Ed. 746. See also Model Code of Evidence, Rule 201(2); Uniform Rules of Evidence, Rule 23(3).

20. One court has held that in order for the removal (search) of a blood sample to be reasonable without a warrant, the officer must first have probable cause to arrest, and that the emergency exception to the warrant requirement will not apply. If an officer is investigating a major accident scene involving death or injury to

several people, he or she may not be able to establish immediately who is responsible. If the officer detects the odor of alcohol emanating from one of the damaged vehicles, but cannot identify the driver, the removal of blood samples from several people may be required. But no arrest can be made at that time because responsibility cannot be established. If a later investigation establishes the identity of the driver, who is then prosecuted, the defendant may assert that he or she was arrested without probable cause, and the search, without a warrant, is therefore unreasonable. In *People* v. *Superior Court* (Hawkins) 6 C. 3d 757, 100 Cal. R. 281, 493 P. 2d 1145, the court seemed to so hold. Later cases have established that the emergency created by the disappearance of alcohol in the blood constitutes sufficient reason for excusing the requirement of probable cause, *Carrington* v. *Superior Court,* 31 Cal. App. 3d 635, 107 Cal. R. 546.

21. See *People* v. *Kovacik,* 128 N.Y.S. 2d 492 for a discussion of this instrument.

22. "If the evidence establishes beyond a reasonable doubt that the amount, by weight, of alcohol in the defendant's blood was one tenth of one percent (0.10%) or more at the time of the test as shown by a chemical analysis of his blood, breath, or urine, you should find that the defendant was under the influence of intoxicating liquor at the time of the alleged offense, unless from all the evidence you have a reasonable doubt that he or she was in fact under the influence of intoxicating liquor at the time of the alleged offense." (California Jury Instructions.)

23. Cases are summarized in 87 A.L.R. 2d 370; see also *State* v. *Bock,* 80 Idaho 296, 328 P. 2d 1065.

24. Recent technical developments in the scientific investigation of crime have made blood and urine tests useful in determining the presence of opiates or barbiturates in the system. These results can be admitted into evidence for narcotic prosecutions without violating the privilege against self-incrimination; see *People* v. *Saldivar,* 249 Cal. App. 2d 670, 57 Cal. R. 731.

25. The manner of driving a car is relevant as circumstantial evidence that the defendant was driving under the influence of alcohol. The jury would be instructed as follows: "The manner in which a vehicle is being operated does not itself establish that the driver of the vehicle either is or is not under the influence of intoxicating liquor. However, the manner in which the vehicle is being operated is a factor to be considered in light of all the proved surrounding circumstances in deciding whether the person operating the vehicle was or was not under the influence of intoxicating liquor." (California Jury Instructions.)

26. Requiring a person to furnish a handwriting sample does not violate any Fourth Amendment right; *United States* v. *Mara* (1973), 410 U.S. 19, 93 S. Ct. 774, 35 L. Ed. 2d 99.

27. *Miranda* v. *Arizona* (1966), 384 U.S. 436, 88 S. Ct. 1602, 16 L. Ed. 2d 649. Moreover, if the defendant does not take the stand at trial to testify, the prosecution cannot comment on his or her refusal because no penalty may be imposed on an accused for the rightful exercise of the Fifth Amendment privilege.

9 Attacking and Supporting the Credibility of Witnesses

Chapter Objectives

After reading this chapter, you will be able to:

1. Describe the methods that may be used to assist a witness in recalling past events.

2. Explain the ways the credibility of a witness may be attacked.

3. Evaluate the strengths and weaknesses of a prospective witness.

4. Describe the rules governing the introduction of a witness's character as relevant evidence.

5. State the rules and statutes that apply when accomplices are used as witnesses.

Recalling Facts to the Witness

Prosecuting attorneys must take their civilian witnesses as they find them. Because many crimes are perpetrated against the aged, the ignorant, and the uneducated citizen, the prosecutor must necessarily expect a large number of witnesses whose testimony will be subjected to extensive cross-examination by the defense counsel. Many of these witnesses will be involved in crimes of violence, such as robbery and homicide. In robbery prosecutions, the prosecutor may present elderly storekeepers or grocery and liquor store clerks; in homicides, the witnesses may vary from respected ciritzens to criminals. Regardless of the character of the witnesses in a case, a prosecutor knows their appearance in court will probably be their first—and perhaps their last. A prosecutor must, therefore, attempt to proceed along a twin trial strategy, selecting those witnesses whose testimony will be accurate, clear, and complete, and supporting that testimony with testimony by officer-witnesses.

It cannot necessarily be assumed that all witnesses have the best interest of the prosecutor at heart. Some prosecuting witnesses may be accomplices, or at least implicated in the crime. Others may be friendly with the defendant and therefore reluctant to provide any testimony which would damage this person's case. The prosecutor and the officer must therefore prepare for a variety of witnesses. Depending upon the kind of witness and the expected content of the testimony, the prosecutor must be prepared to: refresh the failing memory of the witness; revive his or her memory by means of evidence previously prepared by the witness; and impeach the witness if the trial testimony is inconsistent with statements he or she made to peace officers earlier or testified to in a previous criminal proceeding. When attempting to undertake any of these approaches, however, the prosecutor must also be aware of other evidentiary objections to the admissibility of evidence, whether statutory or constitutional.

Refreshing the Witness's Recollection

If a witness is attempting to recall an event, the prosecutor may use virtually unlimited means to refresh the witness's recollection. In most cases, a writing or document of some kind may be shown to the witness as an aid to the memory. If, after examining the document or writing, the witness's recollection is revived, he or she may then testify. The document presented to the witness may be a rent receipt, a newspaper, a calendar, a hotel register, or any other writing; this document need not have been prepared by the witness or under his or her direction.

The method most frequently used is a statement by the witness of the events as recorded in the police report. Whether witnesses need to revive their memories or not, they should be permitted to read such reports prior to their testimony. The reports will contain many details which they related at the time the event was fresh in their memory. Nor should witnesses be embarrassed to state during cross-examination that they have read a report, for such a procedure is entirely permissible.

In jurisdictions which process criminal cases by grand jury or preliminary hearing, the transcript of the witness's testimony may be made available to the witness prior to trial. If the testimony at the earlier proceeding was uncertain or unclear, the witness should call such facts to the attention of the prosecutor prior to testifying. The witness must also alert the prosecutor prior to trial if his or her present testimony is in conflict with that reported in the transcript. In most cases, defense counsel will have access to the police report and the transcript of the previous testimony. Because of liberalized discovery proceedings in criminal cases, the defendant's possession of the report and transcript allow him or her to explore thoroughly any inconsistencies or uncertainties in testimony.

Past Recollection Recorded

If a witness recorded a fact at the time a crime took place but can no longer recollect the fact, can the written record of the fact be admitted as evidence?

For example: A robbery occurred at a liquor store operated by Mr. W. He testified that, after obtaining the money, the robber fled in the direction of Mrs. S's house. Mrs. S then testified that on that day at approximately 4:30 or 5 P.M. she saw a man running away from the vicinity of the liquor store carrying what appeared to be a paper bag. The man got into a car, but before the car was driven away, she obtained the license number of the vehicle. She called Mr. W and informed him of the license number, which she had written down on a piece of paper. She later gave the paper to Mr. W, but could not now remember the number.

After Mrs. S had completed her testimony, Mr. W was recalled to the witness stand. He testified that in a telephone conversation shortly after the robbery, Mrs. S gave him a license number which he wrote down. He further testified that he had with him in court what he had written down. Mr. W was permitted to read aloud the license number. He stated that it was the number which he had received over the telephone from Mrs. S, but that he could not otherwise recall it. In the course of cross-examination, it developed that the notation of the license number which Mr. W had with him in court was not his original notation, but was based on information that he had received from his bookkeeper by telephone as to his original notation, which he had made on an ice cube receipt hanging on a nail near the telephone when Mrs. S telephoned him.

Later, Mr. W resumed the witness stand and testified that a piece of paper he then had before him was the one on which he had written the license number which Mrs. S had given him. Over the defendant's objection, the paper was received in evidence. Was such evidence admissible?

The information which Mr. W had received from his bookkeeper and had noted on a paper did not serve to refresh his recollection so that at the time of his testimony he had an *actual recollection* of the license number given to him by Mrs. S. Consequently, the concept of refreshing memory did not apply.

But, even though the witness could not recall the license number with certainty, the note could still be admissible in evidence as a past recordation of the witness's observation. This rule, which is in reality an exception to the hearsay rule, is important here because of the necessity to assist witnesses in testifying to an event, even if they have no present recollection. Because such a rule can be abused by a careless or hostile witness, several safeguards have been imposed:

1. The statement must be one the witness could testify to if he or she had sufficient recollection of the facts. Thus, the statement would not be admissible if it was in violation of some other rule of evidence.

2. The witness must lack a present recollection of the facts; that is, even a reading of the written statement by the witness does not refresh his or her recollection. Total lack of recollection is not required.

3. The writing must have been made when the fact recorded occurred, or at a time when the fact recorded was still fresh in the witness's memory.

4. The writing must have been made by the witness or by someone under his or her direction.

5. The witness must testify that the prior statement was a true statement of the facts. The witness must testify to personal knowledge of the facts when the statement was made, and must testify that the statement is an accurate recital of these facts.

6. If the witness made the writing, or read it after it was made, he or she must so testify, and must identify the writing.

If all of these tests were met, the testimony of Mr. W would be admissible.

Impeachment of Witnesses

As noted earlier, witnesses are the lifeblood of any case. Their testimony establishes the elements of the crime, identifies the culprit, recounts the conduct of the accused, and repeats the incriminating statements of a defendant. The defendant's witnesses may contradict the prosecution witnesses, cast doubt on their honesty, establish a motive or bias of a prosecution witness, question their integrity, or establish a defense of alibi. Prosecutors and defense counsels review their cases and call those witnesses who are least susceptible to effective cross-examination. Depending upon the crime charged, these witnesses play greater or lesser roles.

As a first step in analyzing the strength of a criminal case, the investigating officer knows that the witness's testimony will be scrutinized by a jury. All of the rules of evidence will be ignored if the jury disbelieves the witness; therefore, the demeanor of a witness is important. Aside from considering demeanor, the jury will also evaluate the extent of a witness's opportunity to observe, recollect, or communicate any matter about which he or she testifies. Thus, any witness who is interviewed before trial must be evaluated as follows:

1. Was the witness in a position to observe or hear the acts or statements to which he or she will testify?

2. If so, was the witness's vision or sense of sound impaired by any physical obstructions?

3. Was the witness's vantage point stationary or from a moving vehicle?

4. Does the event which the witness observed involve a stationary act, or was the person moving?

5. Does the witness suffer any personal physical handicap which may impair vision or sense of sound?

6. Can the witness testify to the entire event or only to a portion of the event?

7. If the witness's opportunity to observe or hear is unimpaired, can he or she recall the event in detail?

8. If so, can the witness relate the event in detail?

9. If the witness's recollection is hazy, can memory be refreshed by reviewing a document or other writing?

10. If the witness cannot refresh his or her recollection, can the witness testify from a document which he or she recorded at the time of the event so that the past recollection of the event may substitute for the current inability to recall?

11. Will the witness be able to recall, relate, and testify before a jury?

Once this initial evaluation has been made, the prosecutor or investigator must know the kinds of evidence which may be used to attack the credibility of a witness. Attacking credibility is referred to as "impeaching" the witness. The most common grounds of impeachment are:

1. Inability of the witness to accurately observe, recall, and relate facts;

2. Lack of opportunity to observe facts;

3. Any bias of the witness for or against the defendant;

4. Any personal interest in the case which might affect testimony;

5. Any motive against the defendant which might affect testimony;

6. A prior inconsistent statement by the witness;

7. Other facts which contradict the witness's testimony;

8. A previous felony conviction.

Evidence to attack a witness's credibility, or "impeach" the witness, may be accomplished by cross-examining the witness or by introducing other evidence which contradicts his or her testimony. In evaluating the testimony of a witness, the jury will be instructed as follows:

"You are the exclusive judges of the credibility of the witnesses who have testified in this case, which means that you must decide which witnesses are to be believed and how much weight, if any, is to be given to the testimony of each witness.

"In determining the credibility of a witness, you may consider anything which tends in reason to prove or disprove the truthfulness of his testimony, such as: his conduct, attitude and manner while testifying; whether the facts testified to by him are inherently believable or unbelievable; his capacity to hear or see that about which he testified and his ability to recollect or to relate such matters; whether or not there was any bias, interest, or other motive for him not to tell the truth; any statement previously made by him that was consistent with his testimony or, conversely, any statement previously made by him that was inconsistent with his testimony; his character for honesty or for dishonesty; any admission by him that he did not tell the truth; or any prior conviction of a felony.

"If you believe that a witness willfully lied as to a material fact, you should distrust the rest of his testimony and you may, but are not obliged, to disregard all of his testimony.

"However, you should bear in mind that discrepancies in a witness's testimony or between his testimony and that of others, if there were any, do not necessarily mean that you should disbelieve the witness, as failure of recollection is a common experience and innocent misrecollection is not uncommon. You are all certainly aware of the fact that two persons witnessing the same incident often will see or hear it differently.

"Also, in considering a discrepancy in a witness's testimony, you should consider whether such discrepancy concerns an important fact or only a trivial detail." (California Jury Instructions.)

Inability to Observe, Recall, and Relate Facts

Using the checklist in this chapter to evaluate the strength of a witness's testimony, the prosecutor will learn how comprehensively the witness may testify. On cross-examination, the defendant will seek to probe in detail the ability of the witness to observe and recall not only those facts elicited on direct examination, but also those facts which were omitted. In this way, counsel seeks to modify or dilute the impact of a witness's testimony by questioning his or her ability to recall significant facts omitted in the prosecutor's direct examination. This occurs most frequently when an officer is examined about an event or statement to which he or she testified on direct examination, but which does not appear in the arrest report. If such evidence is significant—yet appears nowhere in the report—the defendant will suggest that the officer fabricated this testimony to strengthen the prosecution's case.

In drunk driving prosecutions—cases which normally involve only the testimony of the arresting officer—the witness's ability to recall the manner of driving, the appearance of the defendant, the order and manner in which field sobriety tests were administered, and the thickness of the defendant's voice will be examined closely not only to test the witness's memory, but also in an attempt to establish an inconsistency between the officer's field examination and the ultimate scientific reading of the alcoholic content of the blood. The officer must record field observations while the defendant is performing the field sobriety test or shortly thereafter because the officer will never be able to recall the position of the defendant's feet as he or she walked the line, or the manner in which the defendant touched a finger to his or her nose, etc. Because these observations should be recorded well in advance of the blood, breath, or urine test subsequently administered to the defendant, any variance between the officer's description of the defendant's conduct in the field and the scientific measurement of the defendant's blood alcohol will be exploited on cross-examination.

In most cases, the cross-examination will be directed toward establishing either an incomplete recollection, a misrecollection, or a nonrecollection. An incomplete recollection may be established by testing the witness's memory. A misrecollection may be established if other witnesses testify to facts inconsistent with the witness's testimony, or if the witness changes the testimony after other facts are brought to his or her attention. Nonrecollection of unimportant facts is not unusual. But if the facts are of some significance, their absence in the witness's testimony may suggest that the witness is mistaken, possesses a poor memory, or is dishonest. Whether cross-examination establishes impaired recollection ("I couldn't see too well because the room was dark"), misrecollection ("I thought the car was eastbound but I guess it was northbound"), or nonrecollection ("I don't remember telling the defendant I would kill her someday if I got the chance"), the jury will evaluate these factors in determining whether to believe the witness. Note that such techniques are not limited to cross-examination of prosecution witnesses. The prosecution may impeach the defendant or any of the defendant's witnesses by similar methods.

If a witness has used marijuana, drugs, or narcotics, can he or she be impeached on this ground? A prosecutor may be forced to offer the testimony of a prostitute addicted to heroin to establish a pandering case against the defendant. Or the defendant may attempt to offer an addict as a witness in an alibi defense or on the issue of the lawfulness of an arrest or search.

For example: The defendant is charged with robbery. The robbery does not involve drugs or narcotics and none are found on the defendant's person at the time of his arrest. The defendant offers a witness to testify that the defendant was elsewhere at the time and place the robbery occurred. On cross-examination, the prosecutor asks the witness the following questions:

Q: Mrs. A, on June the 7th, were you a narcotic addict?

Q: Were you in a physical condition such that you had some physical craving for narcotics back on that date?

Q: Were you taking hard narcotics, heroin, morphine and the morphine derivatives in June?

Q: By "some drugs," you mean heroin?
Q: Were you shooting them with a needle into your body?
Q: Isn't it true that you were attempting to get a fix of heroin on the 8th of June?
Q: Shortly before you were arrested on the 8th of June, weren't you making an attempt to obtain some heroin?
Q: Did you talk to them (narcotic officers) about your addiction to the use of hard narcotics over a period of time?
Q: Have you mainlined in the past?
Q: What does "mainline" mean?
Q: Does the word "quarter" have significance to you so far as narcotics are concerned, the word "quarter"?

The witness denies any use of narcotics, but the prosecutor offers a witness in rebuttal who testifies that the alibi witness is an addict, describes photos of the witness's arms which reflect scars and puncture wounds, and relates a conversation with the witness about her use of narcotics. Is such testimony admissible?

In this example, the prosecution is attempting to impeach the witness by asking about her narcotic history. Such questions may tend to establish that her ability to recall was impaired by use of narcotics. To impeach a witness on grounds of impaired recollection, misrecollection, or nonrecollection, the evidence must establish that the witness was unable to perceive, recollect, or recall. With respect to the use of narcotics: "The view adhered to by what may be called the weight of authority is that testimony as to narcotic addiction, or expert testimony as to the effects of the use of such drugs, is not considered admissible to impeach the credibility of a witness unless followed by testimony tending to show that he was under the influence while testifying, or when the events to which he testified occurred, or that his mental faculties were actually impaired by the habit. A minority of the decisions take the broad view that evidence of the use of narcotics is generally admissible for impeachment purposes notwithstanding the absence of the qualifying factors mentioned above. (*People* v. *Ortega.*)[1]

Even though the rule may vary in different states, the investigator must alert the prosecutor to the possible use of a witness who is an addict—whether for prosecution or defense—and may be required to provide evidence regarding a witness's use of narcotics, at least during the time of the witness's observation of events pertaining to the case.

Bias, Personal Interest, and Motive

In certain kinds of criminal prosecutions, a witness may never have seen the defendant before the crime occurred. Robberies, burglaries, and rapes are frequently perpetrated against people previously unknown to the defendant. In such cases, the crucial issue will be identification of the suspect.

But in other kinds of crime the identification of the defendant is not in issue. In assault and battery, disturbance of the peace, assaults with force and violence, and even homicide, the parties frequently knew each other prior to the alleged crime. No question of identification is involved, and the key issue becomes the credibility, that is, the believability, of witnesses. In this kind of crime, the bias or prejudice of the witness may emerge. Witnesses can always be questioned about personal relationships with the parties: the nature of these associations, the length of time they have known defendants, and the conditions under which the relationships existed. In homicide cases, for example, defendants often raise the issue of self-defense, based on threats previously made by victims. The very nature of some cases suggests that witnesses will be motivated by friendship or enmity.

For the purposes of such a case, the People must evaluate whether the case can be successfully prosecuted based upon the possible bias of their witnesses. Because such witnesses may not have testified frequently in court, they cannot always be expected to provide a clear picture of the facts. And if, added to this, witnesses display any bias concerning the defendant, their testimony may seriously dilute the strength of such a case. Of course, previous acquaintance with a witness does not insulate the defendant from prosecution for criminal acts; yet the investigator must recognize the possibility of impeaching the witness for bias. In such cases, additional evidence should be offered in an attempt to corroborate the witness's testimony; photographs of injuries or damaged property are useful. And in some cases the visual evidence may tend to discredit the victim's version of the facts and alert the prosecution to the weakness of their case.

The most common example of possible bias in testimony arises from testimony given by an accomplice or by a witness who has been immunized from prosecution. As we will see in greater detail later in this chapter, the prosecution may ask an accomplice to testify to a certain set of facts in exchange for a promise of immunity. Cross-examination will strengthen the witness's anticipation that his or her testimony will guarantee freedom. Such motivation is sufficiently powerful to warrant an inference that the witness will testify to any set of facts which assures release and on cross-examination, the defense will fully exploit the witness's motivation for testifying. Therefore, other corroborating evidence should be offered by the prosecution to support such testimony.

Prior Inconsistent Statements

Because the trial of a criminal case is often delayed for a variety of reasons, the arresting officer must refresh his or her recollection from the arrest report. At the trial, the defense counsel may cross-examine the officer-witness about details of the report in an effort to uncover inconsistencies between the facts stated in the report and the testimony at trial. If such inconsistencies exist, they serve to impeach the witness. Any such impeachment may be argued to the jury in an effort to discredit the officer's testimony.

In response to this tactic, some officers prepare sketchy and incomplete reports, believing that a short description of the facts will eliminate any attempts at impeachment. But not only do incomplete reports increase the difficulty of recollection, they also do not help the officer avoid impeachment. Defense counsel will repeatedly question the officer on the reasons for omitting important details from the report. Counsel will invite the jury to consider the reasons for the failure of a witness to record significant and frequently incriminating facts.

Incomplete reports also prevent the prosecutor from truly evaluating the strengths and weaknesses of a case. Since no purpose is served by forcing a weak case to trial, defense attorneys should be provided with carefully written and complete arrest reports to help them evaluate the strength of their defense.

Civilian witnesses may also be impeached by prior inconsistent statements. In most cases, the victim or witness to a crime will speak to an officer, who summarizes the conversation and records it in a crime report. Not infrequently, the witness does not review what he or she has said, particularly if in shock or injured at the time the report was made. Even if the witness signs the report, he or she may not necessarily read it carefully. Yet these crime reports recording the statements of witnesses may be used at trial for impeachment if the testimony is inconsistent with the pre-trial statement—particularly in robbery prosecutions, if the identity of the suspect is in question.

Defendants and their witnesses may also be impeached by any pre-trial statements which are inconsistent with testimony at trial. Under the rules of *Miranda* v. *Arizona* (see chapter 11, The *Miranda* Decision), the prosecution may not offer into evidence any pre-trial statements given by defendants to police unless they were first advised of their right to counsel and silence. But in some states this rule only applies to statements offered by the prosecution during presentation of its case in chief. If defendants offer themselves as witnesses in their own defense, the prosecution may impeach them by use of any inconsistent pre-trial statements to police, even if the defendants were not advised of their *Miranda* rights or if the advice was incomplete. (*Harris* v. *New York*.) This rule protects defendants in the exercise of their constitutional rights but does not allow them to shield themselves from perjury. Any statements from defendants should be recorded, whether preceded by a *Miranda* admonition or not, for possible use at trial for impeachment.

Whether counsel attempts to impeach an officer, a civilian witness, or the defendant, the threshold question is whether the pre-trial statement is "inconsistent'' with the trial testimony. If a witness has written a pre-trial statement, or if someone has written his or her statement, that statement can be read to the jury to demonstrate any inconsistency. Although the court may be required to rule on whether the statement is ''inconsistent,'' the problem is not difficult if an express inconsistency can be determined. In some cases, however, the prosecution may have difficulty in establishing an ''express'' inconsistency. For example, assume a certain witness relates a set of facts to an officer which implicates the defendant in a crime. At the trial, however, the witness testifies that he has no recollection of the incident. In this case, the prosecution cannot utilize the pre-trial statement because ''the right of impeachment does not exist where the witness states he has no recollection of the facts concerning which he is examined.'' (*People* v. *Sam.*) In other words, a loss of memory is not ''inconsistent'' with a pre-trial statement.

But compare this example:

''[A witness] testifies at the preliminary hearing substantially as follows: About January 5 or 6, defendant had a conversation with him at the latter's house; at that time defendant told the witness he had a kilo of marijuana which he wanted the witness to sell for him; the marijuana was packaged in 29 Baggies (i.e., small, transparent plastic bags) inside a large shopping bag; defendant told the witness where the shopping bag was hidden at his father's house; defendant then directed the witness to go to that location and get the bag. The witness recounted that one morning between January 1 and 10, defendant called him on the phone and told him he had a kilo of 'stuff' or 'grass' which he wanted to leave at the witness's house; the witness replied he could bring it over later in the day; defendant did so, arriving with a shopping bag containing 29 plastic bags of a green, leafy material which the witness recognized as marijuana . . .

''[At the trial,] the witness admitted he had known defendant for some four and a half years; sometime between January 1 and 10, defendant called him on the phone and said he had some 'stuff' that he wanted the witness to sell; the witness understood 'stuff' to mean 'grass or pot, marijuana'; and the witness agreed to sell the marijuana for the defendant. At this point in the proceedings, however, the witness's testimony suddenly became curiously vague. When asked what happened after the phone conversation, the witness claimed he was no longer 'absolutely sure' that defendant had come to his house later that day, adding, 'I think, but I'm not positive.' Asked if defendant brought anything to the house, the witness replied, 'Not that I recall.' To explain this apparent lapse of memory, the witness said he had taken LSD about 20 minutes before defendant phoned him.

''The witness's preliminary hearing testimony, summarized above, was then read to him. Once again he equivocated, claiming 'I can't absolutely say' that after making the phone call defendant came to his house and brought him anything. Nevertheless, the witness then admitted that the same night he had in his possession a shopping bag containing 29 'Baggies' of marijuana, although he alleged he could not recall 'how I actually did get them.'

"When asked if someone had told him where to find the shopping bag, the witness conceded, 'I suppose someone did tell me,' but reiterated that 'I can't say absolutely' who it was. When asked whether he obtained the bag at the house of defendant's father, he replied, 'I might have. You know, I knew [the defendant] called . . .' The prosecutor then asked when was the next time he saw defendant after the phone call and the witness replied, 'I think I might have seen him that day, but I couldn't be positive . . .'

"A dispassionate appraisal of the foregoing testimony . . . leads to but one conclusion: the trial court could properly disbelieve the witness's claim that he no longer remembered how the marijuana came into his possession. The witness's reluctance to testify against defendant was apparent from the outset, as it was necessary to repeatedly warn him to make his voice more audible. When he reached the critical point in his testimony—i.e., whether defendant did in fact give him the marijuana as he agreed to do—the witness first hesitated by saying, 'I just messed around for a while. . . . Well, you know, I mean he didn't come over right away.' Finally the witness unmasked his apparent motive when he protested, 'Like I already said, I mean I've got a conscience, and I don't want to . . .' His voice trailed off, and he was told once again to speak up.

"Thereafter the witness adopted a technique of refraining from flatly denying that defendant either brought the marijuana to his house or pointed out its hiding place to him; instead, the witness evaded all questions to that effect with such equivocations as 'I'm not absolutely sure' and 'I'm not positive.' These evasions are, in the circumstances, inherently incredible. The witness admitted in open court that he clearly remembered every event *before* his acquisition of the marijuana, including the highly incriminating phone call by defendant, and every event after that acquisition, including his possession the same day of the shopping bag containing precisely 29 'Baggies' of marijuana, his consumption of some, his sale of others. His claim to have conveniently forgotten only the actual transfer of the contraband was not believed by the trial judge, who repeatedly castigated him for his 'highly unsatisfactory performance' on the stand.

"In normal circumstances, the testimony of the witness that he does not remember an event is not 'inconsistent' with a prior statement by him describing that event. But justice will not be promoted by a ritualistic invocation of this rule of evidence. Inconsistency in effect, rather than contradiction in express terms, is the test for admitting a witness's prior statement and the same principle governs the case of the forgetful witness. Here the witness admittedly remembered the events both leading up to and following the crucial moment when the marijuana came into his possession, and as to that moment his testimony was equivocal . . . The witness's deliberate evasion of the latter point in his trial testimony must be deemed to constitute an implied denial that defendant did in fact furnish him with the marijuana as charged. His testimony was thus materially inconsistent with his preliminary hearing testimony and his pre-trial statement, in both of which he specifically named defendant as his supplier. Accordingly, the two prior statements of this witness were properly admitted." (*People* v. *Green.*)

When a witness's testimony varies from his or her pre-trial statements, the prosecutor or defense attorney must elect which evidentiary course to take. The lawyer can attempt to refresh the recollection of the witness from a pre-trial statement or can attempt to introduce the statement as past recollection recorded. When the witness still is unable or unwilling to testify according to the pre-trial statement, prosecution or defense attorneys may elect to attack the credibility of the witness, rather than support it, by means of an attempt to impeach. The strategy might be as follows:

1) Counsel may ask the witness to refresh his or her recollection by reading the pre-trial statement.

2) If the witness still has no recollection, he or she may be able to testify that the pre-trial statement was true at the time it was made. If such evidence is absent, the statement is inadmissible as past recollection recorded.

3) If the witness still recalls nothing, but is evasive or equivocal, counsel may then attempt to impeach the witness.

4) If counsel can offer the pre-trial statement to impeach the witness, the advantage is twofold: first, to contradict the witness; and second, to offer the evidence for the truth of the matter asserted.

When a prior inconsistent statement is introduced in evidence, the jury may consider such statement in determining the credibility of a witness. The jury can also consider the inconsistent statement as affirmative evidence; that is, they can regard the contents of the statement as true. (*California* v. *Green.*)

Whenever the prosecution calls a witness whose complicity with the defendant is established, a danger exists that this witness's testimony may vary from pre-trial statements given to the police. If a witness has already pled guilty, he or she can still refuse to answer questions on the ground of self-incrimination, as the privilege expires only upon termination of sentence. But if the prosecution possesses a pre-trial statement by the witness, may the prosecuting attorney attempt to impeach a witness who claims his or her privilege? For example, in a murder prosecution, a witness who claimed his Fifth Amendment privilege was asked the following questions by the prosecutor:

''Isn't it true that you were with the men I just mentioned in the Honda car belonging to James Eric Shipe?

''Isn't it true that James Eric Shipe was wearing a black beret that night, or a dark colored beret?

''Is it not true that when you arrived Katherine and Richard Stinnett were at the Kroupa's with their baby?

''Is it not true that you engaged in an argument with Hugh Kroupa about your being there?

''Is it not true that you told Hugh Kroupa that you did not have a dime with which to call him?

''Is it not true that while you were at the Kroupa residence, the three of you,—that the Stinnetts left the residence?

''Is it not true that after your argument with Kroupa you retired to the front lawn while Marc Setencich and James Eric Shipe remained inside the house with Kroupa?

''Is it not true that when you—you were called back into the house by Marc Setencich and when you arrived you saw the body of Hugh Kroupa on the floor in the living room?

''Is it not true that when you came back and saw the body of Hugh Kroupa that James Eric Shipe was on top of him?

''Is it not true that you saw James Eric Shipe remove the wallet of Hugh Kroupa and take the knife with him?

''Is it not true that then you and Marc Setencich removed the stereo set from the premises?

''Is it not true that with the money that was taken from Hugh Kroupa you were present when James Eric Shipe made a purchase, using $100 of that money, of heroin?

''Is it not true that you told the police about the incidents I have just examined you on?

''Is it not true that you have talked to me and my investigator about the events we have just discussed, I have just asked you questions on that?

''Did you stab Kroupa?

''Did you see James Eric Shipe stab Kroupa?

''Is it not true that on the 18th of August in an interview in the jail with you you told me that you told the police the truth about this matter?

> "Is it not true that at the time you saw the body of Hugh Kroupa on the floor you went up to examine that body and because of your experience in Viet Nam determined the body to be dead?
>
> "Is it not true that at the time of your arrest there [was] blood on your boots?
>
> "Do you know the answers to the questions I have just asked you?
>
> "Have you been advised by anyone not to testify here today?
>
> "What did you three men do with that knife?
>
> "Is it not true that after Kroupa was stabbed that the three of you went over to the house of Doris Ihlenfeldt on La Salle?
>
> "And isn't it true that you were going there to Doris Ihlenfeldt's house to get drugs or narcotics?
>
> "Isn't it true . . . that you and Marc Setencich delivered the stolen stereo set to the residence of Julian and Debbie Lopez?" (*People* v. *Shipe*.)

Is this proper ground for impeachment? In order to impeach a witness, the answer to the question must be inconsistent in effect, or an express contradiction. As the witness in this case answered by invoking his Fifth Amendment privilege, the answers do not qualify under either of these rules. The only purpose of these questions was to use the witness's refusal to answer as an inference that he was responsible for the crimes.

Character Evidence for Impeachment

To the extent that it is possible to do so, the law attempts to limit the introduction of evidence to the facts of the case on trial. Because other facts often illuminate the evidence, exceptions are made to allow introduction of facts which exist independently of the current use. One kind of evidence that often appears to be relevant is evidence concerning the character traits of the parties involved in the case. "Character" connotes the personal qualities of an individual or a disposition towards certain moral conduct. Because the role of "character" in a trial can become relevant, the law attempts to authorize evidence of character, but only under carefully limited circumstances.

The legislature and the courts must determine when and under what circumstances evidence concerning such character traits is admissible. For purposes of impeachment, the only traits of character which are relevant are honesty and veracity, or their opposites, dishonesty and lack of veracity.[2] The credibility of a witness is central to the court's ability to achieve a just verdict. If a witness cannot be believed, the jury must be so informed.

Character traits which bear no relation to integrity are deemed too remote and irrelevant for a jury to consider as grounds for impeachment. To allow evidence of other character traits would distort the central issue in the trial.

A character witness must limit testimony to his or her personal opinion of another witness's reputation, or to the reputation for truth and veracity which the witness enjoys in the community. Either side may cross-examine the witness and determine how long the witness has been acquainted with the party, the number of mutual friends they share, and whether their relationship would include confidences of a personal nature.

It should be noted that the use of character evidence for impeachment is severely limited. But as we will see later in this chapter, character evidence may be offered for other purposes.

Impeachment by Felony Conviction

Most jurisdictions allow impeachment of a witness by evidence that he or she has previously been convicted of a felony. Of course, if the defendant does not take the witness stand, no evidence of the prior conviction may be offered by the prosecution. A defendant who testifies may be impeached because of a prior felony conviction as follows: The prosecution must first establish that the defendant was convicted of a crime which constituted a felony, and that the conviction is constitutionally valid. In some jurisdictions, the felony must involve the character traits of truth and honesty. Under the latter rule, for example, a witness charged with theft could not be impeached by a previous conviction of assault with a deadly weapon—a crime which reflects the character trait of violence, but not dishonesty.

Character Evidence

As noted above, to impeach a witness, only the person's character for truth and veracity is relevant because only those traits relate to the credibility of a witness. But the law admits character evidence for reasons other than credibility:

1. As circumstantial evidence that a person acted or conducted himself in conformity with his character or character trait;[3]

2. To prove a person's character or character trait that is an ultimate issue of disputed fact.[4]

Character as Circumstantial Evidence

All crimes require proof of certain legal elements to establish the defendant's guilt. But underlying these legal elements is an inference concerning defendants' moral character which lead them to commit such crimes. Thus, if the prosecution charges the defendant with assault, the underlying moral charge is the defendant's propensity to commit acts of violence; if the crime alleged was disturbing the peace, the underlying moral charge is a character trait for loud and boisterous conduct.

At trial, a defendant may offer witnesses to testify to his or her good character. The rationale for such evidence is that a person with good character for the trait in issue would not commit the crime alleged. Thus, in an assault case, a witness could testify to the defendant's character for nonviolence or passivity; in a charge of disturbing the peace, a witness could testify to the defendant's character for peace and tranquility. This evidence is offered as affirmative evidence on behalf of the defendant to rebut the underlying accusation of moral lapse. The jury will be instructed to consider such evidence as follows: Evidence of the defendant's character as to those traits which ordinarily would be involved in the commission of an offense such as that with which he is charged is relevant to the question of defendant's guilt or innocence, because it may be reasoned that a person of good character as to such traits would not be likely to commit such offense. Evidence of good character may be sufficient to raise a reasonable doubt whether the defendant is guilty, which doubt otherwise would not exist.

Because the defendant has been charged with the commission of a crime implying bad moral conduct, only the defendant can introduce evidence on his or her own behalf for good character. To introduce this evidence, the defendant will present witnesses to testify that in their opinion the defendant enjoys a good reputation for the character trait in issue, or that the defendant's reputation for the character trait is good among members of the community. If the defendant has introduced evidence of good character, the prosecution may then rebut such evidence by asking witnesses whether they are aware of conduct by the defendant on earlier occasions which may have culminated in an arrest record, or other acts of misconduct. But the prosecution may never introduce such evidence until the defendant has affirmatively put his or her character in issue by the testimony of witnesses.

Because the prosecutor cannot offer evidence of prior misconduct to prove the defendant's bad character unless the defendant puts his or her character in issue, the prosecutor may only introduce acts of prior misconduct which are relevant on some other issue. For example, acts of prior misconduct may be offered as circumstantial evidence to establish an element of the prosecution case, such as identity of the suspect, motive, intent, or lack of knowledge.[5] The court must determine whether acts of prior misconduct are relevant on these issues, and that they are not merely evidence that the defendant is of poor moral character.

Nor may the defendant offer acts of prior "good conduct" to establish his or her good moral character. Only personal opinion and evidence of reputation are admissible to establish the defendant's good character.

Character of the Victim

The defendant may offer character evidence concerning the victim of a crime for which the defendant is being prosecuted. Such circumstantial evidence is offered to prove that the conduct of the victim at the time of the crime is in conformity with his or her character. The evidence may consist of testimony by witnesses of their personal opinion of the victim, testimony as to the victim's reputation in the community for the character trait involved, or testimony concerning specific acts of misconduct by the victim. The prosecutor must determine in advance whether the victim, who is usually the principal witness, is vulnerable to an attack on his or her character. Such an attack may include previous felony convictions as well as other acts of misconduct which relate to the case on trial. Such evidence is most frequently introduced in homicide prosecutions when the defendant offers witnesses to testify that on earlier occasions the victim attacked and assaulted the defendant. This conduct, if believed by the trier of fact, would tend to establish the victim's character trait for force and violence and thereby support the defendant's defense of self-defense.

More recently, defendants have sought access to administrative records of law enforcement agencies to determine whether citizens have complained that arresting officers used excessive force against them. If the defendant has been charged with resisting arrest or battery on a peace officer, the defendant may defend on the ground that the arresting officer—the victim—exerted excessive force in effecting the arrest. To support his or her defense, the defendant may seek the names of other witnesses who were allegedly subjected to excessive force by the arresting officer on earlier occasions. If the court grants the motion to disclose the names of citizens who complained about excessive force, the records are usually submitted to the judge for review. Thereafter, the judge decides whether disclosure of names would serve the defendant's interest. If names are disclosed, the defendant may then subpoena these witnesses to testify in support of his or her defense that the officer exercised excessive force. (*Pitchess* v. *Superior Court.*)

Character of the Victim in Crimes of Sexual Misconduct

Rape prosecutions are one of the most difficult types of cases to try, and the credibility of the witnesses is usually the most important factor in such cases. The courts have long recognized that charges of rape are easily made and difficult to disprove; the jury is often so instructed. The chief defense strategy is to attack the character of the prosecution witness by introducing her prior acts of consenting sexual misconduct. Because the nature of the charge is highly personal to the victim, extensive cross-examination is often acutely embarrassing. For this reason alone, a rape victim is often reluctant to testify. When she does testify, she can anticipate extensive cross-examination concerning her character and conduct.

Recent legislative changes in some jurisdictions have limited the extent to which a victim in a rape case can be impeached by character evidence relating to sexual misconduct. In some cases, character evidence of the victim is inadmissible to prove consent unless the victim was herself involved in prior acts with the defendant. Of course, such legislation does not restrict introduction of any other impeaching evidence offered to attack the credibility of the witness.

Despite any limitation on the use of character evidence, some courts have allowed the defendant to use psychiatric testimony to attack the credibility of a witness in a case alleging sexual misconduct. (*Ballard* v. *Superior Court.*) If the defendant can establish that the victim's emotional or mental stability is in issue, he can request that the court appoint a psychiatrist to examine the witness. The purpose of the examination is to determine whether or not the victim's emotional or psychiatric problems affect her ability to perceive, to recall, and to recollect—that is, her ability to tell the truth. If the ability to tell the truth is impaired, the foundation for her impeachment has been laid.[6]

In order for the court to appoint a psychiatrist, some evidence must exist to justify an examination of the witness. If the court does order the victim examined, she may decide not to submit (or may decide not to testify). The only remedy for the defendant is an instruction to the jury informing them that she was ordered to submit to an examination and refused to do so. If the witness does submit, the court and the prosecution must draft careful guidelines to insure the integrity of the examination.

Accomplices as Witnesses

The prosecutor must often use a witness who was implicated in the crime and is subject to prosecution. Any witness who is liable to prosecution for the same offense charged against the defendant on trial in the cause in which the testimony is given is an accomplice. This rule includes those who conspire with the defendant to do the act or who aid and abet its perpetrator. For the investigator and the prosecutor, the use of an accomplice involves the application of several rules of evidence which have developed over the centuries. In England, the use of accomplices to testify on behalf of the Crown was a familiar technique until about 1700 in prosecuting alleged traitors. Lacking any evidence to connect the accused with the offense, the Crown offered a witness who testified about personal participation in a criminal act with the defendant, and such "evidence" would support a conviction. Moreover, a jury tended to believe the accomplice because of his or her recitation of the details of the criminal act. The testimony sometimes resembled a personal confession, thus carrying the ring of truth.

The abuses of accomplice testimony are manifest. The accomplice may be immunized from prosecution in advance of trial and may testify for the State without being charged with the offense. The accomplice may also be charged with the crime along with a codefendant and be later immunized, and his or her case may be dismissed. Or the accomplice may be charged or tried separately from the defendant, may be acquitted, and thereafter may testify against the defendant. Finally, the accomplice may testify in his or her own behalf and implicate the codefendant in a joint trial. Experience has shown that the testimony of an accomplice ought to be viewed with distrust because it comes from a tainted source and is often given in the hope or expectation of leniency or immunity. The dangers of accomplice testimony are outlined to the jury in a series of legal instructions of which the officer should be aware in the preparation of a case for trial:

1. "An accomplice is a person who is liable to prosecution for the identical offense charged against the defendant.

2. "A person is an accomplice if he knowingly and with criminal intent aided, promoted, encouraged, or instigated by act or advice the commission of such offense. In other words, the person must have guilty knowledge and intent.

3. "A conviction cannot be had upon the testimony of an accomplice unless it is corroborated by such other evidence as shall tend to connect the defendant with the commission of the offense.

4. "Corroborative evidence is evidence of some act or fact related to the offense which, if believed, by itself and without any aid, interpretation, or direction from the testimony of the accomplice, tends to connect the defendant with the commission of the offense charged.

5. "However, it is not necessary that the corroborative evidence be sufficient in itself to establish every element of the offense charged, or that it corroborate every fact to which the accomplice testifies.

6. "In determining whether an accomplice has been corroborated, you must first assume the testimony of the accomplice has been removed from the case. You must then determine whether there is any remaining evidence which tends to connect the defendant with the commission of the offense.

7. "If there is not such independent evidence which tends to connect defendant with the commission of the offense, the testimony of the accomplice is not corroborated.

8. "If there is such independent evidence which you believe, then the testimony of the accomplice is corroborated." (California Jury Instructions.)

One court has said: "Evidence is not sufficient if it requires interpretation and direction to be furnished by the accomplice's testimony to give it value;

the corroborative evidence to be sufficient and of the required substantial value must tend directly and immediately to connect the defendant with the offense; and the corroborative evidence is insufficient when it merely casts a grave suspicion upon the accused. (*People* v. *Lohman.*)

It has been further stated that: "It is the law that the testimony of an accomplice ought to be viewed with distrust. This does not mean that you may arbitrarily disregard such testimony, but you should give to it the weight to which you find it to be entitled after examining it with care and caution and in the light of all the evidence in the case." (California Jury Instructions.)

Feigned Accomplices

In crimes involving vice or narcotics, law enforcement agencies must resort to the use of informants or else pose as willing victims themselves. In either case, officers or informers are feigning complicity, that is, concealing their true identity or purpose in order to apprehend a suspect. They are, in effect, accomplices in the crime. For example: "An officer met Albert Gracia, an employee of the police department, and gave Garcia $40 with which he was to attempt to purchase heroin; the three men went to a Nalline testing center, where Garcia had been enrolled as an addict. Garcia drove to the center in his car, and the two officers followed in another car. Garcia entered the center and there met the defendant. Garcia told him that he wanted to buy a gram of heroin, and asked the defendant to "score" for him. The defendant replied that he would and instructed Garcia to pick it up at his house.

"Garcia then left and drove to a prearranged spot where he met with the officers. After the officers had searched Garcia's person, clothing and car, one of them concealed himself in the trunk of Garcia's car, which Garcia then drove to [the defendant's] house. . . . At approximately 9:25 P.M., Garcia arrived at the defendant's house . . . and parked his car. . . . The defendant came out and Garcia again asked him if he would "score" for him. Defendant replied that he would, and Garcia gave him the $40.00.

"The defendant handed Garcia five bindles of heroin. Although Garcia insisted that he was entitled to ten bindles for his $40.00, the defendant informed him that they had used some themselves and had given some to another fellow, and that was all there was." (*People* v. *Salazar.*)

Garcia was an accomplice. But "one who feigns complicity in the commission of a crime for the purpose of detecting and prosecuting the perpetrator thereof is not an accomplice, and his testimony need not be corroborated. Whenever the commission of a crime by one person involves the cooperation of another person, the latter becomes an accomplice only in the event that his cooperation in the commission of the crime is corrupt. In contacting the defendant and in arranging for the purchase of narcotics, Garcia was acting under specific instructions from police and was at all times kept under the closest surveillance possible; in this situation he was an accomplice and his testimony need not be corroborated."

A further difficulty in using accomplice testimony occurs in cross-examining the accomplice-witness. The defendant will explore the kind of promises which officers or prosecutors offered the witness. If the prosecutor fails to reveal such evidence in advance of trial, the defendant may urge a denial of due process. (*People* v. *Ruthford.*)

CASES AND MATERIALS

Ballard v. *Superior Court,* 64 C. 2d 159, 49 Cal. R. 302, 410 P. 2d 838.

California v. *Green,* 399 U.S. 149, 26 L. Ed. 2d 489, 90 S. Ct. 1930.

Harris v. *New York* (1971), 401 U.S. 222, 91 S. Ct. 643.

People v. *Green,* 3 C. 3d 981, 92 Cal. R. 494, 479 P. 2d 998.

People v. *Lohman,* 6 Cal. App. 3d 760, 86 Cal. R. 221.

People v. *Ortega,* 2 C. 3d 884, 83 Cal. R. 260: 848.

People v. *Perry,* 7 C. 3d 756, 103 Cal. R. 161, 499 P. 2d 129.

People v. *Ruthford,* 14 C. 3d 399, 121 Cal. R. 261, 534 P. 2d 1341.

People v. *Salazar,* 201 Cal. App. 2d 284, 20 Cal. R. 25.

People v. *Sam,* 71 C. 2d 194, 77 Cal. R. 804, 454 P. 2d 780.

People v. *Shipe,* 49 C. 3d 343, 122 Cal. R. 701.

Pitchess v. *Superior Court,* 11 C. 3d 531, 113 Cal. R. 897, 522 P. 2d 305.

1. In certain kinds of cases, the prosecution may be unable to prosecute the defendant without the testimony of a codefendant, accomplice, or other witness. To obtain the necessary testimony and thoroughly overcome the obstacle of the privilege against self-incrimination, the prosecution will offer immunity from prosecution to the witness. The immunity can be offered prior to trial or during the course of the trial. Once immunized from prosecution, the witness must answer the incriminating questions because the purpose of the privilege is not to prevent compulsory discovery of criminal conduct, but to protect against punishment. Thus, if the witness has become immunized from punishment for the crime, the answers will not incriminate this person and the privilege cannot be claimed. (Uniform Rules of Evidence, Rule 24.)

From the prosecution's standpoint, when negotiating with an accomplice or a party deeply involved or having knowledge about the pending criminal prosecution, two dangers are involved:

". . . The first is that of the treacherous witness—who promises to testify in return for a grant of immunity from prosecution and then, having secured immunity, does not testify in the manner he said he would or refuses to testify beyond a certain point. It is a fact of life that quality of veracity and honor among thieves and murderers leaves something to be desired, and an overly trusting district attorney may find that in granting immunity to one he could have prosecuted he has exchanged gold for brass.

"The other danger in the exchange of immunity for testimony is the obverse of the first—a witness may be so influenced by his hopes and fears that he will promise to testify to anything desired by the prosecution in order to obtain a grant of immunity. Because the satisfaction of the prosecutor is the witness's ticket to freedom, the prosecutor, by dangling the promise of immunity, can put the words he wishes into the witness's mouth. This danger is especially grave when the witness knows he is expected to give particular testimony, absent which he will not receive the promised immunity.

"These twin dangers point up the desirability for court approval of immunity bargains with . . . witnesses. . . . In our view, whenever target-area witnesses have been promised immunity in return for their promise to testify, the prosecutor's request for court approval should set out the terms of the agreement, the subject-matter of the testimony, the proceedings at which it will be given, the representations of the witness (or his counsel) as to the specific content of his testimony, and the promise of the witness to testify fully and truthfully in return for the promised grant of immunity. On court approval of the agreement, immunity will be granted the witness *after he has complied with the representations of the agreement*.

"As with plea bargains, terms of a promise of immunity should appear clearly on the record and be supported by court order. Full disclosure of the terms of the bargain not only protects against double-dealing, coercion, and misunderstanding, but it enables an impartial judicial officer to review the propriety of the immunity bargain itself. The court retains ample authority to prevent major abuses in granting immunity. The veto power (serves) as a salutory check against the possible overzealousness, unwisdom, or corruption of local prosecutors. (Commissioner's Prefatory Note, Model State Witness Immunity Act, 9C U.L.A. 192.) True enough, a promise of immunity from prosecution in exchange for particular testimony amounts to a promise by the witness to testify in a certain way, and the witness who does not so testify will not acquire the sought-for immunity. To that extent the witness is vulnerable to the charge that his testimony has been bought. Yet while these factors bear heavily on the weight to be given the witness's testimony, they do not impinge upon the validity of the bargain itself.

"In sum, when an immunity agreement is entered into under court sanction, the witness becomes absolutely entitled to immunity 'provided it appears that he acted in good faith and that he testified fully and fairly.' (*Whiskey Cases* [1878], 99 U.S. 594, 595, 598, 599, 600, 602, 604, 605; 25 L. Ed. 399, 400, 401, 402, 403.) We see no reason why the witness's good faith may not be made a matter of record in advance of his appearance on the stand by requiring him to disclose the nature of his prospective testimony." For a discussion of judicially awarded immunity beyond statutory authorization, see *People* v. *Superior Court* (Kaufman), 12 C. 3d 421, 115 Cal. R. 812, 525 P. 2d 716.

2. The defendant is prosecuted for grand theft auto. During the course of his testimony, he states that he purchased the car with money he won in gambling. To

rebut this testimony, the prosecutor offers in evidence a copy of the defendant's financial statement, which he completed to establish indigency for the purpose of representation by the public defender. In this statement, the only asset listed by the defendant is an old car. Can the prosecution impeach the defendant's testimony by introduction of the financial statement? (*People* v. *Canfield,* 12 C. 3d 699, 117 Cal. R. 81, 527 P. 2d 633.)

3. A witness in a robbery testifies, identifying the defendant as the perpetrator. The defendant calls a psychiatrist to testify about the distorting effects of excitement and fear on the witness's ability to perceive, recall, and relate. Is such testimony admissible? See Juviler, "Psychiatric Opinions as to the Credibility of Witnesses: A Suggested Approach," 48 *California Law Review* 648.

4. Accomplices may be corroborated by independent evidence of flight, concealing identity or whereabouts, or attempted escape. See *People* v. *Perry,* 7 C. 3d 756, 103 Cal. R. 161, 499 P. 2d 129.

5. The Model State Witness Immunity Act is discussed in 9 *UCLA Law Review* 186.

6. The Federal Immunity Statute may be found in 18 U.S.C. 6001.

7. A sample Immunity Statute (Calif. P.C. 1324 & 1324.1) is presented below.

1324: "In any felony proceeding or in any investigation or proceeding before a grand jury for any felony offense, if a person refuses to answer a question or produce evidence of any other kind on the ground that he may be incriminated thereby, and if the district attorney of the county in writing requests the superior court in and for that county to order that person to answer the question or produce the evidence, a judge of the superior court shall set a time for hearing and order the person to appear before the court and show cause, if any, why the question should not be answered or the evidence produced, and the court shall order the question answered or the evidence produced unless it finds that to do so would be clearly contrary to the public interest, or could subject the witness to a criminal prosecution in another jurisdiction, and that person shall comply with the order. After complying, and if, but for this section, he would have been privileged to withhold the answer given or the evidence produced by him, that person shall not be prosecuted or subjected to penalty or forfeiture for or on account of any fact or act concerning which in accordance with the order he was required to answer or produce evidence. But he may nevertheless be prosecuted or subjected to penalty or forfeiture for any perjury, false swearing or contempt committed in answering or failing to answer or in producing or failing to produce evidence in accordance with the order."

1324.1: "In any misdemeanor proceeding in any court, if a person refuses to answer a question or produce evidence of any other kind on the ground that he may be incriminated thereby, the person may agree in writing with the district attorney of the county, or the prosecuting attorney of a city, as the case may be, to testify voluntarily pursuant to this section. Upon written request of such district attorney, or prosecuting attorney, the court having jurisdiction of the proceeding shall approve such written agreement unless the court finds that to do so would be clearly contrary to the public interest. If, after court approval of such agreement, and if, but for this section, the person would have been privileged to withhold the answer given or the evidence produced by him, that person shall not be prosecuted or subjected to penalty or forfeiture for or on account of any fact or act concerning which, in accordance with such agreement, he answered or produced evidence, but he may, nevertheless, be prosecuted or subjected to penalty or forfeiture for any perjury, false swearing or contempt committed in answering or in producing evidence in accordance with such agreement. If such person fails to give any answer or to produce any evidence in accordance with such agreement, that person shall be prosecuted or subjected to penalty or forfeiture in the same manner and to the same extent as he would be prosecuted or subjected to penalty or forfeiture but for this section."

NOTES

1. For a summary of cases supporting majority and minority views, see 52 A.L.R. 2d; also see 16 So. Cal. L. Rev., 333 for a discussion of this issue with appropriate citations. The same rule applies to use of marijuana; see *People* v. *Rocha,* 3 C. 3d 893, 92 Cal. R. 172, 479 P. 2d 372.
2. Evidence Code Section 786: "Evidence of traits of his character other than honesty or veracity, or their opposites, is inadmissible to attack or support the credibility of a witness."
3. Evidence Code Section 1102: "In a criminal action, evidence of the defendant's character or a trait of his character in the form of an opinion or evidence of his reputation is not inadmissible if: A. Offered by the defendant to prove his conduct in conformity with such character trait or character. B. Offered by the prosecution to rebut evidence adduced by the defendant under subdivision."
4. Any otherwise admissible evidence (including evidence in the form of an opinion, evidence of reputation, and evidence of specific instances of such person's conduct) is admissible to prove a person's character or a trait of his or her character.
5. Evidence Code Section 1101: "A. . . . Evidence of a person's character or a trait of his character . . . is inadmissible when offered to prove his conduct on a specified occasion.
   "B. Nothing in this section prohibits the admission of evidence that a person committed a crime, civil wrong, or other act when relevant to prove some fact (such as motive, opportunity, intent, appropriation, plan, knowledge, identity, or absence of mistake or accident) other than his disposition to commit such acts."
6. If the court appoints a psychotherapist, the victim cannot claim the information obtained in such an interview is privileged. If the victim has been examined by a psychiatrist under any other circumstances, she can assert the privilege. See *People* v. *Perry*.

10 Hearsay

Chapter Objectives

After reading this chapter, you will be able to:

1. Discuss the rules prohibiting hearsay evidence and the exceptions to those rules.

2. Explain the circumstances in which an accused's statement is admissible against the accused.

3. Describe the role of confessions in criminal cases.

4. Define voluntariness and explain the factors that determine whether or not a confession is voluntary.

5. Describe the rules governing joint confessions and confessions by co-conspirators.

The General Rule

Rules of evidence are a legislative or judicial attempt to allow the trier of fact to consider testimony and receive exhibits relevant and material to the defendant's guilt or innocence. Some evidentiary rules prohibit a jury from hearing relevant testimony because the prejudicial effect of the evidence outweighs its value in proving the issue in question. Other rules limit the introduction of evidence which, although relevant, is too untrustworthy or unreliable. A most conspicuous example of the latter is hearsay evidence. Generally speaking, hearsay is defined as a statement that was made other than by a witness testifying at a trial which is offered to prove the truth of the matter stated. Or, in other words, hearsay is testimony by a witness on the stand concerning matters told to the witness by a third party. The validity of such evidence depends upon the accuracy of the third party's perception as well as the person's ability to recollect or relate observations. When presented with hearsay evidence, a jury has no opportunity to observe the manner, attitude, and demeanor of the third party in order to evaluate his or her credibility. Nor is the third party under oath to tell the truth. Furthermore, no cross-examination of the third party can be undertaken in his or her absence. All these deficiencies require the general exclusion of such evidence; however, there are some exceptions.

One major exception to the exclusion of hearsay is in pre-trial hearings on motions to suppress evidence based upon an alleged unlawful search and seizure. If the officer is called to testify on the lawfulness of the arrest or search, he or she may rely upon statements made by a third party to establish probable cause to arrest or probable cause to support a search warrant. Such out-of-court statements, however, are not offered to prove the truth of the matter stated, but only to establish the officer's reasonable basis to arrest, detain, or search. The out-of-court statements may originate from informants or fellow officers, or through official enforcement channels. The officer can rely on such statements as a basis to arrest and search, but the same statements are not admissible at a trial on the issue of guilt or innocence.

When an officer testifies on the issue of probable cause and repeats a hearsay statement from an informant, the defendant may still cross-examine the officer-witness to determine the reliability of the information and the informant's accuracy in relating that information. If the officer testifies that he or she received the information through official channels, the defendant may still insist that the witness identify the source of the information. Probable cause cannot be manufactured through the device of relaying information through several officers. But in revealing the original source of the information, the officer need not necessarily disclose the name of the person. Whether disclosure will be required depends upon the materiality of the informant to the defendant's guilt or innocence. (See The Identity of Informant Privilege in chapter 8.)

The exceptions to the general hearsay rule authorize the reception of hearsay because certain kinds of evidence carry an element of trustworthiness. But in order for an exception to be allowed, certain preliminary questions must be asked. Unless these foundational elements are satisfied, the out-of-court statements cannot be admitted. Depending upon the particular rule involved, the prosecution may have to establish out-of-court that the witness is unavailable, dead, insane, or disqualified from testifying.

In terms of prosecuting or defending criminal cases, certain rules of hearsay are more important than others. A number of rules involving exceptions to the hearsay rule arise only in civil cases. Within the category of criminal cases, specific hearsay problems arise in homicide cases, in robbery cases, and in forgery cases. Counsel and investigators for both sides must be alert to the kinds of out-of-court statements which will assist in the prosecution or defense of these cases. If evidence comes within an exception to the hearsay rule, preparation must be made in advance of trial to establish the necessary foundation.

Even if evidence which is offered is admissible because the statement is not offered to prove the truth of the matter asserted—and is therefore not hearsay—or even if it comes within an exception to the hearsay rule, the court must still find that the evidence is relevant and material to the case on trial and that no other rule of evidence is violated by admitting this evidence. (For example, a relevant statement may be a privileged communication.) A preliminary checklist on admissibility of a witness's testimony must be reviewed before the issue of hearsay arises. More specifically, it must be determined if the witness is competent and has personal knowledge of the facts, if his or her testimony is subject to a claim of privilege, etc.

Admissions and Confessions

An *admission* is a statement made by defendants acknowledging one or more facts which tend to connect them with a crime. A *confession* is a statement made by defendants admitting each element of the crime charged against them. An admission or a confession is admissible as an exception to the hearsay rule on the theory that acknowledging guilt of a crime is so adverse to a party's interest that it can be considered reliable.

The most frequent use of out-of-court statements in criminal cases concerns the admission or confession of a defendant. An out-of-court statement by a defendant to an officer admitting implication in a crime may be offered for the truth of that statement. Such statements are hearsay, yet they are admissible as an exception to the hearsay rule. But confessions are subject to numerous other legal objections before they may be received in evidence.

Juries are routinely instructed that although they may consider an oral admission or confession, such statements must be viewed with caution.[1] Too much opportunity exists for mistakes or omissions in repeating oral conversations.[2]

An admission or a confession may not be received in evidence unless the prosecution offers independent evidence of all the elements of the crime charged against the defendant. No part of the crime may be proved by a defendant's statement, although the degree of a crime may be so established. Once the corpus delicti, or elements of the crime, have been proved, the defendant's statement to the officer may be considered by the jury in determining guilt or innocence.

Historical Background

Just as the Fourth Amendment prohibits the court from admitting evidence seized in violation of its prohibition against unreasonable searches and seizures, the Fifth Amendment to the U.S. Constitution excludes evidence obtained in violation of its command that "no person shall be compelled to be a witness against himself." The U.S. Supreme Court has construed this phrase to mean that any statement of a suspect in custody is inadmissible as evidence in a criminal trial if obtained in violation of the Fifth Amendment. Because confessions are heavily incriminating, their admissibility as evidence may be crucial to the prosecution case. Some background is necessary to understand the current law on the admissibility of confessions.

In early American legal history, involuntary confessions were excluded on the ground of their presumed untrustworthiness—that is, not because any wrong was done to the accused in using them, but because the accused might have been induced by the pressure of hope or fear to admit facts unfavorable to him- or herself, without regard to their truth, in order to obtain promised relief or avoid threatened danger.[3] Because of this rule, evidence of physical facts discovered by means of an involuntary confession was uniformly held to be admissible because such evidence tended to corroborate or prove the trustworthiness of the confession.

More recently, the U.S. Supreme Court declared that the older "trustworthiness" test of admissibility is not an acceptable standard. The Court held that admission into evidence of confessions that are involuntary—that is, the product of coercion, either physical or psychological—is prohibited, regardless of the confessions' truth or falsity. According to the Court this is so not because such confessions are unlikely to be true, but because the methods used to extract them offend an underlying principle in the enforcement of criminal law. Ours is an accusatorial, not an inquisitorial system—a system in which the State must establish guilt by evidence which is independently and freely secured; the State may not prove the charge against an accused by means of coercion.

Under this reasoning, the justification for the old rule permitting the introducing of real evidence discovered by means of an involuntary confession—that is, that such evidence tends to prove the "trustworthiness" of the confession—is now constitutionally indefensible. The issue now is whether the introduction of the challenged evidence—the confession itself or its asserted product—denies the accused any essential element of a fair trial or due process of law. Thus, any threat, promise, or reward made by an officer to the defendant voids any subsequent confession, regardless of the truthfulness of the confession or any corroborating facts.

As stated by one court, "the line to be drawn between permissible police conduct and conduct deemed to induce, or to tend to induce, an involuntary statement does not depend on the bare language of inducement, but rather on the nature of the benefit to be derived by the defendant if he speaks the truth, as represented by the police. Advice or exhortation by a police officer to an accused to "tell the truth," or that "it would be better to tell the truth," unaccompanied by either a threat or promise, does not render a subsequent confession involuntary. . . . When the benefit pointed out by the police to a suspect is merely that which flows naturally from a truthful and honest course of conduct, there is nothing improper. On the other hand, if in addition to the foregoing benefit or in place of it, the defendant is given to understand that he might reasonably expect benefits in the nature of more lenient treatment at the hands of the police, prosecution, or court in consideration for making a statement, even a truthful one, such motivation is deemed to render the statement involuntary and inadmissible. The offer or promise of such benefit need not be express, but may be implied from equivocal language not otherwise made clear." (*People* v. *Hill*.)

Often suspects attempt to exonerate themselves or to minimize their responsibility for a criminal act. Their offers to talk may be preceded by questions as to the benefits which will flow to them if they confess. At this point, interrogating officers are on dangerous legal ground. Any temptation to promise a benefit—other than those that come naturally from telling the truth—must be avoided.

Voluntariness

Whenever the prosecution offers a confession, either written or oral, they must first establish the "voluntariness" of the statement. "The most extensive judicial exposition of the meaning of 'voluntariness' has been developed in those cases in which the U.S. Supreme Court has had to determine the 'voluntariness' of a defendant's confession for the purposes of the Fourteenth Amendment. Almost 40 years ago, the court held that a criminal conviction based upon a confession obtained by brutality and violence was constitutionally invalid under the Due Process Clause of the Fourteenth Amendment. In some 30 different cases decided therafter, the court was faced with the necessity of determining whether in fact the confessions in issue had been 'voluntarily' given. It is to that body of case law to which courts turn for initial guidance on the meaning of 'voluntariness.' Those cases yield no talismanic definition of 'voluntariness,' mechanically applicable to the host of situations where the question has arisen. 'The notion of voluntariness, Mr. Justice Frankfurter once wrote, 'is itself an amphibian.' It cannot be taken literally to mean a 'knowing' choice. Except where a person is unconscious or drugged or otherwise lacks capacity for conscious choice, all incriminating statements—even those made under brutal treatment—are 'voluntary' in the sense of representing a choice of alternatives.

". . . 'Voluntariness' has reflected an accommodation of the complex of values implicated in police questioning of a suspect. At one end of the spectrum is the acknowledged need for police questioning as a tool for the effective enforcement of criminal laws. Without such investigation, those who were innocent might be falsely accused, those who were guilty might wholly escape prosecution, and many crimes would go unsolved. In short, the security of all would be diminished. At the other end of the spectrum is the set of values reflecting society's deeply felt belief that the criminal law cannot be used as an instrument of unfairness, and that the possibility of unfair and even brutal police tactics poses a real and serious threat to civilized notions of justice. In cases involving involuntary confessions, this court enforces the strongly felt attitude of our society that important human values are sacrificed where an agency of the government, in the course of securing a conviction, wrings a confession out of an accused against his will.

"This court's decisions reflect a frank recognition that the Constitution requires the sacrifice of neither security nor liberty. The Due Process Clause does not mandate that the police forego all questioning, nor that they be given carte blanche to extract what they can from a suspect. 'The ultimate test remains that which has been the only clearly established test in Anglo-American courts for two hundred years: the test of voluntariness. Is the confession the product of an essentially free and unconstrained choice by its maker? If it is, if he has willed to confess, it may be used against him. If it is not, if his will has been overborne and his capacity for self-determination critically impaired, the use of his confession offends due process.'

"In determining whether a defendant's will was overborne in a particular case, the court has assessed the totality of all the surrounding circumstances—both the characteristics of the accused and the details of the interrogation. In all of these cases, the court has determined the factual circumstances surrounding the confession, assessed the psychological impact on the accused, and evaluated the legal significance of how the accused reacted. The significant fact about all of these decisions is that none of them turned on the presence or absence of a single controlling criterion; each reflected a careful scrutiny of all the surrounding circumstances." (*Schneckloth* v. *Bustamonte*.)[4]

Because interrogation of suspects is conducted within the confines of a governmental facility with few outside witnesses, determining "voluntariness" is difficult. Some independent facts can be ascertained, but often the only witnesses are the defendant and police officers.

Yet in some cases the atmosphere of coercion is obvious; it is apparent that the confession is not the product of a free will. For example, in *Reck* v. *Pate,* the court found that: "At the time of his arrest, the defendant was a nineteen-year-old youth of subnormal intelligence. He had no prior criminal record or experience with the police. He was held nearly eight days without a judicial hearing. Four of those days preceded his first confession. During that period, the defendant was subjected each day to six- or seven-hour stretches of relentless and incessant interrogation. The questioning was conducted by groups of officers. For the first three days the interrogation ranged over a wide variety of crimes. On the night of the third day of his detention the interrogation turned to the crime for which the defendant stands convicted. During this same four-day period he was shuttled back and forth between police stations and interrogation rooms. In addition, defendant was intermittently placed on public exhibition in 'show-ups.' On the night before his confession, defendant became ill while on display in such a 'show-up.' He was taken to the hospital, returned to the police station, and put back on public display. When he again became ill, he was removed from the 'show-up,' but interrogation in the windowless 'handball court' continued relentlessly until he grew faint and vomited blood on the floor. Once more he was taken to the hospital, where he spent the night under the influence of drugs. The next morning he was removed from the hospital in a wheel chair, and intensive interrogation was immediately resumed. Some eight hours later the defendant signed his first confession. The next afternoon he signed a second.

"During the entire period preceding his confessions, defendant was without adequate food, without counsel, and without the assistance of family or friends. He was, for all practical purposes, held incommunicado. He was physically weakened and in intense pain."

The U.S. Supreme Court concluded that the total combination of circumstances was so inherently coercive that the confession was involuntary. The court considered the age of the defendant, his mental ability, and his prior criminal history. Youth is not too significant a factor if balanced by extensive prior police contacts. But immaturity coupled with a low I.Q. is significant. The relentless interrogation over several days does not suggest a repentant criminal ready to confess. The illness and absence of food combined with isolation from friends and inability to contact counsel definitely weakened the accused's will to resist and kept him from making an intelligent choice concerning whether or not to speak.

Greenwald v. *Wisconsin* is another case in which a confession was held to be involuntary. The court summarized the testimony—apart from certain conflicts between the defendant and the officer—as follows:

> Defendant, who has a ninth-grade education, was arrested on suspicion of burglary shortly before 10:45 on the evening of January 20, 1965. He was taken to a police station. He was suffering from high blood pressure, a condition for which he was taking medication twice a day. Defendant had last taken food and medication, before his arrest, at 4 P.M. He did not have medication with him at the time of the arrest. At the police station defendant was interrogated from 10:45 until midnight. He was not advised of his constitutional rights. Defendant repeatedly denied guilt. No incriminating statements were made at this time.
>
> Defendant was booked and fingerprinted and, sometime after 2 A.M., he was taken to a cell in the city jail. A plank fastened to the wall served as his bed. At 6 A.M., defendant was led from the cell to a 'bullpen.' At 8:30 he was placed in a lineup. At 8:45, his interrogation recommenced. It was conducted by several officers at a time. Defendant testified that in the course of the morning he was not offered food and that he continued to be without medication. For an hour or two he refused to answer any questions. When he did speak, it was to deny, once again, his guilt.
>
> Sometime after 10:00 A.M., defendant was asked to write out a confession. He refused, stating that 'it was against my constitutional rights' and that he was 'entitled to have a lawyer.' These statements were ignored. No further reference was made to an attorney, by defendant or by the police officers.

> At about 11:00 A.M., defendant began a series of oral admissions culminating in a full oral confession at about 11:30. At noon he was offered food. The confession was reduced to writing around 1:00 P.M. Just before the confession was reduced to writing, defendant was advised of his constitutional rights. According to his testimony, he confessed because 'I knew they weren't going to leave me alone until I did.'" Under the "totality of circumstances" test, the court found the confession involuntary.

When the court reviews the "totality of the circumstances," no single element may be significant in itself, but due to the combination of elements, the confession may be held involuntary. The *kinds* of evidence the court voices concern about can be identified. They are: the character of the accused, the conduct of the police, the length of the interrogation, the use of deceptive techniques, promises, or threats, and the introduction of outside personnel.

Character of the Accused Defendants who are mature individuals with no history of bizarre conduct or evidence of present mental instability might find difficulty in contending that their confessions are not the product of a rational intellect and a free will. But particularly in homicide prosecutions, investigators frequently confront suspects whose intellectual quotient is low and whose previous history involves commitments in mental institutions. Interrogating such suspects is difficult. Moreover, when such a defendant is brought to court, the defense counsel will probably request the appointment of a psychiatrist to examine the defendant. If the report reflects psychological disorder, it may be used to buttress the defendant's contention that his or her confession was involuntary.

If a defendant is immature, this factor will also be taken into account. Even the sophisticated adolescent who has committed violent crimes must be questioned within the legal guidelines laid down by the U.S. Supreme Court. The Court has urged trial courts to exercise special caution in admitting admissions or confessions of juveniles, not only to scrutinize the possibility of coercion, but also to assure themselves that the confession is not the product of fantasy, fright, or despair. (*In re Gault.*) This rule applies even if the minor is tried in juvenile court. In *Haley* v. *Ohio,* "a 15-year-old boy was arrested shortly after midnight on a robbery-murder charge. He was interrogated by relays of police officers, without being advised of his right to counsel, and at 5:00 A.M., he orally confessed. After being informed that he had a right to remain silent and that his statement might be used against him, he signed a written version of his confession. He was thereafter held incommunicado for three days before being arraigned."

The United States Supreme Court reviewed the foregoing undisputed evidence and held that "the confession was obtained by unconstitutional methods and its introduction in evidence therefore violated due process.'' The court reasoned that ''when, as here, a mere child—an easy victim of the law—is before us, special care in scrutinizing the record must be used. Age 15 is a tender and difficult age for a boy. . . . He cannot be judged by the more exacting standards of maturity. That which would leave a man cold and unimpressed can overawe and overwhelm a lad in his early teens. This is the period of great instability which the crisis of adolescence produces. A 15-year-old lad, questioned through the dead of night by relays of police, is a ready victim of the inquisition. Mature men possibly might stand the ordeal from midnight to 5 A.M. But we cannot believe that a lad of tender years is a match for the police in such a contest. He needs counsel and support if he is not to become the victim first of fear, then of panic. He needs someone on whom to lean. . . .''

The *Haley* case does not hold that age alone is a decisive factor. In fact, the court reiterated the general rule that age constitutes just one of the circumstances to be considered in determining voluntariness. Although some courts differ, most agree that youth alone does not automatically invalidate a minor's voluntary confession of a crime. The prosecution can also offer evidence of the minor's prior experience with the police and courts (including advisement of his or her constitutional rights prior to questioning). But if the record reflects extensive questioning, delayed arraignment, or denial of access to friends or counsel, the defendant's youth would be an additional factor to be considered in determining voluntariness.

The mental subnormality of a defendant is another factor which must be considered in determining whether the defendant could voluntarily confess. In many cases, the subnormal defendant will contend that his or her confession was the product of an inability to resist questioning by officers or the result of susceptibility to pressure; in short, the defendant will raise the issue of coercion. Emotional or mental instability will not automatically foreclose admissibility of a voluntary confession, but the issue will be raised at trial as one of the factors in the ''totality of circumstances'' test.[5]

Note also that the issue of voluntariness is closely related to advising suspects of their constitutional rights prior to questioning. Failure to advise arrestees of their constitutional rights under the *Miranda* decision prevents the introduction of such confessions in evidence during the prosecution case-in-chief, even if the test of voluntariness is met. If such defendants testify and the prosecution attempts to impeach their testimony by offering their confessions in rebuttal, the defendants can still contend that failure to advise them of their *Miranda* rights rendered their confessions involuntary—in which case, if the trial court agrees, such confessions cannot be used for any purpose.

Threats In *Lynumn* v. *Illinois,* the defendant testified as follows: ''I told him (the officer) that I hadn't sold [to] Zeno; I didn't know anything about narcotics and I had no source of supply. He kept insisting I had a source of supply and had been dealing in narcotics. I kept telling him I did not and that I knew nothing about it. Then he started telling me I could get 10 years and the children could be taken away, and after I got out they would be taken away and strangers would have them, and if I could cooperate he would see they weren't; and he would recommend leniency and I had better do what they told me if I wanted to see my kids again. The two children are three and four years old. Their father is dead; they live with me. I love my children very much. I have never been arrested for anything in my whole life before. I did not know how much power a policeman had in a recommendation to the State's Attorney or to the Court. I did not know that a Court and a State's Attorney are not bound by a police officer's recommendations. I did not know anything about it. All the officers talked to me about my children and the time I could get for not cooperating. All three officers did. After that conversation I believed that if I cooperated with them and answered the questions the way they wanted me to answer, I believed that I would not be prosecuted. They had said I had better say what they wanted me to, or I would lose the kids. I said I would say anything they wanted me to say. I asked what I was to say. I was told to say 'You must admit you gave Zeno the package' so I said, 'Yes, I gave it to him.'

". . . The only reason I had for admitting it to the police was the hope of saving myself from going to jail and being taken away from my children. The statements I made to the police after they promised that they would intercede for me, the statements admitting the crime, were false.

". . . My statement to the police officers that I sold the marijuana to Zeno was false. I lied to the police at that time. I lied because the police told me they were going to send me to jail for 10 years and take my children, and I would never see them again; so I agreed to say whatever they wanted me to say."

The Court added: "The police officers did not deny that these were the circumstances under which the (arrestee) told them that she had sold marijuana to Zeno. To the contrary, their testimony largely corroborated (her) testimony."

In this example, the threat was direct and unambiguous. Evidence of threats will render any subsequent confession involuntary because the statement is not the product of a free will. In some cases, the threat may be more subtle, for example, a suggestion that relatives may be arrested unless the defendant admits guilt (*People* v. *Matlock*), or the refusal to release a coarrestee until the defendant confesses. (*People* v. *Trout.*) But the mere fact that a defendant believes or hopes a confession may result in the exoneration of others does not render the confession involuntary as a matter of law. (*People* v. *Haydel.*) To render the confession involuntary, there must be evidence that the officers directly or indirectly indicated that other people would be released or not arrested.

Threats to the defendant may also arise because of the circumstances of the arrest. For example, in *Payne* v. *Arkansas,* the court summarized the facts as follows:

"Defendant testified, concerning the conduct that immediately induced his confession, as follows: 'I was locked up upstairs and Chief Norman Young came up (about 1:00 P.M. on October 7) and he told me that I had not told him all of the story—he said that there was 30 or 40 people outside that wanted to get to me, and he said if I would come in and tell him the truth that he would probably keep them from coming in.' When again asked what the chief of police had said to him on that occasion, defendant testified:

"'Chief Norman Young said thirty or forty people were outside wanting to get in to me and he asked me if I wanted to make a confession he would try to keep them out.' The chief of police, on cross-examination, admitted that he had made the substance of that statement to defendant, and had told him that he would be permitted to confess to the chief 'in private.' In this setting, defendant immediately agreed to make a statement to the chief. The chief then took defendant to his private office, and almost immediately after arriving at that place there was a knock on the door. The chief opened the door and stepped outside, leaving the door ajar, and defendant heard him say 'He is fixing to confess now, and he would like to have me alone.' Defendant did not know what persons or how many were outside the door. The chief re-entered his office and began questioning defendant, who orally confessed that he had committed the crime." Under these circumstances, the implied threat was sufficient to void the confession.

As we have seen, if the confession is the product of threats by law enforcement officers, the confession is excluded as evidence because the Due Process Clause of the U.S. Constitution prohibits unlawful action by government agents. But what if the confession is induced by threats made by civilians? The passage that follows illustrates such a case:

"Defendant was kidnaped at rifle point by Harry Pettit, the victim's husband. He was threatened with imminent death by a vengeful man who believed defendant had aborted his wife and caused her death. Holding a rifle to defendant's head, Pettit forced the defendant to drive to a strange house. Other relatives of Mrs. Pettit bent on revenge were there. Pettit showed the defendant a bullet from the rifle and told him that it was 'his' bullet if he did not confess to killing Mrs. Pettit. He commanded the defendant to stare at the bullet for long periods while Pettit threatened his life. Pettit drummed it into the defendant's mind that he must confess or die. Pettit also threatened defendant's parents with dire consequences if they did anything in his defense. Then, while Pettit pointed his rifle at the defendant, another man beat him with his fists. For almost two hours defendant was kicked and slugged with shoes, fists and furniture. A glass object was hurled at him. The kidnapers pushed his head through a window, cutting him. Pettit struck him in the groin with his rifle butt and hit him other places with it.

Defendant received many blows on the head. This treatment terrorized, numbed, nauseated and caused defendant great pain. During this period the defendant was constantly reminded that unless he confessed he would be murdered.

"In corroboration of this testimony, Officer Peterson, the arresting officer, testified that when he arrived on the scene he observed defendant's condition and that he was bleeding, bruised, perspiring and in a disheveled state. He saw Harry Pettit seated on a chair in front of defendant with a gun in his hands. He knew that defendant had been brought to the house at the point of a gun. He had seen defendant about two hours earlier and knew that his injuries had been inflicted in the meantime.

"Defendant's reaction to being rescued from his tormentors by the police was one of relief.

"The police arrested the defendant, handcuffed him and removed him to the police station. He arrived at the station between 7:30 and 7:45 P.M. and the interview leading to his confession began at 8:11 P.M. Defendant did not receive medical attention or have an opportunity to rest or wash himself. He was given only one cup of water before his confession was complete. During the interview he was so confused that he showed complete temporal disorientation. Defendant testified that he was fatigued, numb, confused and in increasing pain during the entire interview. He testified that he could not recall many of the questions and answers which were recorded. He testified that he was in fear for himself and his parents from further attack by the hoodlums. One of the officers reminded him that he was 'lucky to be alive.' Defendant testified that during the interview: 'I would have agreed with anything in the world just to be left alone. I would have said "Yes" to anything in the world if they had let me lay down and let me rest.'" (*People* v. *Berve.*)

Although an involuntary confession is inadmissible under the Due Process Clause of the U.S. Constitution, the Constitution only prohibits governmental action—not private action. Yet involuntary confessions are so obnoxious to a free society that they will be excluded because they deny a defendant the right to a fair trial. Whether a confession to police officers was induced by the unlawful conduct of civilians or made involuntarily directly to civilians is immaterial. In either case, the confession will be excluded.

Promises Because any admission or confession must be the product of a free mind, a promise to reduce the charge, to seek leniency from the court, or to attempt to provide some benefit to the accused will render any confession involuntary. The nature of such a promise need not be express; the implication may be sufficiently clear to induce the accused to believe the officer is able to promise some benefit. For example: In a prosecution for a homicide, the arresting officer testified he said to the defendant, "You either take it the hard way or you take it the easy way. Now, the hard way is that I am going to get up and walk out of this room and put you before a jury of twelve good and true people, and I am going to bring in a number of medical doctors, a great number of medical doctors, and I am going to bring in the grandparents of that child, and I am going to bring in some of your neighbors, and we are going to put them on the witness stand and swear them in to tell the truth, and they are going to tell everything they know about you, all about your violent temper, about the number of times that you have beat that child, and then the judge is going to pass sentence on you, and before you walk up to that judge to find out what is going to happen to you, he is going to want to know your ability to tell the truth.

"We have a little paper down here that wants to know how your ability is to tell the truth, whether you sit down and told the truth about it, or whether you lied about it, and if we write across there that this person would not tell the truth, on many opportunities, we gave him the chance to tell the truth, but he absolutely refused to tell any truth about it at all—in other words, if we just wrote one word across there, Liar, that would—you can go up before that judge and you can ask him for all the breaks in the world, and he is not going to believe you because when a man tells a lie, then even the truth becomes a lie because he is branded as a liar.

"Now if you want to meet that judge that way, if you want to meet your maker that way, well, brother, that is up to you."

The court said: "The latter part of this statement was both a threat, that unless defendant told the officers what they wanted and were insisting that he tell them they would write 'Liar' on the statement and that defendant could then expect no leniency from the court; and an implied promise, that if defendant told the officers the story that they were insisting that he tell them they would not write 'Liar' on the document and defendant might expect a 'break' from the court." (*People* v. *Brommel.*)

Advice to "tell the truth" or "reveal the facts" is not prohibited as long as such encouragement is not coupled with any promise. ". . . When the benefit pointed out by the police to a suspect is merely that which flows naturally from a truthful and honest course of conduct, there is nothing improper. On the other hand, if in addition to the foregoing benefit or in place of it, the defendant is given to understand that he might reasonably expect benefits in the nature of more lenient treatment at the hands of the police, prosecution, or court in consideration for making a statement, even a truthful one, such motivation is deemed to render the statement involuntary and inadmissible. . . .

"Often a suspect attempts to exonerate himself or minimize his responsibility for a criminal act. His offer to talk may be preceded by queries as to the benefit which will flow to him if he confesses. At this point, the interrogating officer is on dangerous legal ground. Any temptation to promise a benefit—other than that of telling the truth—must be avoided." (*People* v. *Hill.*)

Just as officers might threaten to arrest a spouse or relative unless the accused confesses, they might also promise to release such a person already under arrest. If the other person had been arrested lawfully for participation in the crime, the officer would not be in a position to effect a complete release. If the arrest was unfounded, the release would be forthcoming anyway. Thus, the benefit is illusory.

Often suspects will initiate a request for some benefit in exchange for a confession. Investigation officers can only indicate that they are in no position to provide benefits, but that they will submit all the evidence to the prosecution and court for their evaluation.

Extended Interrogation Most states require that an accused be brought before a magistrate within a reasonable time after the arrest. During that time, usually forty-eight hours, officers must present sufficient evidence to warrant continued incarceration. This period of time will be consumed by investigation and questioning. In a complex or serious case, more time for questioning would be expected, but if the questioning is prolonged or it is conducted by relays of officers without respite for the accused, the circumstances may become coercive in effect. The ability of one person to resist extensive questioning will vary, and age and prior experience with the police and the courts will be relevant as factors applying to the "totality of circumstance." (*Ashcraft* v. *Tennessee.*)

Deception: Defendant Not in Custody The Fifth and Fourteenth Amendments, as construed by the U.S. Supreme Court, require that confessions be the product of a free will and that they be obtained without coercion. When a person is arrested, whether force is used or not a certain element of coercion is present. But when a person is not in custody, or is unaware that he or she is speaking to police officers, the element of coercion disappears. For these reasons, any statements made by a suspect in the field to an undercover officer are not within the protection of the Fifth and Fourteenth Amendments. Thus, incriminating conversations between narcotic sellers and undercover officers would not be excluded from evidence on Fifth and Fourteenth Amendment grounds. Nor would a recording or transcription of such a conversation be excluded.

If officers intend to use witnesses or informants to implicate a defendant during the course of an investigation, for the reasons given above any incriminating statements made to them by a suspect not in custody would be admissible. For example, if a rape victim telephoned a suspect at the request of the police, the conversation could be overheard and recorded without constitutional objection. The absence of custody is the significant factor for Fifth and Fourteenth Amendment purposes.

Although defendants may not be able to invoke a Fifth Amendment claim to prohibit the introduction of incriminating statements made while not in custody, can they object on other constitutional grounds? In *U.S.* v. *White,* an informant entered the defendant's premises at the request of police. Prior to this entry, police had concealed a microphone and transmitter on his person. Unknown to the suspect, the conversation between the informant and the suspect was overheard, recorded, and transcribed by police. At the trial, the prosecutor offered the transcribed statement into evidence. The defendant argued that under the Fourth Amendment to the U.S. Constitution, the actions of the police constituted an unlawful search and seizure (of his conversation).

Under current constitutional theory, verbal evidence as well as physical evidence is within the scope of Fourth Amendment protection. But the court rejected the defendant's agrument for the following reasons: ". . . that 'however strongly a defendant may trust an apparent colleague, his expectations in this respect are not protected by the Fourth Amendment when it turns out that the colleague is a government agent regularly communicating with the authorities. In these circumstances, no interest legitimately protected by the Fourth Amendment is involved, for that amendment affords no protection to a wrongdoer's misplaced belief that a person to whom he voluntarily confides his wrongdoing will not reveal it. No warrant to search and seize is required in such circumstances, nor is it when the Government sends to defendant's home a secret agent who conceals his identity and makes a purchase of narcotics from the accused or when the same agent, unbeknown to the defendant, carries electronic equipment to record the defendant's words and the evidence so gathered is later offered in evidence. . . .'

"Concededly a police agent who conceals his police connections may write down for official use his conversations with a defendant and testify concerning them, without a warrant authorizing his encounters with the defendant and without otherwise violating the latter's Fourth Amendment rights. For constitutional purposes, no different result is required if the agent instead of immediately reporting and transcribing his conversations with defendant, either (1) simultaneously records them with electronic equipment which he is carrying on his person; or (2) carries radio equipment which simultaneously transmits the conversations either to recording equipment located elsewhere or to other agents monitoring the transmitting frequency. If the conduct and revelations of an agent operating without electronic equipment do not invade the defendant's constitutionally justifiable expectations of privacy, neither does a simultaneous recording of the same conversations made by the agent or by others from transmissions received from the agent to whom the defendant is talking and whose trustworthiness the defendant necessarily risks . . ."

The court stated that: "its problem is not what the privacy expectations of particular defendants in particular situations may be or the extent to which they may in fact have relied on the discretion of their companions. Very probably, individual defendants neither know nor suspect that their colleagues have gone or will go to the police or are carrying recorders or transmitters. Otherwise, conversation would cease and the problem with these encounters would be nonexistent or far different. . . . The problem . . . is what expectations of privacy are constitutionally "justifiable"—what expectations the Fourth Amendment will protect in the absence of a warrant. So far, the law permits the frustration of actual expectations of privacy by permitting authorities to use the testimony of those associates who for one reason or another have determined to turn to the police, as well as by authorizing the use of informants. If the law gives no protection to the wrongdoer whose trusted accomplice is or becomes a police agent, neither should it protect him when the same agent has recorded or transmitted the conversations which are later offered in evidence to prove the State's case.

"Inescapably, one contemplating illegal activities must realize and risk that his companions may be reporting to the police. If he sufficiently doubts their trustworthiness, the association will very probably end or never materialize. But if he has no doubts, or allays them, or risks what doubt he has, the risk is his. In terms of what his course will be, what he will or will not do or say . . . he would probably not distinguish between probable informers on the one hand and probable informers with transmitters on the other. Given the possibility or probability that one of his colleagues is cooperating with the police, it is only speculation to assert that the defendant's utterances would be substantially different or his sense of security any less if he also thought it possible that the suspected colleague is wired for sound. At least there is no persuasive evidence that the differences in this respect between the electronically equipped and the unequipped agent is substantial enough to require discrete constitutional recognition, particularly under the Fourth Amendment which is ruled by fluid concepts of 'reasonableness.' "

The Court also stated it "should not be too ready to erect constitutional barriers to relevant and probative evidence which is also accurate and reliable. An electronic recording will many times produce a more reliable rendition of what a defendant has said than will the unaided memory of a police agent. It may also be that with the recording in existence it is less likely that the informant will change his mind, less chance that threat or injury will suppress unfavorable evidence and less chance that cross-examination will confound the testimony. Considerations like these obviously do not favor the defendant, but a defendant who has no constitutional right to exclude the informer's unaided testimony should not have a Fourth Amendment privilege against a more accurate version of the events in question.

"It is thus untenable to consider the activities and reports of the police agent himself, though acting without a warrant, to be a 'reasonable' investigative effort and lawful under the Fourth Amendment but to view the same agent with a recorder or transmitter as conducting an 'unreasonable' and unconstitutional search and seizure. . . .''

Note, that in the example above, the government used an agent or an informant under their direction to converse directly with the defendant. The defendant assumed the risk that no disclosure of the conversation would occur. But if officers attempt to overhear or record conversations between two parties not in custody who are both unaware of police presence, the Fourth Amendment will be relevant even though no Fifth Amendment problems occur. Both electronic eavesdropping and wiretapping are subject to constitutional and statutory limits under federal and state laws. Use of such investigative techniques may either be foreclosed or limited to use only in conjunction with a warrant.

If the defendant has been arrested and arraigned, but is no longer in custody, may officers obtain incriminating statements? For example: ''The defendant, a merchant seaman, was in 1958 a member of the crew of the S.S. Santa Maria. In April of that year federal customs officials in New York received information that he was going to transport a quantity of narcotics aboard that ship from South America to the United States. As a result of this and other information, the agents searched the Santa Maria upon its arrival in New York and found in the afterpeak of the vessel five packages containing about three and a half pounds of cocaine. They also learned of circumstances, not here relevant, tending to connect the defendant with the cocaine. He was arrested, promptly arraigned, and subsequently indicted for possession of narcotics aboard a United States vessel. In July a superseding indictment was returned, charging the defendant and a man named Colson with the same substantive offense, and in separate counts charging the defendant, Colson and others with having conspired to possess narcotics aboard a United States vessel, and to import, conceal, and facilitate the sale of narcotics. The defendant, who had retained a lawyer, pleaded not guilty and was released on bail, along with Colson.

''A few days later, and quite without the defendant's knowledge, Colson decided to cooperate with the governmental agents in their continuing investigation of the narcotics activities in which the defendant, Colson and others had allegedly been engaged. Colson permitted an agent named Murphy to install a radio transmitter under the front seat of Colson's automobile, by means of which Murphy, equipped with an appropriate receiving device, could overhear from some distance away conversations carried on in Colson's car.

''On the evening of November 19, 1959, Colson and the defendant held a lengthy conversation while sitting in Colson's automobile, parked on a New York street. By prearrangement with Colson, and totally unbeknown to the defendant, the agent Murphy sat in a car parked out of sight down the street and listened over the radio to the entire conversation. The defendant made several incriminating statements during the course of this conversation. At the defendant's trial these incriminating statements were brought before the jury through Murphy's testimony, despite the insistent objection of defense counsel. The jury convicted the defendant of several related narcotics offenses." (*Massiah* v. *United States*.)

In *Massiah,* the United States Supreme Court held that no Fourth Amendment violation occurred for the reasons stated in the *White* case. Because the defendant was not in custody, he could not contend that his statements were involuntary. But, the court held, the deliberate and surreptitious attempt to solicit incriminating statements from the accused under these circumstances was in violation of his right to counsel under the Sixth Amendment to the U.S. Constitution. The court concluded that law enforcement agencies have a duty to continue investigating a case even after an arrest, but that they cannot indirectly interrogate the defendant through the use of an agent.

The *Massiah* case has been severely criticized as an unwarranted extension of constitutional law. *Massiah* holds that even though statements by the defendant are voluntary in every sense, the Sixth Amendment warrants exclusion of the defendant's statements under these circumstances. *Massiah* involved the use of federal officers rather than state officials, but the language implies that the principles would apply to state courts as well. Moreover, the rule of *Massiah* applies only if state or federal authorities solicit such incriminating statements and then attempt to use them against the defendant in their case-in-chief. Some courts might allow the use of such statements to impeach a defendant who is testifying in his or her own behalf.

Deception: Defendant in Custody Once the status of a suspect changes from noncustody to custody, the protection of the Fifth and Fourteenth Amendments surround the defendant. Although police must bring an accused before a magistrate for arraignment without any unnecessary delay, most states permit a reasonable time between arrest and arraignment. During this time, the accused will be questioned by the police. May police use deceptive techniques in an effort to secure a confession?

For example: The defendant is indicted for murder. But prior to his arrest, he contacts a police friend by telephone to explain his conduct and ask for assistance. The officer refuses to assist him because of his official position. Shortly therafter, the defendant is arrested.

Prior to the defendant's arraignment, investigating officers solicit the assistance of the police officer whom the defendant called. The officer agrees to help. He falsely tells the accused that the telephone call has placed his job in jeopardy and that the loss of income threatens his marriage. He urges the defendant to confess to avoid these consequences. Although the defendant initially is reluctant, he finally confesses at the urging of his friend. The prosecution offers the confession in evidence.

Note that no force or violence was used, that no promises or threats were made, and that the character of the accused is relatively stable and mature. Assume that the police can verify the truth of the confession independently (even though this element is no longer crucial).

In *Spano* v. *New York,* the U.S. Supreme Court concluded that the willful use of false statements by the defendant's friend was a factor in overcoming the defendant's will. The court did not state that the use of deception alone was forbidden, but that in considering the totality of circumstances, this factor contributed to overbearing the suspect's will. Because other coercive elements were present, the court reversed the conviction.

This raises questions concerning the extent to which investigating officers can use deceptive techniques to induce a confession. In *Leyra* v. *Denno,* the defendant, under arrest, suffered from an acute sinus attack. Police officers provided him medical attention and obtained the service of a psychiatrist skilled in the art of hypnosis. Introduced as a doctor, the psychiatrist used sympathy, held out hope for leniency, and even threatened the suspect. Ultimately, a confession was obtained. Under these facts, the Supreme Court held that the deceptive use of a doctor constituted "mental coercion" in overcoming the defendant's will. The use of the phrase "mental coercion" suggests that this kind of deception is equivalent to physical coercion and is, therefore, a forbidden practice.

But consider a case in which police obtain the assistance of an insurance agent to interview a suspect accused of murdering his wife. The agent does not seek a confession, but only asks questions about the facts of the death so they may be recorded for insurance purposes. The agent, however, would not undertake such questioning absent a police request. No "mental coercion" is present here and no physical force is used. But police do deceive the defendant as to the reason for answering the insurance agent's questions. Under these circumstances, the deception is not likely to procure an untrue statement. In other words, the absence of any circumstances which might induce a suspect to confess in order to obtain a benefit, hold out hope of relief from questioning, or convince a suspect that he or she had been promised something is relevant in determining whether the suspect's will was overborne.

In some cases, the People may offer the testimony of a cellmate who spoke with the defendant while both were in custody. Absent any evidence that the police solicited such conversation, any statements made by the suspect are not considered the product of impermissible deception and are therefore admissible.

If a police officer posed as a cellmate to solicit incriminating statements from the defendant and deceived the defendant as to his or her true identity, the statements would be "voluntary." But under other provisions of the Fifth Amendment, such conversations would be excluded for failure to advise the suspect of the right to counsel under the Sixth Amendment and the right to remain silent under the Fifth Amendment. Both federal constitutional rights are applicable to the states through the Fourteenth Amendment.

If officers listen to conversation between a visitor and an arrestee without their knowledge, such a deception would not be likely to procure an untrue statement. Under the Fifth Amendment, the statement would meet the "voluntariness" test. But under recent interpretations of the Fourth Amendment, officers should not take affirmative steps to lure an inmate falsely into a reasonable expectation of privacy. Even though privacy does not normally attach when a person is in custody, a recent California case holds that the protection of privacy, which is at the core of the Fourth Amendment, may be breached in those cases where the officer actively leads the accused into believing that a conversation with a visitor will be private.[6]

Delay in Arraignment The purpose of arraigning arrestees promptly is to prevent secret police interrogation, to place the issue of probable cause before a judicial officer, and to advise arrestees of their rights—including the appointment of counsel—and provide them with opportunity to apply for bail. In federal courts, the rules on criminal procedure require that arresting officers deliver arrestees to a magistrate immediately. Failure to comply with these rules constitutes an illegal detention, and any statements obtained during this time are inadmissible. (*McNabb* v. *United States*.) In state courts, local statutes require delivery of the accused to a magistrate within a prescribed period of time.[7] Failure to comply with these statements will not necessarily invalidate confessions or admissions obtained during this period of illegal detention, but such a failure will be a factor in determining "voluntariness."

Delays in arraignment may be attributable to several causes. The accused may have been hospitalized after the arrest and unable to come to court; the defendant may have volunteered a defense which was quickly verifiable; or a holiday or Sunday may have intervened. But if confessions are obtained during a delay in arraignment, defendants may contend that the extended period of custody contributed to an "atmosphere of coercion." If defendants can establish that a delay prejudiced their ability to prepare a defense, they might also contend that they were unable to obtain a fair trial and demand dismissal of the charges. Failure to comply with the law requiring prompt arraignment may pose serious problems for the prosecution.

Drugs An admission or confession of a suspect in custody is not automatically involuntary if he or she was under the influence of a drug at the time. But this factor is relevant in considering the "totality of the circumstances." In some cases an officer will interview a suspect who has placed him- or herself under the influence of a drug. In other cases a physician may have injected the defendant with a drug for medical purposes.

Or the defendant may have agreed to submit to a drug injection in conjunction with a psychiatric interview.

As we have seen, if the defendant is under arrest and is interviewed by an investigating officer, the prosecution must establish that any resulting confession is the product of a rational intellect and a free will. A questioner who detects the familiar symptoms of narcotic use must be alert to the legal objections which will ultimately be raised—that the drug-induced condition prevented the defendant from freely choosing whether or not to talk. Initially, the investigating officer must determine to what degree the use of drugs is affecting the accused by noting the objective symptoms of drowsiness, incoherent or slow speech, and inability to understand or respond to questions, and by obtaining an admission of use and the kind of drug used. A tape recording of the conversation may substantiate the voluntariness of a statement by enabling the trier of fact to listen to the voice of the defendant in response to the questioning. The tone and coherence of the voice will corroborate the defendant's ability to articulate.

If the defendant manifests withdrawal symptoms, the issue of voluntariness becomes more difficult. A person in withdrawal suffers acute physical pain. This, combined with the accompanying mental anguish, bears heavily on a person's ability to determine freely whether or not to talk. Expert opinion by a medical doctor may be necessary to support a finding that the defendant's physical condition was stable enough to permit a free choice.

If a suspect has been injured or is in poor health, a specific medication with a narcotic content may have been prescribed. If officers interrogate the defendant while under medication, the defendant may contend at trial that any resulting statements were influenced by the effect of the drug. To a large extent, the kind of drug used and its effect on the human body will be relevant. If the drug tends to reduce the ability to cope with stress, the court may find that the defendant was unable to decide rationally whether or not to speak. If the drug alleviates pain, the court may find that the defendant was indeed able to make a rational choice.

In preparing for trial, both parties may offer the testimony of medical doctors to relate the direct and indirect effects of a specific drug. Investigating officers should determine this fact well in advance of trial.[8]

Various drugs have been administered to suspects in custody for the express purpose of obtaining statements. Sodium amytal and sodium pentathol, known as "truth serums," have generally been held inadmissible even if administered at the request of the defendant.[9]

Alcohol Self-induced intoxication will not automatically render a statement involuntary, yet it is relevant in determining whether the defendant was sufficiently rational to choose freely to speak. A tape recording of the interrogation can help to resolve any conflict between the officer's testimony and that of the defendant. Note that the defendant's use of drugs or alcohol may also be relevant to other issues—such as intent, knowledge, and motive—in a criminal case.

Sanity The mental state of a defendant at the time he or she allegedly committed a crime is a crucial issue in criminal cases. A person's intent, motive, premeditation, and knowledge are key elements in major crimes. When officers question an arrestee, they are interested in learning about the defendant's state of mind at the time the crime was committed. If the defendant states that he or she had been drinking or had used drugs at the time of the crime, this statement will be relevant in establishing the ability to form an intent or to premeditate. In terms of a voluntary confession, the defendant may contend that some mental disability prevented him or her from exercising a free will. Officers should attempt to note any signs of irrationality or mental instability and should be prepared to testify accordingly.

Product of an Involuntary Confession If verbal evidence (a confession) is given after an earlier involuntary confession, this evidence will be inadmissible in court. For example: The defendant was prosecuted for the murder of a prison inmate. At the trial, the captain in charge of the investigation testified that after he had advised the defendant of his constitutional rights, "the defendant stated that he had argued with the victim and that during the course of the argument he had stabbed him. On cross-examination, the defendant inquired about facts which had taken place *before* the defendant had entered the captain's office. The captain testified that at the time the defendant entered the office he appeared to have sustained an injury about the face and was bleeding slightly from the nose. But the captain had seen the defendant a few minutes before the interview while he was being taken . . . to the prison adjustment center, and no injuries were apparent. The defendant testified that his first recollection after the events leading up to the killing was of lying on the floor in the adjustment center and being kicked about the head, face, heart and groin by each of four correctional officers. The defendant maintained that he sustained a broken nose, received some cuts and bumps, and had a lot of bruises on his arms, back, and legs; that he was made dizzy by the abuse; that his clothing was removed; and that on leaving the cell to go to the captain's office he was again kicked in the back. It also appeared that a medical technician was called to attend the defendant while he was in the captain's office, but only after the captain had taken the defendant's statement. The technician closed a laceration around defendant's eye with six stitches and treated him for head injuries. The defendant remained dizzy while he was in the captain's office and was removed to the hospital later that day."

Additionally, evidence was offered that the defendant had already confessed to other officers before his confession to the captain. The court said: "The rule has been long and well settled in this state that where a defendant, subjected to threats, violence or other improper influences, makes a confession or other incriminating statement in such a coercive atmosphere and shortly thereafter again incriminates himself under circumstances not manifestly coercive 'there is a presumption that the influence of the prior improper treatment continues to operate on the mind of the defendant and that the subsequent confession is the result of the same influence which rendered the prior confession inadmissible, and the burden is upon the prosecution to clearly establish the contrary.' The law presumes the subsequent confession to have been made and influenced by the same hopes and fears as the first, and this presumption continues until it is affirmatively established by the prosecution that the influences under which the original confession was made had ceased to operate before the subsequent confession was made.

"The determination of the extent of the influence persisting at the time the subsequent confession is made rests, of course, upon attendant circumstances, and the inquiry is whether, considering the age and intelligence of the defendant, the nature and degree of the influence, and the time intervening between the confessions, it can be said that defendant was not induced to confess by reason of the pressure which motivated him to make the first statement, or was not influenced so to do by reason of the prior confession itself." (*People* v. *Sanchez*.)

Just as a confession will be excluded because of an earlier involuntary statement, real or physical evidence will also be excluded if discovered as a result of an involuntary confession. For example: Police secure an involuntary confession from a suspect in which the accused reveals the location of a weapon used in the commission of the crime. If police had no other independent evidence as to the location of the weapon, the gun would be the product of an involuntarily obtained confession and therefore would be excluded. Had police learned of the weapon from another source, then the knowledge of the gun's location would not be the direct result of the involuntary statement and the gun should be admissible in evidence.

This doctrine may be further applied in cases where a voluntary confession is *preceded* by an unlawful arrest or search. In *Wong Sun* v. *U.S.*, the U.S. Supreme Court said that even though there may be no direct Fifth Amendment issue, ". . . the Fourth Amendment may also protect against the overhearing of verbal statements as well as against the more traditional seizure of papers and effects. Similarly, testimony as to matters observed during an unlawful invasion has been excluded in order to enforce basic constitutional policies. . . . Thus, verbal evidence which derives so immediately from an unlawful entry and an unauthorized arrest . . . is no less the 'fruit' of official illegality than the more common tangible fruits of the unwarranted intrusion.''

The verbal evidence to which the court refers is usually a confession. Thus, an unlawful search that directly results in a confession may taint the confession and exclude an otherwise voluntary statement from evidence. If the original search is unlawful, the investigators' painstaking attempts to obtain a voluntary confession may be wasted.

A fundamental distinction exists between a prior unlawful *arrest* and a prior unlawful *search* in determining whether to admit a subsequent confession. An illegal detention does not necessarily produce a voluntary admission, whereas the evidence obtained by an illegal search or by a coerced confession is the necessary product of the search or of the coercion. In the case of an illegal seizure, the illegality induces the confession by showing the suspect the evidence, and the consequent futility of remaining silent. But when a confession follows a false arrest, the custodial environment is merely one factor (though a significant one) to be considered in determining whether the confession is inadmissible. (*People* v. *Johnson.*)

If an investigating officer reviews the arrest report prior to interviewing the defendant, he or she may note the questionable search or seizure of evidence. Under these circumstances, the officer may initially question the defendant without referring to the illegally seized evidence in any way. If the confession is voluntary and is preceded by an adequate *Miranda* admonition, the arrestee's statement should be admissible even if the arrest and search are unlawful. Thereafter, the officer can take a second statement referring specifically to the questionably seized evidence. At trial, if the court agrees that the search was unlawful, the first confession of the defendant is still admissible, as it is not the product of an unlawful search. If the search is ruled lawful, both statements will be admissible.

Note that if the arrest is unlawful and the search depends on the lawfulness of the arrest for its validity, the physical evidence seized as a consequence of the unlawful arrest will be excluded under the provisions of the Fourth Amendment, but the verbal evidence will not be excluded if the suspect was not confronted with the illegally seized evidence. In other words, the confession must not be the direct product of the prior unlawful search.

Joint Confessions

In cases involving the arrest of multiple suspects, officers often obtain an incriminating statement from one arrestee which implicates another. If the defendants are tried together, the prosecutor will call the interrogating officer to testify to the incriminating conversation. As to the confessing defendant, the confession is admissible as an exception to the hearsay rule.

But as to the nonconfessing defendant, the confession is clearly hearsay and is therefore inadmissible.

Formerly in such cases, the trial court instructed the jury to disregard the confession as to the nonconfessing defendant. Because of the extremely difficult task this imposed on the jury, the U.S. Supreme Court has held that this cautionary instruction could not cure the prejudicial impact on the nonconfessing defendant. In *Bruton* v. *United States,* the court held that, in a joint trial, the introduction of a confession by one defendant which implicates a nonconfessing codefendant violates the latter's right of confrontation under the Sixth Amendment to the U.S. Constitution. The nonconfessing codefendant can cross-examine the officer-witness who is repeating the confession, but cannot cross-examine the confessing defendant.

Under this interpretation, the trial court must determine in advance of trial whether a confession of the *Bruton* type will be offered. If the prosecution proposes to introduce into evidence a statement by one defendant that implicates a codefendant, the trial court can attempt one of the following methods:

"(1) It can permit a joint trial if all parts of the extrajudicial statements implicating any codefendants can be and are effectively deleted without prejudice to the declarant. By effective deletions, we mean not only direct and indirect identifications of codefendants but any statements that could be employed against nondeclarant codefendants once their identity is otherwise established. (2) It can grant a severance of trials if the prosecution insists that it must use the extrajudicial statements and it appears that effective deletions cannot be made. (3) If the prosecution has successfully resisted a motion to sever and thereafter offers an extrajudicial statement implicating a codefendant, the trial court must exclude it if effective deletions are not possible." (*People* v. *Aranda.*)

If the conversation between the defendant and the officer is oral, the prosecution can usually instruct the officer-witness to edit the confession to delete all references to the nonconfessing codefendant. But in some circumstances, depending on the evidence linking both defendants to the crime or on the type of crime involved, such editing may be difficult. If editing cannot be accomplished, the court must order separate trials or the prosecution must forego introducing the evidence.

If the prosecution offers a tape recording of the defendant's confession implicating the codefendant, the editing process may require more technical skill. But officers need not undertake this task until the court orders it.

When confronted by a *Bruton* problem, officers can attempt to obtain two separate confessions from the defendant. In the first confession, the officer questions the defendant concerning all the details of the crime, including the conduct of the nonconfessing codefendant. Thereafter, officers can obtain a second confession from the defendant, carefully limiting the questions to the defendant's conduct only and excluding all references to the codefendant. Of course, this second attempt to limit the confession cannot always be expected to succeed, but multiple confessions are not uncommon, and a more limited second confession may avoid trial problems later.

Recording Confessions

Testimony by a peace officer relating a confession by the defendant is admissible as an exception to the hearsay rule. But juries are instructed to evaluate oral confessions as follows:

"An admission is a statement made by a defendant other than at his trial, which by itself is not sufficient to warrant an inference of guilt, but which tends to prove guilt when considered with the rest of the evidence.

"You are the exclusive judges as to whether an admission was made by the defendant and if the statement is true in whole or in part. If you find that such statement is wholly untrue, you must reject it. If you find it is true in part, you may consider only that part which you find to be true.

"Evidence of an oral admission of the defendant ought to be viewed with caution.

"No person may be convicted of an offense unless there is some proof of each element of the offense independent of any admission made by him outside of his trial.

"However, the identity of the person who committed the offense may be established by an admission." (California Jury Instructions.)

Moreover, cross-examination of the officer-witness will focus on his or her ability to recall exact words, the order of the conversation, and any threatening tone of voice. Of course, the officer can refresh his or her recollection from notes, but the best evidence is a tape recording. The recording captures the voices, the conversation, and the recitation of *Miranda* rights in a way that demonstrates the voluntariness of the confession. The prosecution can play the tape to the jury, transcribe it and allow the jury to read the confession or even re-record an inaudible tape.

Admission of a Co-conspirator

If a conspiracy involving the defendant is proved, a statement made by a co-conspirator is admissible as evidence against the defendant. This exception to the hearsay rule is authorized because a conspiracy involves two or more people who are each other's agents, each agent acting in behalf of the other. During the attempt to reach a common goal, and in furtherance to it, the conspirators' acts and declarations are reliable enough to be competent evidence against each other in a criminal prosecution. Thus, an incriminating statement of one co-conspirator is admissible against this person as an admission of a defendant, and it is also admissible against his or her codefendant as an exception to the hearsay rule. Moreover, even if the co-conspirator is not on trial with the defendant, the co-conspirator's statement is still admissible against the defendant.

In order for this exception to apply, the prosecution must establish three fundamental elements:

1. The declarant was participating in a conspiracy at the time of the declaration.

2. The declaration was in furtherance of the objective of that conspiracy.

3. At the time of the declaration, the party against whom the evidence is offered was participating in the conspiracy.

None of the above facts can be established by evidence of the declaration itself; they must be proved independently by direct or circumstantial evidence of the conspiracy. For example: ''Defendant solicited a 15-year-old boy, Ruben, to burn down his house so that he could collect the insurance proceeds. Ruben died in the fire, and defendant was indicted for murder as well as arson.

''The fire occurred on Saturday, July 7, 1973, at approximately 9:30 P.M. There is no question that the fire was set by Ruben. Linda M, a former neighbor and friend of Ruben, testified to five conversations she had with Ruben prior to his death. Approximately three weeks prior to the fire, Ruben told her [the defendant had asked him to] set fire to his residence. About a week later, Ruben and Linda engaged in a second conversation in which Ruben reiterated his intention to burn the residence, and also told her he would set the fire at 9:30 P.M. on a Saturday within the next two weeks; no one would be at home when he arrived; he would find a gasoline can on the back porch; the back door would be kicked in to suggest that the house had been broken into; all of the windows would be shut; and the gas would be left on inside the house. He told Linda he was to pour gasoline along the outside of the house and ignite it with a fuse constructed of a lit cigarette and a book of matches devised so as to provide him time to get away. Linda was also told that Ruben was to receive one hundred dollars for his efforts.

''A third conversation occurred between Ruben and Linda approximately one week prior to the fire, during which Ruben stated that he would have some money by the following Monday for burning the house.'' (*People* v. *Earnest*.)

In this case, an independent witness (Linda), not a party to the conspiracy, testified to statements by the co-conspirator, Ruben. Assuming that the prosecution can establish the existence of the conspiracy independent of this statement, the hearsay statement by Ruben to Linda is admissible against the defendant as an exception to the hearsay rule.

The co-conspirator exception to the hearsay rule, however, is limited to acts or declarations committed by the conspirator during the course of the conspiracy. When the conspiracy achieves the object of the conspiracy—that is, the commission of the substantive crime—the conspiracy terminates and no further acts or declarations are admissible. Although in most conspiracies the conspirators attempt to avoid detection and apprehension, such conduct is not considered part of the conspiracy and any acts or declarations committed after the conspired act has been completed are inadmissible under this exception to the hearsay rule. (*Krulewitch* v. *United States*.)

Prior Inconsistent Statements

Statements made by a witness prior to trial may be offered at trial for two different reasons: (1) To attack the witness's credibility in an attempt to impeach this person; and (2) As substantive evidence under the hearsay exception for prior inconsistent statements. Under this exception to the hearsay rule, the prosecution or defendant can offer testimony concerning a statement previously made by a witness at a former trial, or while under oath to a grand jury, or as an unsworn oral or written pre-trial statement. If the pre-trial statement is expressly or impliedly inconsistent with the trial testimony, the pre-trial statement may be offered as substantive evidence in support of the charge. In other words, the prior inconsistent statement not only impeaches the witness, but also may be considered by the jury as affirmative evidence.

For example: A witness has testified before a grand jury that the defendant assaulted and sexually molested her at a specific time and place. At the trial, she testifies that the defendant did not assault her or make any sexual advances. The prosecutor then reads the grand jury transcript to the trial jury.

The pre-trial statement is admissible as a prior inconsistent statement. Because the statement was made out of court, the hearsay rule applies. But under the prior inconsistent statement exception to the hearsay rule, the statement is admissible for the truth of the matter. The jury may consider the pre-trial statement and discount the in-trial statement if they wish.

Inconsistent statements are admitted as an exception to the hearsay rule because in such cases the dangers against which the hearsay rule is designed to protect are largely nonexistent. That is: "the declarant is in court and may be examined and cross-examined in regard to his statements and their subject matter. In many cases, the inconsistent statement is more likely to be true than the testimony of the witness at the trial because it was made nearer in time to the matter to which it relates and is less likely to be influenced by the controversy that gave rise to the litigation. The trier of fact has the declarant before it and can observe his demeanor and the nature of his testimony as he denies or tries to explain away the inconsistency. Hence, it is in as good a position to determine the truth or falsity of the prior statement as it is to determine the truth or falsity of the inconsistent testimony given in court. Moreover, such a rule will provide a party with desirable protection against the 'turncoat' witness who changes his story on the stand and deprives the party calling him of evidence essential to his case." (*California* v. *Green.*)

Although a pre-trial statement inconsistent with trial testimony may be considered for its truth, prosecutors will carefully evaluate the weight such statements will carry with the jury. Convincing a juror that he or she should believe one of two inconsistent versions is no easy task. The defense attorney develops the impeachment and attempts to discredit the witness, while the prosecutor tries to rehabilitate the witness.

Prior Consistent Statements

As shown above, a witness will sometimes inform police officers at the time of the arrest of a certain set of facts which he or she subsequently denies at the time of trial. At this point, the prosecution or defendant must contend with the effect of a prior inconsistent statement. If, however, the witness has given another statement prior to trial *consistent* with the trial testimony, the consistent statement is admissible as an exception to the hearsay rule if made *prior* to the inconsistent statement.

A prior consistent statement is also admissible if the testimony of the witness at the trial is apparently the result of recent fabrication or is influenced by bias or other motives, and if the prior consistent statement was made before the bias, motive for fabrication, or other improper motive arose. For example: The defendant is charged with the murder of a fellow prisoner inside a state penal institution. A witness testifies to facts implicating the defendant but is impeached by defense counsel by means of an inconsistent statement which he made to district attorney investigators prior to trial. Defense counsel also develops evidence that the prosecution told the witness that the judge could rehear his case—a statement made before the witness's statement at the trial. The prosecutor can now offer any pre-trial statement consistent with his trial testimony if given prior to the time the prosecutor stated the judge could rehear his case. The prior consistent statement arose before any alleged improper motive to fabricate—that is, the promise held out by the prosecutor.

Prior Identification

Statutory Requirements

A pre-trial statement by a witness identifying the defendant is admissible at trial as an exception to the hearsay rule. A person who is either the victim of a crime or the witness to a crime provides a description of the perpetrator to officers shortly after the crime occurs. The witness may be excited, angry, or afraid, or may be suffering some degree of emotional stress. Under these circumstances, the description may be vague, incomplete, or even completely in error. But this recorded description in a police report is valuable evidence for both the prosecution and the defense. Use of this statement may serve one of the following purposes:

1. To refresh the recollection of the witness if the witness is unable to recall the description

2. To serve as a record of past recollection if the witness cannot recall the prior identification at all

3. To provide a prior inconsistent statement if the witness's trial testimony is impeached by the prior description.

4. To provide a prior consistent statement if the witness is impeached and can be rehabilitated.

5. To provide a prior identification of the defendant as an exception to the hearsay rule.

When a witness identifies a suspect prior to trial, but is unable to identify this person at the time of trial, another witness—usually a police officer—may be able to testify that the witness made a pre-trial identification of the defendant if the following facts can be established:

1. The prior statement identifies the defendant as the person who committed the crime.

2. The prior identification statement was made when the facts were fresh.

3. The witness acknowledges that he or she made an identification and that it was correct at the time.

4. The statement is not otherwise inadmissible because of a statutory or constitutional restriction.

For example: "Following the burglary of an apartment, a police officer arrived and showed Mrs. F seven to ten small photographs. She selected one photograph of defendant Gould as the man inside her apartment. On several subsequent occasions she identified the same . . . photograph or enlargements thereof.

At the trial, Mrs. F pointed out Gould as having "some features but not all of the features" of the man she saw inside her apartment, and added that he seemed thinner than the burglar. She stated that she was unable to point out anyone in the courtroom as the man she saw on the steps. She also said that the pictures she selected shortly after the crime 'looked similar to the men who were in my apartment but not all the features were the same.' Officer Brewer testified, however, that Mrs. F was sure of her identification of the photographs at the time she first selected them.

Although the witness's testimony did not amount to an identification, the evidence of her extrajudicial identification to the officer was nevertheless admissible. "Evidence of an extrajudicial identification is admissible, not only to corroborate an identification made at the trial, but as independent evidence of identity. Unlike other testimony that cannot be corroborated by proof of prior consistent statements unless it is first impeached, evidence of an extrajudicial identification is admitted regardless of whether the testimonial identification is impeached, because the earlier identification has greater probative value than an identification made in the courtroom after the suggestions of others and the circumstances of the trial may have intervened to create a fancied recognition in the witness's mind.

"The failure of the witness to repeat the extrajudicial identification in court does not destroy its probative value, for such failure may be explained by loss of memory or other circumstances. The extrajudicial identification tends to connect the defendant with the crime, and the principal danger of admitting hearsay evidence is not present since the witness is available at the trial for cross-examination." (*People* v. *Gould.*)

In the illustration above, therefore, all the elements of the prior identification are present and the testimony is admissible.

CASES AND MATERIALS

Ashcraft v. *Tennessee,* 322 U.S. 143, 88 L. Ed. 1192, 64 S. Ct. 921.

Brewer v. *Williams,* U.S. Sup. Ct., 3/23/77

Bruton v. *United States,* 391 U.S. 123, 20 L. Ed. 2d 476, 88 S. Ct. 1620.

Greenwald v. *Wisconsin,* 390 U.S. 519, 20 L. Ed. 2d 77, 88 S. Ct. 1152.

Haley v. *Ohio,* 332 U.S. 569, 68 S. Ct. 302, 92 L. Ed. 224.

In re Gault, 387 U.S. 1, 87 S. Ct. 1428, 18 L. Ed. 2d 527.

Krulewitch v. *United States,* 336 U.S. 440, 69 S. Ct. 716, 93 L. Ed. 790.

Leyra v. *Denno,* 347 U.S. 556, 98 L. Ed. 948, 74 S. Ct. 716.

Lynumn v. *Illinois,* 372 U.S. 528, 83 S. Ct. 917, 9 L. Ed. 2d 922.

Massiah v. *United States,* 377 U.S. 201, 12 L. Ed. 2d 246, 84 S. Ct. 1199.

McNabb v. *United States,* 318 U.S. 332, 63 S. Ct. 608, 87 L. Ed. 819.

Payne v. *Arkansas,* 356 U.S. 560, 2 L. Ed. 2d 975, 78 S. Ct. 844.

People v. *Aranda,* 63 C. 2d 518, 47 Cal. R. 353, 407 P. 2d 265.

People v. *Barbaro,* 395 Ill. 264, 69 N.E. 2d 692.

People v. *Berve,* 51 C. 2d 286, 332 P. 2d 97.

People v. *Brommel,* 56 C. 2d 629, 15 Cal. R. 909, 364 P. 2d 845.

People v. *Earnest,* 53 Cal. App. 3d 734, 126 Cal. R. 107.

People v. *Haydel,* 12 C. 3d 190, 115 Cal. R. 394, 524 P. 2d 866.

People v. *Hill,* 66 C. 2d 536, 58 Cal. R. 340, 426 P. 2d 908.

People v. *Johnson,* 70 C. 2d 541, 75 Cal. R. 401, 450 P. 2d 865.

People v. *Matlock,* 51 C. 2d 682, 336 P. 2d 505.

People v. *Sanchez,* 70 C. 2d 562, 75 Cal. R. 642, 451 P. 2d 74.

People v. *Trout,* 54 C. 2d 576, 6 Cal. R. 759, 354 P. 2d 231.

Reck v. *Pate,* 367 U.S. 433, 6 L. Ed. 2d 948, 81 S. Ct. 1541.

Schneckloth v. *Bustamonte,* 412 U.S. 218, 36 L. Ed. 2d 854, 93 S. Ct. 2041.

Spano v. *New York,* 360 U.S. 315, 3 L. Ed. 2d 1265, 79 S. Ct. 1200.

United States v. *White,* 401 U.S. 745, 28 L. Ed. 2d 453, 91 S. Ct. 1122.

Wong Sun v. *United States,* 371 U.S. 471, 9 L. Ed. 2d 441, 83 S. Ct. 407.

1. In a murder prosecution, the People offer the following tape-recorded interview of the defendant, a juvenile, by the investigating officers:

"The first 15 pages of the transcript disclose Roger's effort to avoid confessing to the crime and claim an inability to remember. The interrogating officer then asked: 'How old are you? Sixteen? Seventeen? Seventeen?' and then added: 'You know you could be in jail until you are about twenty-five. That's a long time.' Another officer interjected: 'And then some, cause he might be certified to adult court. . . . And you can be certified adult and get a life sentence on it too.' The original officer said: 'So let's have it out, man. Let's get it straight now. You're still a juvenile yet. You get you certified an adult, you're not gonna be treated as a juvenile; you're gonna be treated as an adult. They sure hold them tight boy. . . .'

"When Roger said 'I've gotta see 'em (the other two accused juveniles) before I say anything,' an interrogating officer replied: 'You ain't gonna see nobody except the court if you want to be that way. I'd see you go to adult court uh, you ain't gonna ride Richard's rap.' Roger said, 'Oh, yeah?' The officer stated: 'You know, if Richard squeezed the trigger and you didn't man, I ain't gonna ride his rap.'

"The interrogating officer continued: 'We ain't askin' you to do the squealing, all we want is your version of what took place. Because, uh, when you go to jail, do time, you're gonna be your own time. You're not gonna be Richard's time, you're not gonna do Jerry's time, you're gonna be your own time. It's your life, man. It's shades. It could be seven or eight or ten or life, you know, sentence out of your life;

not theirs. You're the guy—number one—you'd better start thinking about and talkin' about. We don't want to hear about what they did; only what you did.'

"Another officer entered the questioning. He said: 'Say you and I went to a liquor store, and I have a gun, and you don't. . . . And we go in there in all intents and purposes of robbing the liquor store. OK? . . . I'm just giving you a for instance . . . OK? You and I go in a liquor store and you're gonna be my lookout . . . And I'm gonna pull the job? You know I'm gonna pull the job. So, we get in there and get the money and the liquor store guy reaches under the counter, so I blast him. . . . And tell you and hey, man, let's make it OK. I killed the guy.' Roger answered: 'You gonna get the shades, the shades?' The officer replied: 'That's right. Exactly what I was going to tell you.' Roger said: 'Well, I'll get jes' as much time as he do, won't I?'

"Another officer responded: 'That's exactly right.' The previous officer added: 'But it's gonna help you out for a chance of probation or getting parole if you are honest about the thing.' Roger said, 'Oh, yeah?' The officer continued: 'Tell your side of it, because if you go in there hard-nosed and just lie and, try to cover up, do you think we'd give you a chance at probation or parole? No way.'

"Roger asked: 'What is parole?' The officer responded: 'Well, that's getting out of jail—you know, you might be six months and get out the rest on parole. And do the rest of the time at home. You understand, well, parole's like probation. A parole, you say, well, you see, ah, I get sentenced to, for robbery. They give me a five-to-life sentence. OK? . . . I go to jail and I serve a year or to 18 months. OK, for the next five years, they're gonna put me on parole and let me out, and I'm gonna do my time outside. I'm still really technically in jail, but I'm out a . . . doing everything I do normally, but I've gotta behave myself, cause if I get involved in any more trouble, I go right back and serve that five years out. But—if I go to jail hard-nosed 'n what-have-you, do you think the Parole Board is gonna listen to me? No, man. They're make me do probably the whole damn five years, or more. You know.'

"Roger answered: 'You think I can get parole, I mean, ah, whatcha call it?' The officer responded: 'Not promising it. There's a possibility. But if you go in there with, if, if I was sittin' here and shuckin' with you, and he and I pulled a caper, and he's tellin' me the straight poop, then you're surely gonna listen to him and try to help him more than you are me.'" Shortly thereafter, the defendant confessed.

Is this statement voluntary? (*In re Roger G.*, 53 Cal. App. 3d 198.)

2. "An officer of the State Police investigated a theft at a residence near Pendleton. He asked the lady of the house that had been burglarized if she suspected anyone. She replied that the defendant was the only one she could think of. The defendant was a parolee and a 'close associate' of her son. The officer tried to contact defendant on three or four occasions with no success. Finally, about 25 days after the burglary, the officer left his card at defendant's apartment with a note asking him to call because 'I'd like to discuss something with you.' The next afternoon the defendant did call. The officer asked where it would be convenient to meet. The defendant had no preference, so the officer asked if the defendant could meet him at the state patrol office in about an hour and a half, about 5:00 P.M. The patrol office was about two blocks from defendant's apartment. The building housed several state agencies.

"The officer met defendant in the hallway, shook hands and took him into an office. The defendant was told he was not under arrest. The door was closed. The two sat across a desk. The police radio in another room could be heard. The officer told defendant he wanted to talk to him about a burglary and that his truthfulness would possibly be considered by the district attorney or judge. The officer further advised that the police believed defendant was involved in the burglary and [falsely stated that] defendant's fingerprints were found at the scene. The defendant sat for a few minutes and then said he had taken the property. This occurred within five minutes after defendant had come to the office. The officer then advised defendant of his Miranda rights and took a taped confession.

"At the end of the taped conversation the officer told defendant he was not arresting him at this time; he was released to go about his job and return to his family. The officer said he was referring the case to the district attorney for him to determine whether criminal charges would be brought. It was 5:30 P.M. when the defendant left the office."

How should the court decide? (*Oregon* v. *Mathiason* #76-201, U.S. Sup. Ct. 1/25/77.)

3. In *Davis* v. *North Carolina,* the court reviewed the following facts. How would you vote on the admissibility of the confession?

"Elmer Davis is an impoverished male with a third or fourth grade education. His level of intelligence is such that it prompted the comment by the court below, even while deciding against him on his claim of involuntariness, that there is a moral question whether a person of Davis' mentality should be executed. Police first came in contact with Davis while he was a child when his mother murdered his father, and thereafter knew him through his long criminal record, beginning with a prison term he served at the age of 15 or 16.

"In September 1959, Davis escaped from a state prison camp near Asheville, North Carolina, where he was serving sentences of 17 to 25 years. On September 20, 1959, Mrs. Foy Belle Cooper was raped and murdered in the Elmwood Cemetery in the City of Charlotte, North Carolina. On September 21, police in a neighboring county arrested Davis in Belmont, 12 miles from Charlotte. He was wearing civilian clothes and had in his possession women's undergarments and a billfold with identification papers of one Bishel Buren Hayes. Hayes testified at trial that his billfold and shoes had been taken from him while he lay in a drunken sleep near the Elmwood Cemetery on September 20.

"Charlotte police learned of Davis' arrest and contacted the warden of the state prison to get permission to take Davis into their custody in connection with the Cooper murder and other felonies. Having obtained permission, they took Davis from Belmont authorities and brought him to the detective headquarters in Charlotte. From the testimony of the officers, it is beyond dispute that the reason for securing Davis was their suspicion that he had committed the murder.

"The second and third floors of the detective headquarters building contain lockup cells used for detention overnight and occasionally for slightly longer periods. It has no kitchen facilities for preparing meals. The cell in which Davis was placed measures 6 by 10 feet and contains a solid steel bunk with mattress, a drinking fountain, and a commode. It is located on the inside of the building with no view of daylight. It is ventilated by two exhaust fans located in the ceiling of the top floor of the building. Despite the fact that a county jail equipped and used for lengthy detention is located directly across the street from detective headquarters, Davis was incarcerated in this cell on an upper floor of the building for the entire period until he confessed. Police Chief Jesse James testified: 'I don't know anybody who has stayed in the city jail as long as this boy.'

"When Davis arrived at the detective headquarters, an arrest sheet was prepared giving various statistics concerning him. On this arrest sheet was typed the following illuminating directive: 'HOLD FOR HUCKS & FESPERMAN RE-MRS. COOPER. ESCAPEE FROM HAYWOOD COUNTY STILL HAS 15 YEARS TO PULL. DO NOT ALLOW ANYONE TO SEE DAVIS OR ALLOW HIM TO USE TELEPHONE.' Both at trial and at the habeas corpus hearing the testimony of police officers on this notation was nearly uniform. Each officer testified that he did not put that directive on the arrest sheet, that he did not know who did, and that he never knew of it. The police captain first testified at trial that there had never been an order issued in the police department that Davis was not to see or talk to anybody. He cited as an example the fact that Davis' sister came to see him (after Davis had confessed). He testified later in the trial, however:

"'I don't know, it is possible I could have ordered this boy to be held without privilege of communicating with his friends, relatives and held without the privilege of using the telephone or without the privilege of talking to anybody. . . . No, I did not want him to talk to anybody. For the simple reason he was an escaped convict and it is the rules and regulations of the penal system that if he is a C grade prisoner he is not permitted to see anyone alone or write anyone letters and I was trying to conform to the state regulations.'

"The District Court found as a fact that from September 21 until after he confessed on October 6, neither friend nor relative saw Davis. It concluded, however, that Davis was not held incommunicado because he would have been permitted visitors had anyone requested to see him. In so finding, the District Court noted specifically the testimony that police officers contacted Davis' sister for him. But the court made no mention whatever of the notation on the arrest sheet or the testimony of the police captain.

"During the time Davis was held by Charlotte police, he was fed two sandwiches, described by one officer as 'thin' and 'dry,' twice a day. This fare was occasionally supplemented with peanuts and other 'stuff' such as cigarettes brought to him by a police officer. The District Court found that the food was the same served prisoners held overnight in the detention jail and that there was no attempt by police to weaken Davis by inadequate feeding. The State contends that 'two sandwiches twice a day supplemented by peanuts "and other stuff" was not such a poor diet, for an idle person doing no work, as to constitute a violation of due process of law.'

"From the time Davis was first brought to the overnight lockup in Charlotte on September 21, 1959, until he confessed on the 16th day of detention, police officers conducted daily interrogation sessions with him in a special interrogation room in the building. These sessions each lasted 'forty-five minutes or an hour or maybe a little more,' according to one of the interrogating officers.

"Captain McCall testified that he had assigned his entire force of 26 to 29 men to investigate the case. From this group, Detectives Hucks and Fesperman had primary responsibility for interrogating Davis. These officers testified to interrogating him once or twice each day throughout the 16 days. Three other officers testified that they conducted several interrogation sessions at the request of Hucks and Fesperman.

Although the officers denied that Davis was interrogated at night, one testified that the interrogation periods he directed were held some time prior to 11 P.M. Captain McCall also interrogated Davis once.

"According to each of the officers, no mention of the Cooper murder was made in any of the interrogations between September 21 and October 3. Between these dates they interrogated Davis extensively with respect to the stolen goods in his possession. It is clear from the record, however, that these interrogations were directly related to the murder and were not simply questioning as to unrelated felonies.

"Davis had told the officers that he took the items from houses along the railroad line between Canton and Asheville. To disprove this story, Davis was aroused at 5 A.M. and driven to Canton. There his leg shackles were removed and he walked on the railroad tracks, handcuffed to an officer, 14 miles to Ahseville. When Davis was unable to recognize any landmark along the way or any house that he had burglarized, an officer confronted him with the accusation that his story was a lie. The State points out that Davis was well fed on this day, that he agreed to make the hike, and contends that it was not so physically exhausting as to be coercive.

"On the afternoon of October 3, two officers planned and carried out a ruse to attempt to get Davis to incriminate himself in some manner. They engaged Davis in idle conversation for 10 to 20 minutes and then inquired whether he would like to go out for 'some fresh air.' They then took Davis from the jail and drove him into the cemetery to the scene of the crime in order to observe his reaction.

"The purpose of these excursions and of all of the interrogation sessions was known to Davis. On the day of the drive to the cemetery, the interrogators shifted tactics and began questioning Davis specifically about the murder. They asked him if he knew why he was being held. He stated that he believed it was with respect to the Cooper murder. Police then pressed him, asking, 'Well, did you do it?' He denied it. The interrogation sessions continued through the next two days. Davis consistently denied any knowledge of the crime.

"On October 6, Detectives Hucks and Fesperman interrogated Davis for the final time. Lieutenant Sykes, who had known Davis' family, but who had not taken part in any of the prior interrogation sessions because he had been away on vacation, asked to sit in. During this interrogation after repeated earlier denials of guilt, Davis refused to answer questions concerning the crime. At about 12:45 P.M., Lieutenant Sykes inquired of Davis if he would like to talk to any of the officers alone about Mrs. Cooper. Davis said he would like to talk to Sykes. The others left the room. Lieutenant Sykes then asked Davis if he had been reading a testament which he was holding. Davis replied that he had. Sykes asked Davis if he had been praying. Davis replied that he did not know how to pray and agreed he would like Sykes to pray for him. The lieutenant offered a short prayer; then Davis confessed. He was driven to the cemetery and asked to re-enact the crime. Police then brought him back to the station where he repeated the confession to several of the officers. In the presence of six officers, a two-page statement of the confession Davis had made was transcribed. Although based on the information Davis had given earlier, Captain McCall dictated this statement employing his own choice of format, wording, and content. He paused periodically to ask Davis if he agreed with the statement so far. Each time Davis acquiesced. Davis signed the statement." (*Davis* v. *North Carolina,* 384 U.S. 737, 16 L. Ed. 2d 895, 86 S. Ct. 1761.)

NOTES

1. Sample instruction: An admission is a statement made by a defendant other than at his trial, which by itself is not sufficient to warrant an inference of guilt, but which tends to prove guilt when considered with the rest of the evidence. You are the exclusive judges as to whether an admission was made by the defendant and if the statement is true in whole or in part. If you find that such statement is wholly untrue, you must reject it. If you find it is true in part, you may consider only that part which you find to be true. Evidence of an oral admission of the defendant ought to be viewed with caution.

2. Unless the statement is recorded, the cautionary instruction is mandatory; see *People* v. *Ramirez,* 40 Cal. App. 3d 347, 114 Cal. R. 916.

3. For a vivid description of abuse incident to obtaining a confession, see *Chambers* v. *Florida,* 309 U.S. 277, 84 L. Ed. 716, 60 S. Ct. 472.

4. Because the admissibility of a confession is a mixed question, the trial judge must first determine whether the confession may be read to the jury. The judge makes a determination as a matter of law whether the confession is voluntary. If the statement is allowed into evidence, the judge then instructs the jury that they also may consider whether the confession is voluntary. If the jury finds the confession voluntary, they may then consider what weight, if any, should be given to the evidence. If they find the confession involuntary, the evidence should be ignored. The jury may be instructed as follows: "You are the exclusive judges as to whether an admission or a confession was made by the defendant and if the statement is true in whole or in part. If you should find that such statement is entirely untrue, you must reject it. If you find it is true in part, you may consider that part which you find to be true." (California Jury Instructions.)

5. For a case collecting federal and state cases on admissibility of confessions by minors and the mentally unbalanced, see: *People* v. *Lara,* 67 C. 2d 365, 62 Cal. R. 586, 432 P. 2d 202.

6. *North* v. *Superior Court,* 8 C. 3d 301, 104 Cal. R. 833, 502 P. 2d 1305. An unusual fact situation and a case not likely to be expanded beyond the facts. Note also that local statutes may regulate overhearing conversations in jails.

7. California Penal Code, Section 825: "The defendant must in all cases be taken before the magistrate without unnecessary delay, and, in any event, within two days after his arrest, excluding Sundays and holidays; provided, however, that when the two days prescribed herein expire at a time when the court in which the magistrate is sitting is not in session, such time shall be extended to include the duration of the next regular court session on the judicial day immediately following. . . ."

8. See *In re Cameron,* 68 C. 2d 487, 67 Cal. R. 529, 439 P. 2d 633.

9. See the dissenting opinion in *People* v. *Johnson,* 32 Cal. App. 3d 988, 109 Cal. R. 118.

11 The *Miranda* Decision

Chapter Objectives

After reading this chapter, you will be able to:

1. Explain the effects of the *Miranda* decision on pre-trial questioning of suspects.

2. State the admonition that must be given and explain when it must be administered.

3. Distinguish between "questioning" and obtaining nonverbal evidence.

4. Describe the factors that determine a waiver of rights.

The scope of the Fifth Amendment protection against compelled disclosure of information by an accused was initially construed to prohibit the prosecution from calling the defendant to be questioned as a witness at his or her own trial. But compulsory *pre-trial* disclosures by an accused, either to a grand jury or to police, could not be used against the defendant either, for otherwise the privilege would be a nullity. In *Miranda* v. *Arizona,* the U.S. Supreme Court held that compulsion—that is, involuntariness—may be inherent in any police interrogation unless the suspect is advised of the Fifth Amendment right to remain silent and the right to have an attorney present. This rule was not novel, because suspects in criminal cases have always had the right to remain silent when confronted by official questioning. Suspects who knew of their Fifth Amendment rights—often because of past experience with law enforcement—exercised their rights. But if suspects were unaware of their right to silence or counsel, their ignorance prevented them from intelligently choosing whether or not to exercise their Fifth Amendment privilege. The court in *Miranda* concluded that everyone should be informed of his or her Fifth Amendment rights in order to be advised of the available alternatives.

In order to enforce the provisions of the Fifth Amendment, the Court fashioned certain rules which would implement the privilege against self-incrimination but still not preclude law enforcement officers from questioning suspects and subsequently admitting their answers into evidence. The

Supreme Court held in *Miranda* that if officers intend to question a suspect in "custody" or "deprived of his freedom of action in a significant way," the suspect must be advised of: the right to counsel before any questions are asked, the right to remain silent at any time before or during questioning, and the fact that if he or she does answer questions, any responses made may be used in evidence against the suspect. Having been informed of these rights, the suspect must then waive both rights in order for interrogation to proceed. The Court thought that if suspects knew they could foreclose questioning or discontinue an interrogation, such knowledge would correct the psychological imbalance created by official questioning in an alien environment. If suspects refused to discuss the case, knowing that they could not be penalized for their refusal, no promises or threats would be availing. Law enforcement officers must bear the responsibility of informing defendants of these rights.

To enforce the *Miranda* rule, the courts exclude from evidence any statement obtained from the defendant not in compliance with *Miranda,* unless an exception applies. Noncompliance with *Miranda* does not prevent the State from trying the defendant. The *Miranda* rule is a rule of evidence based on constitutional principles. This rule of evidence precludes not only a statement obtained in violation of *Miranda,* but any product of that statement as well. Any physical evidence discovered directly as a consequence of a *Miranda* violation will be excluded as the fruit of an unlawful confession. An otherwise voluntary consent search obtained as a consequence of a *Miranda* violation would also be inadmissible. In some cases, even the identity of a witness discovered after an unlawful interrogation might be suppressed.

The Admonition

The language of the *Miranda* admonition varies slightly among law enforcement agencies, but the following sample admonition, administered by the Los Angeles Police Department, contains all the elements made necessary by the *Miranda* ruling: "When a suspect in custody is to be interrogated regarding his possible participation in the commission of a criminal offense, he shall be 'warned' exactly as follows:

> 1. You have the right to remain silent.
>
> 2. If you give up the right to remain silent, anything you say will be used against you in a court of law.
>
> 3. You have the right to speak with an attorney and to have the attorney present during questioning.
>
> 4. If you so desire and cannot afford one, an attorney will be appointed for you without charge before questioning.

After the admonition has been given, the following questions shall be asked:

1. Do you understand each of these rights I have explained to you?

2. Do you wish to give up the right to remain silent?

3. Do you wish to give up the right to speak to an attorney and have him present during questioning?

Include in any resulting report or recording of the interview:

1. The admonition of rights in its entirety, AND

2. Statements indicating the subject's understanding of the admonition, AND

3. Statements indicating whether the suspect waived his rights to remain silent and to have an attorney present, and how he waived them."

Conditions under which the Admonition Must Be Given

The *Miranda* admonition must be given whenever either of two conditions arise: 1) the suspect is in custody; or 2) the suspect is deprived of freedom of action in a significant way.

To begin with the first condition, "custody" implies an arrest for a particular charge and advice by the arresting officer of his or her intention to arrest, of the cause of the arrest, and of the officer's authority to make the arrest. Because the precise moment at which an arrest takes place cannot always be determined, the court will review all of the circumstances surrounding the confrontation. An officer cannot, for example, delay informing the suspect of the reason for the arrest as a tactic to avoid *Miranda*. If an officer has learned that there is sufficient evidence upon which to justify an arrest and yet does not inform the suspect that he or she is under arrest, "custody" will be implied from the circumstances.

For example: Officers investigating the robbery of a bar determine that a jacket inside the bar was abandoned by the suspect in his flight. Other witnesses state that they saw the suspect in the vicinity. The officers ask the suspect to come to the station to make a statement. When he arrives, officers ask him to try on the jacket—which fits him perfectly. When confronted by evidence that the coat was found in the location of the robbery, the suspect admits his guilt.

In this example, the officers possessed highly incriminating evidence against the defendant. Witnesses had seen him near the robbery and physical evidence placed him inside the location, since when the defendant tried the coat on, the fit was perfect. At that point, the officers possessed sufficient evidence to justify an arrest. The mere fact that they failed to inform the defendant at that time that he was under arrest did not relieve them of the duty of informing him of his *Miranda* rights before questioning began. Objectively, the facts establish that the officers would have arrested the defendant for the crime in any event. The time of custody, therefore, should be evaluated based on the facts known to the officers prior to the questioning, even if no formal arrest is made.

Confrontations between an officer and a suspect vary considerably. If an officer detains a person involuntarily to inquire about certain conduct, the nature of such a confrontation differs from that of actually observing a crime and placing the suspect under arrest. Suspects who are detained for questioning and are not placed under arrest for a particular crime may not be in custody for purposes of *Miranda*. Such suspects, however, may be "deprived of their freedom of action in a significant way"—the other element of *Miranda*.

If a person has been placed under arrest by an officer and has been involuntarily transported to a local station, "custody" clearly attaches. But if a person is asked to come to the station voluntarily to be interviewed or to discuss a case, the fact that the interview takes place at the station does not necessarily mean that questioning must be preceded by an admonition. The location of the interview is significant because of the potential for coercion inherent in an official building. But if the investigation is an open one and officers are only seeking statements from possible witnesses—as distinct from suspects—the element of custody is absent.

Nothing prevents officers from seeking interviews with witnesses or possible suspects at their residences. Because a residence is a familiar environment, the atmosphere of coercion substantially diminishes in such a place. If the officers do not have a basis to arrest, then questioning can be conducted without the *Miranda* admonition, unless the answers suggest that there is some basis for arrest. If so, custody would then attach and the admonition would be required before any further questioning.

Because the word "custody" and the phrase "deprived of his freedom of action" tend to overlap, a clear line cannot always be drawn between them and, in fact, some courts tend to construe the phrases interchangeably. For purposes of this discussion, the factors which lead to "custodial" status or the status of being "deprived of freedom of action" can be treated similarly.

Just as the factors which determine whether a confession is voluntary are myriad and no single factor may dominate, the elements of custody and being deprived of freedom of action cannot always be determined by a single factor. Of course, if the officer has probable cause for arrest, that factor alone will signal the requirement for *Miranda* admonitions because the subject is, or will be, in custody. When the officer does not have probable cause to arrest, but only sufficient evidence to detain a person, then the issue is whether the person was deprived of freedom of action in a significant way.

The Threshold Issue—Focus

The court in *Miranda* held that police officers can always question people about unsolved crimes without a *Miranda* admonition. But as the investigation begins to "focus" on a particular subject, the emphasis of the case shifts from investigatory to accusatory. The factors which lead to the shift vary, depending upon the amount and kind of information officers possess about the particular suspect. Thus, the first factor in determining whether the defendant is in custody or deprived of freedom of action in a significant way is whether the investigation has narrowed to a particular suspect or if a particular person has been stopped, whether or not the officer has sufficient information to charge this person with a crime. Three kinds of confrontation situations may occur; each will be discussed in turn on the following pages.

1. *The officer is uncertain whether any crime has been committed.* In this type of situation, the officer has no prior information about the suspect and relies only on the conduct he or she observes prior to any detention.

Consider the following example: "About noon, during a heavy rainstorm, [a burglary investigator] for the police department saw the defendant without a raincoat walk by his patrol car, heading west on a sidewalk, and carrying what appeared to be a new portable-typewriter case. Because many burglaries in that area involved stolen typewriters, and because the defendant was apparently exposing a new portable typewriter to a heavy downpour [most typewriter cases are not water-proof], [the officer] followed. [The defendant] continued west and then north toward an area of several pawnshops. From time to time he looked back in the officer's direction. After he crossed an intersection, the officers drove past him, and when they did so, he reversed his direction. As the officers made a u-turn, the defendant turned into a local park. At that point, the officers left their car and stopped the defendant.

"The officer, after identifying himself, asked the defendant where he was going. Santa Monica (a city twenty-five miles away), the latter replied. How would he get there? Walk. What was in the case he had set down? Radios. Did he have a receipt for the radios? No." (*People* v. *Manis.*)

At this point the defendant was arrested and a search of the case revealed four radios with department store tags still attached.

In this case, the officer observed unusual conduct which warranted further investigation. But no particular crime had been reported, nor had he received any prior information about the suspect, so probable cause for the arrest was initially lacking. Under these circumstances, no arrest was justified, and therefore the person detained was not in custody, nor was he deprived of his freedom of action in a significant way. The questioning was brief and casual, as the officers were merely attempting to verify or dispel their suspicions. Only after the subject provided unbelievable answers to questions did the investigation shift from mere suspicion to probable cause to arrest. At this point, the investigation shifted from the inquisatory to the accusatory. "Focus" had narrowed to the suspect and to a particular charge—that is, burglary. It is at this point that a *Miranda* admonition is necessary, before any further questioning begins.

2. *The officer reasonably believes a particular crime has been committed, but the identity of the suspect is unknown.* In this type of case, the officer knows a specific crime has been committed, either from personal investigation or reports from other sources. To begin an inquiry into the unsolved crime, the officer routinely seeks to interview witnesses. If the officer seeks an interview with a witness who is not suspected as a possible culprit, no *Miranda* admonition is necessary prior to questioning because there is no basis to arrest and the officer has not focused the investigation on a particular person. If, during the course of the questioning, the witness's answers suggest implication in the crime, the witness now becomes a suspect. A *Miranda* admonition may be necessary at this point because the focus has shifted from general investigation to suspicion of a specific person.

For example: "The deceased, Danna Gay Scheibler, was alive at 5:30 P.M. on October 28, 1966, when her mother-in-law called tc pick up Danna's children to care for them while Danna worked from 6:30 P.M. to midnight. The following evening the elder Mrs. Scheibler returned, found the house locked, looked through the front window and saw Danna lying 'like a rag doll' on the floor. There were stab wounds in her back, and blood had run down her back, her arms, and around her body. Sheriff's officers were summoned and gained entry by breaking the lock on the door.

"The deceased was lying face down in the center of the living room, nude except for a housecoat that had been pulled over her head and halfway up her arms. There was a large pool of blood under her head and blood on the soles of her feet. There were two knife blades, a table knife blade and a butcher knife blade approximately 7 inches long, on the floor about 4 feet from her head.

"The living room showed signs of a struggle. The coffee table appeared to have been knocked against the couch. One piece of a broken plastic trash container lid was under a leg of the coffee table, another piece was next to the deceased's left arm. There were spots of blood on the television set and on the wall behind it. A pair of torn panties and a black negligee were found near the deceased's legs. A slip was also found near the body.

"A drain pipe in the laundry area of the kitchen had what appeared to be blood on it. The kitchen telephone had been broken from its cord, and there was a red spot on the cord. The officers found an unlighted, regular-size Lucky Strike cigarette among some debris on the floor and another on the kitchen table. A cigarette butt of another brand was also found on the table. In the bathroom, spots resembling blood were found on a damp towel, the wash basin, and the soap. . . .

"James Scheibler, the deceased's husband, was in Seattle at the time of the murder and returned on October 30, 1966. In searching his house with the police he discovered that his wife's purse and two knives were missing. James Scheibler had known defendant for seven or eight years. Defendant had helped the Scheiblers move into their home four or five months before the murder. Mr. Scheibler had seen defendant the day before he left for Seattle, on or about October 7 or 8, and had told defendant he was going there.

"The investigating officers asked Mr. Scheibler for the names and addresses of all the people with whom he and his wife had been friendly, and on the morning of November 3, 1966, he mentioned defendant's name to the officers, who went to defendant's home at 2:25 P.M. on that date. At that point in the investigation the officers had interviewed from 75 to 100 people.

"Sergeant Thornton knocked on the door and when defendant answered the officers informed him that they were from the Sheriff's office and were investigating the death of Danna Scheibler and had information that he was a personal friend. Defendant invited the officers into his home. They observed a 2-inch cut across his right palm, a 1-inch scar on the right side of his nose, two scars across his right temple, a scar on his left temple, and scratches on his inner left arm.

"Defendant stated that he expected to see the officers, inasmuch as they probably had found his fingerprints inside the Scheiblers' home when he helped them move in. (No fingerprints of defendant had, in fact, been discovered at the Scheibler home.) He accounted for his whereabouts at the time of the murder in such a way as to afford himself, in Sergeant Thornton's opinion, a complete alibi. . . .

"Sergeant Thornton noticed that defendant had a limp, and defendant stated that he had hurt his back in connection with his employment at a steel mill. He was asked when he had last been at the Scheibler residence, and at first said it was the day he had helped them move, then corrected himself and said it was the day before Mr. Scheibler went to Seattle. At that point defendant lighted a Lucky Strike cigarette. He appeared nervous and paced up and down. . . ." (*People* v. *Goodridge.*)

In this example, officers knew that a specific crime, homicide, had already occurred, but they did not suspect any particular person. As the crime was investigated and questioning progressed, the focus narrowed to the defendant. "Questioning" is a factor to be considered in determining focus. But the *kinds* of questions asked, whether investigatory or accusatory, will also determine at what point the *Miranda* admonition is necessary. In the example, the officers initially interviewed the defendant because they felt he might have information regarding the crime. The questions were only investigatory until his answers to the questions, his personal appearance, and his possession of the Lucky Strike cigarette all suggested the defendant's possible involvement. At this point focus narrowed, and custody probably followed.

Most investigations are not conducted by a single officer, and investigating officers rely on many sources of information in an attempt to identify a particular suspect. These sources include laboratory reports, crime-scene investigations, and autopsy reports. If any of the evidence focuses suspicion on a particular suspect, a *Miranda* admonition is required before any questioning.

When information identifying a particular suspect comes directly from the victim of a crime or from a witness to a crime, this information may carry enough weight to narrow the focus immediately. Therefore, the officer must first categorize the source of the information if he or she intends to interrogate a possible suspect. If the victim of a crime provides information to officers, such information will not only narrow the focus of the investigation for *Miranda* purposes, but may also provide probable cause to arrest. If the victim's information is sufficient by itself to qualify as probable cause to arrest, then an arrest will occur immediately and prior to any questioning. Similarly, if an eyewitness to a crime identifies a particular suspect or provides information qualifying as probable cause to arrest, a *Miranda* admonition is required prior to any questioning because the suspect is or will be in custody.

When the source of the officer's information is an informant rather than a victim or witness to a crime, the officer may also make an arrest—assuming the informant is reliable and speaks with personal knowledge of the facts. But in this type of case—the so-called informant case—the officer relies solely on the informant for two facts: that a crime has been committed, and that a person who has been specifically described, although possibly unnamed, committed the crime. These cases almost invariably involve narcotic or other so-called "victimless" crimes. It is because no "victim" has reported the commission of any crime that the officer must rely on the informant for the fact of commission as well as for the identity of the person committing the crime.

This category of cases illustrates the clear relationship between probable cause to arrest and the element of custody. If probable cause to arrest exists, the defendant is in custody and the *Miranda* admonition is required before any questioning occurs. Statements made by an informant must be analyzed to ascertain if they provide probable cause for arrest before the *Miranda* issue is raised. The court will review the status of the informant—reliable or untested—and will determine whether probable cause to arrest is present. If probable cause is lacking, the arrest will be invalid and any subsequent questioning may be tainted and excluded. For example: "Police units conducted a surveillance of an automobile body shop which, according to information obtained by police from an informant, would be the site of the delivery by defendant to the informant of 50 pounds of hashish oil. One officer observed defendant arrive at the site in a Mercedes-Benz, driven by one C. G. The two men and the informant then went to the trunk of the vehicle, opened it, and the informant apparently looked inside the trunk before the trunk was closed. The informant then gave a prearranged signal to the police which indicated that he had seen contraband. From the officers' position, however, they could see nothing in the trunk.

"Defendant and the informant then walked away and were out of police sight for three to five minutes. They returned in the defendant's automobile, a Pontiac. Again, the informant was shown something in the trunk of that vehicle, whereupon the informant gave another prearranged signal to the officers which indicated that the presence of all of the narcotics that were to be delivered had been verified. Defendant and the informant then drove to the informant's residence, with C. G. following behind in his vehicle. When they arrived, the informant went into the house while defendant and C. G. remained outside. Officers then rushed over and accosted defendant and C. G. Officers identified themselves and asked defendant if he had any narcotics in the vehicle, to which defendant replied that he did. Officers then searched both vehicles and found a green suitcase in the trunk of the Pontiac and a brown suitcase in the trunk of the nearby Mercedes-Benz. The green suitcase was opened by [police] at that time, and 34 pounds of marijuana, rather than hashish oil, were found therein. The brown suitcase was opened at the police station without a warrant. It contained 16 additional pounds of marijuana. (*People* v. *Herdan.*)

In this case, the officers had information about a particular crime, a narcotic transaction, from an informant along with their observation of conduct. The court must first determine whether the information in addition to the observation of conduct constituted probable cause to arrest. If probable cause to arrest existed, the defendant was in custody for purposes of *Miranda* and an admonition would be required before the officer asked for the incriminating statement. If probable cause to arrest was lacking, the arrest was unlawful, and any statement by the defendant would be excluded as the direct product of an unlawful arrest.

3. *Officers have reason to believe that a particular crime has been committed, and the identity of the suspect is known.* In the earlier example of the robbery suspect who came into the police station and was asked to try on a jacket, officers knew that a particular crime had been committed, and the identity of the robber was reasonably certain. The investigation had already focused on a particular suspect for the commission of a particular crime. In such cases, a *Miranda* admonition is required before any questioning begins.

The Secondary Issue—The Mental Factor

Assuming that the investigation has focused on an accused, the court will review the objective facts to determine whether the defendant was in custody or whether the defendant *reasonably believed* he or she was in custody. Custody will be determined not only by the officer's state of mind, but also by the suspect's state of mind. Despite the officer's statement that he or she did not arrest the defendant, if a person reasonably believed he or she was in custody, the *Miranda* admonition is required before any questioning takes place.

The amount and kind of information possessed by the officer, the location of the questioning, and the length and character of the questioning will be scrutinized by the court to determine whether a person "reasonably believed" he or she was in custody or deprived of freedom of action in a significant way. For example: "Defendant is charged with manslaughter based upon evidence that she had negligently allowed her daughter to die. The most damaging part of the prosecution's case against the defendant consisted of a transcription of an interrogation of defendant by a deputy district attorney in the course of which defendant described Sandra's terminal illness. According to the statement, Sandra became ill on May 2; she complained of stomach pains and vomited several times. Over the following days defendant kept Sandra at home in a specially obtained hospital bed, gave her enemas, and applied compresses. Sandra's condition began to deteriorate, and defendant called members of the Church of the First Born, who came to the Arnold home on May 14 and prayed for Sandra.

"Defendant realized at this time that Sandra was gravely ill, since the girl could not walk unassisted, could not retain liquids fed her, could not normally excrete bodily wastes, and was losing weight. Defendant, although aware that Sandra might die, did not obtain a doctor for her because of defendant's religious convictions against using medical assistance. On May 19 Sandra had a 25-minute convulsion; on May 20 defendant and other members of the church took Sandra to the river, where she was immersed and baptized. Three hours later Sandra died.

"Defendant rendered the questioned statement during an interrogation at the office of the deputy district attorney. The deputy had notified her to come to his office to discuss the circumstances of Sandra's death. She did so; she testified at trial, 'I didn't know I didn't have to come down and talk to you, or I wouldn't have. . . .' The deputy queried her for one hour and forty-five minutes. No one else was present on the occasion except an attaché of the district attorney's office who transcribed the interrogation; he took no part in the questioning. At this point defendant had not been placed under arrest.

"The attaché who transcribed the statement testified that the deputy district attorney did not advise defendant of her right to counsel, but that defendant had not requested an attorney before or during the interrogation. . . ."

In this case "the investigation was no longer a general inquiry into an unsolved crime but had begun to focus on a particular suspect. The record indicates that, prior to the formal interrogation of defendant, the deputy district attorney had determined that Sandra's death resulted from a felony and that defendant perpetrated the crime. The questions asked during the session strongly suggest that *before* the interrogation occurred the deputy had reason to believe that Sandra had been extremely ill for several weeks before her death, that defendant had not obtained medical assistance for Sandra during the terminal illness, that defendant's religious beliefs would not permit the summoning of a doctor for Sandra, that members of defendant's church had immersed Sandra in the river several hours before she died, that Sandra was in the custody of her mother, and that Sandra's father lived in Louisiana. The deputy also had in his possession the autopsy report. Moreover, defendant and other members of the Church of the First Born had previously talked with various law enforcement officials about the death. He therefore had strong reason to believe that defendant was guilty of manslaughter." (*People* v. *Arnold.*)

Was the defendant in "custody"? She was not in actual custody, because no one had placed her under arrest prior to the questioning. But the defendant had testified without contradiction "that she believed she had no alternative other than to comply with an authoritative summoning for interrogation. She might reasonably have believed that if she attempted to leave during the course of the interrogation, the deputy district attorney would have arested her or told police officers to physically detain her. In determining whether the defendant 'reasonably believed' she was in custody or deprived of her freedom of action, the court [will] review the precise language used by the deputy district attorney in summoning the defendant to the office, any statements of the deputy not transcribed and made before or after formal interrogation, and the physical surroundings. The trial court should also consider the extent to which the authorities confronted defendant with evidence of her guilt, the pressures exerted to detain defendant, and any other circumstances which might have led defendant 'reasonably to believe that she could not leave' freely."

The test of whether a person "reasonably believes" he or she is in custody is objective—that is, the test is a review of all of the facts surrounding the interrogation. This test of "reasonable belief" applies whether the investigation is conducted pursuant to category 1, 2, or 3 above.

The Role of Questioning in Determining Custody

The Court in *Miranda* held that the admonition must be given if the defendant is in custody or deprived of freedom of action in a significant way, *and* if the officer carries on a process of questioning. The *Miranda* decision was "not intended to hamper the traditional function of police officers in investigating a crime. . . . General on-the-scene questioning as to facts surrounding a crime or other general questioning of citizens in the fact-finding process is not affected by our holding. It is an act of responsible citizenship for individuals to give whatever information they may have to aid in law enforcement. In such situations, the compelling atmosphere inherent in the process of in-custody interrogation is not necessarily present." (*Miranda* v. *Arizona.*)

In determining whether an investigation has focused on a particular person, the officer may have obtained all the facts necessary for arrest prior to contacting and questioning the suspect. On the other hand, the officer may have collected sufficient evidence to warrant questioning of a person, but not enough evidence to justify an arrest. In the latter case, the officer must resort to questioning in order to proceed with an investigation. Although the investigation has focused on a particular person, the officer need not administer *Miranda* rights at the outset if there are not sufficient facts to justify an arrest. The questioning itself, therefore, will be scrutinized by the court to determine whether the suspect was being deprived of freedom of action or reasonably believed that he or she was deprived of freedom of action. As long as such questions are investigatory rather than accusatory, no Miranda admonition is necessary. For example:

"At approximately midnight on Saturday night, August 12, 1967, Officer S of the Sacramento City Police Department was directed by police car radio to investigate a report of a missing child. He understood this directive to mean that he was to find out where the child had been on Saturday and to find her. He had been informed that she had been with defendant on Saturday. Officers S and W interviewed Mrs. A, the child's mother, in front of the A residence. Accompanied by Mrs. A, the officers went to defendant's residence, but he was not there. They located his car parked on the street, and Mrs. A went into nearby bars in search of him. In the meantime the car had driven away, and the three searchers returned to defendant's residence. Not finding defendant there, they went back to the A residence, where the officers obtained additional information for their written police report. Officer S told Mrs. A that the police department would continue searching for her daughter. The officers then reported to police headquarters that they were going to a nearby restaurant to have lunch. During their lunch, the officers received a phone call from headquarters that defendant had returned to his residence. Upon arriving there, the officers saw defendant in front of his residence, talking with another unit of police officers, who left shortly after the arrival of Officers S and W.

"Mrs. A was there and accused defendant of being responsible for her daughter's disappearance. Defendant asked the officers to keep Mrs. A away from him, and the officers told both defendant and Mrs. A that their arguing would not help the police in their efforts to locate the girl. Defendant told Officer S that he wanted to be helpful and would assist the police in their investigation; he said he was very sorry about the little girl but that he had not taken her from her home; he said he had not visited the A residence on Saturday morning; he had visited a house several doors away and had seen the girl playing with other children around his car but she had not been in it.

"During his conversation with defendant, Officer S suspected that defendant may have been involved in the girl's disappearance, but he also felt that 'there was nothing to go on' as a ground for taking defendant into custody because of the conflicting statements by Mrs. A that defendant had taken the girl in his station wagon Saturday morning and by defendant's denial that he had done so.

"Defendant testified that Officer S said to him, in substance: 'You know, the little girl is missing. . . . Now, at this point I don't have too much reason to believe that anything really happened. We feel it is just a case where she hasn't come home . . . You are not under arrest. But there will be additional officers . . . out to talk to you . . . (in) the next five or six hours. Please be available or let someone know if you go away from home any length of time.' (*People* v. *Miller*.)

In this example, the officers were uncertain that any crime had been committed. They did not have probable cause to arrest prior to questioning and their questions were directed towards finding the child rather than toward soliciting incriminating statements. Absent probable cause to arrest, custody would not attach. Nor was the defendant deprived of his freedom of action in a significant way. The officers were conducting a general on-the-scene investigation, and the questions were not accusatory. Had the questioning shifted from the inquisitory to the accusatory, the *Miranda* admonition would have been necessary.

Moreover, if the answers to inquisitory questions had suggested criminal knowledge or conduct, the *Miranda* admonition would have been necessary because probable cause to arrest would have emerged. But a review of the kinds of questions asked of the defendant by the officers could not be interpreted by the defendant to suggest that he "reasonably believed he was in custody." In short, if the role of questioning is to inquire, rather than to accuse, and probable cause to arrest is not present, no admonition need be given. But once the questioning shifts from the inquisitory to the accusatory, a defendant is in custody for *Miranda* purposes.

Not infrequently, officers are called to the scene of an incident without any knowledge of the circumstances. In order to commence any investigation, they must ask questions to determine the facts. For example, "Police officers responded to a police radio broadcast indicating that a stabbing had occurred at 750 North Twenty-third Street, Apartment 22. When they arrived on the scene, a man waved down the officers and said, 'Apartment 23 upstairs.' En route to Apartment 23 the officers passed Apartment 21, noting that its door was wide open. A voice within Apartment 21 said, 'In here, officers.' The officers entered and observed defendant seated in a chair in the livingroom. The officers asked him 'What happened?' Defendant replied, 'I did it and I'm sorry.'

"After discovering the deceased body of defendant's wife in Apartment 23, the officers informed defendant that he was under arrest for assault with a deadly weapon. As defendant was being handcuffed, the officer asked defendant 'Where is the knife?' Pointing, defendant responded, 'Over on the kitchen sink.' From his location in the living room, the officer could see the knife on the kitchen counter. The officer then went into the kitchen area and obtained the knife which was on the kitchen counter.

"The officer then asked defendant if he had any weapons on his person. Defendant indicated that he had a pocket knife which the officer removed. No further questions were asked of the defendant. The officer instructed another officer to take defendant to the detective bureau and to advise him of his constitutional rights." (*People* v. *Supreme Court* [Mahle].)

Applying the threshold rules, the officers relied on a radio broadcast to investigate a possible assault. When they arrived at the scene, they had no particular suspect in mind nor any knowledge that a crime had actually been committed. No focus on a suspect emerged when they initially talked to the defendant. The brief question, "what happened?" was the first stage of the investigation. Their neutral inquiry was inquisitory, not accusatory.

This typical general on-the-scene investigation was initiated by a routine general question which did not imply any guilt. Since the officers were unaware of any facts justifying an arrest of the defendant, or even that a crime had been committed, they lacked probable cause to arrest, and the element of custody was absent. Nor could the defendant reasonably believe he was in custody based upon this routine inquiry. His statement was not custodial, no *Miranda* admonition was necessary, and the response is admissible.

The Role of Location in Determining Custody

The location where questioning is conducted is relevant in determining whether the defendant was in custody or reasonably believed he or she was in custody. Part of the Supreme Court's concern with police interrogation stems from the atmosphere of coercion implicit in any police facility. An arrestee transported to a total police environment, separated from family or friends, and confronted by officers in authority cannot be unaffected. According to the U.S. Supreme Court, interrogation at a police facility is inherently coercive unless the suspect arrives on his or her own initiative and volunteers to speak. Aside from that exception, however, any questioning of a suspect on whom suspicion has focused which is conducted by police at a police facility must be preceded by a *Miranda* admonition unless other factors dispel the coercive nature of the environment (for example: inviting a person to come to the station, informing this person that he or she is not under arrest, and allowing the person to leave after questioning has been completed).

When questioning is conducted at a location other than a police facility the atmosphere of coercion diminishes, but it does not disappear. The confrontation between a suspect and a police officer always carries a factor of coercion if the suspect is detained involuntarily. Questioning conducted on a public street or sidewalk may be less coercive, but the detention is still relevant in determining custody from the total atmosphere of the facts.

Miranda does not prevent officers from seeking interviews with suspects at their homes. Because the suspect's home is unlikely to allow coercion, the location alone will be relevant. But questioning at home does not necessarily foreclose the necessity of a *Miranda* admonition if the facts warrant it. For example, in *Orozco* v. *Texas,* "the evidence introduced at trial showed that defendant and the deceased had quarreled outside the El Farleto Cafe in Dallas shortly before midnight on the date of the shooting. The deceased had apparently spoken to defendant's female companion inside the restaurant. In the heat of the quarrel outside, the deceased is said to have beaten defendant about the face and called him 'Mexican Grease.' A shot was fired killing the deceased. Defendant left the scene and returned to his boardinghouse to sleep. At about 4 A.M. four police officers arrived at defendant's boardinghouse, were admitted by an unidentified woman, and were told that petitioner was asleep in the bedroom. All four officers entered the bedroom and began to question defendant. From the moment he gave his name, according to the testimony of one of the officers, defendant was not free to go where he pleased but was 'under arrest.' The officers asked him if he had been to the El Farleto restaurant that night and when he answered 'yes' he was asked if he owned a pistol. Defendant admitted owning one. After being asked a second time where the pistol was located, he admitted that it was in the washing machine in a backroom of the boardinghouse. Ballistics tests indicated that the gun found in the washing machine was the gun that fired the fatal shot. At defendant's trial, the trial court allowed one of the officers, over the objection of defendant's lawyer, to relate the statements made by defendant concerning the gun and defendant's presence at the scene of the shooting. The trial testimony clearly shows that the officers questioned defendant about incriminating facts without first informing him of his right to remain silent, his right to have the advice of a lawyer before making any statement, and his right to have a lawyer appointed to assist him if he could not afford to hire one. . . .

"It is true that the Court did say in *Miranda* that 'compulsion to speak in the isolated setting of the police station may well be greater than in courts or other official investigations, where there are often impartial observers to guard against intimidation or trickery.' But the opinion iterated and reiterated the absolute necessity for officers interrogating people 'in custody' to give the described warnings.

"According to the officer's testimony, defendant was under arrest and not free to leave when he was questioned in his bedroom in the early hours of the morning. The Miranda opinion declared that the warnings were required when the person being interrogated was 'in custody at the station or otherwise deprived of his freedom of action in any significant way.'"

The Court held that although the questioning was conducted at the suspect's home, thereby reducing the atmosphere of coercion inherent in a police facility, that factor alone was not sufficient to avoid the *Miranda* rule. In *Orozco,* police possessed sufficient information prior to the questioning to charge the defendant with a specific crime they knew had been committed, and they had probable cause to arrest him. Failure to notify Orozco that he was under arrest is immaterial because the investigation had focused on him and police had a basis to take him into custody.

Secondly, Orozco would have "reasonably believed" he was not free to leave, even in his own home. Confronted by several police officers and questioned specifically about a particular crime, Orozco would have reasonably believed that he was in custody, even though he was not told he was under arrest. Both the factor of focus and the factor of the defendant's belief that he was in custody were present, and a *Miranda* admonition was required before any questioning commenced.[1]

The Role of Officers' Conduct in Determining Custody

The conduct of officers while questioning a suspect is another factor which is relevant in determining whether the defendant was in custody or reasonably believed he or she was in custody. At trial, the court will review the events preceding the questioning and the conduct of the officers during the confrontation. If an officer routinely stops a lone motorist for a simple traffic violation and begins the process of determining the status of his driver's license and vehicle registration, such conduct is only barely coercive. But this example may be contrasted with a situation in which the officer uses physical restraint on a suspect or draws a weapon. These objective factors of force will be relevant in determining whether the suspect reasonably believed he was in custody.

Noncustodial Questioning

Because defendants must be in custody or reasonably believe they are in custody in order for the *Miranda* ruling to apply, incriminating statements may be obtained from suspects without a *Miranda* admonition if the element of custody is missing. Police may record incriminating statements solicited by an informant or a suspect unaware of police presence in narcotics transactions (*Hoffa* v. *United States*), may overhear conversations between the victim of the crime and the suspect if the victim consents (*People* v. *Ing*), and may record the conversation of the defendant and an accomplice who has agreed to testify for the prosecution (*People* v. *Murphy*). In all of these cases, the defendants are not in actual custody or even aware of police presence and could not reasonably believe that they were in custody. Even though police had focused on the defendants as suspects, the absence of custody nullifies the requirement of a *Miranda* admonition.

The Requirement of Questioning

Voluntary Statements

Just as the determination of whether a confession is voluntary turns upon a number of factors, the determination of whether a suspect is in custody depends upon a variety of circumstances. As we have seen, these circumstances are: the amount and kind of information the officer possesses about the crime and/or the suspect; whether the investigation has narrowed to a particular person or whether the investigation is an open one; the kinds of questions asked, whether investigatory or accusatory; the length and time of the questioning; the location of the questioning; and the conduct of the officers during the questioning.

As noted earlier, questioning is an important factor in determining whether the defendant was in custody or reasonably believed he or she was in custody. But questioning is also important in another context: The Miranda admonition needs to be given only if the officer intends to question the suspect. If no questions are to be asked, then no admonition needs to be given, even if the suspect is under arrest and in custody. Under this interpretation, therefore, a statement submitted voluntarily by a suspect in custody and not in response to questioning will be admissible.

Physical Evidence

Because the Fifth Amendment only prohibits compulsory testimony or compelled pre-trial statements, the *Miranda* rules are inapplicable when police request or obtain physical evidence rather than questioning the defendant. Handwriting samples, blood, breath, or urine tests, or voice tests may be obtained from suspects without advising them of their rights under *Miranda*. The *Miranda* case is an interpretation of the Fifth Amendment and, as noted earlier, the Fifth Amendment applies to statements, not to physical evidence. Only if the officers intend to obtain a voice sample must they explain the distinction between speaking for identification and speaking for incrimination.

Waivers

If the defendant is in custody or is deprived of freedom of action in a significant way, and if the officer intends to question this person, the *Miranda* admonition is necessary. But the officer must now obtain a waiver of the defendant's right to silence and counsel before the questioning can proceed in order to admit the defendant's answers into evidence on the People's case in chief. As noted earlier in this chapter, the admonition must request that the defendant give up the right to counsel and silence. Once the waiver has been obtained, the questioning may begin.

Waivers will not be presumed from a silent record and officers must be able to testify that they advised defendants of their rights and that defendants agreed to discuss the case and to do so without counsel. Courts throughout the United States differ on whether defendants must affirmatively state that they do not desire counsel and desire to speak to the officer, or whether statements by defendants that they understand these rights and choose to respond to questions are sufficient (*United States* v. *Hayes.*) But a stronger case for admissibility can always be made if defendants expressly state that they do not desire counsel and wish to speak. (*Miranda* v. *Arizona.*)

The burden is on the prosecution to establish that waivers are knowingly, intelligently, and voluntarily given by defendants. If defendants are under the influence of alcohol or drugs at the time of questioning, they may contend that their mental state prevented them from knowingly and intelligently waiving their rights. The courts will analyze the facts in a manner similar to that used in determining the voluntariness of a confession. A promise or threat directed towards the defendant affects not only the voluntariness of the confession, but also the voluntariness of the waiver.

Just as the voluntariness of a confession involving a minor requires special consideration, so the waiver of rights by a minor is often in issue. If a defendant suffers from a physical or mental impairment, the difficulty of establishing voluntariness of a waiver also increases. One method of establishing a knowing, intelligent, and voluntary waiver is to tape-record the interview which includes the defendant's personal waiver. Although the law does not require corroboration of a waiver by tape, by writing, or even by corroborative evidence from other witnesses, trial courts can more easily determine the validity of a waiver when it is presented with strong evidence.

Invoking the Privilege

The Right to Remain Silent

Once the *Miranda* warnings have been administered, the arrestee can elect to speak or to remain silent. But even if the arrestee commences speaking, he or she can retract the decision to speak and stop responding at any time. According to the U.S. Supreme Court, the admissibility of a statement obtained once a person in custody has invoked the privilege to remain silent depends upon whether the person's right to cut off questioning was scrupulously honored.

For example, in *Michigan* v. *Mosley,* the following facts occurred: "The defendant was arrested in Detroit, Michigan, on the early afternoon of April 8, 1971, in connection with robberies that had recently occurred at the Blue Goose Bar and the White Tower Restaurant on that city's lower east side. The arresting officer, Detective Cowie of the Armed Robbery Section of the Detroit Police Department, was acting on a tip implicating Mosley and three other men in the robberies. After effecting the arrest, Detective Cowie brought Mosley to the Robbery, Breaking and Entering Bureau of the Police Department, located on the fourth floor of the departmental headquarters building. The officer advised Mosley of his rights under this Court's decision in *Miranda* v. *Arizona,* and had him read and sign the department's constitutional rights notification certificate. After filling out the necessary arrest papers, Cowie began questioning Mosely about the robbery of the White Tower Restaurant. When Mosley said he did not want to answer any questions about the robberies, Cowie promptly ceased the interrogation. The completion of the arrest papers and the questioning of Mosley together took approximately 20 minutes. At no time during the questioning did Mosley indicate a desire to consult with a lawyer, and there is no claim that the procedures followed to this point did not fully comply with the strictures of the *Miranda* opinion. Mosley was then taken to a ninth-floor cell block.

"Shortly after 6 P.M., Detective Hill of the Detroit Police Department Homicide Bureau brought Mosley from the cell block to the fifth-floor office of the Homicide Bureau for questioning about the fatal shooting of a man named Leroy Williams. Williams had been killed on January 9, 1971, during a holdup attempt outside the 101 Ranch Bar in Detroit. Mosley had not been arrested on this charge nor interrogated about it by Detective Cowie. Before questioning Mosley about this homicide, Detective Hill carefully advised him of his '*Miranda* rights.' Mosley read the notification form both silently and aloud, and Detective Hill then read and explained the warnings to him and had him sign the form. Mosley at first denied any involvement in the Williams murder, but after the officer told him that Anthony Smith had confessed to participating in the slaying and had named him as the 'shooter,' Mosley made a statement implicating himself in the homicide. The interrogation by Detective Hill lasted approximately 15 minutes, and at no time during its course did Mosley ask to consult with a lawyer or indicate that he did not want to discuss the homicide. . . . The statement was admitted at a trial which resulted in the defendant's conviction."

The Court said that, "a review of the circumstances leading to Mosley's confession reveals that his 'right to cut off questioning' was fully respected in this case. Before his initial interrogation, Mosley was carefully advised that he was under no obligation to answer any questions and could remain silent if he wished. He orally acknowledged that he understood the Miranda warnings and then signed a printed notification of rights form. When Mosley stated that he did not want to discuss the robberies, Detective Cowie immediately ceased the interrogation and did not try either to resume the questioning or in any way persuade Mosley to reconsider his position. After an interval of more than two hours, Mosley was questioned by another police officer at another location about an unrelated holdup murder. He was given full and complete Miranda warnings at the outset of the second interrogation. He was thus reminded again that he could remain silent and could consult with a lawyer, and was carefully given a full and fair opportunity to exercise these options. The subsequent questioning did not undercut Mosley's previous decision not to answer Detective Cowie's inquiries. Detective Hill did not resume the interrogation about the White Tower Restaurant robbery or inquire about the Blue Goose Bar robbery, but instead focused exclusively on the Leroy Williams homicide, a crime different in nature and in time and place of occurrence from the robberies for which Mosley had been arrested and interrogated by Detective Cowie. Although it is not clear from the record how much Detective Hill knew about the earlier interrogation, his questioning of Mosley about an unrelated homicide was quite consistent with a reasonable interpretation of Mosley's earlier refusal to answer any questions about the robberies.

"This is not a case, therefore, where the police failed to honor a decision of a person in custody to cut off questioning, either by refusing to discontinue the interrogation upon request or by persisting in repeated efforts to wear down his resistance and make him change his mind. In contrast to such practices, the police here immediately ceased the interrogation, resumed questioning only after the passage of a significant period of time and the provision of a fresh set of warnings, and restricted the second interrogation to a crime that had not been a subject of the earlier interrogation." Under this interpretation, police had scrupulously honored Mosley's desire to cut off questioning.

Despite its holding, the *Mosley* case should not be construed as a license to reinterview a suspect after he or she has initially refused to discuss the case. Once a defendant has expressed unwillingness to speak about the case at hand, officers cannot question the defendant further unless counsel is present. To allow reinterview would only serve to intimidate the person. But if officers obtain information incriminating the defendant in a separate crime, *Mosley* authorizes a reinterview as long as the questioning is preceded by an adequate admonition and waiver. Or, if the defendant reverses the decision to remain silent and requests the opportunity to give a statement, this decision to solicit the interview will be construed as a valid waiver.

In *Mosley,* the defendant expressly stated that he did not want to discuss the case. Had he been reinterviewed on the original charges, the Court undoubtedly would have held that the invocation of the privilege to remain silent foreclosed any further interrogation. For example: The prosecutor offers a confession of the defendant at trial under the following circumstances: "After defendant was brought into the police station, he was administered the standard advice now required by the *Miranda* decision. The detective who so informed defendant then asked him to sign a waiver of the constitutional rights. Defendant refused. Almost immediately thereafter the officers confronted defendant with his two accomplices, both juveniles who had confessed and had implicated defendant. In the presence of the officers, one of the juveniles and the defendant engaged in a heated argument over an $8.00 loan. The juveniles were then taken out, and the detective again advised defendant of his rights, inquiring anew if he would like to sign a waiver and confess. Defendant then signed the waiver and confessed to the crime." (*People* v. *Fioritto.*)

Not all courts may agree on whether the defendant's initial refusal to sign a waiver was an invocation of the right to remain silent. The defendant did not state that he was unwilling to discuss the case—he only refused to sign the waiver. But the burden is on the prosecution to establish that this conduct was not reasonably inconsistent with a present unwillingness to discuss the case.

If the defendant does not expressly state that he or she declines to discuss the case, the court must determine from all the facts and circumstances whether the defendant has invoked the privilege to remain silent. For example: "[The defendant] was apprehended by Denver, Colorado police on November 26, 1972. At about 6:30 P.M. on that date, the Denver police sought to question him concerning the crime. Reading from a printed form, the Denver police advised defendant of his *Miranda* rights. Rather than consenting to a waiver of the right, defendant wrote on the form in the space designated for a signature of the 'Person Advised,' 'You are in as much in the dark as I am. I'll just wait.' Two Los Angeles Police Department officers interviewed defendant in Denver on November 29 at about noon. They read his rights per *Miranda* and asked if he understood them. The interviewing officer asked defendant if he wished to talk about the crime. Defendant stated that he wanted to talk to 'somebody.' The officer asked who he meant by 'somebody.' Defendant replied that he wished to see a prison doctor or a psychiatrist. The officer arranged an interview for the defendant with the chief psychologist at the Denver County Jail. The doctor spoke with defendant for about ten minutes beginning at 2:45 P.M. The psychologist noted that defendant was 'apparently under pressure, stress, and that's why he wanted to talk matters over with a psychologist or a minister, as he stated. And the pressure was that he could not decide whether he would make a confession to the detectives or not.' [The doctor] gave defendant no advice as to whether or not he should confess. Following the interview, however, [the doctor] told Los Angeles police officers that he had 'this boy ready to make his confession.' Without repeating the *Miranda* warning, the officer then asked defendant if he would be willing to discuss his role in the 'attempted robbery and murder.' He responded that he would. After further questioning, defendant wrote out a confession.'' (*People* v. *Parker*.)

At no time did the defendant actually state that he declined to discuss the case. But the combination of custody, the desire to speak to ''somebody,'' the statement by the doctor that the defendant was under stress, and the second statement that the doctor had apparently convinced him to confess, all combined to suggest that any waiver of rights was not freely and voluntarily made—that is, the defendant was attempting to invoke his privilege to remain silent.

The Right to an Attorney

If the defendant expresses the desire for an attorney before any questioning begins, police must discontinue the questioning until an attorney is present. Law enforcement officers are under no affirmative obligation to provide counsel; the officer must only cease any questioning. In *Miranda,* the Court said:

''If the individual states that he wants an attorney, the interrogation must cease until an attorney is present. At that time the individual must have an opportunity to confer with the attorney and to have him present during any subsequent questioning. If the individual cannot obtain an attorney and he indicates that he wants one before speaking to the police, they must respect his decision to remain silent.

''This does not mean, as some have suggested, that each police station must have a 'station house lawyer' present at all times to advise prisoners. It does mean, however, that if police propose to interrogate a person they must make known to him that he is entitled to a lawyer and if he cannot afford one, a lawyer will be provided for him prior to any interrogation. If authorities conclude that they will not provide counsel during a reasonable period of time in which the investigation in the field is carried out, they may refrain from doing so without violating the person's Fifth Amendment privilege so long as they do not question him during that time.''

Just as a suspect's desire to remain silent may not be expressly stated, the request for counsel may be ambiguous or only inferred by conduct. And when minors are involved, other factors come into play. For example: A defendant, 16 years old, was arrested for murder. During the booking process, the defendant asked if he could see his parents. The officers refused his request. Later, he was advised of his *Miranda* rights and confessed. Was the minor's request to see his parents an invocation of the privilege? In

People v. *Burton,* the court said that, "It appears to us most likely and most normal that a minor who wants help on how to conduct himself with the police and wishes to indicate that he does not want to proceed without such help would express such desire by requesting to see his parents. For adults, removed from the protective [influence] of parental guidance, the desire for help naturally manifests in a request for an attorney. For minors, it would seem that the desire for help naturally manifests in a request for parents. It would certainly severely restrict the 'protective devices' required by Miranda in cases where the suspects are minors if the only call for help which is to be deemed an invocation of the privilege is the call for an attorney. It is [absurd] to assume that a minor in custody will be in a position to call an attorney for assistance and it is unrealistic to attribute no significance to his call for help from the only person to whom he normally looks—a parent or guardian. It is common knowledge that this is the normal reaction of a youthful suspect who finds himself in trouble with the law."

As we have seen, the *Miranda* admonition advises a suspect of the right to silence and counsel, and if a suspect requests counsel, officers are under no obligation to provide such counsel; they must only discontinue the questioning. Once the defendant has been arraigned in court, however, counsel will be appointed by the court and at that point no further interrogation may be conducted in the absence of counsel unless the defendant initiates or volunteers a statement.

Under the *Miranda* case, the defendant is entitled to be advised of the right to counsel whenever in custody. If officers know that the defendant is already represented by an attorney at the time custody attaches, but prior to arraignment, can they question the defendant, or is all questioning completely barred until counsel arrives? In some states, notably New York (*People* v. *DiBiasi*), custodial interrogation initiated by police is prohibited if the suspect is known by them to be represented by an attorney and the attorney is not present. Even a valid *Miranda* warning is not sufficient; without the presence of an attorney, only statements volunteered by the suspect would be admitted. Because not all jurisdictions subscribe to this rule, local court cases must be considered. (*Dillon* v. *United States.*)

Exceptions to the *Miranda* Rule

As noted earlier, the Court held that the rules they fashioned were designed to implement the protection afforded by the Fifth Amendment. The scope of that protection, however, must be related to the reason for the rules. The rules were preventative—that is, they were intended to eliminate coercive questioning by enjoining police to advise suspects that they could remain silent without penalty and that legal counsel was available to assist them. But in some cases, the urgent need for questioning outweighs the rule.

Impeachment of the Defendant

As a general rule, the prosecution cannot offer evidence of the defendant's admission or confession in their case in chief until they establish compliance with the *Miranda* rules. But an admission or confession may be admissible if the defendant elects to testify in his or her own defense, even if the *Miranda* rules have been violated. The prosecution may impeach the defendant—that is, contradict his or her testimony—by means of a prior inconsistent statement to police, even if a defective admonition or no admonition at all was given. In *Harris* v. *New York,* the defendant was charged by the State in a two-count indictment with twice selling heroin to an undercover police officer. The prosecution introduced evidence of the two sales. When Harris took the stand in his own defense, he denied the first sale and described the second as one of baking powder utilized as part of a scheme to defraud the purchaser. On cross-examination, Harris was asked whether he had made specific statements to the police immediately following his arrest which partially contradicted his present testimony. In response, Harris testified that he could not remember the questions or answers recited by the prosecutor. After the defense rested, the prosecution presented testimony by a police officer concerning a pre-trial statement in which Harris had implicated himself. The officer testified that he had not given a proper *Miranda* admonition. The trial court then instructed the jury that the statements attributed to Harris could be used only in passing on his credibility and not as evidence of guilt. The jury returned a verdict of guilty on the second count of the indictment.

The prosecution had not sought to use the statements in its case in chief, for it conceded that they were inadmissible under *Miranda* because Harris had not been advised of his right to appointed counsel. The Chief Justice, speaking for the Supreme Court, observed, "It does not follow from *Miranda* that evidence inadmissible against an accused in the prosecution's case in chief is barred for all purposes, provided of course that the trustworthiness of the evidence satisfies legal standards. We hold the impeachment process here undoubtedly provided valuable aid to the jury in assessing petitioner's credibility; that the benefits of this process should not be lost; that, assuming that the exclusionary rule has a deterrent effect on proscribed police conduct, sufficient deterrence flows when the evidence in question is made unavailable to the prosecution in its case in chief, and that the shield provided by *Miranda* cannot be perverted into a license to use perjury by way of a defense, free from the risk of confrontation with prior inconsistent utterances. Harris' credibility was appropriately impeached by the use of his earlier conflicting statements."[2]

Under the *Harris* rule, a failure to advise a suspect of the right to counsel, or silence, authorizes the use of the defendant's incriminating pre-trial statements by police for the purpose of impeaching the defendant if he or she testifies. However, not all courts have agreed with the *Harris* rule. In California, for example, the defendant cannot be impeached by inconsistent pre-trial statements unless he or she has received the *Miranda* warning. (*People* v. *Disbrow*.)

Lifesaving

If the evidence established that a life was in danger and the defendant possessed information which would assist officers in saving that life, most courts would undoubtedly approve noncompliance with the *Miranda* rules. For example: The defendant and his wife kidnapped an eighteen-year-old girl from the home of her parents and kept her captive in their home while making ransom calls to her parents. These calls were monitored by F.B.I. agents while waiting at the drop point the defendant had specified. Before the ransom money was dropped off, the defendant, waiting in the bushes, was apprehended, disarmed, and handcuffed. The arresting officer holstered his weapon and asked the defendant the location of the kidnap victim without advising him of his *Miranda* rights. The defendant replied that she was at a specific address. Not knowing whether the defendant was or was not telling the truth, the agent asked whether the defendant's car was nearby, believing the kidnap victim might be in the car. The defendant stated that he did not have a car but would be picked up by a confederate driving a specified vehicle. No promises or threats were made to the defendant to obtain this information. The defendant's accomplice in the pickup vehicle was apprehended, and the agents proceeded to the defendant's home and rescued the kidnap victim.

"The *Miranda* opinion provides no guidance to police officers when they are confronted with balancing the life of a victim against a protection of a suspect's constitutional rights. Although the *Miranda* decision was designed to protect basic constitutional rights, even more fundamental than the right against self-incrimination is the right of a citizen to *life*.

"One solution would be to decide that the police may ask questions concerning the location of a kidnap victim, but that the defendant's answers could not be used against him in a court of law. The problem here, of course, is that in some cases a rule excluding the defendant's answers might well allow him to go free, and that "while a premium must be placed on rescue of the victim, this must not occur in a setting that will merely turn the criminal loose again to work his evil upon others." (*People* v. *Dean*.)

Although each court must determine whether an incriminating statement is admissible under these circumstances, the questioning should be designed to assist in the preservation of human life. The interrogating officers should have a reasonable belief that the victim is alive, and that the information they obtain may save the victim's life. Coercion must not be used to obtain the answers, and the objective of the questioning should not be a confession. Once information has been obtained to enable the officer to locate the kidnap victim, interrogation should cease until *Miranda* warnings can be given.

The "rescue" doctrine is similar to the "emergency" search doctrine. The trial court will determine factually whether or not the appropriate circumstances exist to disregard *Miranda* warnings, and the absence of a reasonable belief that the victim may still be alive, for example, might cause a court to exclude evidence of answers given to questions.

The rescue doctrine appears to apply in a limited set of circumstances. Aside from kidnapping, officers could question a suspect in a bomb case as to the location of the explosive device. In this circumstance, *Miranda* warnings might be unnecessary, particularly if the bomb endangers human life.

Careful application of these principles will allow law enforcement officers to perform vital functions while not being forced to choose between saving a human life and possibly endangering the conviction of a criminal.

Miranda and the Implied Consent Law

Many states have adopted laws—called implied consent laws—which require that a motorist arrested for driving under the influence of alcohol or drugs submit to a chemical test of his or her blood, breath, or urine. Under this legislation, the motorist has no right to refuse to submit to these tests, because physical evidence is not protected by the Fifth Amendment. But a motorist could refuse to answer *questions* by invoking the right to silence or requesting counsel. What happens when the defendant requests counsel after the officer has informed the motorist of his or her chemical rights as well as of the *Miranda* rights?

For example: The defendant is arrested for driving under the influence of alcohol and the officer informs her that she must submit to a chemical test of her blood, breath, or urine. The officer also advises the motorist that she has a right to silence and counsel. The defendant states that she will not submit to a field sobriety test, a chemical test, a blood test, or a urine test without her lawyer. At trial, she testifies that the officer told her she had a right to have an attorney and that she need not answer any questions without her lawyer. The defendant testifies that she was confused by the officer's admonition and as a consequence she refused to submit to any test without the presence of her lawyer.

This confusion is understandable. Even though the motorist has no constitutional right to refuse to submit to either a field sobriety test or a chemical test because of the laws governing physical evidence, the officer may have misled her by the use of the *Miranda* admonition. The *Miranda* admonition informs a person of the right to counsel, and the motorist might have assumed that she had a right to counsel during the administration of any test.

Because of the possible confusion, some states have modified the implied consent law to include in the officer's statement a provision informing defendants that they have no right to counsel during any tests. (For further discussion, see chapter 13, Driving Under the Influence Prosecutions.)

Readvisement of Rights

In *Michigan* v. *Mosley,* the U.S. Supreme Court noted that the second interrogation of the defendant was preceded by a second advisement of rights before questioning began. If the officer had not readvised Mosely, would his confession have been admissible? For example: Officers arrest a suspect for murder and properly advise him of his constitutional rights under *Miranda*. The arrestee states that he understands his rights, waives them, and agrees to talk to the officers. Officers transport the arrestee to the police station and interview him there approximately thirty minutes later without readvising him of his *Miranda* rights. The defendant implicates himself in the murder.

Generally speaking, one warning is sufficient to cover a subsequent interrogation if there is no substantial lapse in time and the defendant understands that the subsequent interview is directly related to the reason for the arrest. This rule obviously requires an independent factual review by the court to determine whether the defendant reasonably understands that he or she could have remained silent or obtained counsel before talking to the officer. The issue is waiver, a knowing and understanding one, and the burden is on the prosecution to establish waiver. To avoid these legal issues, officers can merely readvise the arrestee or inquire whether other officers have previously administered the *Miranda* admonition. Officers should receive an acknowledgment thereof from the suspect.

Another method used to avoid problems of readvisement is to have police agencies instruct their uniformed personnel not to advise an arrestee of his or her *Miranda* rights at all. Instead, the *Miranda* admonitions are given only once, and then by the investigating officers—not uniformed officers. No legal difficulty arises from this practice because the *Miranda* admonition must be given only if the officer intends to *question* the suspect. If no questioning is intended, no *Miranda* admonition is necessary.

In cases involving lineups, officers must advise a suspect of two different sets of rights; that is, if officers intend to display the defendant in a lineup, he or she must be advised of the right to counsel *during the lineup*. A *Miranda* admonition will not suffice for this purpose because *Miranda* only applies to interrogation (*People* v. *Banks*), and does not sufficiently inform an arrestee of the right to counsel during the lineup. Note also that if the officer intends to ask the arrestee in the lineup to submit a sample of his or her voice for *identification* only, and not in response to questioning, the arrestee has no right under the Fifth Amendment to refuse (see chapter 12, Pre-trial Identification and Lineups).

CASES AND MATERIALS

Brewer v. *Williams,* U.S. Sup. Ct., 3/23/77.

Butter v. *State* (Texas), 493 S.W. 2d 190.

Dillon v. *United States,* 391 F. 2d 433.

Harris v. *New York,* 401 U.S. 222, 28 L. Ed. 2d 1, 91 S. Ct. 643.

Hoffa v. *United States* (1966), 385 U.S. 293, 87 S. Ct. 408, L. Ed. 2d 374.

Michigan v. *Mosley,* 46 L. Ed. 2d 313.

Miranda v. *Arizona,* 384 U.S. 436, 86 S. Ct. 1602, 16 L. Ed. 2d 694.

Orozco v. *Texas,* 394 U.S. 324, 22 L. Ed. 2d 311, 89 S. Ct. 1095.

People v. *Anonymous,* 58 Misc. 2d 132, 94 N.Y.S. 2d 248.

People v. *Arnold,* 66 Cal. 2d 438, 58 Cal. R. 115, 426 P. 2d 515.

People v. *Banks,* 2 C. 3d 127, 84 Cal. R. 367, 465 P. 2d 263.

People v. *Burton,* 6 C. 3d 375, 99 Cal. R. 1, 491 P. 2d 793.

People v. *Dean,* 39 Cal. App. 3d 875, 114 Cal. R. 555.

People v. *DiBiasi,* 7 N.Y. 2d 544, 200 N.Y.S. 2d, 21 166 NE2nd 825.

People v. *Disbrow,* 16 C. 3d 101, 127 Cal. R. 360, 545 P. 2d 272.

People v. *Duck Wong,* 18 C. 3d 178.

People v. *Fioritto,* 68 C. 2d 714, 68 Cal. R. 617, 441 P. 2d 625.

People v. *Goodridge,* 70 C. 2d 824, 76 Cal. R. 421, 452 P. 2d 637.

People v. *Herdan,* 42 Cal. App. 3d 300, 116 Cal. R. 641.

People v. *Ing.* 65 C. 2d 603, 55 Cal R. 902, 422 P. 2d 590.

People v. *Manis,* 268 Cal. App. 2d 653, 74 Cal. R. 423.

People v. *Miller,* 71 C. 2d 459, 78 Cal. R. 449, 455 P. 2d 377.

People v. *Murphy,* 8 C. 3d 349, 105 Cal. R. 138, 503 P. 2d 594.

People v. *Parker,* 45 Cal. App. 3d 24, 119 Cal. R. 49.

People v. *Supreme Court* (Mahle), 3 Cal. App. 3d 476, 83 Cal. R. 771.

United States v. *Hayes,* 385 F. 2d 375.

1. Is this an invocation of the right to counsel?

"After the *Miranda* admonition, but before the actual discussion of the case, the following colloquy took place between appellant and Sergeant Voorhies: Q: Do you understand each of these rights that were explained to you? A: Yes, I do. Q: Having these rights in mind, which were just read and which you understand, do you wish to talk about the issue at hand right now? A: Uh, yes . . . attorneys and stuff like that, I can't afford one right at the moment. Q: Well, this says that an attorney can be appointed for you. You know if you can't afford one, one will be appointed to represent you. A: Well, I feel I need one. Q: OK, you'd rather not talk about the case. A: No, I don't mind talking about the case, but I just feel I want it noted that I want an attorney. Q: OK, you want it noted that you do want an attorney? A: Yes, but I don't mind talking to you. Q: OK. You understand, then, everything that we've talked about and that you do want an attorney but not necessarily at this particular second. Is that right? A: "Yes." See *People* v. *Turnage*, 45 Cal. App. 3d 201, 119 Cal. R. 237.

2. Is a parole officer a law enforcement officer within the meaning of *Miranda* v. *Arizona?* See: *State* v. *Johnson* (1972), 87 S.D. 43, 202 N.W. 2d 132-133; *Nettles* v. *State* (Fla. App. 1971), 248 So. 2d 259-160; *People* v. *West* (1969), 24 N.Y. 2d 732, 302 N.Y.S. 2d 260, 249 N.E. 2d 882.

3. Do the following facts invoke the right to counsel?

"Defendant testified that he had informed one of the arresting officers that he wanted to talk to his attorney during the initial interview conducted immediately after arriving at the substation and that they discontinued the questioning at that point and took him over to the booking room. His account of the events in the booking room corresponds to that of [the arresting officer] to the extent that it is more fully detailed than that of the officer, and is uncontradicted. According to his testimony, he asked the uniformed deputy on duty at the booking desk to look up the correct spelling of [a local attorney's name] and to place a call to his residence. During the ensuing conversation, defendant informed [the attorney] of his predicament. [The attorney] advised defendant of his constitutional rights, assured him that he would bring proceedings to secure his release, and stated that he would talk to him later and advise him further at that time. While this discussion was proceeding, [a deputy sheriff] was present at the booking desk and listening to them. Thereafter, the defendant confessed." See *People* v. *Randall,* 1 C. 3d 948, 83 Cal. R. 658, 464 P. 2d 114.

NOTES

1. For a different analysis of the facts, consider the dissenting opinion in *Orozco*.
2. If the defendant remains silent after the admonition, this silence cannot be used by the prosecution either as evidence of guilt or impeachment. *Doyle* v. *Ohio,* 49 L. Ed. 2d 91.

12 Pre-trial Identification and Lineups

Chapter Objectives

After reading this chapter, you will be able to:

1. Describe the constitutional restrictions on eyewitness identifications.

2. State the constitutionally correct procedures to be used in identifying suspects in the field, by photograph, and by lineup.

3. Explain how to conduct a proper pre-trial identification.

4. State the model lineup regulations and procedures.

Constitutional Requirements

In recent years, the U.S. Supreme Court has analyzed procedures used by police officers in identifying suspects and has imposed constitutional restrictions on the use of these methods. The most common pre-trial methods of identification are: photographs, in-the-field lineups and in-the-station lineups. Officers responsible for robbery and homicide investigations must be particularly well informed of the rules imposed by the Court. The penalty for noncompliance is a possible exclusion of the witness's identification in court.

Identification by Photograph

Impermissibly Suggestive Techniques

Law enforcement agencies commonly use photographs of potential suspects in an attempt to identify the person responsible for a particular crime. It is always possible, however, that the particular procedures employed in displaying the photographs may inadvertently suggest an identification to a witness. Because eyewitness identification is so critical in many criminal prosecutions, the courts require that pre-trial identifications be conducted fairly, without the use of any suggestive techniques. To do otherwise would deprive the defendant of his or her right to a fair trial.

For example, in a robbery prosecution, the U.S. Supreme Court reviewed these facts: "The evidence at trial showed that at about 1:45 P.M. on February 27, 1964, two men entered a Chicago savings and loan association. One of them pointed a gun at a teller and ordered her to put money into a sack which the gunman supplied. The men remained in the bank about five minutes. After they left, a bank employee rushed to the street and saw one of the men sitting on the passenger side of a departing white 1960 Thunderbird automobile with a large scrape on the right door. Within an hour police located in the vicinity a car matching this description. They discovered that it belonged to a Mrs. Rey, sister-in-law of defendant Simmons. She told the police that she had loaned the car for the afternoon to her brother, William Andrews.

"The following morning the FBI obtained from another of Andrews' sisters some snapshots of Andrews and of defendant Simmons, who was said by the sister to have been with Andrews the previous afternoon. These snapshots were shown to the five bank employees who had witnessed the robbery. Each witness identified pictures of Simmons as representing one of the robbers. A week or two later, three of these employees identified photographs of defendant Garrett as depicting the other robber. The other two witnesses stated that they did not have a clear view of the second robber.

"During the trial, all five bank employee witnesses identified Simmons as one of the robbers. Three of them identified Garrett as the second robber, the other two testifying that they did not get a good look at the second robber.

"The facts as to the identification claim are these. As has been noted previously, FBI agents on the day following the robbery obtained from Andrews' sister a number of snapshots of Andrews and Simmons. There seem to have been at least six of these pictures, consisting mostly of group photographs of Andrews, Simmons, and others. Later the same day, these were shown to the five bank employees who had witnessed the robbery at their place of work, the photographs being exhibited to each employee separately. Each of the five employees identified Simmons from the photographs. At later dates, some of these witnesses were again interviewed by the FBI and shown indeterminate numbers of pictures. Again, all identified Simmons. . . .

"It must be recognized that improper employment of photographs by police may sometimes cause witnesses to err in identifying criminals. A witness may have obtained only a brief glimpse of a criminal, or may have seen him under poor conditions. Even if the police subsequently follow the most correct photographic identification procedures and show him the pictures of a number of individuals without indicating whom they suspect, there is some danger that the witness may make an incorrect identification. This danger will be increased if the police display to the witness only the picture of a single individual who generally resembles the person he saw, or if they show him the pictures of several persons, among which the photograph of a single such individual recurs or is in some way emphasized. The chance of misidentification is also heightened if the police indicate to the witness that they have other evidence that only one of the persons pictured committed the crime. Regardless of how the initial misidentification comes about, the witness thereafter is apt to retain in his memory the image of the photograph rather than of the person actually seen, reducing the trustworthiness of subsequent lineup or courtroom identification.

"Despite the hazards of initial identification by photograph, this procedure has been used widely and effectively in criminal law enforcement, from the standpoint both of apprehending offenders and of sparing innocent suspects the ignominy of arrest by allowing eyewitnesses to exonerate them through scrutiny of photographs. The danger that use of the technique may result in convictions based on misidentification may be substantially lessened by a course of cross-examination at trial which exposes to the jury the method's potential for error. We are unwilling to prohibit its employment, either in the exercise of our supervisory power or, still less, as a matter of constitutional requirement. Instead, we hold that each case must be considered on its own facts, and that convictions based on eyewitness identification at trial following a pre-trial identification by photograph will be set aside on that ground only if the photographic identification procedure was so *impermissibly suggestive as to give rise to a very substantial likelihood of irreparable misidentification*." (*Simmons* v. *United States*.)

In *Simmons,* the Court held that procedures used to identify the suspect were not impermissibly suggestive. But compare the judgment in this robbery prosecution: "On the evening of July 10, 1968, two men entered a pharmacy shortly before closing time. The pharmacist (Gleason) and the clerk (Carol Pankovich) were the only other persons present. While one of the men made a small purchase from Miss Pankovich, the other moved rapidly toward the rear of the store where Gleason was working. The two men then cooperated in robbing the store of money and narcotics, and forced both employees to lie down on the floor before binding their wrists and ankles with adhesive tape. At this point two prospective customers entered the store; one of the robbers went to the front and said that the pharmacy was closed. The customers were later identified as Marsha Cariglia and Mary Vanderwerff. After the robbers left, Miss Pankovich managed to free herself and Gleason, who then called the police.

"Approximately two months later, on September 14, a police officer displayed to Miss Pankovich 10 photographs, one of which she picked out as looking 'like the man who I saw the most during the robbery.' Miss Pankovich had earlier described this individual to investigators as having long hair and glasses. The picture she identified is the only photograph of the 10 shown to her which portrays a man with long hair and glasses.

"Within a few days the officer returned and showed Miss Pankovich the same set of pictures. At that time Miss Pankovich picked out the same picture and was then asked to find another photograph of the same man. After studying the pictures for about 15 minutes, and looking through them several times, she tentatively identified another as showing the same man. She was then informed that her identification was correct and that the two photographs were indeed of the same man. The newly identified picture shows the defendant with short hair and without glasses. A lineup was then conducted in which the defendant was presented along with five other men. After five to seven minutes, Miss Pankovich identified the defendant. At trial she identified the defendant in court as one of the robbers, declaring 'it's not a positive identification.'

"On the day before trial, witnesses Cariglia and Vanderwerff were brought to the district attorney's office and shown a group of five photographs, and were asked if they could identify the man they had seen at the pharmacy. Three of the five photographs depicted the defendant. One of the pictures of defendant was attached to a fingerprint identification card which indicated that he had already been twice convicted of burglary. The witnesses picked out one of the photographs of the defendant. Both witnesses had seen the man at the drug store only briefly and both were uncertain in their courtroom identification of defendant.

The Court said: "Miss Pankovich's identification of defendant was uncertain. The procedure used to procure this identification was, in certain aspects, obviously suggestive. Miss Pankovich had described the man without the gun as having long hair and glasses. Of the photographs shown to Miss Pankovich, defendant's was the only one depicting a man with long hair and glasses. In addition, there was a second picture of defendant with short hair and no glasses which, together with the officer's assurance that it was the same man, may have aided Miss Pankovich in her subsequent identifications of defendant at the lineup and in court, in both of which defendant appeared with short hair and no glasses. . . .

"As to the witnesses Cariglia and Vanderwerff, defendant made a strong showing that the photographic identification procedure used was impermissibly suggestive. On the day before trial, when there had been no previous identification and several months had elapsed since the witnesses had briefly seen one of the robbers, the witnesses were shown five photographs, three of which depicted defendant. One of the three pictures of defendant was attached to a fingerprint card indicating that defendant had previously been convicted of two counts of burglary. The witnesses were thereby inevitably made aware that the police suspected defendant and that defendant was a criminal. Moreover, even if the witnesses did not draw these obvious conclusions, the statistical chance for error was greatly increased by the procedure adopted; a mere random choice from among the five pictures would have been subject to the likelihood that one of the three pictures of defendant would be selected. The prosecution, on the other hand, could defend the identification only by showing that the witnesses had briefly seen the man they identified as defendant and that their identification was uncertain. Nothing further was shown by the prosecution to justify the procedure employed to substantiate the identifications, or to show that they had a source independent of the photographs.'' (*People* v. *Citrino*.)

The availability and number of photographs of possible suspects will vary depending upon the crime. At the time of the display of photographs to witnesses, officers must adopt a technique which will not impermissibly suggest a particular suspect to the witnesses. At the time of trial, the witnesses will be cross-examined and asked what method officers used to display the photographs of them. Often a witness will not recall the facts of pre-trial identification in detail; in such cases, officers must use a simple and fair technique which will enable the witness to remember the pre-trial identification as clearly as possible.

The following techniques are suggested as a means of avoiding legal problems arising from the display of photographs to a witness or to a group of witnesses:

1. Select a minimum of six photographs, none of which duplicates the others.

2. Arrange the photographs under a cardboard so as to leave only the face visible and to block out any identification numbers or letters which suggest prior arrest (as in booking photos).

3. If police photos are unavailable, attempt to display available photographs of the suspect with similar kinds of photographs.

4. Attempt to obtain photographs of suspects who resemble each other as much as possible in terms of physical and racial characteristics.

5. Display the groups of photographs to one witness at a time and ask each witness not to discuss his or her identification of the suspect with any other witness.

6. Inform the witness that the suspect may not necessarily be included in the display because investigating officers are attempting to eliminate suspects as well as to identify them.

7. Ask the witness to initial the photograph he or she can identify on the back.

8. Keep a list of the names of all suspects whose photographs are shown to a witness and write the position of the photograph in the display on the back of the photo.

9. Keep the entire display card in the file for use at trial.

10. Avoid the temptation of confirming that the identification made by the witness is correct.

Right to Counsel

The U.S. Supreme Court has held, as have many state courts, that an accused has no right to counsel during the display of photographs to witnesses.[1] The Court reasoned that the pictures displayed to witnesses could be made available to the trial court at the time of trial and that any possible unfairness could be detected through cross-examination at that time. As long as officers scrupulously observe proper pre-trial identification techniques, evidence of a witness's identification should be admissible. Moreover, the proper use of pre-trial identification techniques strengthens the prosecution of the case.

Identification by Photographic Lineup

As we have seen, the U.S. Supreme Court has held that when officers display groups of several individual photographs to witnesses for possible identification, no impermissibly suggestive techniques may be used. If officers arrange a formal lineup at the station and then *photograph* the lineup, the same rule applies. Just as counsel is not required for the display of individual photographs, so the defendant has no right to counsel at a photographic lineup. (*United States* v. *Ash*.)

Identification by Lineup

For many years, law enforcement agencies conducted lineups at police facilities to aid in the pre-trial identification process. Because lineups enable witnesses to view suspects in person and observe their height, weight, race, facial characteristics, body movements, and voice, police officers generally considered them more satisfactory than a display of still photographs. Yet the possibility of unfairly suggesting the identity of the suspect to witnesses, even unintentionally, was always present. Participants in the lineup could be substantially dissimilar, the same suspect could be used repeatedly in a series of lineups, the number of participants in a lineup could be reduced or the officer could suggest to the witness the person who was suspected.

Because eyewitness identification is so critical, and because the errors in identification by eyewitnesses are so common, the U.S. Supreme Court reviewed this practice to determine whether the potential for unfairness created any constitutional questions. In *United States* v. *Wade,* the Court considered the following facts: "The federally insured bank in Eustace, Texas, was robbed on September 21, 1964. A man with a small strip of tape on each side of his face entered the bank, pointed a pistol at the female cashier and the vice president, the only persons in the bank at the time, and forced them to fill a pillowcase with the bank's money. The man then drove away with an accomplice who had been waiting in a stolen car outside the bank. On March 23, 1965, an indictment was returned against Wade and two others for conspiring to rob the bank, and against Wade and the accomplice for the robbery itself. Wade was arrested on April 2, and counsel was appointed to represent him on April 26. Fifteen days later an FBI agent, without notice to Wade's lawyer, arranged to have the two bank employees observe a lineup made up of Wade and five or six other prisoners and conducted in a courtroom of the local county courthouse. Each person in the line wore strips of tape such as allegedly worn by the robber and upon direction each said something like 'put the money in the bag,' the words allegedly uttered by the robber. Both bank employees identified Wade in the lineup as the bank robber.

"At trial, the two employees, when asked on direct examination if the robber was in the courtroom, pointed to Wade. The prior lineup identification was then elicited from both employees on cross-examination. . . .

"The confrontation compelled by the State between the accused and the victim or witnesses to a crime to elicit identification evidence is peculiarly riddled with innumerable dangers and variable factors which might seriously, even crucially, derogate from a fair trial. The vagaries of eyewitnesses' identification are well-known; the annals of criminal law are rife with instances of mistaken identifications. Mr. Justice Frankfurter said: 'What is the worth of identification testimony even when uncontradicted? The identification of strangers is proverbially untrustworthy. The hazards of such testimony are established by a formidable number of instances in the records of English and American trials. These instances are recent—not due to the brutalities of ancient criminal procedures.' A major factor contributing to the high incidence of miscarriage of justice from mistaken identification has been the degree of suggestion inherent in the manner in which the prosecution presents the suspect to witnesses for pretrial identification. A commentator has observed that 'The influence of improper suggestion upon identifying witnesses probably accounts for more miscarriages of justice than any other single factor—perhaps it is responsible for more such errors than all other factors combined.' Suggestion can be created intentionally or unintentionally in many subtle ways. And the dangers for the suspect are particularly grave when the witness's opportunity for observation was insubstantial, and thus his susceptibility to suggestion the greatest.

"Moreover, 'it is a matter of common experience that, once a witness has picked out the accused at the lineup, he is not likely to go back on his word later on, so that in practice the issue of identity may (in the absence of other relevant evidence) for all practical purposes be determined there and then, before the trial.'

"The pretrial confrontation for purposes of identification may take the form of a lineup, also known as an 'identification parade' or 'showup,' as in the present case, or presentation of the suspect alone to the witness. . . . It is obvious that risks of suggestion attend either form of confrontation and increase the dangers inherent in eyewitness identification. But as is the case with secret interrogations, there is serious difficulty in depicting what transpires at lineups and other forms of identification confrontations: 'Privacy results in secrecy and this in turn results in a gap in our knowledge as to what in fact goes on . . .'

"For the same reasons, the defense can seldom reconstruct the manner and mode of lineup identification for judge or jury at trial. Those participating in a lineup with the accused may often be police officers; in any event, the participants' names are rarely recorded or divulged at trial. The impediments to an objective observation are increased when the victim is the witness. Lineups are prevalent in rape and robbery prosecutions and present a particular hazard that a victim's understandable outrage may excite vengeful or spiteful motives. In any event, neither witnesses nor lineup participants are apt to be alert for conditions prejudicial to the suspect. And if they were, it would likely be of scant benefit to the suspect since neither witness nor lineup participants are likely to be schooled in the direction of suggestive influences. Improper influence may go undetected by a suspect, guilty or not, who experiences the emotional tension which we might expect in one being confronted with potential accusers. Even when he does observe abuse, if he has a criminal record he may be reluctant to take the stand and open up the admission of prior convictions. Moreover, any protestations by the suspect of the fairness of the lineup made at the trial are likely to be in vain; the jury's choice is between the accused's unsupported version and that of the police officers present. In short, the accused's inability effectively to reconstruct at trial any unfairness that occurred at the lineup may deprive him of his only opportunity meaningfully to attack the credibility of the witness's courtroom identification.

"What facts have been disclosed in specific cases about the conduct or pretrial confrontations for identification illustrate both the potential for substantial prejudice to the accused at that stage and the need for its revelation at trial. . . .

"State reports, in the course of describing prior identifications admitted as evidence of guilt, reveal numerous instances of suggestive procedures. For example: that all in the lineup but the suspect were known to the identifying witness; that the other participants in a lineup were grossly dissimilar in appearance to the suspect; that only the suspect was required to wear distinctive clothing which the culprit allegedly wore; that the witness is told by the police that they have caught the culprit, after which the defendant is brought before the witness alone or is viewed in jail; that the suspect is pointed out before or during a lineup; and that the participants in the lineup are asked to try on an article of clothing which fits only the suspect.

"In the present case, the testimony of the identifying witnesses elicited on cross-examination revealed that those witnesses were taken to the courthouse and seated in the courtroom to await assembly of the lineup. The courtroom faced on a hallway observable to the witnesses through an open door. The cashier testified that she saw Wade 'standing in the hall' within sight of an FBI agent. Five or six other prisoners later appeared in the hall. The vice president testified that he saw a person in the hall in the custody of the agent who 'resembled the person that we identified as the one that had entered the bank.'

"The few cases that have surfaced therefore reveal the existence of a process attended with hazards of serious unfairness to the criminal accused and strongly suggest the plight of the more numerous defendants who are unable to ferret out suggestive influences in the secrecy of the confrontation. We do not assume that these risks are the result of police procedures intentionally designed to prejudice an accused. Rather we assume they derive from the dangers inherent in eyewitness identification and the suggestibility inherent in the context of the pretrial identification.

"The accused's conviction may rest on a courtroom identification which is, in fact, the fruit of a suspect pretrial identification which the accused is helpless to subject to effective scrutiny at trial. The accused is deprived of that right of cross-examination which is an essential safeguard to his right to confront the witnesses against him. And even though cross-examination is a precious safeguard to a fair trial, it cannot be viewed as an absolute assurance of accuracy and reliability. Thus, in the present context, where so many variables and pitfalls exist, the first line of defense must be the prevention of unfairness and the lessening of the hazards of eyewitness identification at the lineup itself. The trial which might determine the accused's fate may well not be that in the courtroom but at the pretrial confrontation, with the State aligned against the accused, the witness the sole jury, and the accused unprotected against overreaching, intentional or unintentional, and with little or no effective appeal from the judgment there rendered by the witness—'that's the man.'

"Since it appears that there is grave potential for prejudice, intentional or not, in the pretrial lineup, which may not be capable of reconstruction at trial, and since presence of counsel itself can often avert prejudice and assure a meaningful confrontation at trial, there can be little doubt that for Wade the post-indictment lineup was a critical stage of the prosecution at which he was 'as much entitled to such aid [of counsel] . . . as at the trial itself.' Thus both Wade and his counsel should have been notified of the impending lineup, and counsel's presence should have been a requisite to conduct of the lineup, absent an 'intelligent waiver.'"

The most significant rule of the *Wade* case is the Supreme Court's decision that all lineups must be conducted in the presence of the suspect's counsel unless the suspect waives the right to counsel.[2] After reviewing earlier cases which held that counsel must be present at any critical stage of the proceedings, the Court held that a lineup was indeed a critical stage, and that the right to counsel therefore attaches.

The obligation to inform the suspect of the right to counsel rests on law enforcement. The admonition may be couched in the following language: "Later on today we will have a lineup in which you will take part. Witnesses will observe you and determine whether you are responsible for the crime of _______________ or if you are not involved. You have a right to have your attorney present at the lineup to observe the proceedings. If you do not have an attorney and are unable to afford one, we will obtain an attorney for you to be at the lineup at no cost to you. If you wish, you need not have an attorney present at the lineup. Do you understand what I have just told you? What do you want to do? Do you want to have an attorney present at the lineup?"

The Court in *Wade* rejected the contention that counsel would interefere with the conduct of a lineup. Attorneys at lineups are observers—not participants. Although they can recommend procedures to police, they cannot impose them as conditions to their presence. Generally, they record their observations and preserve them for future cross-examination of witnesses and officers.

In order to comply with the law requiring the presence of counsel at lineups, investigating officers must contact the defendant's attorney or the public defender to arrange for the presence of counsel. Despite the difficulties of this requirement, the penalty for noncompliance may be the loss of a witness's testimony at the trial; the U.S. Supreme Court held in *Wade* that if a lineup is held in the absence of counsel, any pre-trial identification may taint the in-trial identification and possibly exclude the witness's testimony entirely.

If counsel agrees to attend and is late, every effort should be made to determine the reason for this tardiness, and due consideration should be given to problems related to travel and the weather. Even if the witnesses are inconvenienced, the defendant's rights are paramount. (*People* v. *Collins.*) If counsel refuses to attend, or is unable to attend, or is unreasonably delayed, prosecuting authorities may contact substitute counsel to be present. Or, the prosecution could require the court to appoint counsel, if possible. If police do proceed without counsel, detailed records of their attempts to contact counsel should be maintained.

Upon arrival, counsel will frequently request an opportunity to interview the suspect. Normally, a brief interview should be allowed, as long as this does not cause an unreasonable delay in the lineup. No reason exists, however, to interview other participants in a lineup.

Prior to the lineup, counsel may wish to interview victims or witnesses. Because witnesses are often fearful of the proceedings, such interviews should be postponed until the conclusion of the lineup. At that time, police officers can inform witnesses that counsel may wish to speak to them if the witnesses agree. If, however, police interview the witnesses after a lineup, one court has held that defense counsel may be present as an observer. (*People* v. *Williams*.)

Although no law requires that counsel preview lineups before the witnesses see them, investigating officers may agree if this does not cause an unreasonable delay. If counsel notes objections, a possible correction may assure the fairness of the lineup.

With some exceptions, the presence of counsel should not interfere with the conduct of the lineup. Ample authority exists to allow officers to discharge their duties properly, without interference. In some jurisdictions, a deputy prosecutor also attends the lineup. All objections by counsel are referred to the prosecutor, who deals directly with counsel. By including the prosecutor, police can proceed with the course of their investigation without interference.

Aside from advising a suspect that a lineup will be conducted and that the suspect has a right to have counsel present as an observer during the lineup, the investigating officer must also advise a suspect that if he or she cannot afford counsel, an attorney will be appointed at no cost. Officers may also solicit a waiver of counsel. If the suspect refuses to participate in the lineup, a further admonition should be given: "There is no right to refuse to take part in a lineup. Refusal to take part in a lineup can and will be used as evidence against you. The legality of the lineup can be decided by a judge if the case goes to court and any objections can be made to him. If you persist in refusing to take part in the lineup, we will show photographs to the witnesses. Do you still refuse to take part in the lineup?"

The investigating officer must arrange for the presence of witnesses. When witnesses arrive, they should be advised as follows:

1. Several persons will be shown at a lineup.
2. To determine which, if any, of these persons may be involved in a particular crime, witnesses are asked to come down and observe.
3. The enforcement agency desires to eliminate suspects from consideration as well as implicate them.
4. Witnesses should not discuss identification with friends, family, or anyone else prior to the lineup, as such evidence might jeopardize the fairness of the trial.
5. Witnesses should make no statement or outward identification or sign of recognition when an identification is made.

When witnesses arrive, officers should space them as far apart as possible. After generally explaining the procedure of the lineup, officers should tell witnesses not to communicate with anyone except the investigating officer, and then to do so in private. If witnesses state that they wish a person in the lineup to repeat something, investigating officers should ask the entire lineup to do so. The witnesses should be instructed not to speak out loud, but rather to raise their hands to request a private talk with the investigating officer.

Witnesses should be furnished with cards on which they can write their own names. On these cards, they should be asked to mark down whether or not they can identify a suspect. If they can identify someone, they should write the number of the suspect identified. Witnesses can then deliver the cards to the investigating officers. These cards should be retained for possible further use as evidence.

A sample explanation of procedure to witnesses may be as follows: "Ladies and gentlemen: In a few moments several men will appear on the stage. (You will be able to see them, but they will not be able to see you.) Each man will be assigned a number and will be referred to only by number. Each will be asked to do certain things, such as turning, speaking, etc. When the entire line has completed this process, I will ask whether anyone desires one or more of the suspects to repeat something. If you do, please raise your hand and an officer will talk with you. In the event one of the suspects is asked to repeat, we will ask the entire line to repeat. Please do not talk with each other at any time. Communicate only with the officer, and then do so in private. When the lineup is completed, please fill out the card we have given you and hand it to the officer whether you have made an identification or not. If you cannot identify anyone, please so indicate. If you can identify a suspect, mark the card with his number in the line. You received an instruction sheet when you entered. Please read it carefully. At the end of the lineup, fill out the back-side and return it to one of the officers conducting this lineup."

Inform the witnesses that there may be attorneys present who represent the suspect, but that the presence of attorneys should not influence their judgment. Inform the witnesses that after the lineup is concluded they may or may not discuss the case with the attorneys, as they choose.

Lineup Procedures

In *Wade,* the court held that the Fifth Amendment prohibits the compelled use of "testimony" or oral "communications" only. Therefore, as we saw in chapter 8, a suspect may be asked to speak for purposes of identification, or to walk, turn, assume a stance or a gesture, or don clothing. A refusal to do any of these should be followed by a statement that such refusal will be used in evidence against the suspect.

If suspects specifically refuse to speak, they should be informed that the constitutional right to remain silent does not include a refusal to speak for purposes of identification and that this refusal can and will be used as evidence against them. But suspects should not be asked questions which might lead to self-incriminatory answers. They should not be asked where they were arrested, whether they had weapons on their person at the time of the arrest, or similar questions which call for incriminating statements or which would tend to prejudice the witnesses. But participants in a lineup may be directed to utter words purportedly used for the commission of the crime under investigation—for example, "Freeze!" or "Hold it! This is a stick-up!"

To preserve a record of the procedures used at the lineup for trial, the investigating officer should maintain a record of all those who appear in the lineup, including names, addresses, booking numbers, and positions in the lineup. The officer should also be prepared to present booking photographs of all those who appear in the lineup. Finally, the officer should photograph the entire lineup if facilities are available—preferably front and side views—and be prepared to print the negative for trial.

Although *Wade* established a defendant's right to counsel at a lineup, the defendant also has a right under the Due Process Clause of the Constitution to contest any identification confrontation which is unfairly conducted. In *Stovall* v. *Denno* the U.S. Supreme Court wrote: "Dr. Paul Behrendt was stabbed to death in the kitchen of his home in Garden City, Long Island, about midnight August 23, 1961. Dr. Behrendt's wife, also a physician, had followed her husband to the kitchen and jumped at the assailant. He knocked her to the floor and stabbed her 11 times. The police found a shirt on the kitchen floor and keys in a pocket which they traced to defendant. They arrested him on the afternoon of August 24. An arraignment was promptly held but was postponed until defendant could retain counsel.

"Mrs. Behrendt was hospitalized for major surgery to save her life. The police, without affording defendant time to retain counsel, arranged with her surgeon to permit them to bring defendant to her hospital room about noon of August 25, the day after the surgery. Defendant was handcuffed to one of five police officers who, with two members of the staff of the District Attorney, brought him to the hospital room. Defendant was the only Negro in the room. Mrs. Behrendt identified him from her hospital bed after being asked by an officer whether he 'was the man' and after defendant repeated at the direction of an officer a 'few words for voice identification.' None of the witnesses could recall the words that were used. Mrs. Behrendt and the officers testified at the trial to her identification of the defendant in the hospital room, and she also made an in-court identification of the defendant in the courtroom. . . .

"The practice of showing suspects singly to persons for the purpose of identification, and not as part of a lineup, has been widely condemned. However, a claimed violation of due process of law in the conduct of a confrontation depends on the totality of the circumstances surrounding it, and the record in the present case reveals that the showing of Stovall to Mrs.

Behrendt in an immediate hospital confrontation was imperative. Here was the only person in the world who could possibly exonerate Stovall. Her words, and only her words, 'He is not the man' could have resulted in freedom for Stovall. The hospital was not far distant from the courthouse and jail. No one knew how long Mrs. Behrendt might live. Faced with the responsibility of identifying the attacker, with the need for immediate action and with the knowledge that Mrs. Behrendt could not visit the jail, the police followed the only feasible procedure and took Stovall to the hospital room. Under these circumstances, the usual police station line-up, which Stovall now argues he should have had, was out of the question.''

The due process rule of *Stovall* applies not only to one-on-one confrontations but to lineups as well. For example: Following a robbery, the defendant was arrested and placed in a lineup with four other men. ''The defendant is of imposing stature, being 6′1″ tall and weighing 238 pounds. He is of Italian descent with a very dark complexion and has dark wavy hair. The two victims, the officers in charge of the investigation, Sergeant Allen, and defendant, all testified that the other lineup participants did not physically resemble defendant. They were not his size, not one had his dark complexion, and none had dark wavy hair. During the robbery both victims had noted the driver's large size and dark complexion. . . .'' (*People* v. *Caruso.*)

Under the *Stovall* rule, the court must consider the ''totality'' of circumstances surrounding the lineup. This ''totality'' test is similar to the factors used in assessing the voluntariness of a confession or waiver of *Miranda* rights. In reviewing the fairness of a lineup, the court will consider the number of participants in the lineup, their race, their height, their weight, the clothing worn, pre-lineup conversations with victims or witnesses, and the procedures used by police during the lineup. In the example above, the court concluded that the defendant was so dissimilar in height, weight, and race to other lineup participants that the lineup was unfair under the *Stovall* rule.

In-the-Field Identification

More common to patrol officers than the lineup is the in-the-field identification procedures which are used in an attempt to identify someone soon after a crime has been committed. For example: A witness testifies that he was robbed by a man he then describes. Another witness identifies the car used by the robber in his flight. Thereafter, the defendant is arrested in the car when he collides with another vehicle. The defendant is returned to the scene of the robbery, where the victim identifies him. Is counsel necessary in such a case? Is this confrontation impermissibly suggestive?

In a California case, the court wrote: ''We think there are cogent reasons the *Wade* right-to-counsel rule should not be extended to apply to the pretrial identification in the present case. Here the witness identified defendant as the man who had robbed him only minutes after the holdup occurred, five or six blocks from the liquor store, at a place where defendant became involved in an automobile accident as he fled from the scene of the crime. There are present in this timely, in-the-field identification public policy considerations wholly absent from the circumstances presented in *Wade,* where the staged lineup identification procedures took place days after indictment, days after arrest and days after counsel had been appointed to represent the defendant.

"Through good police work, good fortune, or a combination of the two, a criminal suspect may be apprehended so close in proximity to the time and place of the crime itself [that] the exigencies of the situation and over-riding public policy make it neither practical nor necessary to afford counsel for an in-the-field identification. It is not necessary to our decision to define the actual limits of time or distance which circumscribe the procedure. It is sufficient that we be satisfied, as we are, the in-the-field identification in the instant case falls well within those limits.

"Timely in-the-field identification is a procedure which enhances the reliability of the identification and 'aids in quickly exonerating the innocent and discovering the guilty.' The public benefit which flows from such procedures should not be underestimated. Where, as here, a serious crime has been committed, it is important to the public well-being that law enforcement officers know with speed and certainty the culprit has been apprehended. Once that fact has been ascertained, they may cease their efforts to catch the criminal—usually greatest and requiring most manpower immediately following the crime—and devote themselves to their other public duties. The general public in the area, although not directly involved, may have its apprehension put at rest by knowledge the perpetrator of the crime has been arrested and identified. Nor should we lose sight of the public interest in avoiding at this very early stage inconvenience and injustice to an innocent person if the use of the procedure results, as it frequently may, in the witness to the crime stating: 'This is not the man.' And, if an innocent man has been apprehended, should the police 'await the assembling of a lineup, and the summoning of counsel, while the real perpetrators put more time, and presumably distance, between [themselves] and the focal point of the offense'?

"While we have stressed the public benefit to be derived from early in-the-field identifications, we are not unmindful of the serious prejudice a defendant may suffer by reason of any improperly carried out pretrial identification procedure. But the impracticability of furnishing counsel for in-the-field identifications, close in time and place to the commission of the offense, is apparent on the surface. To require the presence of counsel under the circumstances would so hinder, delay and obstruct the procedure as to make it unworkable. To apply the *Wade* rule to identifications comparable to that made in the instant case would, as a practical matter, require the police to discontinue the procedure or run the substantial risk of invalidating later in-court identifications.

"We believe the public benefit derived from prompt in-the-field identification need not be sacrificed to the *Wade* rule of right to counsel. . . . Such identifications should be permitted in the absence of counsel without legal impairment to the witness' later in-court identification, and testimony concerning such identifications should be admissible, except upon a showing in a given case the procedure was conducted unfairly or in such an impermissively suggestive manner as to amount to a denial of due process of law." (*People* v. *Colgain.*)

Thus, in-the-field identifications may be conducted without counsel if there is an immediate identification under emergency circumstances, or if the field identification occurs so immediately after the crime that the victim's or witness's identification is based entirely on recollection of the suspect at the time of the crime.

Although counsel need not be provided in field identifications, officers must still consider the *Stovall* rule of "fairness." If an in-the-field identification is conducted so as to suggest identification unfairly, the defendant may object on due process grounds. To avoid potential unfairness in identifying a person shortly after a crime has been committed, in-the-field identifications may be conducted under the guidelines listed below.

Prior to confronting the suspect and the witness, advise the witness as follows:

1. A person is in our custody for the purpose of determining whether or not he is responsible for committing the crime.

2. Because we did not see the crime occur, we need to determine whether you can identify the suspect or not.

3. It is as important for you to tell us that you cannot identify the suspect as it is that you can identify him or her, because if you cannot identify the suspect we will continue our search.

4. (If applicable) Please ignore the handcuffs on the defendant. This is for security reasons only.

These admonitions should be noted in the report and referred to at the time of trial.

CASES AND MATERIALS

California v. *Green,* 399 U.S. 149, 90 S. Ct. 1930, 26 L. Ed. 2d 489.

People v. *Caruso,* 68 C. 2d 183, 65 Cal. R. 336, 436 P. 2d 336.

People v. *Citrino,* 11 Cal. App. 3d 778, 90 Cal. R. 80.

People v. *Colgain,* 276 Cal. App. 2d 118, 80 Cal. App. 2d 118, 80 Cal. R. 569.

People v. *Collins,* 20 Cal. App. 3d 601, 97 Cal. R. 821.

People v. *Gould,* 54 C. 2d 621, 7 Cal. R. 273, 354 P. 2d.

People v. *Williams,* 3 C. 3d 853, 92 Cal. R. 6, 478 P. 2d 942.

Simmons v. *United States,* 390 U.S. 377, 19 L. Ed. 2d 1247, 88 S. Ct. 967.

Stovall v. *Denno,* 388 U.S. 293, 18 L. Ed. 2d 1199, 87 S. Ct. 1967.

United States v. *Ash,* 413 U.S. 380, 37 L. Ed. 2d 619, 93 S. Ct. 2568.

United States v. *Wade,* 388 U.S. 218, 87 S. Ct. 1926, 18 L. Ed. 2d 1149.

1. For a proposed model statute on lineups, consider the following: "Any proposed statute should provide for the right to counsel during any lineup or during any confrontation. Provision should be made that any person, whether a victim or a witness, must give a description of the suspect before he views any arrested person. A written record of this description should be required, and the witness should be made to sign it. This written record would be available for inspection by defense counsel for copying before the trial and for use at the trial in testing the accuracy of the identification made during the lineup and during the trial.

"This ideal statute would require at least six persons in addition to the accused in a lineup, and these persons would have to be of approximately the same height, weight, coloration of hair and skin, and bodily types as the suspect. In addition, all of these men should, as nearly as possible, be dressed alike. If distinctive garb was used during the crime, the suspect should not be forced to wear similar clothing in the lineup unless all of the other persons are similarly garbed. A complete written report of the names, addresses, descriptive details of the other persons in the lineup, and of everything which transpired during the identification would be mandatory. This report would include everything stated by the identifying witness during this step, including any reasons given by him as to what features, etc., have sparked his recognition.

"This statute should permit voice identification tests by having each person in the lineup repeat identical innocuous phrases, and it would be impermissible to force the use of words allegedly used during a criminal act.

"The statute would enjoin the police from suggesting to any viewer that one or more persons in the lineup had been arrested as a suspect. If more than one witness is to make an identification, each witness should be required to do so separately and should be forbidden to speak to another witness until all of them have completed the process.

"The statute could require the use of movie cameras and tape recorders to record the lineup process in those states which are financially able to afford these devices. Finally, the statute should provide that any evidence obtained as the result of a violation of this statute would be inadmissible." Murray, "The Criminal Lineup at Home and Abroad," 1966 *Utah Law Review* 610, 627-628.

2. Sample Lineup Report

Date:

Time:

Location:

Suspect:

Enforcement Agency Conducting the Lineup:

Complaint, if any, to be filed by: ______________________
(Enforcement Agency or Agencies)

Complaint, if any, to be filed by: ______________________
DISTRICT ATTORNEY'S OFFICE

Number of Persons in Lineup:

PERSONS IN LINEUP	RACE	HEIGHT	WEIGHT	CLOTHING WORN	DISTINCTIVE CHARACTERISTICS
1.					
2.					
3.					
4.					
5.					
6.					

1. Was suspect asked to speak or repeat a phrase? If so, what was said by police and suspect?

2. Were those in the line asked to do anything? If so, what?

3. To your knowledge was suspect advised of his right to the presence of counsel during the lineup?

4. Names and addresses of other attorneys present at the lineup.

5. How did the witnesses communicate their identification of the suspect to police (i.e., privately or publicly)? Describe:

6. To your knowledge were witnesses shown photographs of suspects at any time?

7. Describe any other significant facts of benefit to the trial deputy; i.e., tape recordings, photos of lineup, etc.

3. Sample Instructions for a Lineup Witness

YOU ARE ABOUT TO SEE AND PARTICIPATE IN A LINEUP CONDUCTED BY THE [NAME OF LAW ENFORCEMENT AGENCY]. THE FOLLOWING INFORMATION MAY BE HELPFUL TO YOU IN UNDERSTANDING THE PROCEDURE TO BE USED:

1. The lineup will be conducted by____
____
2. The place of this lineup is____
____
3. Please use the seats closest to the stage, keeping one vacant seat between you and other persons.
4. Do not discuss the case with other witnesses.
5. There may be deputy district attorneys present who may wish to speak to you regarding your case. If so, they will identify themselves.
6. There may be defense attorneys for various prisoners present. They may wish to speak to you regarding your case. You may or may not discuss the case with them, as you choose.
7. Do not call out a suspect's number or do or say anything which might show you have identified someone in the line.
8. The individuals you will be shown will not be named; they will be assigned numbers. If the suspect or suspects in your case are in the line, remember their numbers.
9. If you identify anyone, please tell the investigating officer if he has changed his appearance in any way.
10. If you wish to have a certain person in the line do certain things (speak, wear a hat, walk rapidly, etc.) make this request to the investigator or the officer conducting the show-up and all members of the line will be asked to do the same thing. No member of the line will be singled out to speak or perform a certain act.
11. Do not be hesitant in making an identification because you think a person can see you; he cannot see through the screen. [Omit, if inapplicable.]
12. Remember it is the investigator's desire to remove persons from suspicion as well as implicate them when guilty.
13. Please fill out the identification card provided and return it to the investigator in your particular case.
14. Complete other side of this form and return it along with the identification card.

DATE: ____

DAY OF WEEK: ____

TIME OF LINEUP: ____

1. Did you hear the instructions? Yes ______ No _____
2. Where were you seated (which row)? Row No. _____
3. How many persons were in the lineup? _____
4. If you identified someone, what was his number? _____

____
Signature

NOTES

[This instruction sheet is to be returned by the lineup witness and included in the case file.]

4. For articles on the problems of lineups, see *United States* v. *Wade* (388 U.S. 218, 87 S. Ct. 1926, 18 L. Ed. 2d 149), footnotes 6, 7, and 8.

5. What defect, if any, do you see in this lineup?

"The lineup occurred on March 26, 1964, after Gilbert had been indicted and had obtained counsel. It was held in an auditorium used for that purpose by the Los Angeles Police. Some ten to thirteen prisoners were placed on a lighted stage. The witnesses were assembled in a darkened portion of the room, facing the stage and separated from it by a screen. They could see the prisoners but could not be seen by them. State and federal officers were also present and one of them acted as 'moderator' of the proceedings.

"Each man in the lineup was identified by number, but not by name. Each man was required to step forward into a marked circle, to turn, presenting both profiles as well as a face and back view, to walk, to put on or take off certain articles of clothing. When a man's number was called and he was directed to step into the circle, he was asked certain questions: where he was picked up, whether he owned a car, whether, when arrested, he was armed, where he lived. Each was also asked to repeat certain phrases, both in a loud and in a soft voice, phrases that witnesses to the crimes had heard the robbers use: 'Freeze, this is a stickup; this is a holdup; empty your cash drawer; this is a heist; don't anybody move.'

"Either while the men were on the stage, or after they were taken from it, it is not clear which, the assembled witnesses were asked if there were any that they would like to see again, and told that if they had doubts, now was the time to resolve them. Several gave the numbers of men they wanted to see. . . . While the other prisoners were no longer present, [the defendant] and 2 or 3 others were again put through a similar procedure. Some of the witnesses asked that a particular prisoner say a particular phrase, or walk a particular way. After the lineup, the witnesses talked to each other; it is not clear that they did so during the lineup. They did, however, in each other's presence, call out the numbers of men they could identify." *Gilbert* v. *United States,* 366 F. 2d 923.

NOTES

1. Not all states agree: See *United States* v. *Ash,* 413 U.S. 380, 37 L. Ed. 2d 619, 93 S. Ct. 2568.
2. The U.S. Supreme Court has held that the right to counsel does not apply to preindictment or preinformation lineups; *Kirby* v. *Illinois,* 406 U.S. 682, 32 L. Ed. 2d 411, 92 S. Ct. 1877. But not all state courts agree; see cases cited in *Kirby*.

13 Driving under the Influence Prosecutions

Chapter Objectives

After reading this chapter, you will be able to:

1. Describe the evidence needed to establish the elements of a driving under the influence case.

2. State constitutional objections to the admissibility of evidence.

3. Discuss the physical tests used to determine sobriety.

4. Describe the conditions surrounding a refusal to submit to tests and the consequences of such an action in a criminal case.

5. Explain the proof needed in administrative proceedings to suspend drivers' licenses.

Pre-trial Procedures

Before the trial of any criminal case, the defendant will attempt to discover the evidence which will be produced against him or her in court. Although the practice varies, the defendant usually serves notice on the prosecutor prior to trial that the defense will move that the court require disclosure of prosecution evidence. This motion may be written or oral. The court must then determine which evidence in the possession of the prosecutor must be disclosed. In driving under the influence cases, defense attorneys routinely obtain copies of arrest reports, evidence reports, pre-trial statements, results of chemical tests administered to the defendant, lists of prosecution witnesses expected to testify, and any reports by expert witnesses. The defendant may also demand the maintenance and calibration records of any instrument used to administer a breath test as well as the maintenance records of laboratory equipment used to measure the alcoholic content of blood or urine samples. Thus, defense lawyers will rarely be surprised by any prosecution evidence at the trial.

Discovery of these materials is granted largely as a matter of due process. The law recognizes that the defendant cannot adequately prepare a defense to a criminal case without knowledge of the prosecution case. (This has been called the "fundamental fairness" law.)

Prior Convictions

In most jurisdictions, an allegation of a defendant's prior conviction on a charge of driving under the influence increases the possible penalty for the second conviction. Defendants who entered a guilty plea in the earlier case will often attempt to attack the prior conviction on the grounds that it is constitutionally defective—that the defendants were not advised by the court of their right to counsel, their right to a jury trial, their right to remain silent, their right to confront and cross-examine the witnesses who testify against them, or their right to compel the production of witnesses in their own behalf.

Although the practice may differ in some states, prosecutors generally must establish the validity of a prior conviction by offering the docket—the summary of the proceedings—of the previous case. If the docket fails to establish a knowing and intelligent waiver of constitutional rights, such a conviction is invalid for sentencing purposes and cannot be used to increase punishment. But a prior conviction is not necessarily invalid for all purposes, because in some states the state agency which regulates licensing of motorists may still rely on the prior conviction in determining whether to suspend or revoke driving privileges.

Presentation of Evidence

The Statute

Driving under the influence statutes are frequently similar to one another in language. A representative statute, Oregon Revised Statutes §483.99s(s), provides that: "Any person who, while being under the influence of intoxicating liquor, dangerous drugs or narcotic drugs, drives any vehicle upon any highway, street or thoroughfare within this state, shall be punished, upon conviction, by imprisonment in the county or municipal jail for not more than one year, or by fine of not more than $1,000.00 or both."

"California Vehicle Code §23102(a) provides that: "It is unlawful for any person who is under the influence of intoxicating liquor, or under the combined influence of intoxicating liquor and any drug, to drive a vehicle upon any highway."

Elements of the Offense

Driving a Motor Vehicle Although evidence of "driving" is usually established by testimony of the arresting officer, the prosecution may also establish the defendant's driving circumstantially. For example: The defendant was found seated in an automobile located in the center of the street. He was seated in the driver's seat clutching the steering wheel and apparently unconscious. The engine of the vehicle was running and the headlights were on. No other persons were about. There was a strong odor of alcohol about the person of the defendant, but no witness saw the defendant driving the car. The court said: ". . . (T)here was ample evidence from which the jury could have inferred that the defendant had been driving his vehicle on the public highway at a time when he was intoxicated. From the combination of circumstances—defendant's sitting in a vehicle in the center of the street, behind the wheel, engine running, lights on—it can be inferred that defendant must have placed himself in such a position, and that he accomplished this by driving the car to the place at which he was found." (*People* v. *Hanggi.*)

When a traffic accident has occurred and the officer arrives at the scene, he or she may not have observed the defendant driving even though there is evidence that the defendant is under the influence of alcohol. To establish the fact that the defendant was "driving," the prosecution must subpoena any eyewitnesses to the accident. If the witness was unconscious after the accident or otherwise unable to identify the driver of the defendant's vehicle, the prosecutor may be able to establish the case circumstantially. If not, the defendant cannot be convicted in the absence of evidence that he or she was driving.

Driving under the Influence of Alcohol or Drugs A person is considered "under the influence of intoxicating liquor"—or under the influence of a drug—when, as a result of drinking such liquor—or using a drug—the person's physical or mental abilities are impaired so that he or she no longer has the ability to drive a vehicle with the caution characteristic of a sober person of ordinary prudence under the same or similar circumstances.

To establish that the defendant was under the influence of alcohol or drugs, the prosecutor must therefore prove that the driver of the motor vehicle was impaired in the manner described above. To establish impairment, the prosecutor usually relies on the manner of driving, the conduct of the driver, and on sobriety tests as evidence.

The manner in which a vehicle is being operated does not itself establish that the driver of the vehicle either is or is not under the influence of intoxicating liquor or drugs. However, the manner in which the vehicle is being operated is a factor to be considered in light of the surrounding circumstances in determining whether or not a person is intoxicated. Absent some evidence of an accident, the officer usually testifies to observations of those movements of the defendant's vehicle which alerted his or her attention to a possible traffic violation.

Officers who stop drivers on the suspicion of driving while intoxicated should be on the alert for symptoms of intoxication in the following areas: the defendant's conduct in exiting from the vehicle, the ability to locate and withdraw his or her driver's license, balance and coordination while conversing with the officer, clarity of speech, the condition of face and eyes, the condition of clothing, and alcoholic breath. Because the officer has not observed the defendant actually drinking, all of these symptoms may be circumstantial evidence that the defendant has been drinking. As a consequence, the court must give an instruction to the jury defining circumstantial evidence as follows:

"The word 'evidence,' as used in these instructions, means the testimony of witnesses offered to prove the existence or nonexistence of a fact.

"Evidence is either direct or circumstantial. Direct evidence means exactly what the term says—that is, it is evidence that directly proves a fact, without having to infer that fact from some other fact, and is evidence which in itself, if true, conclusively establishes that fact. Circumstantial evidence, on the other hand, means evidence that proves a fact from which you may logically and reasonably infer the existence of another fact.

"Both direct and circumstantial evidence are acceptable means of proof. Neither is entitled to any greater weight than the other.

"You may not find the defendant guilty based on circumstantial evidence unless the proved circumstances are not only consistent with an assumption that defendant is guilty, but cannot be reconciled with any other rational conclusion, and each fact of the circumstantial evidence necessary to establish defendant's guilt has been proven beyond a reasonable doubt.

"Also, if the evidence is susceptible of two reasonable interpretations, one of which points to defendant's guilt and the other to his innocence, you must adopt that interpretation which points to his innocence and reject the other which points to his guilt." (California Jury Instructions.)

Field Sobriety Tests

In an attempt to measure the impairment of the driver, the officer usually asks the defendant to perform a field sobriety test. The officer typically demonstrates certain tests which he or she asks the defendant to perform (finger to nose, walking an imaginary straight line, etc.). From an observation of the defendant's performance, the officer determines whether the defendant should be arrested for driving under the influence. Note that there are no constitutional objections to administering a field sobriety test because the defendant's *conduct* is not a verbal statement, and only verbal statements are protected by the Fifth Amendment.

In some cases, the defendant may refuse to perform any field tests. In the absence of any satisfactory explanation for the refusal, the officer will probably arrest and transport the defendant for a chemical test. At trial, evidence of such refusal is admissible against the defendant unless a state statute prohibits such evidence.

Breath or Chemical Tests

Most police agencies are equipped to offer the defendant a chemical or breath test to measure the alcohol in the system. If an agency utilizes a breathalyzer instrument or Gas Chromatrograph Intoximeter machine (G.C.I.) the officer will testify to the administration of the test. If the result of the test exceeds a prescribed statutory percentage of alcohol in the blood, the defendant is presumed to be under the influence of alcohol. Based on this evidence, the prosecutor will submit an instruction to the jury as follows: "If the evidence established beyond a reasonable doubt that the amount, by weight, of alcohol in the defendant's blood was 1/10th of 1% (0.10%) or more at the time of the test as shown by a chemical analysis of his blood, breath, or urine, you should find that the defendant was under the influence of intoxicating liquor at the time of the alleged offense, unless from all the evidence you have a reasonable doubt that he was in fact under the influence of intoxicating liquor at the time of the alleged offense." (California Jury Instructions.)[1]

At the trial, the prosecutor will call an expert witness to explain the operation of the instrument used, its ability to translate a breath sample into a percentage of alcohol in the bloodstream, and the reliability of the test. The expert may also testify that anyone whose blood alcohol (B/A) exceeds a certain percentage (.10%) is under the influence of alcohol. Cross-examination of the expert will be directed towards the proper maintenance of the machine prior to the administration of the test to the defendant, towards the ability of the arresting officer to alter the result, and towards the strength of the expert's opinion that a certain blood alcohol percentage impairs the defendant's ability to drive. Because expert opinion differs as to the percentage of blood alcohol which impairs a driver, most prosecutors are reluctant to prosecute cases if the reading is under .10%. Most experts testify that at a B/A reading of .10% or above, all persons are under the influence of alcohol.

If blood or urine tests are offered, the prosecutor must subpoena any medical personnel who administered the tests. Blood tests always require medical or paramedical assistance. The officer must testify to the chain of evidence—that is, trace the evidence from original acquisition to its production in court to assure that no tampering occurred—if he or she took the blood sample elsewhere for analysis.

A urine test is frequently administered by an officer. The nature of the test requires some degree of privacy for the arrestee, but the officer must be assured that the integrity of the test is not violated. For example: "An arrestee, who had been shown to a urinal in a restroom, endeavored to produce a specimen with his back to an open door while the arresting officer and a laboratory attendant remained about five or six feet behind him. The officer and attendant refused a request to leave the restroom and shut the door. After about 15 minutes, the arrestee threw the empty sample container to the floor and stated that he could not take the test because he was too modest. Blood and breath tests were then offered but were refused.'' (*Quesada* v. *Orr.*) The court pointed out that leaving the arrestee alone with the door closed would have presented the opportunity to dilute the specimen and that once he had refused to give a urine specimen for any purpose, the defendant was obligated to select another test or be deemed to have refused to take a test.

Refusal to Submit to Tests

In the event that a driver refuses to submit to a breath or chemical test, the evidence of this refusal is admissible because the inference may be drawn that the refusal was based on the driver's consciousness of guilt. In some states, the prosecutor may comment on the refusal and the judge may instruct the jury to consider such evidence as follows: ''If you find that the defendant was offered and refused a choice of a blood, urine or breathalyzer sobriety test after he had been made aware of the nature of such tests and their purpose, such refusal is not sufficient, standing alone and by itself, to establish the guilt of the defendant but it is a fact which, if proved, may be considered by you in the light of all other proved facts in deciding whether defendant is guilty or not guilty. The weight to which such a circumstance is entitled and whether or not such conduct shows a consciousness of guilt are matters for your determination.'' (California Jury Instructions.)

Whether or not a driver ''refused'' a test can be the subject of much controversy. As we have seen, in a criminal prosecution, the defendant has no right to refuse to provide a sample of blood, breath, or urine, because no privilege against self-incrimination is involved. (*Schmerber* v. *California.*) The officer need not even advise the person that a chemical or breath test will be offered, and may administer any such test whether the suspect desires to take it or not. (But see Compulsion to Provide Real or Physical Evidence in chapter 8.) For further discussion of ''refusal,'' see the section entitled Implied Consent Laws in this chapter.

Constitutional Limitations on the Admissibility of Evidence

The Fourth and Fifth amendments to the U.S. Constitution provide certain limitations on the admissibility of evidence in driving under the influence cases. For convenience's sake, these limitations are listed below.

Fifth Amendment: Field Sobriety Test

A motorist is not entitled to consult with an attorney prior to determining whether he or she should submit to a field sobriety test. A field sobriety test is designed to elicit physical evidence, not testimonial evidence.

Fifth Amendment: Breath or Chemical Test

A person has no Fifth Amendment right to refuse to submit to a breath or chemical test. Such evidence is physical, not testimonial, and the privilege against self-incrimination is not involved.

Fifth Amendment: The Driver

Under *Miranda* v. *Arizona,* a suspect in custody who is subjected to incriminating questions by police officers must be advised of the Fifth Amendment right to counsel and silence. In the context of driving under the influence prosecutions, the preliminary questions asked by an arresting officer in the field are usually not incriminating. Questioning undertaken to determine whether a crime has been committed need not be preceded by any constitutional admonition. Similarly, the administration of a field sobriety test need not be preceded by any *Miranda* warnings, nor need the suspect be advised before submitting to any chemical or breath test. Perhaps the only incriminating questions are: "How much have you had to drink? When was your last drink? What kind of drink did you consume?" Even assuming that such questions must be preceded by a *Miranda* admonition, the penalty for nonadmonition extends only to exclude the questions and answers during the prosecution's case in chief. Noncompliance with *Miranda* does not foreclose criminal prosecution, affect the balance of the officer's testimony, or prevent reception of evidence of the chemical or breath tests. Moreover, in some jurisdictions, if defendants elect to testify in their own behalf, they may be impeached by any prior statements they made to officers inconsistent with their present testimony—even if the *Miranda* admonition was not given.

Assuming that a defendant is in custody and the officer solicits incriminating statements, the prosecution must offer evidence that the defendant understood and waived the Fifth Amendment rights. (*Harris* v. *New York.*) The defendant may contend, in a hearing outside the presence of the jury, that he or she was affected by alcohol to the extent of being unable to waive the right to counsel and silence knowingly and understandingly. This issue is a question of fact to be resolved by the trial judge.

Confusion may arise when officers do advise defendants of their right to counsel and silence, and then request that the defendants submit to chemical or breath tests. The defendants may assert that they refused to submit to the tests because they thought that their right to counsel, as stated by the officers, included the right to counsel before submitting to a test or the right to counsel during administration of the test. The court must determine whether the instructions confused the defendants. If the defendants refused to submit because they interpreted the advice to allow them counsel, their failure to submit to a test is not a "refusal" within the meaning of the statute.[2]

Fifth Amendment: The Passenger

In some cases, the occupants of a car may flee, and officers may temporarily lose sight of the vehicle. If officers subsequently locate the vehicle and it contains more than one occupant, the driver at the time of the arrest may contend at trial that a passenger was driving the car at the time police first sighted the vehicle. If the defendant offers the passenger as a witness who intends to testify and admit to driving the vehicle, the court must determine whether the witness should be advised of the Fifth Amendment right not to answer incriminating questions. The court must hold a hearing out of the presence of the jury and determine whether an admission of driving will incriminate the witness. Fairness to the witness requires that the inquiry be held by the trial court without interference by counsel. Ideally, the trial court should appoint counsel to represent the witness and advise him or her whether or not to assert the privilege.

Fourth Amendment: Arrest

Although state statutes authorize an officer to arrest for a misdemeanor committed in the officer's presence, or on probable cause if a felony has been committed, any "seizure of the person" must be conducted within the requirements of the Fourth Amendment to the Constitution. (*Terry* v. *Ohio.*) In driving under the influence cases, the commission of the offense in the officer's presence authorizes an arrest within the meaning of the Fourth Amendment. An officer is also justified in detaining a motorist, without necessarily arresting this person, to determine whether a crime has been committed.[3]

Fourth Amendment: Search of the Person

If the officer arrests the defendant, a thorough search of the defendant's person and vehicle ("effects") is authorized as a lawful incident of the arrest. A second "booking" search of the defendant is also constitutionally reasonable.

If the officer directs the administration of a blood test, the intrusion of the needle into the arm constitutes a "search" within the meaning of the Fourth Amendment; similarly, the emission of a urine sample also constitutes a "search." In almost all cases, such evidence is obtained without a warrant, but may be admitted under the emergency exception to the warrant requirement.

Officers cannot always determine the identity of the driver, and they do not always know who, if anyone, is at fault in a traffic accident. If a blood sample is removed without an arrest, the sample should still be admissible under the emergency exception.

Fourth Amendment: Search of the Vehicle

Officers can search the interior of the car at the location of the arrest to determine whether any evidence reasonably related to the arrest may be seized. But if the car is impounded, a search of the trunk at a later time and place may not be a search incidental to the arrest. Whether an impoundment is lawful may depend on local statutes or court cases. (*South Dakota* v. *Opperman.*) An emergency, or probable cause to search the vehicle independent of the arrest, may also authorize a later search without a warrant. If the search is reasonable under the Fourth Amendment, any seizable evidence may be introduced in a subsequent criminal trial, even if unrelated to the original charge.

Implied Consent Laws

Most states have enacted legislation which requires that a motorist arrested for driving under the influence of alcohol submit to a chemical test of the blood, breath, or urine. Such statutes, commonly called "implied consent" laws, penalize a driver's refusal to submit to a test by administratively revoking or suspending the driver's license. This administrative sanction is unrelated to the criminal penalties for driving under the influence of alcohol, although some of the procedures are similar.

Although the statutory language varies, the following requirements are usually necessary:

1. *Lawful arrest:* The motorist must be lawfully arrested. If the arrest is unlawful, either statutorily or constitutionally, the first element of the implied consent law is absent and no administrative sanctions can be imposed.

2. *The admonition:* The arresting officer must inform a person driving under the influence of alcohol of the statutory requirements as follows:

—that the law requires the driver to submit to a chemical test to determine the alcoholic content of his or her blood;

—that the driver has a choice of a blood, breath, or urine test;

—that the driver must submit to and complete a test or his or her driver's license will be suspended;

—that if the driver is unable to complete a test, he or she must submit to another test;

—that the driver has no right to counsel at any time prior to or during the administration of the test.

The Refusal

If a driver refuses to submit to a chemical test, the officer merely completes the arrest procedure. Later, at an administrative hearing, the officer's testimony of the "refusal" will form the basis for license suspension or revocation. The "refusal" is also admissible against the defendant in a subsequent criminal prosecution. What evidence constitutes a "refusal" and what action, if any, should the officer take upon a "refusal"?

1. A qualified consent is, in fact, a refusal to take the test provided by statute. Thus, consent conditioned upon the test being administered by or in the presence of the motorist's own physician or in presence of counsel is a refusal.

2. The rule that the officer need only advise the motorist in the statutory language is subject to one important qualification. Where the accused manifests confusion or lack of understanding, the officer has a duty to clarify the situation for the arrestee. Further, as a practical matter, dialogue between the police officer and the arrestee will probably arise due to questions or statements by the arrestee. In either case, the officer should not say anything which in any way negates an absolute duty to submit to and complete one of the three tests *at the time the request is made* by the officer.

3. Case law concerning confusion generated by the *Miranda* warning has centered on the right to counsel. This confusion has been met by statute and most states specifically provide that the subject be advised that he or she does not have the right to counsel before or during the chemical test.

At some stage of the investigation, the officer may advise the suspect of the *Miranda* rights. The motorist may construe advice concerning the right to remain silent and the right to counsel as a right to refuse to submit to a blood alcohol test. If police-initiated confusion should arise, the motorist should be advised that the right to remain silent does not relieve a person of the duty to submit to and complete one of the three tests, prevent the refusal from being used against this person in a subsequent criminal prosecution, or entitle the person to counsel.

4. In setting forth the consequences of a refusal, vehicle codes often refer to "privilege to operate a motor vehicle" rather than "license." In many cases the terms could be considered synonymous, but great care should be exercised in so using them. If an accused holds an out-of-state license, the officer's reference to "privilege" rather than "license" is more accurate. Therefore references to the term "license" should either be avoided or used with great care.

5. Delay in submitting to the test has been held to be contrary to the policy of the statute. With this basic policy in mind, the arrestee should not

be told anything which might imply that a right to delay exists or that a change of mind is possible. Once an accused has refused a request to submit to a test, a later change of mind will not excuse the original refusal.

6. If the motorist gives consent to the test on the condition that he or she take all three tests, this is considered a refusal.

7. Where an accused agrees to take one of the three tests and merely declines to choose among the three tests, there is no refusal. In this case, the officer should suggest one of the tests. A refusal would only occur if the driver then declined the suggested test without stating a valid reason for the refusal.

8. There are two separate problem areas related to the arrestee's demand for a doctor. These problems occur: first, when the accused wishes the initial test to be performed or witnessed by his or her own physician; and second, when the accused requests that *an additional test* be given by his or her own physician.

As discussed earlier, an accused has no right to have the *initial* test witnessed or performed by a private physician; placing such conditions on the test constitutes a refusal. If such a request is made, the motorist should be advised that no such right exists. The language is set forth in the admonition in the Cases and Materials section at the end of this chapter.

Whereas officers have no duty to take the initiative and advise arrestees of their right to an *additional* test by their own physician at their own expense, denial of the opportunity to take such a test is a denial of due process. If drivers make statements which can be construed as a request for an additional test, they should be advised as set forth in the admonition below. To avoid confusion, they should be advised that they have no right to have their own doctor witness or perform the initial test. Then they may be advised that they do have a right to obtain an additional test at their own expense and that an opportunity will be provided for them to obtain one. But motorists should also be advised that this right does not excuse them from submitting to and completing one of the tests *now*.

Most implied consent statutes provide that a motorist must submit to *and* complete one of the three tests. If the motorist is unable to complete the test chosen, he or she must submit to and complete one of the other two tests. Inability to complete any test does not excuse a refusal or a failure to complete a different test. But it should be noted that if the motorist is unable to complete the first test taken, failure to advise the motorist of the availability of the other two tests may result in a finding that no refusal occurred.

Administration of Chemical Tests

In the administration of the breath test, the officer usually follows a checklist which instructs him or her to complete certain steps in numerical order to insure the integrity of the test. Such a checklist is discoverable by the defendant in advance of trial. At trial, the officer will identify the graph paper which prints out the results of the test and records the level of alcohol in the defendant's system (also discoverable). Because the officer is not an expert in the internal operation of the machine, he or she can only testify to following certain steps correctly and to the fact that the machine printed out a certain result.

To insure an accurate reading, many agencies regularly service the breathalyzer or G.C.I. (Gas Chromatograph Intoximeter machine) and correct any defects in operation. These records of maintenance are available to the defendant.

In the case of blood or urine samples, the instrument which measures the alcohol content of the sample also must be serviced and maintained. These records are also available at trial and through discovery.

Many implied consent laws require that an administrative agency publish regulations which must be complied with by police departments before they use chemical testing methods. For example, each instrument used in such testing must be approved by the Department of Public Health and must be regularly maintained, with service records available on a weekly basis. Officers who use the instrument must have been instructed in its correct operation. Officers must also allow twenty minutes to elapse prior to administering the test. Furthermore, in cases of blood samples, a preservative and an anticoagulant must be added to the container to assure purity of the sample and a preservative alone must be added to urine samples. Finally, the testing laboratory must be properly licensed.

The defendant may be entitled to a hearing on compliance with administrative regulations. In the event of noncompliance, the court may exclude the results of the test.

Blood tests and urine samples may be tested for alcoholic content without destroying the entire sample; not all the blood or urine in a sample is used at the time of testing and the balance of the material may be tested by another agency. Defense attorneys often subpoena the sample for retesting by an independent lab.

But in the case of instruments which capture a breath sample, the procedure is different. Although breath testing instruments vary, most use a small ampoule containing premixed chemicals. When the motorist exhales into the instrument, the breath sample causes the chemicals to react, and this reaction substantially destroys the contents of the ampoule. As a consequence, any attempt to retest the ampoule is impaired. Nevertheless, there is some opportunity for the defendant to retest the ampoule. Under a recent California case, the arresting agency must take steps to preserve the ampoule, and if they do not, the test results may not be admitted; of course, the prosecution may still proceed to trial without such results, relying on the officer's testimony alone. (*People* v. *Hitch.*)

CASES AND MATERIALS

Harris v. *New York,* 401 U.S. 222, 28 L. Ed. 2d 1, 91 S. Ct. 643.

People v. *Hanggi,* 265 Cal. App. 2d Supp. 969.

People v. *Hitch,* 12 C. 3d 641, 117 Cal. R 9, 527 P. 2d 361.

Quesdada v. *Orr,* 14 Cal. App. 3d 866, 92 Cal. R. 640.

Schmerber v. *California,* 384 U.S. 757, 16 L. Ed. 2d 908, 86 S. Ct. 1826.

South Dakota v. *Opperman,* 49 L. Ed. 2d 1000.

Terry v. *Ohio,* 392 U.S. 1, 20 L. Ed. 2d 889, 88 S. Ct. 1868.

1. The following is a sample implied consent admonition:

The Basic Admonition

You have been arrested for driving a motor vehicle while under the influence of intoxicating liquor.

You are required to submit to a chemical test to determine the alcoholic content of your blood.

You have a choice of either a blood, breath, or urine test to determine the alcoholic content of your blood.

If you fail to submit to and complete one of these tests, your privilege to operate a motor vehicle *will* be suspended for a period of six months.

You do not have the right to have an attorney present nor to consult one before stating whether you will submit to a test or deciding which test to take.

You do not have the right to have an attorney present during the administration of the test you choose.

If Urine Test Is Chosen

You have chosen the urine test.

The law requires that you satisfactorily complete the test chosen.

In the urine test you are required to empty your bladder twenty minutes before you provide a sample. You are then required to give a sample of your urine. If you do not provide a sample, you will not have completed the urine test.

If Subject Requests His Own Doctor to Be Present or Take the Test

You do not have the right to have your own doctor present to administer the test or during the administration of the test you choose.

If Subject Requests an Additional Test or a Test by His Own Physician

You do not have the right to have your own doctor present to administer the test or during the administration of the test you choose.

If you so request you will be given an opportunity to secure an additional test at your own expense, but this does not excuse you from submitting to and completing one of these three tests at this time.

On Inability to Complete the Chosen Test

You are (have stated that you are) incapable of completing the ____________ test.

An inability to complete this test does not excuse you from submitting to and completing one of the other two tests.

You therefore must submit to and complete either the ______________ or ______________ test.

If you do not do so your privilege to operate a motor vehicle *will* be suspended for six months.

Which test do you want?

In Case of a Refusal to Take or Complete Any Test

Your refusal to submit to and complete some of these three tests will result in the suspension of your privilege to operate a motor vehicle for six months.

2. The following Oregon Revised Statutes provide a sample implied consent law.

483.634 *Implied consent to chemical test; police report of refusal; evidence of refusal inadmissible*

"(1) Any person who operates a motor vehicle upon the highways of this state shall be deemed to have given consent, subject to ORS 483.634, to a chemical test of his breath for the purpose of determining the alcoholic content of his blood if arrested for driving a motor vehicle while under the influence of intoxicating liquor in violation of subsection (2) of ORS 483.992 or of a municipal ordinance. A test shall be administered upon the request of a police officer having reasonable grounds to believe the person arrested to have been driving while under the influence of intoxicating liquor in violation of subsection (2) of ORS 483.992 or of a municipal ordinance.

"(2) If a person under arrest for driving a motor vehicle while under the influence of intoxicating liquor in violation of subsection (2) of ORS 483.992 or of a municipal ordinance, refuses the request of a police officer to submit to a chemical test of his breath as provided in subsection (1) of this section, and if the person has been informed of the consequences of such refusal as provided by ORS 482.540 to 482.560 and of his rights as provided in ORS 483.638, no test shall be given, but the police officer shall prepare a sworn report of the refusal and cause it to be delivered to the division. The report shall disclose:

"(a) Whether the person at the time he was requested to submit to a test was under arrest for driving a motor vehicle while under the influence of intoxicating liquor in violation of subsection (2) of ORS 483.992 or of a municipal ordinance;

"(b) Whether the police officer had reasonable grounds to believe, at the time the request was made, that the person refusing to submit to the test had been driving under the influence of intoxicating liquor in violation of subsection (2) of ORS 483.992 or of a municipal ordinance;

"(c) Whether the person refused to submit to a test;

"(d) Whether such person was informed of the consequences, under ORS 482.540 to 482.560, of his refusal to submit to the test; and

"(e) Whether such person was informed of his rights as provided in ORS 483.638.

"(3) If a person under arrest refuses to submit to a chemical test of his breath under the provisions of subsection (2) of this section or refuses to consent to chemical tests as provided by ORS 483.636, evidence of his refusal shall not be admissible in any civil or criminal action, suit or proceeding arising out of acts alleged to have been committed while the person was driving a motor vehicle on the highways while under the influence of intoxicating liquor."

483.636 *Chemical test by consent of arrested person*
"Nothing in ORS 483.634 is intended to, in lieu of a request for and administration of a breath test, preclude the administration of a chemical test of the blood, urine or saliva of any person if, when requested by a police officer, the person expressly consents to such a test."

483.638 *Chemical test at request of arrested person*
"In addition to a chemical test of the breath, blood, urine or saliva administered upon the request of a police officer, a person arrested for driving a motor vehicle upon the highways of this state while under the influence of intoxicating liquor shall be permitted, upon request, at his own expense, reasonable opportunity to have any licensed physician and surgeon, licensed professional nurse or qualified technician, chemist or other qualified person of his own choosing administer a chemical test or tests for the purpose of determining the alcoholic content of his blood. The failure or inability to obtain such a test or tests by a person shall not preclude the admission of evidence relating to a test taken upon the request of a police officer."

483.640 *Administering blood test*
"In conducting a chemical test of the blood, only a duly licensed physician or a person acting under his direction or control may withdraw blood or pierce human tissues."

483.644 *Manner of conducting chemical analyses; duties of Health Division*
"(1) Chemical analyses of the person's breath, blood, urine or saliva, to be valid under ORS 483.642, shall be performed according to methods approved by the Health Division and by an individual possessing a valid permit to perform such analyses issued by the Health Division.

"(2) The Health Division shall:

"(a) Approve techniques or methods of performing chemical analyses that are satisfactory for determining alcoholic content of a person's blood.

"(b) Prepare manuals and conduct courses throughout the state for the training of police officers in chemical analyses of a person's breath, which courses shall include, but are not limited to, approved methods and techniques of chemical analyses, use of approved equipment and interpretation of test results together with a written examination on these subjects.

"(c) Test and certify the accuracy of equipment to be used by police officers for chemical analyses of a person's breath before regular use of such equipment and periodically thereafter at intervals of not more than 60 days, such tests and certification to be conducted by trained technicians.

"(d) Ascertain the qualifications and competence of individuals to conduct such analyses in accordance with one or more methods or techniques approved by the board.

"(e) Issue permits to individuals according to their qualifications. Permits shall be issued to police officers only upon satisfactory completion of the prescribed training course and written examination and the permit shall state the methods and equipment which the police officer is qualified to use. Permits shall be subject to termination or revocation at the discretion of the Health Division."

483.646 *Reports of chemical analyses; expenses of conducting chemical tests*

"(1) An individual who performs a chemical analysis of breath, blood, urine or saliva under ORS 483.634 or 483.636 shall prepare and sign a written report of the findings of the test which shall include the identification of the police officer upon whose request the test was administered.

"(2) Any individual having custody of the report mentioned in this section shall, upon request of the person tested, furnish that person or his attorney a certified copy of the report.

"(3) The expense of conducting a chemical test as provided by ORS 483.634 and 483.636 shall be paid by the governmental unit on whose equipment the test is conducted."

483.648 *Implied consent law not to limit introduction of evidence in certain proceedings*

"The provisions of the implied consent law, ORS 483.634 to 483.646, except subsection (3) of ORS 483.634 and ORS 483.642, shall not be construed by any court to limit the introduction of otherwise competent, relevant evidence in any civil action, suit or proceedings or to any criminal action other than a violation of subsection (2) of ORS 483.992 or a similar municipal ordinance in proceeding under ORS 482.540 to 482.560."

3. California Vehicle Code §13553, which applies to chemical blood, breath, or urine tests, is as follows:

"(a) Any person who drives a motor vehicle upon a highway shall be deemed to have given his consent to a chemical test of his blood, breath or urine for the purpose of determining the alcoholic content of his blood if lawfully arrested for any offense allegedly committed while the person was driving a motor vehicle under the influence of intoxicating liquor. The test shall be incidental to a lawful arrest and administered at the direction of a peace officer having reasonable cause to believe such person was driving a motor vehicle upon a highway while under the influence of intoxicating liquor. Such person shall be told that his failure to submit to or complete such a chemical test will result in the suspension of his privilege to operate a motor vehicle for a period of six months.

"The person arrested shall have the choice of whether the test shall be of his blood, breath or urine, and he shall be advised by the officer that he has such choice. If the person arrested either is incapable, or states that he is incapable, of completing any chosen test, he shall then have the choice of submitting to and completing any of the remaining tests or test, and he shall be advised by the officer that he has such choice.

"Such person shall also be advised by the officer that he does not have the right to have an attorney present before stating whether he will submit to a test, before deciding which test to take, or during administration of the test chosen.

"Any person who is dead, unconscious, or otherwise in a condition rendering him incapable of refusal shall be deemed not to have withdrawn his consent and such tests may be administered whether or not such person is told that his failure to submit to or complete the test will result in the suspension of his privilege to operate a motor vehicle.

"(b) If any such person refuses the officer's request to submit to, or fails to complete, a chemical test, the department, upon receipt of the officer's sworn statement that he had reasonable cause to believe such person had been driving a motor vehicle upon a highway while under the influence of intoxicating liquor and that the person had refused to submit to, or failed to complete, the test after being requested by the officer, shall suspend his privilege to operate a motor vehicle for a period of six months. No such suspension shall become effective until 10 days after the giving of written notice thereof, as provided for in subdivision (c).

"(c) The department shall immediately notify such person in writing of the action taken and upon his request in writing and within 15 days from the date of receipt of such request shall afford him an opportunity for a hearing in the same manner and under the same conditions as provided in Article 3 (commencing with Section 14100) of Chapter 3 of this division. For the purposes of this section the scope of the hearing shall cover the issues of whether the peace officer had reasonable cause to believe the person had been driving a motor vehicle upon a highway while under the influence of intoxicating liquor, whether the person was placed under arrest, whether he refused to submit to, or failed to complete, the test after being requested by a peace officer and whether except for the persons described in paragraph (a) above who are incapable of refusing, he had been told that his driving privilege would be suspended if he refused to submit to, or failed to complete, the test.

"An application for a hearing made by the affected person within 10 days of receiving notice of the department's action shall operate to stay the suspension by the department for a period of 15 days during which time the department must afford a hearing. If the department fails to afford a hearing within 15 days, the suspension shall not take place until such time as the person is granted a hearing and is notified of the department's action as hereinafter provided. However, if the affected person requests that the hearing be continued to a date beyond the 15 day period, the suspension shall become effective immediately upon receipt of the defendant's notice that said request for continuance has been granted.

"If the department determines upon a hearing of the matter to suspend the affected person's privilege to operate a motor vehicle, the suspension herein provided shall not become effective until five days after receipt by said person of the defendant's notification of such suspension.

"(d) Any person who is afflicted with hemophilia shall be exempt from the blood test required by this section.

"(e) Any person who is afflicted with a heart condition and is using an anticoagulant under the direction of the physician and surgeon shall be exempt from the blood test required by this section.

"(f) A person lawfully arrested for any offense committed while the person was driving a motor vehicle under the influence of intoxicating liquor may request the arresting officer to have a chemical test made of the arrested person's blood, breath or urine for the purpose of determining the alcoholic content of such person's blood, and, if so requested, the arresting officer shall have the test performed."

4. If prosecuting authorities suppress material evidence favorable to an accused, the defendant's right to a fair trial is impaired and no conviction for the crime would stand. (*Brady* v. *Maryland,* 373 U.S. 83, 10 L. Ed. 2d 215, 83 S. Ct. 1194.) If the evidence still exists, the appellate court can determine its materiality and can decide whether the suppression deprived the defendant of a fair trial. But what occurs if the evidence is no longer in existence?

As noted in this chapter, law enforcement agencies may be under a duty in some cases to preserve evidence for a subsequent re-examination by the defendant prior to trial. Failure to do so deprives the defendant of the right to a fair trial. What "fair trial" arguments would the defendant make in the following examples?

Example A

The defendant is charged with burglary: "During the early morning hours of February 7, 1974, an intruder broke into the Yettem Learning Center, a school for trainable mentally retarded children and, among other things, removed a typewriter, an adding machine, a camera, a record player and a toaster.

"Later, the police found a film-strip viewer, a 'Joe Namath' popcorn popper and a deep-fat fryer, all belonging to the school, on the floor just inside the front door of the center. Latent fingerprints were discovered on the bottom of the fryer and on the side of the fryer near the bottom; the latent fingerprints were lifted by Sergeant H and were placed upon a card." The defendant's arrest was based on the fingerprint identification.

"At the trial, Sergeant H testified that the latent fingerprints found on the bottom of the deep-fat fryer were made by defendant's right ring finger and his right index finger; he said that the latent fingerprints on the side near the bottom were made by defendant's right thumb. In addition, it was established that defendant had never been in the Center prior to the night of the crime.

"Sergeant H, who lifted the latent fingerprints from the deep-fat fryer, admitted that he made no attempt to preserve the latent fingerprints in place or to photograph the appliance while the latent fingerprints still were on it; the sergeant also admitted that it is possible to lift latent fingerprints more than once if they are found on a shiny, smooth-surfaced object, like the exterior of the deep-fat fryer, and that they can be preserved in place if they are covered with transparent cellophane tape. The police did not seize the fryer and place it in an evidence locker; the appliance was lost when a salvage company cleaned up the center." (*People* v. *Vero,* 62 Cal. App. 3d 293.)

Example B

The defendant is charged with possession of narcotics: "Officer P, working in an undercover capacity, was present at a residence for the purpose of buying some heroin from one Muns. Also present were the tenant of the house and [the defendant].

"Muns had removed 17 capsules from a cigarette package and placed them on a coffee table. Officer P noticed that all the small clear gelatin capsules contained a white powdery substance and that all were full with the exception of one which was half full or more than half full. Muns took the capsule which was half full and handed it to defendant stating, 'There's a half a cap for you, man.' In the jargon of narcotics users, a 'cap' means a capsule of heroin.

"Defendant took the capsule and immediately placed it in his mouth. He quickly removed it and raked his tongue across his teeth, indicating a bitter taste, and placed the capsule in his pocket.

"Muns then handed the package containing the 16 capsules to Officer P, who at that time made a partial payment for the narcotics.

"A short conversation then occurred between Muns and Officer P, in which Muns stated that the 'stuff' was of a good quality, indicating how many shots he had obtained from a single capsule. Defendant was present throughout the conversation.

"Muns and defendant left the house together. The capsule which defendant was handed was not found thereafter. The 16 capsules delivered to P all contained heroin." The defendant was arrested later. (*People* v. *Ihm,* 247 Cal App. 2d 388, 55 Cal R. 599.)

NOTES

1. Some states have a separate offense prohibiting anyone from driving while intoxicated. The statutes covering this offense presume that a motorist is intoxicated, as distinct from being under the influence, if the blood alcohol exceeds a certain percentage. For example: "Any person who drives any vehicle upon a highway of this state when that person has .15 percent or more by weight of alcohol in his blood as shown by chemical analysis of the person's breath, blood, urine or saliva made pursuant to ORS 483.634 to 483.646 shall be punished, upon conviction, by imprisonment in the county or municipal jail for not less than six days and not more than one year and, at the discretion of the court, by a fine of not more than $2,000. However, when the person has had no prior conviction under this section within five years of the date of violation, he shall be punished upon conviction by either such imprisonment or such fine or both, or, at the direction of the court, by such imprisonment or participation in an appropriate rehabilitation program or both." [Oregon Revised Statutes 483.999(1).]
2. Some states have added statutory language which attempts to clarify this problem. For example: "Such person shall be advised by the officer that he does not have the right to have an attorney present before stating whether he will submit to a test, before deciding which test to take, or during the administration of the test chosen." (California Vehicle Code Section 13353.)
3. "The right of the people to be secure in their persons, houses, papers and effects against unreasonable searches and seizures shall not be violated. . . ." (U.S. Constitution, Amendment IV.)

14 Homicide Investigations

Chapter Objectives

After reading this chapter, you will be able to:

1. Describe the law of homicide as it relates to problems of evidence.

2. Name various defenses to homicide and describe the evidence that is necessary to support these defenses.

3. Explain the special rules of evidence relating to the defenses of not guilty by reason of insanity and diminished capacity.

Homicide prosecutions have distinctive evidentiary problems because all states have divided the crime of homicide into varying degrees to reflect as exactly as possible the culpability of the person charged. Evidentiary problems also occur because prosecution for homicide depends extensively upon circumstantial evidence rather than upon direct evidence. As a consequence, the elements of the crime of homicide are important with respect to the evidence offered to support them.

A representative homicide statute would provide as follows: "Murder is the unlawful killing of a human being . . . with malice aforethought. Malice may be express or implied. It is express when there is manifested a deliberate intention unlawfully to take away the life of a fellow creature. It is implied when no considerable provocation appears or when the circumstances attending the killing show an abandoned and malignant heart."

In an attempt to differentiate between the varying states of mind of people responsible for the act of homicide, statutes related to this crime are divided into first-degree murder, second-degree murder, voluntary manslaughter, and involuntary manslaughter.

First-Degree Murder

First-degree murder is "all murder which is perpetrated by means of a bomb, poison, lying in wait, torture, or by any kind of willful, deliberate, and premeditated killing, or which is committed in the perpetration of, or attempt to perpetrate, arson, rape, robbery, burglary, mayhem, or felony child molesting.

First-degree murder is divided into three major categories: murder committed by certain means, murder committed with a certain state of mind, and murder committed during the commission of a felony.

Murder Committed by Certain Means

A murder committed by means of a bomb, poison, lying in wait, or torture is first-degree murder.

Use of Bombs A bomb is defined as: "any device, substance or preparation other than sticks, ammunition, or fireworks, which is designed to cause an explosion and is capable of causing death or serious bodily injury." Under this statute, officers must provide evidence that someone was killed by a "bomb" as that word is defined by statute. The testimony of an expert will therefore be required for this type of prosecution, and investigating officers must carefully record and collect evidence which will assist that expert in making the decision as to whether the device in question is indeed a bomb.

Use of Poison In murder by poison, the prosecution must prove that the defendant intended to give the victim poison, but the prosecution need not prove that the defendant specifically intended to take human life. For example, if the evidence shows only that a defendant gave the victim poison, but the prosecution cannot prove that the defendant *intended* to give the victim poison, the defendant would not be guilty of first-degree murder. On the other hand, if the prosecution proves that the defendant *knowingly* gave the victim poison, this would be sufficient evidence for first-degree murder, regardless of the defendant's state of mind. Invariably, the element of the defendant's knowledge will require circumstantial evidence in the absence of an admission or confession.

What precisely is a "poison"? A poison is any substance which, when applied to the body externally or in any way introduced into the system, is capable of destroying life without acting mechanically, but by its own inherent qualities.

To be a poison, the substance must not be only harmful or injurious when administered, but must also be capable of destroying life. Pulverized glass or boiling water would not qualify as "poison," although the use of these substances to kill another person could be murder in the first degree under one of the other theories of murder.

Determination of whether a particular substance is poison within the meaning of the statute will require expert testimony, usually by a toxicologist. If investigators suspect that poison was administered to a victim, expert witnesses should be contacted at the earliest possible moment.

Lying in Wait Murder committed by lying in wait takes place when the defendant positions him- or herself and waits for an opportune time to kill. Ambush is a good example of lying in wait. If a defendant waits in the lobby of a hotel where he knows his victim will arrive at any time and subsequently kills the victim, he has committed murder in the first degree on a theory of lying in wait. The prosecution need not prove that the defendant had a specific intent to kill the victim, but merely that he waited and that he intended to inflict bodily injury under circumstances likely to cause death. There is no need for a defendant to surprise a victim for this theory to apply.

Torture In order to establish murder by torture, the defendant must actually have intended to cause pain and suffering apart from the act of killing the victim. The torture must be the cause of death; showing that the victim felt pain or suffering is not sufficient. A severe beating, due to which the victim dies, may not be enough in itself to establish a murder by torture. A severe beating could result from rage or some other motive in which the premeditated intent to cause pain and suffering would be completely absent. Therefore, statements by the defendant, the means by which the defendant killed the victim, or the probable relationship between the defendant and the victim would be relevant to show murder by torture.

Murder Committed with a Certain State of Mind

In order to establish proof of murder, the prosecution must offer evidence of the act of murder, and, in this category—murder committed with a certain state of mind—of the defendant's state of mind at the time the act was committed. The act itself is usually not difficult to establish because the dead body and the wounds inflicted thereon establish the killing. The key question therefore becomes: "What was the killer's state of mind?

To possess the mental state required for a conviction of first-degree murder, the defendant must willfully intend to kill, must deliberate, and must premeditate. For the murder to be willful, it must be an intentional act by the person committing the crime. Deliberation means careful examination and consideration of the reasons for and against the choice or measure. Premeditation means to think about the act beforehand and to contrive and design it prior to its commission. In short, the terms "willfully," "deliberate," and "premeditate" mean that the defendant must reflect upon the killing and not act upon impulse. There need not be any appreciable space of time before the forming of the intent to kill and the murder.

Although murder in the first degree often is accompanied by careful planning and reflection, there is no need to prove motive. Proof of a willful, deliberate, and premeditated murder is sufficient grounds to obtain a conviction of first-degree murder.

Often the element of premeditation can be established by the type of weapon employed, the time and manner in which the weapon was acquired, the way the weapon was used, the nature and number of wounds, facts concerning whether or not the victim was armed, and the type of attack.

Murder Committed During the Perpetration of a Felony

Whenever someone is killed during the perpetration of certain enumerated felonies, or during the attempt to perpetrate them, the killing is first-degree murder. This is true even if the killing is accidental and unintended. The felonies in this category are arson, rape, robbery, burglary, mayhem, or felony child molesting. A defendant who robs a liquor store without intending to harm the proprietor, yet accidentally kills him during the robbery, would be guilty of first-degree murder under a robbery felony-murder theory.

In order to establish felony-murder, the prosecution must first prove that the defendant intended to commit the underlying felony. In a case of robbery-murder, for example, the prosecution must prove that the defendant intended to rob in order to sustain a conviction on a felony-murder theory. Proving the underlying felony in felony-murder is no different than proving that same felony in any felony trial.

Evidence of First-Degree Murder

Prosecutors who wish to prove murder in the first degree must obtain proper evidence from the law enforcement officers investigating the crime. The following guidelines for obtaining evidence are therefore quite important.

Scene of the Crime Law enforcement officers know better than anyone else that a thorough investigation of a crime scene is necessary and extremely important. Often investigators are most concerned initially with identifying the suspect, but they should also examine the crime scene with the theories of criminal liability for homicide in mind. A quick mental checklist would be:

> What were the means used? What mental state could possibly be involved? Is one of the specific first-degree felony-murder statutes involved? For example, is there any evidence that the killing was the result of a burglary, a robbery, or a rape?
>
> Is there any intimation of a murder by torture? Whereas a beating may be some evidence of murder by torture, death by means of cigarette burns or other such horrible methods would be probative on this issue.

Is the body mutilated? This might establish murder by torture or mayhem.

What weapon was used? The location of wounds and the nature of the weapon may be relevant on the issue of deliberation.

Although extensive still photographs or films of the crime scene are routine techniques for assisting investigators in reviewing the evidence, they are equally valuable to the prosecutor and jury at the time of trial. Pictures also can establish visually the elements of the crime that the prosecutor is attempting to prove.

Interviewing Witnesses Keeping the various elements of first-degree murder in mind, the law enforcement officer can talk to various witnesses of the crime, or to witnesses who were near the scene of the crime. For example, one witness may have seen a suspect waiting around the victim's home for the victim to return, suggesting a lying-in-wait theory. Another witness may have seen a suspect ''casing'' a home or office, evidencing lying in wait or burglary, or perhaps even robbery or rape.

Ask any witnesses who saw the crime being committed if the defendant appeared to act in a rational, preplanned manner. An example of this is a defendant who went into the office to shoot a certain victim after asking the receptionist if he could speak to the victim.

Technical Experts In any homicide, a thorough autopsy is indispensable to the investigator and the prosecutor. Investigators attend autopsies to learn about the size and nature of all wounds, the type of bullet found in the body, the wound track or body damage which cannot be observed externally. Lab tests, which reflect liver temperature, toxicity, presence of alcohol, and stomach contents are also useful. Any one or all of these factors may provide clues which help to determine the correct theory of homicide. For example, if a person appears to have been poisoned, proof of this fact as well as confirmation of the nature of the poison would be indispensable evidence in proving that the defendant intended to give the victim a substance which could cause death.

In bombing cases, the aid of bomb squads is important in determining whether the explosive device is a ''bomb'' within the definition of the Penal Code. Experts are also used to determine the cause of fires in arson investigations. And medical experts are necessary to prove murder in the perpetration or attempted perpetration of a rape.

Preparation for Possible Defenses A defendant who is charged with premeditated murder may attempt to show that the act of killing was accidental or impulsive. Both witnesses and the defendant should be questioned with these defenses in mind. In fact, an investigating officer should be prepared for all defenses which the defendant may try to raise in court. If the defendant has no alibi, he or she may plead that: the homicide was excusable, that the homicide was justifiable for reasons of self-defense, or that he or she did not have the requisite mental state to commit the crime because of either insanity or diminished capacity.

It is important that investigating officers be aware of the various defenses so that they can warn the prosecutor of the defenses open to a particular defendant. Also, it is important to note that since most homicide victims are known to the defendant, the victim's background and the relationship between the defendant and the victim are extremely important.

After a suspect has been properly advised of his or her rights and has properly waived them, the officer can ask questions which establish the rudimentary elements of first-degree murder. For example, did the defendant know the victim? Did he or she wait for the victim? Exactly how was the murder committed? Did the defendant want to take vengeance on the victim by causing suffering? What was the defendant's state of mind before, during, and after the crime?

Because the crime of homicide lacks the testimony of the victim, investigating officers must depend on witnesses other than the deceased to identify the person responsible and to establish the elements of first-degree murder. Officers must evaluate witnesses objectively—whether their vision and hearing was complete and unobstructed; whether they may assert any privilege to avoid testifying; their general level of intelligence; whether they can testify directly to evidence or only secondarily (hearsay); whether they are subject to impeachment; whether they are accomplices; and whether they give a correct pre-trial identification of the suspect.

Investigating officers should also consider a number of other factors as they collect their evidence. If physical evidence has been seized, they should ask themselves if any constitutional objections to its admissibility will be raised under search and seizure rules. They should consider whether any confessions that are obtained meet the standard of voluntariness, and they should ascertain that the *Miranda* admonitions are proper. Officers should also question whether other offenses committed by the defendant may be admitted to establish the identification of the killer or his or her state of mind at the time of the murder. Only if evidence is admissible at trial can the jury properly assess whether a first-degree murder conviction should result.

Second-Degree Murder

Second-degree murder is defined negatively rather than affirmatively. Section 187 of the California Penal Code defines murder as: "the unlawful killing of a human being . . . with malice aforethought. . . . Malice may be express or implied. It is express when there is manifested a deliberate intention unlawfully to take away the life of a fellow creature. It is implied when no considerable provocation appears, or when the circumstances attending the killing show an abandoned and malignant heart.'' Second-degree murder is the unlawful killing of a human being with malice aforethought which is *not* within the definition of first-degree murder. In other words, second degree murder is *not* committed by a destructive device or explosive, *not* by a poison, *not* by lying in wait, *not* by torture, *not* by willfulness, deliberation, or premeditation, and *not* in the perpetration or attempted perpetration of arson, rape, robbery, burglary, mayhem, or felony child molesting.

When a killing occurs, malice is presumed. In order to establish a lack of malice and thereby avoid a charge of murder, the defendant must bear the burden of proof. Conversely, in order to establish murder in the first degree, the prosecutor must bear the burden of establishing the proof necessary to escalate the degree of the crime. For example: A body is found dead inside a home and the defendant is apprehended. The prosecution is able to prove that the defendant killed the victim, but cannot prove any of the elements of first-degree murder. The defense, however, introduces no evidence to show an absence of malice. If the jury believes that the defendant killed the victim, they must find him guilty of second-degree murder.

A classic example of second-degree murder is the case in which the defendant kills a victim for no apparent reason, without provocation, and without any prior deliberation or premeditation. For example, a defendant is in his home with the victim when they get into a verbal argument. The defendant suddenly grabs for a gun and shoots the victim. There appears to be no evidence of deliberation or premeditation, although some might exist, but there is also insufficient evidence of provocation to reduce the crime to manslaughter. The homicide would, therefore, appear to be murder in the second degree.

Another important factor concerning second-degree murder is that no specific intent to kill is required. For example: A defendant shoots into a crowd of people, not intending to kill anybody, but does kill someone while shooting. The defendant can be found guilty of second-degree murder because second-degree murder is committed in the perpetration of an intentionally performed unlawful act, the natural consequences of which are dangerous to human life.

Like first-degree murder, second-degree murder also has a felony murder rule. But unlike the statutes governing first-degree murder, those governing second-degree felony-murder do not list specific felonies. Therefore, an unlawful killing committed during the perpetration or attempted perpetration of any inherently dangerous felony—other than first-degree felonies—is murder of the second degree. Which felonies are inherently dangerous to human life is always a close question. Examples of felonies inherently dangerous to human life include driving under the influence of intoxicating liquor or drugs, larceny from the person, and other such crimes. Furnishing a narcotic or any type of illegal drug to a person who voluntarily ingests that drug or narcotic, which causes death, is second-degree felony-murder. Therefore, sellers of narcotics or illegal drugs can be found guilty of the second-degree murder of a buyer if that buyer dies as a result of consuming those narcotics or drugs.

To recapitulate, certain rules can be followed in determining whether a homicide is second-degree murder:

1. The killing is not within the definition of first-degree murder;

2. If a killing occurs and no other evidence is offered, second-degree murder is presumed;

3. Specific intent is not required for second-degree murder; and

4. Second-degree murder may be committed in the course of an inherently dangerous felony which is neither a felony as listed in first-degree felony-murder nor an assault.

Manslaughter

Manslaughter is defined as the unlawful killing of a human being *without malice*. It is divided into two major categories, voluntary and involuntary manslaughter.

Voluntary Manslaughter

Voluntary manslaughter is a homicide committed without malice as the result of a sudden quarrel or in the "heat of passion." It is the absence of malice which distinguishes manslaughter from murder. In most cases of manslaughter, the killing occurs during a quarrel or because the defendant was provoked by the words or conduct of the decedent. At trial, the defendant often attempts to justify his or her provocation by introducing negative aspects of the victim's character as evidenced by past conduct, including the victim's potential for violence.

To reduce a homicide to manslaughter, the "heat of passion" must be such as would naturally be aroused in the mind of an ordinary, reasonable person or in the mind of a person of ordinary self-control under the given facts and circumstances. The classic example of "heat of passion" is that of the husband who, returning home suddenly, finds his wife in bed with a lover and kills the lover and/or the wife. A court would probably find these facts sufficient to arouse the "heat of passion" naturally in an ordinary person. This example should be distinguished from that of the defendant who comes home, finds his wife in bed with a lover, leaves, thinks about it, and returns later with a gun to shoot the lover and/or the wife. Under those facts the defendant would probably be guilty of murder, because under a voluntary manslaughter theory the "heat of passion" must not have cooled. Once it has cooled and time has allowed the defendant an opportunity to premeditate and deliberate, the crime becomes murder. Unlike second-degree murder, voluntary manslaughter requires a specific intent to kill, even though malice is not required.

Involuntary Manslaughter

Involuntary manslaughter is defined as the unlawful killing of a human being without malice in the commission of an unlawful act not amounting to a felony or in the commission of a lawful act which produces death in an unlawful manner, or without due caution and circumspection. Because the statute refers to the "commission of an unlawful act not amounting to a felony," this crime is called "misdemeanor manslaughter." Thus, if the defendant kills someone during the perpetration of a misdemeanor, he or she may be guilty of misdemeanor manslaughter. For this reason, it is important to collect evidence which establishes the specific underlying crime, whether misdemeanor or felony.

For example, a person who unlawfully exhibits a loaded gun in an angry manner—a misdemeanor—causing the gun to be discharged and killing someone, would be guilty of involuntary manslaughter. Involuntary manslaughter may also exist through acts of gross, reckless, and aggravated negligence, even though the act may be lawful. An example of this type of offense would be a person playing with a loaded weapon in the presence of other persons in such a negligent manner that someone is shot and killed.

When investigating homicides, officers must determine from witnesses, including the defendant, whether there is evidence which would help to indicate the degree of murder—that is, indications or evidence of: (a) a quarrel, (b) heat of passion, (c) death as the result of an unlawful act not a felony, (d) death as the result of gross negligence, or (e) a homicide committed in the course of an inherently dangerous felony.

Defenses to Homicide

A suspect charged with the crime of homicide can raise the following defenses: (a) Alibi, (b) Excusable homicide, (c) Justifiable homicide, or (d) Diminished capacity or insanity.

In an alibi defense the defendant attempts to establish that he or she did not commit the crime. In mental defenses, such as diminished capacity or insanity, the defendant does not deny committing the crime, but tries to prove that he or she did not possess a mental state permitting him or her to commit homicide. The rules of evidence governing excusable homicide, justifiable homicide, and diminished capacity will be discussed below.

Excusable Homicide

Section 195 of the California Penal Code defines excusable homicide as follows:

> 1. When committed by accident and misfortune, in lawfully correcting a child or servant, or in doing any other lawful act by lawful means, with usual and ordinary caution, and without any unlawful intent.
> 2. When committed by accident and misfortune, in the heat of passion, upon any sudden and sufficient provocation, or upon a sudden combat, when no undue advantage is taken, nor any dangerous weapon used, and when the killing is not done in a cruel or unusual manner.

Thus, in certain cases a killing will be excused, even though it is a homicide, because of the above factors.

A homicide is ''accidental'' only when it is committed by someone in doing a lawful act by lawful means and with usual and ordinary caution. There must also be an absence of unlawful intent.

For example: A mother wishes to discipline her young child, who has been mischievous, by giving that child a spanking. The spanking is the normal spanking a mother would give a child, and it is not given in a cruel or negligent manner. However, because of a physical defect unknown to the mother, the child dies. This tragic set of facts would be a classic example of excusable homicide. There is no negligence on the part of the mother; the mother was acting in a lawful manner and performing a lawful act, namely, disciplining her child within reason. Yet she was the cause of the death of the child.

Another example of excusable homicide is as follows: The driver of a car runs over and kills a pedestrian unlawfully darting out into the street. If the driver is acting with due caution and driving in a non-negligent manner, yet cannot stop in time to prevent the accident, the homicide is excused. However, if the driver is negligent, he may be guilty of involuntary manslaughter.

As stated earlier, if a killing is caused by accident or misfortune, in the heat of passion, upon any sudden and sufficient provocation, or upon a sudden combat with no undue advantage taken nor any dangerous weapon is used, and if the killing is not done in a cruel or unusual manner, it may be excusable homicide. This definition of excusable homicide is similar to one of the definitions of voluntary manslaughter, that is, the killing of a human which occurs ''upon a sudden quarrel or heat of passion.''

In voluntary manslaughter, however, there is a specific intent to kill, whereas in excusable homicide the killing is accidental. For example: Two parties enter into mutual combat, and during the fight one dies of a heart attack. Mutual combat was initiated by both parties, but the death was accidental and the courts would probably consider the act excusable homicide. Outside of this example, it is difficult to distinguish excusable homicide from manslaughter committed in the heat of passion. The major difference is the presence or absence of intent.

Justifiable Homicide

Justifiable homicide, more commonly known as self-defense, is defined as follows: "Homicide is also justifiable when committed by any person in any of the following cases:

> 1. When resisting any attempt to murder any person, or to commit a felony, or to do some great bodily injury upon any person; or
> 2. When committed in defense of habitation, property, or person, against one who manifestly intends and endeavors, in a violent, riotous or tumultuous manner, to enter the habitation of another for the purpose of offering violence to any person therein; or,
> 3. When committed in the lawful defense of such person, or of a wife or husband, parent, child, master, mistress, or servant of such person, when there is reasonable ground to apprehend a design to commit a felony or to do some great bodily injury, and imminent danger of such design being accomplished; but such person, or the person in whose behalf the defense was made, if he was the assailant or engaged in mutual combat, must really and in good faith have endeavored to decline any further struggle before the homicide was committed; or,
> 4. When necessarily committed in attempting, by lawful ways and means, to apprehend any person for any felony committed, or in lawfully suppressing any riot, or in lawfully keeping and preserving the peace. (California Penal Code § 195.)

Whether a person may justifiably plead self-defense depends on the circumstances. A person may claim self-defense only when he or she used the reasonable force necessary under the facts of the case. Fear of the suspect alone is not enough; rather, the fear must be justified and the defender's actions must be reasonable under the circumstances.

Defense of Person The most common example of self-defense is the attempt to prevent an attack by another on the person of the defender. For example: A is walking along the street. B comes up behind A with a knife in his hand and attempts to kill A. A draws a gun and shoots B, killing him. The court will most likely say that to a reasonable person it would appear that A's life was in great danger from B and that to protect herself she reasonably had to use deadly force.

But a plea of self-defense is not justified unless a person is responding to an imminent threat of danger. For example: A is in his automobile and is tailgating B. B looks behind at A and shakes his fist at him. A then draws his gun in his car and shoots B. In court, A testifies that he shot B because he was afraid of him, his fear stemming from the fact that B made a fist at him. A court most likely would not find self-defense because, to a reasonable person, no imminent or immediate danger existed, and there was therefore no need for deadly force. B merely shook his fist at A from a distance and from a different vehicle. Reasonableness of imminent danger and necessity for deadly force would appear to be missing.

Another example is as follows: A and B have an argument. B tells A, "Someday I'm going to kill you," and A subsequently shoots B. In court, A says she shot B because B said that someday he was going to kill her. Again the court would not find self-defense since the threat of death was not imminent and, to a reasonable person, there was no apparent need for A to use deadly force to save herself.

If a person is faced with the choice of fleeing an assailant or fighting, possibly to the death, does that person have a duty to retreat rather than fight? For example: A and B are inside a bar. B threatens to kill A and draws a gun. A has two choices: He has time enough to run out the door to save himself or he may stand his ground, draw his gun, and attempt to shoot B. A decides to shoot B, and kills him. A testifies to the above in court. If A is believed, he has presented a good case of self-defense. A person faced with imminent peril of death or great bodily harm may stand his or her ground and use deadly force if necessary, even if there is a possible avenue of retreat. There is no duty to retreat because of any threat. Once a case of necessity for self-defense is shown, the person attacked may not only stand his or her ground, but may also pursue the attacker until the person attacked reasonably believes that he or she is safe from danger.

If an assailant attempts to withdraw an attack, but is subsequently forced to kill his or her victim, who continues the struggle, can the assailant successfully plead self-defense? For example: A attacks B. A and B fight, and A gets the worst of it. A communicates to B that he wants to stop the fight, which B hears and ignores. A is in reasonable fear of imminent great bodily harm or death and is forced to kill B to protect himself. In this situation, the courts have held that if an attacker who begins a fight desires to stop the fight and communicates this fact to the person attacked, yet the victim of the attack still continues to fight, the assailant may use deadly force if reasonably convinced that he or she is in imminent danger of great bodily harm or death. An assailant who wishes to take advantage of this rule must establish that he or she communicated a desire to stop the fight to the person who was assailed.

Defense of Home In dealing with self-defense and homicide, the law recognizes the old cliché that a man's home is his castle. A person may defend his or her home with deadly force against an intruder if: (a) the intruder intends or tries by violence or surprise to commit a felony, or (b) the intruder intends or endeavors in a violent or riotous or tumultuous manner to enter the habitation of another for the purpose of offering violence to any person inside the habitation.

For example, H and W are married and are about to go to bed. H leaves the darkened bedroom for a few minutes to go to the bathroom. When he returns, he sees a figure with a knife over W's body. H pulls a gun out from the dresser drawer and kills the figure. Under the facts, the court would find justifiable homicide in H's attempt to protect his wife and property.

Suppose the figure with the knife was a neighbor trying to play a practical joke? The courts would still probably find justifiable homicide, since it appeared to a reasonable man that an intruder had entered his house and was attempting to harm his wife.

But how violent must an intruder be to warrant a plea of justified homicide? For example: A drunken bum enters A's house in broad daylight and sits on A's couch. A shoots the intruder. A cannot avail himself of the defense of self or habitation unless he can show that he reasonably thought that the drunken bum was going to commit a felony by violence or surprise or unless he reasonably believed that this intruder would attempt to offer violence to someone in the home.

What if the drunken bum sits on the sofa and A tries to eject him? During this attempt, the bum hits A, and A kills him. If A has reason to believe—and does believe—that his own life is in danger or that he is in danger of receiving great bodily harm, then A may avail himself of the defense of justifiable homicide.

Defense of Third Persons The law allows a person to protect a "wife or husband, parent, child, master, mistress or servant" and any person inside the defender's habitation. A person may also rely upon justifiable homicide to prevent the commission of a felony harming anyone, but the felony must be one involving the possibility of either serious injury or death.

Homicide may also be justified when necessarily committed by lawful means to apprehend any person for any felony committed, or when committed in the course of lawfully suppressing any riot or keeping or preserving the peace.

Investigation Techniques

The defenses of justifiable and excusable homicide are technical; therefore, it is important that law enforcement officers follow certain guidelines in order to test the weaknesses or strengths of this defense.

1. When working at the scene of the crime, check for the possibilities of an accident or self-defense as suggested by the location of the body and/or the wounds. Could the manner of death be consistent with self-defense? Is the physical evidence surrounding the scene of the death consistent with self-defense?

2. Interview witnesses for details as to the movements and statements of the parties. Movements of the parties are extremely important in self-defense, especially in cases of mutual combat. Find out who started the fight, if there was a separation, and any details that could confirm or deny the possibility of self-defense.

3. Interview the suspect with an awareness of the strict rules of self-defense. Often a suspect will attempt to fabricate a defense of excusable or justifiable homicide without knowing the law. In interrogating the suspect, officers should note every detail relevant to excusable or justifiable homicide.

4. The autopsy report reciting the number of wounds, the wound tracks, and their size and location are all relevant in determining the validity of the defense. Of course, any wounds on the suspect are equally relevant.

Diminished Capacity

At one time, the law enforcement officer in a homicide prosecution typically had two investigative responsibilities: to identify the suspect and to obtain evidence to establish the degree of the crime. In defending such a case, the defendant typically tried to show that: (a) he or she did not do it (alibi), (b) the homicide was of a lesser degree than charged, (c) the homicide was committed in self-defense, or (d) he or she was insane. In fact, the defendant often relied on two or more of these defenses at the same time. Recently the defendant has added a new plea to the armory: not guilty by reason of diminished capacity.

As a consequence, the law enforcement officer now has an added responsibility. In investigating a homicide, he or she must be prepared to rebut affirmative defenses other than alibi or self-defense. The investigator must also be prepared to meet an additional defense that reduces the degree of the crime of murder.

Traditionally, the defense attorney tries to show lack of premeditation or deliberation to reduce the crime from first-degree to second-degree murder, or the defense attorney may introduce evidence of provocation to reduce the murder to manslaughter. The defense of diminished capacity, if successful, will reduce first-degree murder to second-degree murder or voluntary manslaughter, or even to a finding of not guilty. The investigator must obtain evidence in order to be able to rebut this defense.

In many respects, the defense of diminished capacity resembles the defense of insanity. And in most states, the defense of insanity is based on the "McNaughton Rule." This standard labels the person legally insane if at the time of the offense he or she was laboring under defective reasoning from a disease of the mind so as not to know the nature and quality of the act, or, if the person did know its nature, that he or she did not know that the act was wrong. This test has also been called the "right, wrong test." A defendant who commits a crime while suffering from some form of mental illness can still be guilty unless he or she falls under the narrow definition of the "right, wrong test." The sanity test is applied on a strict guilt-innocence basis. If the defendant is found to have been insane at the time of the commission of the crime, he or she cannot be found guilty. If, on the other hand, the defendant was found sane at the time of the commission of the crime, he or she may be found guilty.

Unlike insanity, diminished capacity is not applied on a strict guilt-innocence basis. The defendant introduces evidence of diminished mental capacity in order to reduce the degree of murder by rebutting certain elements of the crime charged. For example, if the defendant can establish an *inability* to premeditate, he or she could remove a critical element in the crime of first-degree murder and reduce the crime to second-degree murder or involuntary manslaughter. This differs from the traditional attempts of a defendant to establish that he or she in fact did not premeditate in the sense that in a diminished capacity defense, the defendant contends that he or she was *disabled* in such a way as to prohibit premeditation. Unlike insanity, diminished capacity need not be specially pleaded, so the prosecutor must attempt to anticipate that this defense will be used. Because of inadequate discovery procedures on the part of the prosecution, the responsibility for anticipating this defense rests heavily on the law enforcement officer.

Diminished capacity originates from the two major propositions of criminal law: first, that to be guilty of a crime, the defendant must commit a criminal act; and second, that when the act was committed the defendant harbored a criminal intent. The defendant is not guilty of first-degree murder merely because of the act of pulling the trigger; he or she must also intend to kill. The criminal law considers both the physical and mental causes of the criminal act, and unless there is a joining of the act and the mental intent, no crime is committed. A multitude of witnesses can see an individual kill the victim, yet the individual may be found guilty of a lesser offense or possibly freed because of an inability to establish the requisite mental state.

Murder is the unlawful killing of a human being with malice aforethought—that is, with a wanton disregard for human life. The definition of malice as used in diminished capacity, however, is much broader than that used in the definition of first-degree murder. As used in the context of diminished capacity, malice aforethought means that a person is capable of achieving such a mental state that he or she is normally capable of comprehending the duties society places on all persons to act within the law. If, despite such awareness, this person commits an act likely to cause serious injury or death to another, he or she exhibits that wanton disregard for human life or antisocial motivation that constitutes malice aforethought. Malice aforethought, either express or implied, is therefore manifested by the commission of an act by a person who is able to comprehend prohibition of this act by society and has an obligation to conform his or her conduct to society's rules. If, because of mental illness, mental defect, or intoxication, the defendant does not have the capacity to harbor malice as defined above, he or she cannot be found guilty of murder (which requires malice). The defendant can only be convicted of involuntary manslaughter, which does not require malice.

In cases of first-degree *felony-murder*, if the defendant could not attain the specific intent needed to commit the underlying felony because of a mental defect or intoxication, he or she cannot be found guilty of homicide. In some crimes, the prosecutor must establish that the person who committed an act did so with a particular state of mind. For example, in a burglary prosecution, the prosecutor must establish that an entry into a structure was made by a person who intended to commit theft. If police respond to a burglar alarm and discover a broken window and a man in the act of stealing, the unlawful entry is established. But if officers enter and find a drunken intruder sleeping on the floor, the defendant can contend that he fell through the window accidentally or only entered to sleep. If believed, his state of mind would not be to commit the felony of theft. Under the felony-murder rule, the homicide committed is incidental to the felony, implying the malice necessary to establish first-degree murder. Without the specific intent to commit the underlying felony—for example, robbery, burglary, or arson—the felony-murder rule dissolves.

Voluntary intoxication is a defense to felony-murder only if the underlying felony requires a specific intent—such as robbery, which requires a specific intent to steal. Thus the defense of intoxication in diminished capacity for felony-murder is the same as the general defense of intoxication in a felony.

Voluntary intoxication, whether by alcohol or drugs, is not a defense to any crime unless that crime requires a specific intent. If a defendant was unconscious at the time he or she committed the offense because of a mental illness or defect, this person cannot be found guilty of any crime. If, on the other hand, a defendant was unconscious at the time he or she committed the crime because of *voluntary intoxication,* the defendant is guilty of involuntary manslaughter.

Diminished capacity is a defense principally involving the courtroom and the psychiatrist. The law enforcement officer, however, has a function in investigation the truth of the defense of diminished capacity. The following guidelines can be used by the officer to help determine the validity of the defense of diminished capacity:

1. *Look carefully at the appearance and conduct of a suspect.* Does he or she speak clearly, coherently, and rationally? Does the suspect answer questions in a straightforward, normal manner? These are clues which can create or destroy a defense of diminished capacity. If a defendant appears to act rationally, this evidence is an important means of negating the defense. If, on the other hand, the suspect appears unable to control him- or herself or is unable to speak clearly, this may also be important.

This is true whether the defendant has just been arrested, is being transported after arrest, or is being interrogated. The defendant must be viewed at all times to see if there are any indications of the existence or nonexistence of diminished capacity.

2. *Look carefully to see whether the suspect is possibly under the influence of any liquor or drugs.* If an arrest is made shortly after the crime, the law enforcement officer should always look specifically to see whether or not the defendant is under the influence of any liquor or drugs. For example, the defendant may say at trial that he or she was under the influence of heroin when committing the homicide. An expert police officer who checks carefully may be able to establish that it was unlikely that the defendant was under the influence at the time.

A blood or urine test should be given to a homicide suspect arrested shortly after the commission of the crime to rebut the defense of intoxication or drug use. These tests should be given incidental to the arrest. Any hospital records should be supplied to the prosecutor, as this will often establish the existence or nonexistence of diminished capacity at the outset.

3. *Talk to witnesses and gather information about the demeanor and appearance of a suspect.* The law enforcement officer should always talk to any witnesses at the scene of the crime. No longer can law enforcement officers limit their questioning to, "Did this person do it?" They must also ask the witnesses about the demeanor and appearance of the defendant at the time of the homicide or at the time surrounding the killing. In other words, when the crime was committed, did the suspect scream or act irrationally, or did this person act in a completely unemotional, cold-blooded manner? Details from witnesses as to the defendant's appearance and actions aside from the killing are relevant.

4. *Look carefully at the scene of the crime.* When checking evidence of a homicide, a law enforcement officer should also look carefully to see whether the manner in which the crime was committed suggests that the

person who committed the crime could possibly have been suffering from diminished capacity, as courts look very carefully into this manner in determining whether or not diminished capacity existed. In determining the existence or nonexistence of diminished capacity, look for signs such as mutilation, decapitation, castration, etc., which might be indicative of that defense.

5. *Look for signs of possible diminished capacity when warning a suspect of his or her rights or gaining consent to search.* When warning a suspect of *Miranda* rights or gaining consent to search, the officer should note the person's appearance and demeanor. Defense counsel may raise the question of whether or not the defendant could intelligently waive rights or give consent to search because of mental illness, a defect, or intoxication. If, because of the above factors, the defendant could not waive rights or give consent, the defendant's statements or the objects found in a search cannot be admitted into evidence. More importantly, the defendant's ability to understand and/or waive constitutional rights will also have a bearing on whether he or she can establish a defense of diminished capacity.

6. *Check carefully to see whether or not the defendant may be ''faking'' in order to prepare in advance a defense of diminished capacity.* Although the defendant may not be suffering from diminished capacity, he or she may try to feign illness in order to raise the defense if apprehended. If the defendant is acting strangely, the officer should try to determine whether this is a true sign of diminished capacity or whether the defendant is just pretending. The officer should note the observations in his or her report.

Although all the general rules of evidence apply to homicide prosecutions, the elements of the crime are technical and require special consideration. Because of the degrees of homicide, the absence of critical evidence may substantially affect the ultimate result of a case. Failure to establish malice or premeditation because evidence is ruled inadmissible is the difference between first-degree murder and involuntary manslaughter—or perhaps an acquittal.

Glossary

Accomplice: A witness liable to prosecution for the same crime charged against the defendant.

Admission: Statement by an accused conceding partial responsibility for a criminal act.

Admonition: Statement to an accused advising the person of his or her constitutional rights.

Affidavit: Sworn statement, usually accompanying an application for an arrest warrant or a search warrant.

Arraignment: A judicial procedure informing the accused of his or her constitutional rights and of the charges brought against the accused.

Autopsy: Medical examination of a deceased body.

Case in Chief: By prosecutor—basic elements of the crime charged against the defendant; by defendant—evidence by the defendant to negate the prosecution's case.

Circumstantial Evidence: Evidence from which a logical and reasonable inference of another fact may be drawn.

Competency: Ability of the witness to understand the nature of the oath and the duty to tell the truth.

Confession: Statement by an accused admitting all the elements of the crime.

Corroboration: Evidence from another source in support of a witness's testimony.

Credibility: The degree of truthfulness established by a witness.

Cross-Examination: Questions asked of witnesses who have testified for the opposing side.

Custody: Combination of facts in which the accused's freedom of voluntary action is significantly impaired.

Direct Evidence: Evidence offered which, if true, conclusively establishes a fact without inference.

Direct Examination: Questions posed to a witness testifying for the side which offers his or her testimony.

Discovery: Pre-trial procedure to compel disclosure of prosecution evidence.

Dominion and Control: Access to and power to dispose of items, usually contraband.

Due Process: Governmental procedures which assure the accused of a fair trial.

Emetic: Substance introduced through the mouth to compel involuntary regurgitation.

Expert Witness: A person whose training, background, or experience qualifies him or her to render an opinion at trial rather than stating facts.

Foundation: Questions posed to a witness to authenticate an exhibit.

Gas Chromatograph Intoximeter: Electronic instrument which measures alcoholic content in the human body.

Hearsay: Statement made by a person who is not testifying to a witness testifying in court.

Immunity: Judicially approved order initiated by the prosecution foreclosing use of a witness's testimony against this person in future criminal proceedings.

Impeachment: Contradiction of a witness's testimony.

Implied Consent Law: Legislation which presumes that all motorists agree in advance of driving a motor vehicle that they will submit to a chemical test to reflect the alcoholic content in their body if they are arrested for driving under the influence of alcohol.

In Camera: In chambers; a hearing held outside the courtroom by the judge.

Informant: A person who supplies information to law enforcement agencies, often in exchange for some promise or benefit.

Interrogate: To question.

Joinder of Courts: Alleging more than one criminal act committed by one or more defendants in the same complaint.

Joinder of Defendants: Charging multiple defendants with the commission of the same act or acts.

Material Witness: Eyewitness, or a witness who can testify to significant facts relating to the crime charged.

Materiality: Evidence offered relating to the crime charged.

Personal Knowledge: Events personally seen or heard by the witness.

Privilege: Option held by a witness to withhold his or her testimony.

Probable Cause (reasonable cause): A strong suspicion that a person is guilty of a crime.

Real Evidence: Physical items, such as documents, bullets, knives, or contraband.

Rebut: To offer evidence in support of testimony previously contradicted by the other side.

Relevancy: Items of evidence that establish the defendant's connection with the crime charged.

Search: Act by a law enforcement officer conducted with the intent of observing that which is concealed from view.

Search Warrant: Judicial order to enter and search residences or vehicles.

Severance: Judicial procedure to separately try defendants jointly charged with the same crime.

Voluntariness: Unencumbered choice made without threats or promises.

Waiver: Voluntary relinquishment of a right.

Index